Logic and Computation

Logic and Computation

Editor

Răzvan Diaconescu

MDPI • Basel • Beijing • Wuhan • Barcelona • Belgrade • Manchester • Tokyo • Cluj • Tianjin

Editor
Răzvan Diaconescu
Simion Stoilow Institute of
Mathematics of the Romanian
Academy
Romania

Editorial Office
MDPI
St. Alban-Anlage 66
4052 Basel, Switzerland

This is a reprint of articles from the Special Issue published online in the open access journal *Mathematics* (ISSN 2227-7390) (available at: https://www.mdpi.com/si/mathematics/Log_Comput).

For citation purposes, cite each article independently as indicated on the article page online and as indicated below:

LastName, A.A.; LastName, B.B.; LastName, C.C. Article Title. *Journal Name* **Year**, *Volume Number*, Page Range.

ISBN 978-3-0365-7376-2 (Hbk)
ISBN 978-3-0365-7377-9 (PDF)

© 2023 by the authors. Articles in this book are Open Access and distributed under the Creative Commons Attribution (CC BY) license, which allows users to download, copy and build upon published articles, as long as the author and publisher are properly credited, which ensures maximum dissemination and a wider impact of our publications.

The book as a whole is distributed by MDPI under the terms and conditions of the Creative Commons license CC BY-NC-ND.

Contents

About the Editor vii

Preface to "Logic and Computation" ix

Liping Xiong and Sumei Guo
Representation and Reasoning about Strategic Abilities with ω-Regular Properties
Reprinted from: *Mathematics* **2021**, *9*, 3052, doi:10.3390/math9233052 1

Mohd Shareduwan Mohd Kasihmuddin, Siti Zulaikha Mohd Jamaludin, Mohd. Asyraf Mansor, Habibah A. Wahab and Siti Maisharah Sheikh Ghadzi
Supervised Learning Perspective in Logic Mining
Reprinted from: *Mathematics* **2022**, *10*, 915, doi:10.3390/math10060915 25

Uwe Wolter
Logics of Statements in Context-Category Independent Basics
Reprinted from: *Mathematics* **2022**, *10*, 1085, doi:10.3390/math10071085 61

Răzvan Diaconescu
Representing 3/2-Institutions as Stratified Institutions
Reprinted from: *Mathematics* **2022**, *10*, 1507, doi:10.3390/math10091507 127

Răzvan Diaconescu
The Axiomatic Approach to Non-Classical Model Theory
Reprinted from: *Mathematics* **2022**, *10*, 3428, doi:10.3390/math10193428 149

About the Editor

Răzvan Diaconescu

Răzvan Diaconescu is a Research Professor at Simion Stoilow Institute of Mathematics of the Romanian Academy. His research revolves around the categorical abstract model theory (i.e., the institution theory) and its applications to logic-based computing science, especially formal specification and declarative programming. Using the model theory methods, he designed three formal specification and verification languages, namely, CafeOBJ, H and COMP. All these have been implemented as actual software systems. Dr. Diaconescu is the author of two books and of many papers scattered over 29 different international journals. His publications have received nearly 4000 citations on Google Scholar, while his book "Institution-independent Model Theory" is widely considered as the authoritative monograph in the respective area.

Preface to "Logic and Computation"

Logic and computation are highly interdependent areas of research. On the one hand, logic plays an important role in computation both at the foundational and applied levels. For instance, several well-known programming and specification languages and systems have been developed as computational implementations of logical systems. Computing paradigms, such as declarative programming or formal specification and verification, owe much to logic. On the other hand, there are lots of computing-driven studies on logic.

The present book contains five articles accepted for publication and submitted to the Special Issue "Logic and Computation" of the MDPI "Mathematics" journal. These appeared in Volumes 9 (2021) and 10 (2022). They cover topics such as the model theory for formal logic-based formal specification and programming, logic mining and logic for games. It is hoped that the book will be interesting and useful for those working in the area of applying logic to computing.

As the Guest Editor of the Special Issue, I am grateful to the authors of the papers for their quality contributions, to the reviewers for their valuable comments towards the improvement in the submitted works and to the administrative staff of MDPI for their support in completing this project. Special thanks are due to the Managing Editor of the Special Issue, Dr. Syna Mu, for his excellent collaboration, encouragement and valuable assistance.

Răzvan Diaconescu
Editor

Article

Representation and Reasoning about Strategic Abilities with ω-Regular Properties

Liping Xiong [1,*] **and Sumei Guo** [2,*]

[1] School of Computer, South China Normal University, Guangzhou 510631, China
[2] School of Computer Technology, Beijing Institute of Technology, Zhuhai, Zhuhai 519000, China
* Correspondence: xiongliping@scnu.edu.cn (L.X.); guo_sm@bitzh.edu.cn (S.G.)

Abstract: Specification and verification of coalitional strategic abilities have been an active research area in multi-agent systems, artificial intelligence, and game theory. Recently, many strategic logics, e.g., Strategy Logic (SL) and alternating-time temporal logic (ATL*), have been proposed based on classical temporal logics, e.g., linear-time temporal logic (LTL) and computational tree logic (CTL*), respectively. However, these logics cannot express general ω-regular properties, the need for which are considered compelling from practical applications, especially in industry. To remedy this problem, in this paper, based on linear dynamic logic (LDL), proposed by Moshe Y. Vardi, we propose LDL-based Strategy Logic (LDL-SL). Interpreted on concurrent game structures, LDL-SL extends SL, which contains existential/universal quantification operators about regular expressions. Here we adopt a branching-time version. This logic can express general ω-regular properties and describe more programmed constraints about individual/group strategies. Then we study three types of fragments (i.e., one-goal, ATL-like, star-free) of LDL-SL. Furthermore, we show that prevalent strategic logics based on LTL/CTL*, such as SL/ATL*, are exactly equivalent with those corresponding star-free strategic logics, where only star-free regular expressions are considered. Moreover, results show that reasoning complexity about the model-checking problems for these new logics, including one-goal and ATL-like fragments, is not harder than those of corresponding SL or ATL*.

Keywords: strategic abilities; ω-regular properties; linear dynamic logic; strategic logics; model checking; concurrent game structure

Citation: Xiong, L.; Guo, S. Representation and Reasoning about Strategic Abilities with ω-Regular Properties. *Mathematics* **2021**, *9*, 3052. https://doi.org/10.3390/math9233052

Academic Editor: Răzvan Diaconescu

Received: 22 September 2021
Accepted: 24 November 2021
Published: 27 November 2021

Publisher's Note: MDPI stays neutral with regard to jurisdictional claims in published maps and institutional affiliations.

Copyright: © 2021 by the authors. Licensee MDPI, Basel, Switzerland. This article is an open access article distributed under the terms and conditions of the Creative Commons Attribution (CC BY) license (https://creativecommons.org/licenses/by/4.0/).

1. Introduction

For the specification of ongoing behaviours of reactive systems, the use of temporal logics has become one of the significant developments in formal reasoning [1–3]. However, interpreted over Kripke structures, traditional temporal logics can only quantify the computations of the closed systems in a universal/existential manner. In order to reason in multi-agent systems, we need to specify the ongoing strategic behaviours [4].

Since Alur and Henzinger [5] proposed alternating-time temporal logic (ATL/ATL*) in 2002, strategy specification and verification has been an active research area in multi-agent systems, artificial intelligence, and game theory. In recent years, there have been many extensions or variants of strategic logics proposed to reason about coalitional strategic abilities. For instance, in [6], Chatterjee et al. proposed strategy logic, which treats strategies as explicit first-order objects in turn-based games with only two agents; Mogavero et al. extended this logic with explicit strategy quantifications and agent bindings in multi-agent concurrent systems [7]; in order to reason about uniqueness of Nash Equilibria, Aminof et al. introduced a graded strategic logic [8]; in [9], Bozzelli et al. considered strategic reasoning with linear past in alternating-time temporal logic; and in [10], Belardinelli et al. studied strategic reasoning with knowledge. These logics are interpreted over concurrent game structures, in which agents act concurrently and instantaneously. Each agent acts independently and interacts with other agents. Formulas of these logics are used to specify an individual's or a group's strategic abilities.

In ATL/ATL*, strategic abilities for coalition A (i.e., a set of agents) are expressed as $\langle\langle A \rangle\rangle \psi$, representing that coalition A has a group strategy to make sure that goal ψ holds, no matter which strategies are chosen by other agents outside of A, here ψ can be any temporal formula. A much more expressive strategic logic is Strategy Logic (SL) [6,7], which is a multi-agent extension of linear-time temporal logic (LTL) [11] with the concepts of agent bindings and strategy quantification. In SL, we can explicitly reason about the agent's strategy itself, allow different agents to share the same strategy, and also represent the existence of deterministic multi-player Nash equilibria.

However, on one hand, existing strategic logics are mainly based on the classical temporal logics. For instance, the underlying logics of ATL, ATL*, alternating-time mu-calculus (AMC) [5], and SL are temporal logic computational tree logic CTL [12], CTL* [3], μ-calculus [13], and LTL, respectively. However, they cannot express general ω-regular properties, such as "property p holds in any even steps in an infinite sequence, and holds in odd steps or not" [14].

On the other hand, the need of a declarative and convenient temporal logic, which can express any general ω-regular expression, is considered compelling from a practical viewpoint in industry [15]. In some papers, e.g., [16], the authors introduce regular expressions or automaton directly into LTL to express ω-regular properties. However, regular expressions or automaton are all too low level as a formalism for expressing temporal specifications. In 2011, Moshe Y. Vardi proposes a novel logic, named linear dynamic logic (LDL) [17], which merges LTL with regular expression in a very natural way and adopts exactly the syntax of propositional dynamic logic (PDL) [18]. LDL has three advantages:

(1) It has the same expressive power as ω-regular expression, which is also equivalent with monadic second-order logic over infinite traces [19];
(2) It retains the declarative nature and intuitive appeal of LTL [20];
(3) The model checking complexity of LDL is PSPACE-complete [17,21], which is the same as that of LTL.

In order to express any ω-regular properties in strategic logic, in [22], Liu et al. propose a logic JAADL to specify joint abilities of coalitions, which combines alternating-time temporal logic with LDL. However, in JAADL, the authors consider a very complex semantics and study the model checking complexity with imperfect recall for JAADL.

Similarly, to remedy the inability to express any general ω-regular temporal goal in strategic abilities in SL, we propose a novel strategic logic, called LDL-based Strategy Logic, abbreviated as LDL-SL. It can explicitly represent and reason about strategies and specify expressive strategic abilities for coalitions about more representative temporal goals, which can be general ω-regular properties. By combining LDL and SL, LDL-SL becomes a natural and intuitive strategic logic to specify more expressive properties. (In [23], the authors propose a strategy logic based on LDL interpreted over interpreted systems with bounded private actions.).

In this paper, we show that LDL-SL is much more expressive than SL and LDL and prove that the model checking complexity of LDL-SL is nonelementary-hard [24]. Moreover, we study fragments of LDL-SL and their model-checking complexities, and we define three types of strategic logics: ATL-like, one-goal, and star-free. The former two, which are fragments for LDL-SL, have the same expressivity as those based on LTL or CTL*, and the model-checking problems are also the same. As for the last, firstly, we formally define the star-free LDL logic and prove it is equivalent with LTL. By this, we know that the corresponding star-free strategic logics are equivalent with those based on LTL/CTL*. Furthermore, the model-checking problems of these new logics, based on LDL, are the same as those based on LTL/CTL*. Furthermore, we show that the model-checking problem complexities of these logics are either 2EXPTIME-complete or nonelementary-hard.

Therefore, in any case, LDL can be viewed as a good and natural underlying temporal logic of strategic logics.

The paper is organized as follows. Section 2 introduces LDL, and its classical temporal logic fragments and then introduces the syntax and semantics of strategic logics. Section 3 indicates that LTL is equivalent with star-free fragment of LDL. In the next section, we propose the LDL-based strategy logic (LDL-SL) and give fragments of LDL-SL. Furthermore, we present the relations for expressivity among strategic logics. Moreover, the model checking problems for these new proposed strategic logics are considered. Finally, we present conclusions and future work.

2. Preliminaries

In this section, firstly, we introduce temporal logics including such as CDL* and its fragments LDL, LTL, and CTL*. Then we introduce strategic logics whose underlying logics are LTL and CTL*.

In this paper, we fix two non-empty finite sets, which are atomic proposition set AP, agent set Ag, and one nonempty countable set of strategy variable Var. By $\mathcal{L}(AP)$, we denote the set of propositional formulas over AP. In this paper, we use *true* (resp. *false*) to refer to valid (resp. contradiction) formula.

2.1. Temporal Logics

Computational-tree dynamic logic (CDL*) [25] is a branching-time extension of LDL, which adopts the syntax from propositional dynamic logic (PDL).

Definition 1 (Syntax of CDL*). *The syntax of is defined inductively by:*

$$\text{State formula } \varphi ::= p \mid \neg\varphi \mid \varphi \wedge \varphi \mid \mathbf{E}\psi$$

$$\text{Path formula } \psi ::= \varphi \mid \neg\psi \mid \psi \wedge \psi \mid \langle\rho\rangle\psi$$

$$\text{Path expression } \rho ::= \Phi \mid \psi? \mid \rho+\rho \mid \rho;\rho \mid \rho^*$$

where, $p \in AP$, and $\Phi \in \mathcal{L}(AP)$.

Intuitively, the path formula $\langle\rho\rangle\psi$ means that from the current instant, there exists an execution satisfying the path expression ρ s.t. Its last instant satisfies ψ, and the state formula $\mathbf{E}\psi$ means that there exists a reachable path that makes the path formula ψ hold.

Let $\mathbf{A}$ define the dual of $\mathbf{E}$, i.e., $\mathbf{A} = \neg\mathbf{E}\neg$, and let $[\rho]$ define the dual of $\langle\rho\rangle$, i.e., $[\rho] = \neg\langle\rho\rangle\neg$.

LDL is a linear-time fragment of CDL*, just as LTL is a fragment of CTL* The syntax of LDL is

$$\psi ::= p \mid \neg\psi \mid \psi \wedge \psi \mid \langle\rho\rangle\psi, \quad \text{and} \quad \rho ::= \Phi \mid \psi? \mid \rho+\rho \mid \rho;\rho \mid \rho^*. \tag{1}$$

Furthermore, CTL*(resp. LTL) is a fragment of CDL*(resp. LDL), where $\langle\rho\rangle$ is replaced by *next-time* $\bigcirc$, *eventuality* $\Diamond$, and *until* $\mathcal{U}$, three temporal operators.

Any LTL formula can be linearly expressed in LDL, for instance, $\bigcirc p \doteq \langle true \rangle p$, $\Diamond p \doteq \langle true^* \rangle p$, and $p\mathcal{U}q \doteq \langle(p; true)^*\rangle q$, when $p, q \in \mathcal{L}(AP)$.

Definition 2 (Kripke Model). *A Kripke model M is a tuple (W, R, V), where W is a finite non-empty set of possible worlds; $R \subseteq W \times W$, which is a left-total relation over W, i.e., for any $w \in W$, there exists a $w' \in W$ s.t., $w R w'$; and $V : W \to 2^{AP}$ is a valuation function.*

In a Kripke model $M = (W, R, V)$, by $Path(w)$ we denote the set of infinite reachable sequences (i.e., path) $\pi = w_0 w_1 \cdots$ from w, where $w_0 = w$ and $w_i R w_{i+1}$ for all $i \in \mathbb{N}$. Let π_i denote the i-th element w_i in π, and $\pi_{\geq i}$ denote the suffix of π, i.e., $\pi_{\geq i} = w_i w_{i+1} \cdots$, and let $\pi_{\leq i}$ denote the prefix of π, i.e., $\pi_{\leq i} = w_0 w_1 \cdots w_i$.

The semantics of CDL* is defined inductively as follows.

Given a CDL* state formula φ, a Kripke model M and a state w in M, the relation $M, w \models \varphi$ is defined as follows.
- $M, w \models p$ iff $p \in V(w)$, here $p \in AP$;
- $M, w \models \neg \varphi$ iff $M, w \not\models \neg \varphi$;
- $M, w \models \varphi_1 \wedge \varphi_2$ iff $M, w \models \varphi_1$ and $M, w \models \varphi_2$;
- $M, w \models E\psi$ iff there exists $\pi \in Path(w)$ s.t. $\pi, 0 \models \psi$.

Given a CDL* path formula ψ, a path π in M, and $i \in \mathbb{N}$, the relation $\pi, i \models \psi$ is defined as follows.
- $\pi, i \models \varphi$ iff $M, \pi_i \models \varphi$, here φ is a CDL* state formula;
- $\pi, i \models \neg \psi$ iff $\pi, i \not\models \psi$;
- $\pi, i \models \psi_1 \wedge \psi_2$ iff $\pi, i \models \psi_1$ and $\pi, i \models \psi_2$;
- $\pi, i \models \langle \rho \rangle \psi$ iff there exists j such that $(i, j) \in \mathcal{R}(\rho, \pi)$ and $\pi, j \models \psi$.

Given a path expression ρ and a path π in M, for $i, j \in \mathbb{N}$, the relation $(i, j) \in \mathcal{R}(\rho, \pi)$ is defined as follows:
- $(i, j) \in \mathcal{R}(\Phi, \pi)$ iff $j = i + 1$, and $\pi, i \models \Phi$, here $\Phi \in \mathcal{L}(AP)$;
- $(i, j) \in \mathcal{R}(\psi?, \pi)$ iff $j = i$, and $\pi, j \models \psi$;
- $(i, j) \in \mathcal{R}(\rho_1 + \rho_2, \pi)$ iff $(i, j) \in \mathcal{R}(\rho_1, \pi)$ or $(i, j) \in \mathcal{R}(\rho_2, \pi)$;
- $(i, j) \in \mathcal{R}(\rho_1; \rho_2, \pi)$ iff there exists $k \in \mathbb{N}$, $i \leq k \leq j$, satisfying that $(i, k) \in \mathcal{R}(\rho_1, \pi)$ and $(k, j) \in \mathcal{R}(\rho_2, \pi)$;
- $(i, j) \in \mathcal{R}(\rho^*, \pi)$ iff $j = i$, or $(i, j) \in \mathcal{R}(\rho; \rho^*, \pi)$.

2.2. Strategic Logics Based on Classical Temporal Logics

SL [24] is an expressive logic, which can explicitly reason about agents' strategies in multi-agent concurrent systems. In [26], Knight and Maubert propose a branching-time version BSL of SL, which is equivalent to SL. Here we introduce BSL with some minor changes, still equivalent with SL.

Definition 3 (BSL Formula). *BSL formulas are defined inductively by:*

$$\text{State formula } \varphi ::= p \mid \neg\varphi \mid \varphi \wedge \varphi \mid (a, x)\varphi \mid \langle\langle x \rangle\rangle \varphi \mid E\psi$$

$$\text{Path formula } \psi ::= \varphi \mid \neg\psi \mid \psi \wedge \psi \mid \bigcirc\psi \mid \Diamond\psi \mid \psi \mathcal{U} \psi,$$

here $p \in AP$, $a \in Ag$, and $x \in Var$.

Syntactically, BSL extends linear-time temporal logic LTL with two operators. Intuitively, $\langle\langle x \rangle\rangle$ (resp. (a, x)) means "there exists a strategy x" (resp. "bind agent a to the strategy associated with variable x"). Here, let $[\![x]\!] = \neg\langle\langle x \rangle\rangle \neg$, which means "for all strategies x".

For a BSL formula φ, let $free(\varphi) \subseteq Var \cup Ag$ denote the set of *free strategy variables and agents* of φ. Informally, $free(\varphi)$ contains all strategy variables (resp. agents) for which there exists an agent binding but no quantifications (resp. no agent binding after the occurrence of a temporal operator). Here the formal definition refers to [24].

Since CTL* (resp. ATL*) is a fragment of ATL* [5] (resp. SL [24]), and BSL is equivalent with SL [26], then both CTL* and ATL* are fragments of BSL.

Now we introduce the semantics model of BSL based on the notion of *concurrent game structure* [5].

Definition 4 (Concurrent Game Structure). *A concurrent game structure (CGS) $\mathcal{G}$ has five components $\langle Act, W, \lambda, \tau, w^0 \rangle$:*
- *Act (resp. W) is a non-empty finite sets of actions (resp. states);*
- *w^0 is an initial state in W;*
- *$\lambda : W \to 2^{AP}$ is a valuation function;*
- *transition function $\tau : W \times Act^{Ag} \to W$ maps a state and a decision to next state.*

A decision is a function from Ag to Act, by Act^{Ag} we denote Dc.

In fact, a concurrent game structure can be viewed as a multi-player game, in which all agents strategically perform joint actions. Before defining the semantics of BSL, first we present relevant notations and definitions, namely *track*, *strategy*, *strategy assignment*, and *outcome*.

Definition 5 (Track). *In a CGS $\mathcal{G} = \langle Act, W, \lambda, \tau, w^0 \rangle$, a finite state sequence $h = w_0 w_1 ... w_k$ is called a track in $\mathcal{G}$ if, for each i with $0 \leq i < k$, there exists $d \in Dc$ s.t. $w_{i+1} = \tau(w_i, d)$.*

Given a track $h = w_0 w_1 ... w_k$, let $len(h)$ denote the length $k+1$ of h, and $lst(h)$ denote the last state w_k of h.

Definition 6 (Strategy). *In a CGS $\mathcal{G} = \langle Act, W, \lambda, \tau, w^0 \rangle$, a strategy in $\mathcal{G}$ is a function mapping a track in $\mathcal{G}$ into an action.*

Intuitively, a strategy of one agent can be viewed as a plan for this agent, which contains the unique choice of action for each track in $\mathcal{G}$.

For brevity, let $Trk(\mathcal{G})$ (resp. $Str(\mathcal{G})$) denote the set of all tracks (strategies) in a CGS $\mathcal{G}$, and let $Trk(\mathcal{G}, w)$ denote the set of all tracks starting with w.

Like the definition of variable assignment in first-order logic, a partial function $\chi : Var \cup Ag \rightharpoonup Str(\mathcal{G})$ is called a *strategy assignment* or just *assignment* in $\mathcal{G}$, which maps a variable or an agent to a strategy. Let $Asg(\mathcal{G})$ denote the set of all strategy assignments in CGS $\mathcal{G}$. If $Ag \subseteq dom(\chi)$, χ is called *complete*, here $dom(\chi)$ is the domain of χ. For each agent a, χ is called w-total, if $Track(\mathcal{G}, w) \subseteq dom(\chi(a))$. Let $Asg(\mathcal{G}, w)$ denote the set of all w-total assignments in $\mathcal{G}$. Let $\chi[x \mapsto g]$ denote a new strategy assignment almost like χ, where the only difference is that it maps x into g.

Let $out(\mathcal{G}, \chi, w)$ denote the set of outcomes (or paths) from w, which is determined by χ. If $\mathcal{G}$ is explicit, we omit the $\mathcal{G}$ in $out(\mathcal{G}, \chi, w)$.

Definition 7 (Outcome). *For any $\pi = w_0 w_1 ...$, $\pi \in out(\mathcal{G}, \chi, w)$ iff $w_0 = w$, for any $i \in \mathbb{N}$, there exists a joint action d, such that $\tau(w_i, d) = w_{i+1}$, satisfying $d(a) = \chi(a)(\pi_{\leq i})$ for each $a \in dom(\chi) \cap Ag$.*

Given a collective strategy g_A of A, i.e., $\{g_a : a \in A\}$, by $out(w, g_A)$ we denote the set of legal executions from w where agents in A perform actions according to g_A. Formally,

$$out(w, g_A) = \{\pi | \pi(0) = w \wedge \exists d \in DC. d(A) = g_A(\pi_{\leq k}) \wedge \tau(\pi_k, d) = \pi_{k+1}, \forall k.\} \quad (2)$$

When χ is complete and w-total, there exists just one path in $out(w, \chi(Ag))$, which we call (χ, w)-play.

Given a CGS $\mathcal{G} = \langle Ac, W, \lambda, \tau, w^0 \rangle$, a BSL state formula φ, an assignment χ, and a state w, the relation $\mathcal{G}, \chi, w \models \varphi$ is inductively defined as follows.

- $\mathcal{G}, \chi, w \models p$ if and only if $p \in \lambda(w)$;
- $\mathcal{G}, \chi, w \models \neg \varphi$ if and only if $\mathcal{G}, \chi, w \not\models \varphi$;
- $\mathcal{G}, \chi, w \models \varphi_1 \wedge \varphi_2$ if and only if $\mathcal{G}, \chi, w \models \varphi_1$ and $\mathcal{G}, \chi, w \models \varphi_2$;
- $\mathcal{G}, \chi, w \models (a, x)\varphi$ if and only if $\mathcal{G}, \chi[x \mapsto \chi(a)], w \models \varphi$;
- $\mathcal{G}, \chi, w \models \langle\langle x \rangle\rangle \varphi$ if and only if   there exists $g \in Str(\mathcal{G})$, s.t., $\mathcal{G}, \chi[x \mapsto g], w \models \varphi$;
- $\mathcal{G}, \chi, w \models E\psi$ if and only if   there exists $\pi \in out(\mathcal{G}, \chi, w)$, s.t., $\mathcal{G}, \chi, \pi, 0 \models \psi$.

Given a path formula ψ in BSL, $i \in \mathbb{N}$, and a path π, the relation $\mathcal{G}, \chi, \pi, i \models \psi$ is defined by:

- $\mathcal{G}, \chi, \pi, i \models \bigcirc \psi$ if and only if $\mathcal{G}, \chi, \pi, i+1 \models \psi$;
- $\mathcal{G}, \chi, \pi, i \models \Diamond \psi$ if and only if $\exists j$ with $i \leq j$, satisfying that $\mathcal{G}, \chi, \pi, j \models \psi$;

- $\mathcal{G}, \chi, \pi, i \models \psi_1 \mathcal{U} \psi_2$ if and only if $\exists j \in \mathbb{N}$ with $i \leq j$, such that for each $k, i \leq k < j$ satisfying that $\mathcal{G}, \chi, \pi, k \models \psi_1$, and $\mathcal{G}, \chi, \pi, j \models \psi_2$.

BSL state formula φ is called a *sentence* if $free(\varphi) = \emptyset$. Clearly, $\mathcal{G}, \chi, w \models \varphi$ does not depend on χ; hence, we can omit χ without confusion.

In order to define the syntax of BSL[1G], we introduce the notions of *quantification prefix* and *binding prefix* [24]. A sequence $\wp = ((x_1))((x_2)) \cdots ((x_n))$ is called quantification prefix, if $((x_i)) \in \{\langle\langle x_i \rangle\rangle, [\![x_i]\!]\}$ is either an existential or universal quantification. Given a fixed set of agents $Ag = \{a_1, \cdots, a_m\}$, a sequence $\flat = (a_1, x_1), \cdots, (a_m, x_m)$ is called a binding prefix if every agent in Ag occurs exactly once. A combination $\wp\flat$ is *closed* if every variable occurring in $\flat$ occurs in some quantifier of $\wp$.

Now the syntax of one-goal fragment BSL[1G] of BSL is defined as follows.

$$\varphi ::= p \mid \neg\varphi \mid \varphi \wedge \varphi \mid \mathrm{E}\psi \mid \wp\flat\varphi, \quad \text{and} \quad \psi ::= \varphi \mid \neg\psi \mid \psi \wedge \psi \mid \bigcirc\psi \mid \Diamond\psi \mid \psi\mathcal{U}\psi, \quad (3)$$

where $\wp\flat$ is a closed combination of a quantification/binding prefix [24].

ATL*, whose underlying logic is CTL*, is a fragment of BSL[1G] [24]. Its syntax is defined by ($A \subseteq Ag$)

$$\text{State formula } \varphi ::= p \mid \neg\varphi \mid \varphi \wedge \varphi \mid \langle\langle A \rangle\rangle \psi$$

$$\text{Path formula } \psi ::= \varphi \mid \neg\psi \mid \psi \wedge \psi \mid \bigcirc\psi \mid \Diamond\psi \mid \psi\mathcal{U}\psi.$$

For details about the semantics of ATL* and BSL[1G], see [5,24].

Here, consider the semantics of the case $\varphi = \langle\langle A \rangle\rangle \psi$: given a CGS $\mathcal{G}$ and a state w,

$$\mathcal{G}, w \models \langle\langle A \rangle\rangle \psi \quad \text{iff} \quad \text{there exist } g_A, \text{s.t.}, \forall \pi \in out(w, g_A), \mathcal{G}, \pi, 0 \models \psi. \quad (4)$$

3. Star-Free Logic of LDL

In this section, we first define star-free logic LDL$_{sf}$ (resp. CDL$^*_{sf}$) of LDL (resp. CDL*), and then show that their expressive abilities are equivalent with LTL (resp. CTL*).

We conjecture that if regular expressions are replaced by star-free regular expressions in LDL, then the expressivity of this new temporal logic is equivalent with that of LTL. In fact, in this section, we show that it is indeed true by Theorem 1.

Definition 8 (Star-free Logic LDL$_{sf}$). *The star-free logic LDL$_{sf}$ is defined inductively by:*

$$LDL_{sf} \text{ formula } \psi ::= p \mid \neg\psi \mid \psi \wedge \psi \mid \langle \rho \rangle \psi$$

$$\textit{Star-free path expression } \rho ::= \Phi \mid \psi? \mid \rho + \rho \mid \rho;\rho \mid \overline{\rho}$$

where $p \in AP$ and $\Phi \in \mathcal{L}(AP)$.

Here $\overline{\rho}$ is the complement of ρ. In the star-free logic CDL$^*_{sf}$ of CDL*, the path expressions in CDL* are just replaced by star-free path expressions as follows:

$$\text{Star-free path expression } \rho ::= \Phi \mid \psi? \mid \rho + \rho \mid \rho;\rho \mid \overline{\rho} \quad (5)$$

In a Kripke model M, given a path π and path expression ρ, for any $i \geq j$, define

$$(i, j) \in \mathcal{R}(\overline{\rho}, \pi) \quad \text{if and only if} \quad (i, j) \notin \mathcal{R}(\rho, \pi). \quad (6)$$

Easily, the following simple property holds.

Lemma 1. *For any path π in a Kripke model, the following holds,*

$$\mathcal{R}(\overline{false}, \pi) = \mathcal{R}(true^*, \pi) = \{(i, j) : j \geq i, i, j \in \mathbb{N}\}. \quad (7)$$

Proof. Firstly, $(i,j) \in \mathcal{R}(\overline{false}, \pi)$ iff $(i,j) \notin \mathcal{R}(false, \pi)$ iff $j \geq i$; secondly, $(i,j) \in \mathcal{R}(true^*)$ iff $j \geq i$. □

Hence, the following two equivalent results are correct.

Corollary 1. *Given an LDL formula ψ, the following are valid*

$$\langle true^* \rangle \psi \equiv \langle \overline{false} \rangle \psi \quad and \quad [true^*]\psi \equiv [\overline{false}]\psi. \tag{8}$$

Since first-order logic (FO) over naturals has the expressive power of star-free regular expressions [27], and LTL over the naturals has precisely the expressive power of FO [28], then LTL over naturals has the same expressivity as star-free regular expression. Now we consider the relation between LTL and LDL_{sf}.

In fact, for each LTL formula ψ, we can translate it into a star-free LDL formula $SF(\psi)$ by function $SF : LTL \rightarrow LDL_{sf}$ as follows:

- $SF(p) = p \quad SF(\neg \psi) = \neg SF(\psi)$
- $SF(\psi \wedge \psi') = SF(\psi) \wedge SF(\psi')$
- $SF(\bigcirc \psi) = \langle true \rangle SF(\psi) \quad SF(\Diamond \psi) = \langle \overline{false} \rangle SF(\psi)$
- $SF(\psi \mathcal{U} \psi') = SF(\psi') \vee \langle \overline{false; \neg SF(\psi)?; false}; true \rangle SF(\psi')$

Obviously, the function SF is well-defined; i.e., for any ψ in LTL, $SF(\psi) \in LDL_{sf}$. Then the following result holds.

Lemma 2. *In a Kripke model M, for any LTL formula ψ, a path π, and $i \in \mathbb{N}$,*

$$\pi, i \models \psi \quad \text{if and only if} \quad \pi, i \models SF(\psi). \tag{9}$$

Proof. We show this lemma inductively as follows. Here we just consider the following cases; the others are routine.

For case $\bigcirc \psi$: $\pi, i \models SF(\bigcirc \psi)$ iff $\pi, i \models \langle true \rangle SF(\psi)$ iff $\pi, i+1 \models SF(\psi)$ iff $\pi, i+1 \models \psi$ (by induction) iff $\pi, i \models \bigcirc \psi$.

For case $\Diamond \psi$: $\pi, i \models SF(\Diamond \psi)$ iff $\pi, i \models \langle \overline{false} \rangle SF(\psi)$ iff $\exists j. (i,j) \in \mathcal{R}(\overline{false}, \pi)$, s.t., $\pi, j \models SF(\psi)$ iff $\exists j. i \leq j$ and $\pi, j \models SF(\psi)$ (by Lemma 1) iff $\exists j. i \leq j$ and $\pi, j \models \psi$ (by induction) iff $\pi, i \models \Diamond \psi$.

For case $\psi_1 \mathcal{U} \psi_2$:

$\pi, i \models SF(\psi_1 \mathcal{U} \psi_2)$ iff
$\pi, i \models SF(\psi_2) \vee \langle \overline{false; \neg SF(\psi_1)?; false}; true \rangle SF(\psi_2)$ iff
$\pi, i \models SF(\psi_2)$ or $\langle \overline{false; \neg SF(\psi_1)?; false}; true \rangle SF(\psi_2)$.

For the latter,

$\pi, i \models \langle \overline{false; \neg SF(\psi_1)?; false}; true \rangle SF(\psi_2)$ iff
$\exists j. (i,j) \in \mathcal{R}(\overline{false; \neg SF(\psi_1)?; false}; true, \pi)$ and $\pi, j \models \psi_2$ iff
$\exists j. \exists k. i \leq k \leq j$, s.t., $(i,k) \in \mathcal{R}(\overline{false; \neg SF(\psi_1)?; false}, \pi)$
and $(k,j) \in \mathcal{R}(true, \pi)$, and $\pi, j \models SF(\psi_2)$ iff
$\exists j. (i, j-1) \in \mathcal{R}(\overline{false; \neg SF(\psi_1)?; false}, \pi)$ and $\pi, j \models SF(\psi_2)$.

Then we show that

$$(i, j-1) \in \mathcal{R}(\overline{false; \neg SF(\psi_1)?; \overline{false}}, \pi) \text{ iff}$$
$$(i, j-1) \notin \mathcal{R}(false; \neg SF(\psi_1)?; \overline{false}, \pi) \text{ iff}$$
$$\forall k.(i \leq k \leq j-1 \to (i,k) \notin \mathcal{R}(\overline{false}) \lor$$
$$(k, j-1) \notin \mathcal{R}(\neg SF(\psi_1)?; \overline{false}, \pi)) \text{ iff}$$
$$\forall k.(i \leq k \leq j-1 \to (k, j-1) \notin \mathcal{R}(\neg SF(\psi_1)?; \overline{false}, \pi)) \text{ iff}$$
$$\forall k.(i \leq k \leq j-1 \to \forall k'.(k \leq k' \leq j-1 \to (k,k') \notin$$
$$\mathcal{R}(\neg SF(\psi_1)?, \pi) \lor (k', j-1) \notin \mathcal{R}(\overline{false}, \pi))) \text{ iff}$$
$$\forall k.(i \leq k \leq j-1 \to \pi, k \models SF(\psi_1)).$$

Therefore, we have that $\pi, i \models SF(\psi_1 \mathcal{U} \psi_2)$ iff $\pi, i \models SF(\psi_2)$ or there exists j, $\forall k.(i \leq k \leq j-1 \to \pi, k \models SF(\psi_1))$ and $\pi, j \models SF(\psi_2)$ iff there exists j, such that for all $k.i \leq k < j$ s.t. $\pi, k \models \psi_1$ and $\pi, j \models \psi_2$ (by induction) iff $\pi, i \models \psi_1 \mathcal{U} \psi_2$. □

By this lemma, LTL can be linearly embedded into LDL_{sf}. Conversely, in order to express an LDL_{sf} formula ψ by an LTL formula, we first express ψ by a first-order logic FO(AP) formula under linear order over natural numbers $\mathbb{N}$ [16]. In FO(AP), the language is formed by the binary predicate $<$, a unary predicate for each symbol in AP.

The first order logic FO(AP) interpretation is the form $\mathcal{I} = (\Delta^\mathcal{I}, \cdot^\mathcal{I})$, where the interpretation of the following binary predicates and the constant are fixed,

- $\Delta^\mathcal{I} = \mathbb{N}$; $0^\mathcal{I} = 0$
- $<^\mathcal{I} = \{(i,j) : i,j \in \mathbb{N}, i < j\}$;
- $succ^\mathcal{I} = \{(i, i+1) : i \in \mathbb{N}\}$;
- $=^\mathcal{I} = \{(i,i) : i \in \mathbb{N}\}$.

In fact, the following properties hold.

- $succ(x,y) \doteq (x < y) \land (\neg \exists z. x < z < y)$
- $x = y \doteq \forall z. x < z \equiv y < z$
- $x \leq y \doteq x < y \lor x = y$
- 0 can be defined as one x, which satisfies that $\neg \exists y. succ(y, x)$ or $\forall y. x \leq y$.

Intuitively, $succ(x,y)$ means that y is an immediate successor of x.

Given a path π in a Kripke model $M = (W, R, V)$, we define a corresponding first order logic interpretation I^π with that for each $p \in AP$,

$$p^{I^\pi} = \{k | p \in V(\pi_k)\} \qquad (10)$$

and interpretations of the other predicates or constant are fixed.

Now we define two functions FO and G, which translate an LDL_{sf} formula into a first-order logic FO(AP) formula by induction.

- $FO(p, x) = p(x), p \in AP$;
- $FO(\neg \psi, x) = \neg FO(\psi, x)$;
- $FO(\psi_1 \land \psi_2, x) = FO(\psi_1, x) \land FO(\psi_2, x)$;
- $FO(\langle \rho \rangle \psi, x) = \exists y.(G(\rho, x, y) \land FO(\psi, y))$;
- $G(\Phi, x, y) = succ(x, y) \land FO(\Phi, x)$, here $\Phi \in \mathcal{L}(AP)$;
- $G(\psi?, x, y) = (y = x) \land FO(\psi, x)$;
- $G(\rho_1 + \rho_2, x, y) = G(\rho_1, x, y) \lor G(\rho_2, x, y)$;
- $G(\rho_1; \rho_2, x, y) = \exists z.(x \leq z \land z \leq y \land G(\rho_1, x, z) \land G(\rho_2, z, y))$;
- $G(\overline{\rho}, x, y) = x \leq y \land \neg G(\rho, x, y)$.

The function $FO(\psi, x)$ and auxiliary function $G(\rho, x, y)$ are well-defined. Intuitively, here the function G is used to specify the relation $\mathcal{R}(\rho, \pi)$ by formulas in FO(AP).

It is shown that the following lemma holds by induction of structures about LDL_{sf} formula.

Lemma 3. *For any path π in a Kripke model M and $i \in \mathbb{N}$, given an LDL_{sf} formula ψ, we have*

$$\pi, i \models \psi \quad \text{if and only if} \quad I^\pi(i \mapsto x) \models FO(\psi, x), \qquad (11)$$

where I^π is the corresponding first order interpretation of path π.

Proof. By induction of the formula LDL_{sf} formula ψ, we can show this lemma.

For case $\psi = p$: $\pi, i \models p$ iff $p \in V(\pi_i)$ (by semantics) iff $i \in p^{I^\pi}$ iff $I^\pi \models p(i)$ iff $I^\pi(i \mapsto x) \models FO(p, x)$ iff $I^\pi(i \mapsto x) \models FO(\psi, x)$;

for case $\psi = \neg \psi_1$: $\pi, i \models \neg \psi_1$ iff $\pi, i \models \psi_1$ does not hold iff $I^\pi(i \mapsto x) \models FO(\psi_1, x)$ does not hold (by induction) iff $I^\pi(i \mapsto x) \models \neg FO(\psi_1, x)$ iff $I^\pi(i \mapsto x) \models FO(\neg \psi_1, x)$;

for case $\psi = \psi_1 \wedge \psi_2$: $\pi, i \models \psi_1 \wedge \psi_2$ iff $\pi, i \models \psi_1$ and $\pi, i \models \psi_2$ iff $I^\pi(i \mapsto x) \models FO(\psi_1, x)$ and $I^\pi(i \mapsto x) \models FO(\psi_2, x)$ (by induction) iff $I^\pi(i \mapsto x) \models FO(\psi_1 \wedge \psi_2, x)$;

In order to show the case $\psi = \langle \rho \rangle \psi_1$, we should show the following mutually with the above (11) by induction.

$$I^\pi(i \mapsto x, j \mapsto y) \models G(\rho, x, y) \quad \text{if and only if} \quad (i, j) \in \mathcal{R}(\rho, \pi). \tag{12}$$

For case $\rho = \Phi$: $I^\pi(i \mapsto x, j \mapsto y) \models G(\Phi, x, y)$ iff $I^\pi(i \mapsto x, j \mapsto y) \models succ(x, y) \wedge FO(\Phi, x)$ iff $j = i + 1$ and $\pi, i \models \Phi$ iff $(i, j) \in \mathcal{R}(\Phi, \pi)$.

For case $\rho = \psi?$: $I^\pi(i \mapsto x, j \mapsto y) \models G(\psi?, x, y)$ iff $j = i$ and $I^\pi(i \mapsto x) \models FO(\psi, x)$ iff $j = i$ and $\pi, i \models \psi$ by induction iff $(i, j) \in \mathcal{R}(\psi?, \pi)$.

For case $\rho = \rho_1 + \rho_2$: $I^\pi(i \mapsto x, j \mapsto y) \models G(\rho_1 + \rho_2, x, y)$ iff $I^\pi(i \mapsto x, j \mapsto y) \models G(\rho_1, x, y) \vee G(\rho_2, x, y)$ iff $(i, j) \in \mathcal{R}(\rho_1, \pi)$ or $(i, j) \in \mathcal{R}(\rho_2, \pi)$. The last is because by induction, we have $I^\pi(i \mapsto x, j \mapsto y) \models G(\rho_1, x, y)$ iff $(i, j) \in \mathcal{R}(\rho_1, \pi)$, and $I^\pi(i \mapsto x, j \mapsto y) \models G(\rho_2, x, y)$ iff $(i, j) \in \mathcal{R}(\rho_2, \pi)$.

For case $\rho = \rho_1; \rho_2$: $I^\pi(i \mapsto x, j \mapsto y) \models G(\rho_1; \rho_2, x, y)$ iff $I^\pi(i \mapsto x, j \mapsto y) \models \exists z (x \leq z \wedge z \leq y \wedge G(\rho_1, x, z) \wedge G(\rho_2, z, y))$ iff there exists k, with $i \leq k \leq j$, satisfying that $(i, k) \in \mathcal{R}(\rho_1, \pi)$ and $(k, j) \in \mathcal{R}(\rho_2, \pi)$ by induction iff $(i, j) \in \mathcal{R}(\rho_1; \rho_2, \pi)$.

For case $\rho = \overline{\rho_1}$: $I^\pi(i \mapsto x, j \mapsto y) \models G(\overline{\rho_1}, x, y)$ iff $I^\pi(i \mapsto x, j \mapsto y) \models x \leq y \wedge \neg G(\rho_1, x, y)$ iff $i \leq j$ and $I^\pi(i \mapsto x, j \mapsto y) \models \neg G(\rho_1, x, y)$ iff $i \leq j$ and $(i, j) \notin \mathcal{R}(\rho_1, \chi)$ iff $(i, j) \in \mathcal{R}(\overline{\rho_1}, \chi)$.

Now we show the case $\psi = \langle \rho \rangle \psi_1$: $\pi, i \models \langle \rho \rangle \psi_1$ iff there exists j, $(i, j) \in \mathcal{R}(\rho, \pi)$ satisfying that $\pi, j \models \psi_1$ iff there exists j, $I^\pi(i \mapsto x, j \mapsto y) \models G(\rho, x, y)$ and $I^\pi(j \mapsto y) \models FO(\psi_1, j)$ by induction iff $I^\pi(i \mapsto x) \models FO(\langle \rho \rangle \psi_1, x)$ by definition. □

In [28], Gabbay et al. have shown that first-order logic FO for linear order over natural numbers is equivalent with LTL over infinite traces. In addition, one of the most familiar LDL formulas is $[(true; true)^*]p$, which cannot be expressed in LTL [14]. Therefore, with the addition of Lemma 2 and 3, the following result holds.

Theorem 1. *LTL has exactly the same expressive power as the star-free logic LDL_{sf}, and strictly less expressive than LDL.*

Moreover, LTL formulas can be linearly translated into LDL_{sf} formulas, but the converse procedure is not. Some star-free LDL formulas are hard to encode by LTL formulas, even by LDL formulas.

4. Strategic Logics Based on LDL/LDL_{sf}

In this section, we introduce two new classes of expressive strategic logics, whose underlying logic is LDL and LDL_{sf}, respectively. The former can express ω-regular properties, and the latter has the same expressivity as star-free regular properties. Firstly, LDL-based Strategy Logic (abbr. LDL-SL) is introduced.

4.1. LDL/LDL_{sf}-Based Strategic Logics

Definition 9 (LDL-SL Formula). *LDL-SL formulas are defined inductively as follows.*

$$\text{State formula } \varphi ::= p \mid \neg \varphi \mid \varphi \wedge \varphi \mid (a, x)\varphi \mid \langle\!\langle x \rangle\!\rangle \varphi \mid E\psi;$$

$$\text{Path formula } \psi ::= \varphi \mid \neg\psi \mid \psi \wedge \psi \mid \langle \rho \rangle \psi;$$

$$\text{Path expression } \rho ::= \Phi \mid \psi? \mid \rho + \rho \mid \rho;\rho \mid \rho^*,$$

where $a \in Ag$, $x \in Var$, $p \in AP$, and $\Phi \in \mathcal{L}(AP)$.

In fact, LDL-SL is a logic that combines BSL with LDL. LDL-SL formula is defined recursively by three components: state formula, path formula, and path expression. Now we present the complete definition about the semantics of LDL-SL formula.

Given a CGS $\mathcal{G}$, a state formula φ, a strategy assignment χ, and a state w, the relation $\mathcal{G}, \chi, w \models \varphi$ is defined as follows.

- $\mathcal{G}, \chi, w \models p$ if and only if $p \in \lambda(w)$;
- $\mathcal{G}, \chi, w \models \neg\varphi$ if and only if $\mathcal{G}, \chi, w \not\models \varphi$;
- $\mathcal{G}, \chi, w \models \varphi_1 \wedge \varphi_2$ if and only if $\mathcal{G}, \chi, w \models \varphi_1$ and $\mathcal{G}, \chi, w \models \varphi_2$;
- $\mathcal{G}, \chi, w \models (a, x)\varphi$ if and only if $\mathcal{G}, \chi[a \mapsto \chi(x)], w \models \varphi$;
- $\mathcal{G}, \chi, w \models \langle\langle x \rangle\rangle \varphi$ if and only if $\exists g \in Str(\mathcal{G})$ s.t. $\mathcal{G}, \chi[x \mapsto g], w \models \varphi$;
- $\mathcal{G}, \chi, w \models E\psi$ if and only if $\exists \pi \in out(\mathcal{G}, \chi, w)$ s.t. $\mathcal{G}, \chi, \pi, 0 \models \psi$.

Given a CGS $\mathcal{G}$, a path formula ψ, a strategy assignment χ, a path π and some $i \in \mathbb{N}$, the relation $\mathcal{G}, \chi, \pi, i \models \psi$ is defined as follows.

- $\mathcal{G}, \chi, \pi, i \models \varphi$ if and only if $\mathcal{G}, \chi, w \models \varphi$, here $w = \pi_i$;
- $\mathcal{G}, \chi, \pi, i \models \neg\psi$ if and only if $\mathcal{G}, \chi, \pi, i \not\models \psi$;
- $\mathcal{G}, \chi, \pi, i \models \psi_1 \wedge \psi_2$ if and only if $\mathcal{G}, \chi, \pi, i \models \psi_1$ and $\mathcal{G}, \chi, \pi, i \models \psi_2$;
- $\mathcal{G}, \chi, \pi, i \models \langle \rho \rangle \psi$ if and only if $\exists j.(i,j) \in \mathcal{R}(\mathcal{G}, \rho, \pi, \chi)$ and $\mathcal{G}, \chi, \pi, j \models \psi$.

The relation $(i,j) \in \mathcal{R}(\mathcal{G}, \rho, \pi, \chi)$ is defined as follows:

- $(i,j) \in \mathcal{R}(\mathcal{G}, \Phi, \pi, \chi)$ if and only if $j = i+1$ and $\mathcal{G}, \chi, \pi, i \models \Phi$;
- $(i,j) \in \mathcal{R}(\mathcal{G}, \psi?, \pi, \chi)$ if and only if $j = i$ and $\mathcal{G}, \chi, \pi, j \models \psi$;
- $(i,j) \in R(\mathcal{G}, \rho_1 + \rho_2, \pi, \chi)$ if and only if $(i,j) \in \mathcal{R}(\mathcal{G}, \rho_1, \pi, \chi)$ or $\mathcal{R}(\mathcal{G}, \rho_2, \pi, \chi)$;
- $(i,j) \in \mathcal{R}(\mathcal{G}, \rho_1; \rho_2, \pi, \chi)$ if and only if there exists k, $i \leq k \leq j$, satisfying $(i,k) \in \mathcal{R}(\mathcal{G}, \rho_1, \pi, \chi)$ and $(k,j) \in \mathcal{R}(\mathcal{G}, \rho_2, \pi, \chi)$;
- $(i,j) \in \mathcal{R}(\mathcal{G}, \rho^*, \pi, \chi)$ if and only if $j = i$, or $(i,j) \in \mathcal{R}(\mathcal{G}, \rho; \rho^*, \pi, \chi)$.

In the above, we omit $\mathcal{G}$ in $\mathcal{R}(\mathcal{G}, \rho, \pi, \chi)$ when there is no confusion. Intuitively, $(i,j) \in \mathcal{R}(\mathcal{G}, \rho, \pi, \chi)$ means that the sequence $\pi_i ... \pi_j$ is a legal execution of ρ under assignment χ in CGS $\mathcal{G}$.

For two special path expressions, $\psi?; true$ and its nondeterministic iteration $(\psi?; true)^*$, the following properties hold, where ψ is an LDL-SL path formula.

Lemma 4. *Given a CGS $\mathcal{G}$, a path formula ψ, a path π, a strategy assignment χ, and $i, j \in \mathbb{N}$,*

$$(i,j) \in \mathcal{R}(\mathcal{G}, \psi?; true, \pi, \chi) \quad \text{if and only if} \quad j = i+1 \text{ and } \mathcal{G}, \chi, \pi, i \models \psi. \tag{13}$$

Proof. $(i,j) \in \mathcal{R}(\mathcal{G}, \psi?; true, \pi, \chi)$ iff there exists k with $i \leq k \leq j$ such that $(i,k) \in \mathcal{R}(\mathcal{G}, \psi?, \pi, \chi)$ and $(k,j) \in \mathcal{R}(\mathcal{G}, true, \pi, \chi)$ iff there exists k with $i \leq k \leq j$ such that $k = i$ and $\mathcal{G}, \chi, \pi, k \models \psi$ and $j = k+1$ iff $j = i+1$ and $\mathcal{G}, \chi, \pi, i \models \psi$. □

Corollary 2. *Given a CGS $\mathcal{G}$, a path formula ψ, a path π, a strategy assignment χ, and $i, j \in \mathbb{N}$,*

$$(i,j) \in \mathcal{R}(\mathcal{G}, (\psi?; true)^*, \pi, \chi) \quad \text{if and only if} \quad j = i \text{ or } (\forall k. i \leq k < j, \mathcal{G}, \chi, \pi, k \models \psi). \tag{14}$$

Proof. $(i,j) \in \mathcal{R}(\mathcal{G}, (\psi?; true)^*, \pi, \chi)$ iff $j = i$ or there exists k ($i \leq k \leq j$) s.t. $(i,k) \in \mathcal{R}(\mathcal{G}, (\psi?; true), \pi, \chi)$ and $(k,j) \in \mathcal{R}(\mathcal{G}, (\psi?; true)^*, \pi, \chi)$ iff $j = i$ or $(\mathcal{G}, \chi, \pi, i \models \psi$ and $(i+1, j) \in \mathcal{R}(\mathcal{G}, (\psi?; true)^*, \pi, \chi))$ by Lemma 4 iff $j = i$ or $(\mathcal{G}, \chi, \pi, i \models \psi, \mathcal{G}, \chi, \pi, i+1 \models \psi$ and $(i+2, j) \in \mathcal{R}(\mathcal{G}, (\psi?; true)^*, \pi, \chi))$ iff $j = i$ or $(\mathcal{G}, \chi, \pi, i \models \psi, \mathcal{G}, \chi, \pi, i+1 \models \psi, ...,$ and $(j-1, j) \in \mathcal{R}(\mathcal{G}, (\psi?; true)^*, \pi, \chi))$ iff $j = i$ or $(\mathcal{G}, \chi, \pi, i \models \psi, \mathcal{G}, \chi, \pi, i+1 \models \psi, ...,$ and $\mathcal{G}, \chi, \pi, j-1 \models \psi)$ repeatedly iff $j = i$ or $(\forall k. i \leq k < j, \mathcal{G}, \chi, \pi, k \models \psi)$. □

Secondly, LDL$_{sf}$-based Strategy Logic (abbr. LDL-SL$_{sf}$ is introduced).

Definition 10 (LDL-SL$_{sf}$ Formula). *The LDL-SL$_{sf}$ formulas are defined as follows:*

$$\text{State formula } \varphi ::= p \mid \neg \varphi \mid \varphi \wedge \varphi \mid \langle\!\langle x \rangle\!\rangle \varphi \mid (a,x)\varphi \mid \mathbf{E}\psi$$

$$\text{Path formula } \psi ::= \varphi \mid \neg \psi \mid \psi \wedge \psi \mid \langle \rho \rangle \psi$$

$$\text{Star-free path expression } \rho ::= \Phi \mid \psi? \mid \rho + \rho \mid \rho;\rho \mid \overline{\rho}$$

where $a \in Ag$, $x \in Var$, $p \in AP$, and $\Phi \in \mathcal{L}(AP)$.

For the semantics of star-free fragment, given a CGS $\mathcal{G}$, a star-free path expression ρ, and a strategy assignment χ, for any $i \leq j$,

$$(i,j) \in \mathcal{R}(\mathcal{G}, \overline{\rho}, \pi, \chi) \quad \text{if and only if} \quad (i,j) \notin \mathcal{R}(\mathcal{G}, \rho, \pi, \chi). \tag{15}$$

4.2. Fragments of LDL-SL and LDL-SL$_{sf}$

In this subsection, we consider fragments for both LDL-SL and LDL-SL$_{sf}$, including SL-like, one-goal fragments, and ATL-like fragments.

Firstly, we consider the SL-like fragment BSL of LDL-SL.

Since LTL is a sublogic of LDL, then by Corollary 2 it is easily shown that BSL is a fragment of LDL-SL by induction and semantics definition. In the following, suppose a logic $\mathcal{L} \in \{BSL, LDL\text{-}SL, ATL^*, ADL^*\}$, let $\mathcal{L}^s$ (resp. $\mathcal{L}^p$) denote all the set of state (resp. path) formulas in $\mathcal{L}$.

Theorem 2. *LDL-SL is strictly more expressive than BSL.*

Proof. Firstly, we define two functions $T^s : BSL^s \to LDL-SL^s$ and $T^p : BSL^p \to LDL-SL^p$ by induction of structures of state formulas and path formulas.
- $T^s(p) = p$; $T^s(\neg \varphi) = \neg T^s(\varphi)$; $T^s(\varphi_1 \wedge \varphi_2) = T^s(\varphi_1) \wedge T^s(\varphi_2)$;
- $T^s((a,x)\varphi) = (a,x)T^s(\varphi)$; $T^s(\langle\!\langle x \rangle\!\rangle \varphi) = \langle\!\langle x \rangle\!\rangle T^s(\varphi)$; $T^s(\mathbf{E}\psi) = \mathbf{E}(T^p(\psi))$.
- $T^p(\varphi) = T^s(\varphi)$; $T^p(\neg \psi) = \neg T^p(\psi)$; $T^p(\psi_1 \wedge \psi_2) = T^p(\psi_1) \wedge T^p(\psi_2)$;
- $T^p(\bigcirc \psi) = \langle true \rangle T^p(\psi)$; $T^p(\diamond \psi) = \langle true^* \rangle T^p(\psi)$;
- $T^p(\psi_1 \mathcal{U} \psi_2) = \langle (T^p(\psi_1)?; true)^* \rangle T^p(\psi_2)$.

By induction, both T^s and T^p are well-defined; i.e., for any $\varphi \in BSL^s$ and $\psi \in BSL^p$, $T^s(\varphi) \in LDL\text{-}SL^s$ and $T^p(\psi) \in LDL\text{-}SL^p$.

Moreover, for any CGS $\mathcal{G}$, a BSL state formula φ, a strategy assignment χ, and a state w, the following holds:

$$\mathcal{G}, \chi, w \models \varphi \quad \text{if and only if} \quad \mathcal{G}, \chi, w \models T^s(\varphi). \tag{16}$$

For any CGS $\mathcal{G}$, a BSL path formula ψ, a strategy assignment χ, a path π, and some $i \in \mathbb{N}$, the following holds:

$$\mathcal{G}, \chi, \pi, i \models \psi \quad \text{if and only if} \quad \mathcal{G}, \chi, \pi, i \models T^p(\psi). \tag{17}$$

We can show the above two mutually by induction.

It is easy to see that for the Boolean cases, the above two are obvious.

For case $\varphi = (a,x)\varphi'$: $\mathcal{G}, \chi, w \models T^s((a,x)\varphi')$ iff $\mathcal{G}, \chi, w \models (a,x)T^s(\varphi')$ by definition of T^s iff $\mathcal{G}, \chi[a \mapsto \chi(x)], w \models T^s(\varphi')$ by semantics definition iff $\mathcal{G}, \chi[a \mapsto \chi(x)], w \models \varphi'$ by induction iff $\mathcal{G}, \chi, w \models (a,x)\varphi'$ by semantics definition.

For case $\varphi = \langle\!\langle x \rangle\!\rangle \varphi'$: $\mathcal{G}, \chi, w \models T^s(\langle\!\langle x \rangle\!\rangle \varphi')$ iff $\mathcal{G}, \chi, w \models \langle\!\langle x \rangle\!\rangle T^s(\varphi')$ by definition of T^s iff $\exists g \in Str(\mathcal{G})$, $\mathcal{G}, \chi[x \mapsto g], w \models T^s(\varphi')$ iff $\exists g \in Str(\mathcal{G})$, $\mathcal{G}, \chi[x \mapsto g], w \models \varphi'$ iff $\mathcal{G}, \chi, w \models \langle\!\langle x \rangle\!\rangle \varphi'$.

For case $\varphi = \mathbf{E}\psi$: $\mathcal{G}, \chi, w \models T^s(\mathbf{E}\psi)$ iff $\mathcal{G}, \chi, w \models \mathbf{E}(T^p(\psi))$ by definition of T^s iff $\exists \pi \in out(\mathcal{G}, \chi, w)$ s.t. $\mathcal{G}, \chi, \pi, 0 \models T^p(\psi)$ iff $\exists \pi \in out(\mathcal{G}, \chi, w)$ s.t. $\mathcal{G}, \chi, \pi, 0 \models \psi$ iff $\mathcal{G}, \chi, w \models \mathbf{E}\psi$.

For case $\psi = \varphi \in BSL^s$: $\mathcal{G}, \chi, \pi, i \models T^p(\varphi)$ iff $\mathcal{G}, \chi, \pi, i \models T^s(\varphi)$ by definition of T^p iff $\mathcal{G}, \chi, \pi_i \models T^s(\varphi)$ iff $\mathcal{G}, \chi, \pi(i) \models \varphi$ iff $\mathcal{G}, \chi, \pi, i \models \varphi$.

For case $\psi = \bigcirc \psi'$: $\mathcal{G}, \chi, \pi, i \models T^p(\bigcirc \psi')$ iff $\mathcal{G}, \chi, \pi, i \models \langle true \rangle T^p(\psi')$ by definition of T^p iff $\mathcal{G}, \chi, \pi, i+1 \models T^p(\psi')$ iff $\mathcal{G}, \chi, \pi, i+1 \models \psi'$ iff $\mathcal{G}, \chi, \pi, i \models \bigcirc \psi'$.

For case $\psi = \diamond \psi'$: $\mathcal{G}, \chi, \pi, i \models T^p(\diamond \psi')$ iff $\mathcal{G}, \chi, \pi, i \models \langle true^* \rangle T^p(\psi')$ by definition of T^p iff there exists $j \geq i$, $\mathcal{G}, \chi, \pi, j \models T^p(\psi')$ iff there exists $j \geq i$, $\mathcal{G}, \chi, \pi, j \models \psi'$ iff $\mathcal{G}, \chi, \pi, i \models \diamond \psi'$.

For case $\psi = \psi_1 \mathcal{U} \psi_2$: $\mathcal{G}, \chi, \pi, i \models T^p(\psi_1 \mathcal{U} \psi_2)$ iff $\mathcal{G}, \chi, \pi, i \models \langle (T^p(\psi_1)?; true)^* \rangle T^p(\psi_2)$ by definition of T^p iff there exists j with $(i, j) \in \mathcal{R}(\mathcal{G}, (T^p(\psi_1)?; true)^*, \pi, \chi)$, such that $\mathcal{G}, \chi, \pi, i \models T^p(\psi_2)$ iff there exists j with $j = i$ or ($\forall k, i \leq k < j$, satisfying that $\mathcal{G}, \chi, \pi, k \models T^p(\psi_1)$), such that $\mathcal{G}, \chi, \pi, i \models T^p(\psi_2)$ by semantics definition and Corollary 2 iff there exists j with $j = i$ or ($\forall k, i \leq k < j$, satisfying that $\mathcal{G}, \chi, \pi, k \models \psi_1$), such that $\mathcal{G}, \chi, \pi, i \models \psi_2$ by induction iff $\mathcal{G}, \chi, \pi, i \models \psi_1 \mathcal{U} \psi_2$.

Secondly, according to a well-known property $even(q)$ "a proposition q has to be true in each even state of one sequence" cannot be expressed in LTL [14], which can be expressed in LDL by $[(true; true)^*]q$. Considering those CGSs with only one agent, LDL-SL formula $\langle\langle x \rangle\rangle (a, x) \mathbf{E}[(true; true)^*]q$ cannot be expressed by any BSL formula.

Hence we have shown that LDL-SL is more expressively than BSL. □

Secondly, we consider a one-goal fragment LDL-SL[1G] and an ATL-like fragment ADL* of LDL-SL.

The syntax of LDL-SL[1G] is the same as that of LDL-SL, except for state formulas:

$$\text{State formula } \varphi ::= p \mid \neg \varphi \mid \varphi \wedge \varphi \mid \mathbf{E}\psi \mid \wp \flat \varphi, \qquad (18)$$

where $p \in AP$, and $\wp \flat$ is a closed combination of a quantification/binding prefix.

The following is ATL-like fragment ADL* of LDL-SL, of which the path formulas are different from those of ATL*.

Definition 11 (ADL* Syntax). *The syntax of ADL* is defined as follows:*

$$\text{State formula } \varphi ::= p \mid \neg \varphi \mid \varphi \wedge \varphi \mid \langle\langle A \rangle\rangle \psi$$

$$\text{Path formula } \psi ::= \varphi \mid \neg \psi \mid \psi \wedge \psi \mid \langle \rho \rangle \psi$$

$$\text{Regular expression } \rho ::= \Phi \mid \psi? \mid \rho + \rho \mid \rho; \rho \mid \rho^*,$$

where $p \in AP$, $A \subseteq Ag$, and $\Phi \in \mathcal{L}(AP)$.

By the following lemma, any ATL* formula can be expressed in ADL*.

Lemma 5. *Any ATL* formula can be linearly encoded by one ADL* formula.*

Proof. Define two translation functions $T^s : ATL^{*s} \to ADL^{*s}$, $T^p : ATL^{*p} \to ADL^{*p}$:

- $T^s(p) = p$; $T^s(\neg \varphi) = \neg T^s(\varphi)$; $T^s(\varphi_1 \wedge \varphi_2) = T^s(\varphi_1) \wedge^s (\varphi_2)$;
- $T^s(\langle\langle A \rangle\rangle \psi) = \langle\langle A \rangle\rangle T^p(\psi)$.
- $T^p(\varphi) = T^s(\varphi)$; $T^p(\neg \psi) = \neg T^p(\psi)$; $T^p(\psi_1 \wedge \psi_2) = T^p(\psi_1) \wedge T^p(\psi_2)$;
- $T^p(\bigcirc \psi) = \langle true \rangle T^p(\psi)$; $T^p(\diamond \psi) = \langle true^* \rangle T^p(\psi)$;
- $T^p(\psi_1 \mathcal{U} \psi_2) = \langle (T^p(\psi_1)?; true)^* \rangle T^p(\psi_2)$.

Here to show this lemma, similarly with those in Theorem 2, the only different case is $\varphi = \langle\langle A \rangle\rangle \psi$. Given a CGS $\mathcal{G}$, a state w, a state formula φ,

- for the case $\varphi = \langle\langle A \rangle\rangle \psi$: $\mathcal{G}, w \models T^s(\langle\langle A \rangle\rangle \psi)$ iff $\mathcal{G}, w \models \langle\langle A \rangle\rangle T^p(\psi)$ by definition of T^s iff there exist collective strategies g_A s.t. for each $\pi \in out(w, g_A)$, $\mathcal{G}, \pi, 0 \models T^p(\psi)$

by semantics iff there exist collective strategies g_A s.t. for each $\pi \in out(w, g_A)$, $\mathcal{G}, \pi, 0 \models \psi$ by induction iff $\mathcal{G}, w \models \langle\!\langle A \rangle\!\rangle \psi$ by semantics.

Obviously, for any $\varphi \in \text{ATL}^{*s}$, the size of $T^s(\varphi)$ is $O(|\varphi|)$. □

Thirdly, we consider one-goal fragment LDL-SL[1G]$_{sf}$ and ATL-like fragment ADL$^*_{sf}$ of LDL-SL$_{sf}$. The syntax of LDL-SL[1G]$_{sf}$ is the same as that of LDL-SL[1G] except for regular expressions:

$$\text{Regular expression } \rho ::= \Phi \mid \psi? \mid \rho + \rho \mid \rho;\rho \mid \overline{\rho}, \tag{19}$$

where $\Phi \in \mathcal{L}(AP)$, and ψ is a path formula in LDL-SL[1G]$_{sf}$.

The syntax of ADL$^*_{sf}$ is the same that of ADL* except for regular expressions,

$$\text{Regular expression } \rho ::= \Phi \mid \psi? \mid \rho + \rho \mid \rho;\rho \mid \overline{\rho}, \tag{20}$$

where $\Phi \in \mathcal{L}(AP)$ and ψ is a path formula in ADL$^*_{sf}$.

Here we consider three kinds of fragments of LDL-SL: one-goal fragment, star-free, and ATL-like. The semantics of these logics are the same as those of LDL-SL and LDL-SL$_{sf}$, respectively.

5. Expressivity Relations among Fragments of LDL-SL and LDL-SL$_{sf}$

In this section, we study the expressivity relations among mentioned fragments of LDL-SL and LDL-SL$_{sf}$. Firstly, we give the following definitions about the expressive power between two logics.

Logic L_1 is *at least as expressive as* logic L_2, denoted as $L_2 \subseteq L_1$, if given a model M, for any formula φ in L_2, there exists a formula φ' in L_1, satisfying that $M \models \varphi$ iff $M \models \varphi'$. L_1 is *strictly more expressive than* L_2, denoted as $L_2 \subsetneq L_1$, if $L_2 \subseteq L_1$, but $L_1 \subseteq L_2$ does not hold. L_1 has *the same expressive power as* L_2, denoted as $L_1 \equiv L_2$, if $L_1 \subseteq L_2$ and $L_2 \subseteq L_1$. L_1 and L_2 are incomparable if neither $L_2 \subseteq L_1$ nor $L_1 \subseteq L_2$.

According to Theorem 1, star-free type strategic logics have the same expressive power as their corresponding strategic logics based on LTL or CTL*.

Theorem 3. *Star-free strategic logics have the same expressive power as their corresponding strategic logics whose underlying logic is LTL or ATL*.*
1. ADL$^*_{sf} \equiv$ ATL*;
2. LDL-SL$_{sf} \equiv$ BSL;
3. LDL-SL[1G]$_{sf} \equiv$ BSL[1G].

Proof. By applying Lemma 2 that LDL$_{sf}$ is equivalent with LTL, these results can be shown by induction of the structures of formulas similarly. Here, we just sketch the ideas of proofs as follows.

In order to show that ADL$^*_{sf} \subseteq$ ATL*, by induction hypothesis, we just consider the case $\varphi = \langle\!\langle A \rangle\!\rangle \psi$, which is an ADL$^*_{sf}$ formula. Suppose for each maximal state subformulas φ' in φ, by induction, there is an ATL* formula equivalent with φ'. If we use a new atom $p_{\varphi'}$ to replace it, then make ψ be equivalent with a pure LDL formula. By Lemma 2, replace ψ with one LTL formula; and further replace those new atoms $p_{\varphi'}$ with original ATL* state formulas. Hence the resulting formula is an ATL* state formula, equivalent with φ.

Similarly, we can show that LDL-SL$_{sf} \subseteq$ BSL and LDL-SL[1G]$_{sf} \subseteq$ BSL[1G].

For item 1: In order to show ATL* $\subseteq$ ADL$^*_{sf}$, define two functions T^s and T^p similarly with those in Lemma 5 except the following two cases in T^p.

$$T^p(\diamond\psi) = \langle \overline{false} \rangle T^p(\psi), T^p(\psi_1 \mathcal{U} \psi_2) = T^p(\psi_2) \vee \langle \overline{false;\neg T^p(\psi_1)?;\overline{false}};true \rangle T^p(\psi_2) \tag{21}$$

Here, the proof for case $\psi = \diamond \psi_1$ or $\psi = \psi_1 \mathcal{U} \psi_2$ about $\mathcal{G}, \pi, i \models T^p(\psi)$ iff $\mathcal{G}, \pi, i \models \psi$ is the same as that of Lemma 2.

Similarly to Item 1, and by Theorem 2, BSL $\subseteq$ LDL-SL$_{sf}$ and BSL[1G] $\subseteq$ LDL-SL[1G]$_{sf}$ can be shown. □

Theorem 4. *The following fragments are incomparable.*
1. *BSL and LDL-SL[1G] are incomparable.*
2. *BSL[1G] and ADL* are incomparable.*

Proof. Here, we just sketch the ideas of proofs.

For item (1), we consider the following formulas:
- $\varphi_1 = \langle\langle x \rangle\rangle [\![y]\!] \langle\langle z \rangle\rangle ((a,x)(b,y)\mathbf{E} \bigcirc p \vee (a,y)(b,z)\mathbf{E} \bigcirc \neg p)$
- $\varphi_2 = \langle\langle x \rangle\rangle (a,x)(\mathbf{E}[(true; true)^*]p)$

where φ_1 is a BSL formula, but it cannot be expressed in LDL-SL[1G]; = conversely, φ_2 is a LDL-SL[1G] formula, but it cannot be expressed in BSL.

In order to show that φ_2 cannot be expressed in BSL, we consider all the CGSs with just one agent and an action. So in these CGSs, each BSL sentence is equivalent with one CTL* state formula. Suppose φ is a CTL* state formula with m $\bigcirc$ temporal operators; then, consider the following two CGSs with just one agent and an action—see Figure 1. In $\mathcal{G}_1$, p holds in all states, and in $\mathcal{G}_2$, p does not hold only in state w_{2m+1}. Due to unique path starting from the initial state, we can see that φ is equivalent with an LTL formula ψ under each $\mathcal{G}_i, i \in \{1,2\}$. Then by the following theorem given by Wolper,

Theorem 4.1 ([14]) *Given an atomic proposition q, any LTL formula $f(q)$ containing m $\bigcirc$ temporal operators has the same truth value on all sequences such as $q^k(\neg q)q^\omega$, here $k > m$ and $f(q)$ is a LTL formula containing only atomic q.*

It holds that $\mathcal{G}_1 \models \psi$ iff $\mathcal{G}_2 \models \psi$. However, $\mathcal{G}_1 \models \varphi_2$, but $\mathcal{G}_2 \not\models \varphi_2$. Therefore, φ_2 cannot be expressed in BSL.

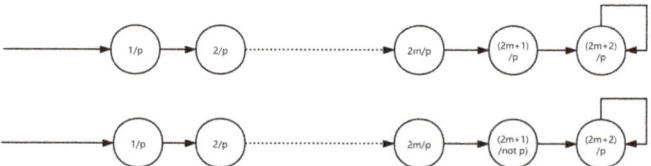

Figure 1. Two CGSs for φ_2: the top is $\mathcal{G}_1$ and the bottom is $\mathcal{G}_2$.

For item (2), we consider the following two formulas:
- $\varphi_3 = [\![x]\!] \langle\langle y \rangle\rangle [\![z]\!] (a,x)(b,y)(c,z) \mathbf{E} \bigcirc p$
- $\varphi_4 = \langle\langle \{a\} \rangle\rangle ([(true; true)^*]p)$

Here, φ_3 is a BSL[1G] formula, but it cannot be expressed in ADL*; conversely, φ_4 is a ADL* formula, but cannot be expressed in BSL[1G].

Like in [24], consider two concurrent game structures CGSs with $AP = \{p\}$ and $Ag = \{a,b,c\}$, $\mathcal{G}_1 = \langle Ac_1, W_1, \lambda_1, \tau_1, w_0 \rangle$, and $\mathcal{G}_2 = \langle Ac_2, W_2, \lambda_2, \tau_2, w_0 \rangle$, where $Ac_1 = \{0,1\}$, $Ac_2 = \{0,1,2\}$, $W_1 = W_2 = \{w_0, w_1, w_2\}$, $\lambda_1 = \lambda_2$, and $D_1 = \{00*, 11*\}$, $D_2 = \{211, 202, 200, 00*, 11*, 12*\}$. $\lambda_1(w_0) = \lambda_1(w_2) = \varnothing$, $\lambda_1(w_1) = \{p\}$. $\forall d \in D_i$, $\tau_i(w_0, d) = w_1$; $\forall d \in Dc_i \setminus D_i, \tau(w_0, d) = w_2$; $\forall d \in Dc_i, w \in \{w_1, w_2\}, \tau_i(w, d) = w$, here $i \in \{1,2\}$ and $Dc_i = Ac_i^{Ag}$. We can show that $\mathcal{G}_1 \models \varphi_3$, but $\mathcal{G}_2 \not\models \varphi_3$. Inspired by the approach in [24], it can be shown that any ADL* formula cannot distinguish between $\mathcal{G}_1$ and $\mathcal{G}_2$.

In order to show that φ_1 cannot be expressed in LDL-SL[1G], we can adopt the same two CGSs like for φ_3 here. The proof that φ_4 cannot be expressed in BSL[1G] is similar with that for φ_2. □

Theorem 5. *Inclusion relations among existing strategic logics:*
1. $ADL^*_{sf} \subsetneq ADL^* \subsetneq LDL\text{-}SL[1G] \subsetneq LDL\text{-}SL$;
2. $LDL\text{-}SL[1G]_{sf} \subsetneq LDL\text{-}SL[1G]$;
3. $BSL \subsetneq LDL\text{-}SL$.

Proof. By Lemma 1, the star-free logic ADL^*_{sf} (resp. $LDL\text{-}SL[1G]_{sf}$) is less expressive than ADL^* (resp. LDL-SL[1G]). One-goal fragment LDL-SL[1G] is obviously less expressive than LDL-SL, due to the restriction about the alternations about strategy variables and agent bindings. Furthermore, the ATL-like fragment ADL^* of LDL-SL is less than one-goal fragment LDL-SL[1G] of LDL-SL, since the coalition operators $\langle\langle A \rangle\rangle$ can be specified by the $\wp\flat$ prefix. □

According to Theorems 3–5, as well as $CL \subsetneq ATL \subsetneq ATL^* \subsetneq BSL[1G] \subsetneq SL$, we can obtain an expressivity graph; see Figure 2.

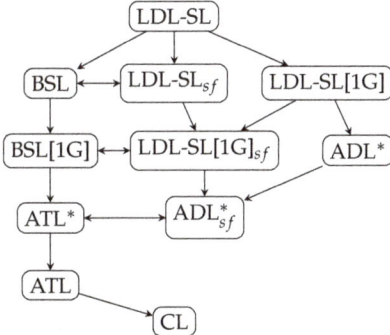

Figure 2. Expressivity Graph.

Here, coalition logic (CL) [29] is a logic, which just has coalition operators without temporal operators.

$$\varphi ::= p \mid \neg\varphi \mid \varphi \wedge \varphi \mid \langle\langle A \rangle\rangle\varphi. \tag{22}$$

6. Positive and Negative Properties for LDL-SL

In this section, similar with those results about BSL in [30], we state negative/positive results about LDL-SL.

Firstly, as in [30], for LDL-SL, we introduce four basic definitions, including bisimilarity between two CGSs, local isomorphism between two CGSs, state-unwinding, and decision-unwinding.

Definition 12 ([30]). *CGSs $\mathcal{G}_1 = \langle Act_1, W_1, \lambda_1, \tau_1, w_1^0 \rangle$ and $\mathcal{G}_2 = \langle Act_2, W_1, \lambda_2, \tau_2, w_2^0 \rangle$ are called bisimilar, denoted as $\mathcal{G}_1 \sim \mathcal{G}_2$, if and only if (1) there exists one relation $\sim \subseteq W_1 \times W_2$, named as bisimulation relation, and (2) there exists a function $f : \sim \to 2^{Act_1 \times Act_2}$, named as bisimulation function, satisfying that:*
1. $w_1^0 \sim w_{1'}^0$;
2. *for each state pair $(w_1, w_2) \in W_1 \times W_2$, if $w_1 \sim w_2$ then*
    (a) $\lambda_1(w_1) = \lambda_2(w_2)$;
    (b) *for each $ac_1 \in Act_1$, there exists $ac_2 \in Act_2$ satisfying $(ac_1, ac_2) \in f(w_1, w_2)$;*
    (c) *for each $ac_2 \in Act_2$, there exists $ac_1 \in Act_1$ satisfying $(ac_1, ac_2) \in f(w_1, w_2)$;*

(d) for each decision pair $(d_1, d_2) \in \hat{f}(w_1, w_2)$, it holds that $\tau_1(w_1, d_1) \sim \tau(w_2, d_2)$.

Here, $\hat{f}: \sim \to 2^{Dc_1 \times Dc_2}$ is the lifting of function f from actions to decisions, satisfying

$$(d_1, d_2) \in \hat{f}(w_1, w_2) \text{ iff it holds that } (d_1(a), d_2(a)) \in f(w_1, w_2), \forall a \in Ag. \quad (23)$$

Obviously, according to the definition of bisimulation relation, the bisimulation of two CGSs can imply the existence of a bismulation between two decisions in them.

Proposition 1. *Suppose that two concurrent game structures $\mathcal{G}_1 = \langle Act_1, W_1, \lambda_1, \tau_1, w_1^0 \rangle$ and $\mathcal{G}_2 = \langle Act_2, W_1, \lambda_2, \tau_2, w_2^0 \rangle$ are bisimilar with a bisimulation relation $\sim$ and a bisimulation relation f, for each state pair $(w_1, w_2) \in W_1 \times W_2$ with $w_1 \sim w_2$, it holds that:*
1. *for each $d_1 \in Dc_1$, there exists $d_2 \in Dc_2$ satisfying that $(d_1, d_2) \in \hat{f}(w_1, w_2)$;*
2. *for each $d_2 \in Dc_2$, there exists $d_1 \in Dc_1$ satisfying that $(d_1, d_2) \in \hat{f}(w_1, w_2)$.*

Next, we define the notion of local isomorphism relation between two CGSs.

Definition 13 ([30]). *Two CGSs $\mathcal{G}_1 = \langle Act_1, W_1, \lambda_1, \tau_1, w_1^0 \rangle$ and $\mathcal{G}_2 = \langle Act_2, W_1, \lambda_2, \tau_2, w_2^0 \rangle$ are locally isomorphic, denoted as $\mathcal{G}_1 \cong \mathcal{G}_2$, if and only if there exists a bisimulation relation $\sim \subseteq W_1 \times W_2$ between these two CGSs, satisfying that, for each state pair $(w_1, w_2) \in W_1 \times W_2$ with $w_1 \sim w_2$*

$$\sim \cap (\{\tau_1(w_1, d) : d \in Dc_1\} \times \{\tau_2(w_2, d) : d \in Dc_2\}) \quad (24)$$

is bijective between the successors of w_1 and those of w_2.

Now we extend the definition of locally isomorphic to tracks, paths, strategies, and assignments as follows.

Definition 14. *Let $\sim$ (resp. f) be a bisimulation relation (resp. function) between two CGSs $\mathcal{G}_1 = \langle Act_1, W_1, \lambda_1, \tau_1, w_1^0 \rangle$ and $\mathcal{G}_2 = \langle Act_2, W_1, \lambda_2, \tau_2, w_2^0 \rangle$.*
- *Two tracks $h_1 \in Trk(\mathcal{G}_1)$ and $h_2 \in Trk(\mathcal{G}_2)$ are locally isomophic, denoted as $h_1 \sim h_2$, if (1) $len(h_1) = len(h_2)$; (2) $\forall i. 0 \leq i < len(h_1), (h_1)_i \sim (h_2)_i$ holds.*
- *Two paths $\pi_1 \in Path(\mathcal{G}_1)$ and $\pi_2 \in Trk(\mathcal{G}_2)$ are locally isomorphic, denoted as $\pi_1 \sim \pi_2$, if $\forall i \in \mathbb{N}, (\pi_1)_i \sim (\pi_2)_i$ holds.*
- *Two strategies $g_1 \in Str(\mathcal{G}_1)$ and $g_2 \in Str(\mathcal{G}_2)$ are locally isomorphic, denoted as $g_1 \sim g_2$, if $\forall k \in \{1, 2\}$ and $h_k \in dom(g_k)$, there exists $h_{3-k} \in dom(g_{3-k})$ with $\pi_1 \sim \pi_2$ satisfying $(g_1(h_1), g_2(h_2)) \in f(lst(h_1), lst(h_2))$.*
- *Two assignments $\chi_1 \in Asg(\mathcal{G}_1)$ and $\chi_2 \in Asg(\mathcal{G}_2)$ are locally isomorphic, denoted as $\chi_1 \sim \chi_2$, if (1) $dom(\chi_1) = dom(\chi_2)$ and (2) $\chi_1(h) \sim \chi_2(h), \forall h \in dom(\chi_2)$.*

In Definition 14, obviously, if $\chi_1 \sim \chi_2$ and $g_1 \sim g_2$, then $\chi_1[x \mapsto g_1] \sim \chi_2[x \mapsto g_2]$. Further, if $\forall i \in \{1, 2\}, \chi_i$ is a complete w_i-total assignment, and $w_1 \sim w_2$, then it holds that $\pi_1 \sim \pi_2$ and $(\chi_1)_{(\pi_1) \leq k} \sim (\chi_2)_{(\pi_2) \leq k'} \forall k \in \mathbb{N}$, where π_i is the (χ_i, w_i)-play.

To show whether LDL-SL has tree model properties, consider two unwinding forms of concurrent game structures; one is about state-unwinding, and another is about decision-unwinding.

Definition 15 ([30]). *Given a CGS $\mathcal{G} = \langle Act, W, \lambda, \tau, w^0 \rangle$, the state-unwinding of $\mathcal{G}$ is the new CGS $\mathcal{G}_{su} = \langle Ac, W_{su}, \lambda_{su}, \tau_{su}, \epsilon \rangle$, where*
- $W_{su} = \{h_{\geq 1} \in W^* : h \in Trk(\mathcal{G}, w^0)\}$;
- $\tau_{su}(h, d) = h \cdot \tau(last(w^0 \cdot h), d)$, *here $d \in Dc$;*
- *there exists a surjective function $surj : W_{su} \to W$, satisfying that for each $h \in W_{su}$ and $d \in Dc$, (1) $surj(h) = last(w^0 \cdot h)$; (2) $\lambda_{su}(h) = \lambda(surj(h))$.*

From Definition 15, the state-unwinding $\mathcal{G}_{su}$ of a CGS $\mathcal{G} = \langle Act, W, \lambda, \tau, w^0 \rangle$ is a tree, whose direction set is just the set W of states in $\mathcal{G}$.

Definition 16 ([30]). *Given a CGS $\mathcal{G} = \langle Act, W, \lambda, \tau, w^0 \rangle$, the decision-unwinding of $\mathcal{G}$ is the new CGS $\mathcal{G}_{du} = \langle Act, W_{du}, \lambda_{du}, \tau_{du}, \epsilon \rangle$, where*

- $W_{du} = Dc^*$ and $\tau_{du}(h, d) = h \cdot d$;
- *there exists a surjective function* $surj : W_{du} \to W$, *satisfying that for each* $h \in W_{du}$ *and* $d \in Dc$, (1) $surj(\epsilon) = w^0$; (2) $surj(\tau_{du}((h,d))) = \tau(surj(h), d)$; (3) $\lambda_{du}(h) = \lambda(surj(h))$.

From Definition 16, the decision-unwinding $\mathcal{G}_{du}$ of a CGS $\mathcal{G} = \langle Act, W, \lambda, \tau, w^0 \rangle$ is a tree, whose direction set is just the set Dc (i.e., Act^{Ag}) in $\mathcal{G}$.

Theorem 6 ([30]). *Given a CGS $\mathcal{G}$, the following properties hold:*

1. *$\mathcal{G}$ and its state-unwinding $\mathcal{G}_{su}$ are locally isomorphic;*
2. *$\mathcal{G}$ and decision-unwinding $\mathcal{G}_{du}$ are bisimilar;*
3. *there exists a CGS $\mathcal{G}'$, satisfying that $\mathcal{G}'$ and $\mathcal{G}'_{du}$ are not locally isomorphic.*

We note that any CGS $\mathcal{G}$ just has a unique associated state-unwinding $\mathcal{G}_{su}$ and a unique associated decision-unwinding $\mathcal{G}_{du}$.

For BSL logic, the following negative properties hold.

Theorem 7 ([30]). *Four negative properties for BSL:*

- *it holds that BSL is not decision-unwinding invariant;*
- *it holds that BSL does not have the bounded tree model property;*
- *it holds that BSL does not have the finite model property;*
- *it holds that BSL is not bisimulation invariant.*

These negative results can be extended into LDL-SL.

Theorem 8. *Four negative properties for LDL-SL:*

- *it holds that LDL-SL is not decision-unwinding invariant;*
- *it holds that LDL-SL does not have the bounded tree model property;*
- *it holds that LDL-SL does not have the finite model property;*
- *it holds that LDL-SL is not bisimulation invariant.*

Proof. By Theorems 2 and 7, these results are the same as those for BSL. □

Similar with those positive properties for BSL [30], the following properties also hold for LDL-SL.

Theorem 9. *Three positive properties for LDL-SL:*

1. *it holds that LDL-SL is local isomorphism invariant;*
2. *it holds that LDL-SL is state-unwinding invariant;*
3. *it holds that LDL-SL has the unbounded tree model property.*

Proof. For item 1:

For any LDL-SL formula φ, given any two CGSs $\mathcal{G}_1$ and $\mathcal{G}_2$ with $\mathcal{G}_1 \cong \mathcal{G}_2$, two states $w_1 \in W_1$ and $w_2 \in W_2$ with $w_1 \sim w_2$, two assignments $\chi_1 \in Asg(\mathcal{G}_1, w_1)$, and $\chi_2 \in Asg(\mathcal{G}, w_2)$ with $\chi_1 \sim \chi_2$, here $free(\varphi) \subseteq dom(\chi_1) = dom(\chi_2)$, we inductively show that

$$\mathcal{G}_1, \chi_1, w_1 \models \varphi \quad \text{if and only if} \quad \mathcal{G}_2, \chi_2, w_2 \models \varphi. \tag{25}$$

From the bisimulation definition and the inductive hypothesis, the cases of atoms and Boolean connectives are easy. As for the cases of existential quantification $\langle\!\langle x \rangle\!\rangle$ and agent binding (a, x), the proofs are the same as those in [30]. Here we just show the case of $\mathbf{E}\psi$, here ψ is a path formula. $\mathcal{G}_1, \chi_1, w_1 \models \mathbf{E}\psi$ iff there exists a $\pi \in out(\mathcal{G}_1, \chi_1, w_1)$ such that $\mathcal{G}_1, \chi_1, \pi_1, 0 \models \psi$.

That means we should mutually show with state formulas by induction, i.e.,

$$\mathcal{G}_1, \chi_1, \pi_1, i \models \psi \quad \text{if and only if} \quad \mathcal{G}_2, \chi_2, \pi_2, i \models \psi. \tag{26}$$

For the case $\psi = \varphi'$: $\mathcal{G}_1, \chi_1, \pi_1, i \models \varphi'$ iff $\mathcal{G}_1, \chi_1, (\pi_1)_i \models \varphi'$ iff $\mathcal{G}_2, \chi_2, (\pi_2)_i \models \varphi_2$ by induction iff $\mathcal{G}_2, \chi_2, \pi_2, i \models \varphi'$.

For the cases of Boolean connectives, these are easy from the definitions and the inductive hypothesis.

For the case $\psi = \langle \rho \rangle \psi'$: we need to show the following by induction,

$$(i, j) \in \mathcal{R}(\mathcal{G}_1, \rho, \pi_1, \chi_1) \quad \text{if and only if} \quad (i, j) \in \mathcal{R}(\mathcal{G}_2, \rho, \pi_2, \chi_2). \tag{27}$$

For case $\rho = \Phi$: $(i, j) \in \mathcal{R}(\mathcal{G}_1, \Phi, \pi_1, \chi_1)$ iff $j = i + 1$ and $\mathcal{G}_1, \chi_1, \pi_1, i \models \Phi$ by definition iff $j = i + 1$ and $\mathcal{G}_2, \chi_2, \pi_2, i \models \Phi$.

For case $\rho = \psi?$: $(i, j) \in \mathcal{R}(\mathcal{G}_1, \psi?, \pi_1, \chi_1)$ iff $j = i$ and $\mathcal{G}_1, \chi_1, \pi_1, i \models \psi$ by definition iff $j = i$ and $\mathcal{G}_2, \chi_2, \pi_2, i \models \psi$ by induction.

For case $\rho = \rho_1 + \rho_2$: $(i, j) \in \mathcal{R}(\mathcal{G}_1, \rho_1 + \rho_2, \pi_1, \chi_1)$ iff $(i, j) \in \mathcal{R}(\mathcal{G}_1, \rho_1, \pi_1, \chi_1)$ or $(i, j) \in \mathcal{R}(\mathcal{G}_1, \rho_2, \pi_1, \chi_1)$ iff $(i, j) \in \mathcal{R}(\mathcal{G}_2, \rho_1, \pi_2, \chi_2)$ or $(i, j) \in \mathcal{R}(\mathcal{G}_2, \rho_2, \pi_2, \chi_2)$ by induction iff $(i, j) \in \mathcal{R}(\mathcal{G}_2, \rho_1 + \rho_2, \pi_2, \chi_2)$.

For case $\rho = \rho_1; \rho_2$: $(i, j) \in \mathcal{R}(\mathcal{G}_1, \rho_1; \rho_2, \pi_1, \chi_1)$ iff there exists $k, i \leq k \leq j$, satisfying that $(i, k) \in \mathcal{R}(\mathcal{G}_1, \rho_1, \pi_1, \chi_1)$ and $(k, j) \in \mathcal{R}(\mathcal{G}_1, \rho_2, \pi_1, \chi_1)$ iff there exists k, $i \leq k \leq j$, satisfying that $(i, k) \in \mathcal{R}(\mathcal{G}_2, \rho_1, \pi_2, \chi_2)$ and $(k, j) \in \mathcal{R}(\mathcal{G}_2, \rho_2, \pi_2, \chi_2)$ by induction iff $(i, j) \in \mathcal{R}(\mathcal{G}_2, \rho_1; \rho_2, \pi_2, \chi_2)$.

For case $\rho = \rho_1^*$: $(i, j) \in \mathcal{R}(\mathcal{G}_1, \rho_1^*, \pi_1, \chi_1)$ iff $j = i$ or $(i, j) \in \mathcal{R}(\mathcal{G}_1, \rho_1; \rho_1^*, \pi_1, \chi_1)$ iff $j = i$ or $(i, j) \in \mathcal{R}(\mathcal{G}_2, \rho_2; \rho_2^*, \pi_1, \chi_1)$ by induction iff $(i, j) \in \mathcal{R}(\mathcal{G}_2, \rho_1^*, \pi_2, \chi_2)$.

Therefore, it implies that LDL-SL is indeed invariant under local isomorphism.

For item 2: by item 1 in Theorem 6, for any CGS $\mathcal{G}$, it holds that $\mathcal{G} \cong \mathcal{G}_{su}$. So by item 1, each LDL-SL sentence φ is an invariant for CGS $\mathcal{G}$ and its state-unwinding $\mathcal{G}_{su}$.

For item 3: let the LDL-SL sentence φ be satisfiable. Therefore, there exists one CGS $\mathcal{G} \models \varphi$, and by item 2, it holds that $\mathcal{G}_{su} \models \varphi$. Since $\mathcal{G}_{su}$ is a tree model, this means that LDL-SL has the (unbounded) tree model property. □

7. Complexities of Model Checking

In this section, we analyse the computational complexities of the model checking problems for these strategic logics. Firstly, we present the definition about the model checking problem. Secondly, we study the model-checking complexities for ADL*, LDL-SL[1G], and LDL-SL. Then we apply expressivity results to infer other logics' model-checking complexities. Due to space restriction, we omit the introduction about automaton theory; please refer to, e.g., [31].

Let $|\mathcal{G}|$ (resp. $|\varphi|$) denote the number of transitions in $\mathcal{G}$ (resp. the length of φ).

Problem 1 (Model-Checking Problem (MCP) for Strategic Logic). *given a concurrent game structure CGS $\mathcal{G}$, a sentence φ in strategic logic $\mathcal{L}$, and a state w, decide whether $\mathcal{G}, w \models \varphi$.*

7.1. Model-Checking for ADL*

Before considering the MCP for ADL*, remember that a state formula in a test in a ADL* state formula φ is also a state subformula of φ.

Theorem 10. *The computational complexity of model-checking for ADL* is 2EXPTIME-complete, in time polynomial w.r.t. the size of CGS model and double exponential in the size of ADL* formula.*

Proof. Firstly, because the MCP for ATL* is 2EXPTIME-complete [5], which can be linearly encoded by that for ADL* by Lemma 5, then the MCP for ADL* is 2EXPTIME-hard. Next we show that the complexity of model checking for ADL* is in 2EXPTIME.

Given a CGS model $\mathcal{G} = \langle Ac, W, \lambda, \tau, w^0 \rangle$ and an ADL* formula φ, as in the model-checking algorithm for CTL, we adopt the labelling algorithm, in a bottom-up fashion, starting from the innermost state subformulas of φ. We label each state w of $\mathcal{G}$ by all state subformulas of φ that are satisfied in w. To give this algorithm, we only consider the case $\varphi = \langle\!\langle A \rangle\!\rangle \psi$, for each subformula φ' such as $\langle\!\langle B \rangle\!\rangle \psi'$ in ψ, introduce a new atomic proposition $p_{\varphi'}$ in $\mathcal{G}$, where for each state w, $p_{\varphi'} \in \lambda(w)$ iff $\mathcal{G}, w \models \varphi'$. Therefore, assume that ψ is just an LDL formula.

Now we mainly consider $\varphi = \langle\!\langle A \rangle\!\rangle \psi$, where ψ is an LDL formula.

1. Construct a Büchi tree automaton $\mathcal{A}_{\mathcal{G},w,A}$ as in [5].

   Here, $\mathcal{A}_{\mathcal{G},w,A}$ accepts exactly the (w, A)-execution trees, which are trees induced by $out(w, g_A)$, where g_A is a collective strategy of A. Automaton $\mathcal{A}_{\mathcal{G},w,A}$ is bounded by $O(|\mathcal{G}|)$.

2. Construct a Rabin tree automaton $\mathcal{A}_{\mathbf{A}\psi}$.

   Here, $\mathcal{A}_{\mathbf{A}\psi}$ accepts all trees that satisfy the CDL* formula $\mathbf{A}\psi$. $\mathcal{A}_\psi$ has $2^{2^{O(|\psi|)}}$ states and $2^{O(|\psi|)}$ Rabin pairs.

   - For LDL formula ψ, construct an alternating Büchi automaton (ABA) $\mathcal{A}_\psi$ with linearly many states in ψ [21].
   - Turn automaton $\mathcal{A}_\psi$ into a nondeterministic Büchi automaton (NBA) $\mathcal{A}'_\psi$ of exponential size of $|\psi|$ [32].
   - Turn automaton $\mathcal{A}'_\psi$ into a deterministic Rabin automaton $\mathcal{A}''_\psi$ (DRA) of double-exponential size of $|\psi|$ [33].
   - According to automaton $\mathcal{A}''_\psi$, build the Rabin tree automaton $\mathcal{A}_{\mathbf{A}\psi}$ for $\mathbf{A}\psi$ in a relatively obvious method; this tree automaton is designed to simply run the deterministic string automaton for ψ down every path from the root.

3. Construct product automaton $\mathcal{A} = \mathcal{A}_{\mathbf{A}\psi} \times \mathcal{A}_{\mathcal{G},w,A}$, which is a Rabin tree automaton with $n = O(|\mathcal{A}_{\mathbf{A}\psi}| \cdot |\mathcal{A}_{\mathcal{G},w,A}|)$ many states and $r = 2^{O(|\psi|)}$ many Rabin pairs. The decidable problem is to determine whether $L(\mathcal{A}) \neq \emptyset$ can be done in time $O(n \cdot r)^{3r}$ [34,35].

   The automata $\mathcal{A}$ is a Rabin tree automaton that accepts precisely the (w, A)-execution trees that satisfy $\mathbf{A}\psi$.

Since $\mathcal{G}, w \models \langle\!\langle A \rangle\!\rangle \psi$ iff there is a collective strategy g_A so that all w-computations in $out(w, g_A)$ satisfy ψ. Since each $\langle w, A \rangle$-execution tree corresponds to a set g_A of strategies, it follows that $\mathcal{G}, w \models \langle\!\langle A \rangle\!\rangle \psi$ iff the product automaton is nonempty. According to the above steps, the whole algorithm runs in polynomial time in the size of model and double exponential time in the size of formula. □

In fact, according to the above algorithm, since both CTL* satisfiability-checking [36] and module-checking [37] problems are 2EXPTIME-complete, then CDL* satisfiability and module checking problems are also 2EXPTIME-complete.

7.2. Model-Checking for LDL-SL[1G]

To give a model-checking algorithm for LDL-SL[1G], we adopt a similar approach proposed in [4], which is used to show that $SL_{1G}[\mathcal{F}]$ model checking is 2EXPTIME-complete.

First, we introduce the concept of *concurrent multi-player parity game* (CMPG) $\mathcal{P} = (Ag, Ac, S, s_0, \mathrm{p}, \Delta)$ [38], here $Ag = \{1, \cdots, n\}$, Δ is a transition function, and $\mathrm{p} : S \to N$ is a priority function. In a CMPG $\mathcal{P}$, there are n agents playing concurrently with infinite rounds. Informally, in a CMPG $\mathcal{P}$, if there exists one strategy for agent 0, s.t., for any strategy for agent 1, there exists one strategy for agent 2, and so forth, which make all the induced plays satisfy the parity condition, and then the existential coalition wins; otherwise, the universal coalition wins.

In a CMPG, $\mathcal{P} = (Ag, Ac, S, s_0, \mathrm{p}, \Delta)$, the winners of which can be determined in polynomial-time with respect to $|S|$ and $|Ac|$ and exponential-time with respect to $|Ag|$ and max p [38].

Theorem 11. *The MCP for LDL-SL[1G] is 2EXPTIME-complete.*

Proof. Firstly, Hardness follows from the fact that the MCP for BSL[1G] is 2EXPTIME-complete [24]. Then, we consider the lower bound of LDL-SL[1G].

Consider a CGS $\mathcal{G} = \langle Ac, W, \lambda, \tau, w_0 \rangle$ and a LDL-SL[1G] sentence φ. As in ADL*, we present a labelling algorithm to solve LDL-SL[1G] model checking. Like in [4], here we just consider the case sentence $\wp \flat \psi$, where quantifiers perfectly alternate between existential and universal $\langle\langle x_1 \rangle\rangle [\![x_2]\!] \cdots [\![x_n]\!]$, and ψ is an LDL formula. Now ψ can be interpreted over paths of the pointed Kripke model $M = (W, R, \lambda, w_0)$, where $R = \{(w_1, w_2) | \exists d \in Ac^{Ag}, w_2 = \tau(w_1, d)\}$.

In [21], for LDL formula ψ, construct an ABA $\mathcal{B}_\psi$ with linearly many states in ψ, and then turn $\mathcal{B}_\psi$ into an NBA $\mathcal{A}_\psi$ of exponential size of $|\psi|$ [32]. Combining $\mathcal{A}_\psi$ with Kripke model M, we get a new NBA $\mathcal{A}_{M,\psi}$, which accepts exactly all the infinite paths π of M s.t. $\pi, 0 \models \psi$. Then, by [39], we convert $\mathcal{A}_{M,\psi}$ into a deterministic parity automaton (DPA) $\mathcal{A}_{M,\psi} = (W, Q, q_0, \delta, \mathrm{p})$ of size in $2^{2^{O(|\psi|)}}$ and index bounded by $2^{O(|\psi|)}$.

Now as in [4], combining CGS $\mathcal{G}$ with $\mathcal{A}_{M,\psi}$, we use the same approach to define the following CMPG $\mathcal{P} = (Ag', Ac, S, s_0, \mathrm{p}, \Delta')$, where Ag' is a set of agents, one for every variable occurring in $\wp$; $S = W \times Q$. Firstly, game $\mathcal{P}$ emulates a path π generated in $\mathcal{G}$; secondly, if the generated path π in $\mathcal{G}$ is read, then the game emulates the execution of $\mathcal{A}_{M,\psi}$. Hence, each execution $(\pi, l) \in W^\omega \times Q^\omega$ in game $\mathcal{P}$ satisfies the parity condition determined by the p$'$ in $\mathcal{G}$ iff $\pi, 0 \models \psi$. In addition, because $\mathcal{A}_{M,\psi}$ is deterministic, for each possible track $h \in Trk(\mathcal{G})$, there is one unique partial path l_h that makes the partial execution (h, l_h) possible in $\mathcal{P}$. This makes the strategies from w_0 in $Str(\mathcal{G})$ one-to-one with the strategies from s_0 in $Str(\mathcal{P})$. Then $\mathcal{P}$ has a winning strategy if and only if $\mathcal{G}, w_0 \models \wp \flat \psi$.

As for complexity, the size of $\mathcal{P}$ is $O(|W| \cdot |Q|)$, where W is the state space of $\mathcal{G}$ and $|Q| = 2^{2^{O(|\psi|)}}$, i.e., doubly exponential in the size of ψ. Since $\mathcal{A}_{M,\psi}$ results from one NGBW $\mathcal{B}_{M,\psi}$, whose size is $2^{O(|\psi|)}$, transformed into a DPW, which needs another exponential in ψ. Moreover, since the transformation from an NGBW to a DPW just needs $2^{O(|\psi|)}$ priorities, so the number of priorities in $\mathcal{P}$ is $2^{O(|\psi|)}$. Hence, the constructed CMPG $\mathcal{P}$ can be solved in time polynomial with respect to the size of the CGS model $\mathcal{G}$ and double exponential in formula $|\psi|$. □

In fact, according to Theorem 11, since ADL* and BSL[1G] can both be linearly embedded into LDL-SL[1G], then the MCPs for both logics are in 2EXPTIME.

7.3. Model-Checking for LDL-SL

Since the MCP for BSL is non-elementary-complete [24], in addition to Theorem 2, then the lower bound of the MCP for LDL-SL is non-elementary.

Theorem 12. *The MCP for LDL-SL is non-elementary-hard.*

As for the upper bound of MCP for LDL-SL, we conjecture that we could reduce the MCP for LDL-SL into that for QCTL* under the tree semantics [40], inspired by the approach proposed in [41].

Conjecture 1. *The MCP for LDL-SL is non-elementary-complete.*

In addition, since ATL*, BSL, and BSL[1G] can be linearly embedded into their corresponding star-free strategic logics ADL$^*_{sf}$, LDL-SL$_{sf}$, and LDL-SL[1G]$_{sf}$, respectively,

MCPs for ATL* [5] and BSL[1G] [24] are 2EXPTIME-complete, and MCP for BSL is non-elementary-complete [24], then the following holds.

Corollary 3. *The MCPs for both ADL^*_{sf} and $LDL\text{-}SL[1G]_{sf}$ are 2EXPTIME-hard. The MCP for $LDL\text{-}SL_{sf}$ is non-elementary-hard.*

Although similar expressive power by Theorem 3, we do not know how to linearly translate star-free logics to the corresponding logics. For the time being, the upper bounds of these star-free strategic logics are not known.

The main complexity results about the MCPs are given in Table 1.

Table 1. Complexity of Model Checking for Strategic Logics.

Strategic Logics	Complexity of Model-Checking
CL	PTIME-complete [42]
ATL	PTIME-complete [5]
ATL*	2EXPTIME-complete [5]
ADL^*_{sf}	2EXPTIME-hard (Corollary 3)
ADL*	2EXPTIME-complete (Theorem 10)
BSL[1G]	2EXPTIME-complete ([24])
BSL	non-elementary-complete ([24])
$LDL\text{-}SL_{sf}[1G]$	2EXPTIME-hard (Corollar 3)
$LDL\text{-}SL_{sf}$	non-elementary-hard (Corollary 3)
LDL-SL[1G]	2EXPTIME-complete (Theorem 11)
LDL-SL	non-elementary-hard (Theorem 12)

8. Conclusions and Future Work

In this paper, we propose logic LDL-SL, an expressive new strategic logic based on linear dynamic logic, which can naturally express ω-regular properties. This logic is a branching-time extension of SL based on linear-time temporal logic. We show that LDL-SL is more expressive than SL, whose model-checking complexity is non-elementary-complete. Moreover, based on LDL, we define similar fragments of LDL-SL, which are more expressive than corresponding strategic logics based on LTL. However, all these fragments have the same model checking complexity, i.e., are 2EXPTIME-complete. At the same time, we define star-free-like strategic logics, based on star-free regular expressions. We show that these logics have the same expressivity as those corresponding strategic logics based on LTL or CTL*.

In short, based on LDL, we propose a new class of strategic logics. These logics have the same model-checking complexities as, but more expressivity than, current mainstream strategic logics. Furthermore, these logics can extend the application areas in multi-agent systems.

However, until now, the upper bounds of LDL-SL and its star-free fragments (ADL^*_{sf}, $LDL\text{-}SL[1G]_{sf}$, and $LDL\text{-}SL_{sf}$) are not known. In future, we will study the compact bounds of these logics. As in [43,44], we will consider concrete implementations about these model checking problems. In addition, here we just consider perfect recall strategies in multi-agent concurrent games with complete information. Next, we will further study these new proposed strategic logics under incomplete information [45–47], where the strategies of agents maybe memoryless or perfect recall [48]. In this paper, we present formal frameworks and show technical results; in the future, we will also present case studies or practical applications to illustrate these theories, such as information security [49], solving winning strategies [50], and voting protocol [51].

Author Contributions: Conceptualization, L.X. and S.G.; methodology, L.X. and S.G; validation, L.X. and S.G.; formal analysis, L.X.; investigation, L.X.; resources, L.X.; writing—original draft preparation, L.X.; writing—review and editing, L.X. and S.G.; project administration, S.G. All authors have read and agreed to the published version of the manuscript.

Funding: This research received no external funding.

Institutional Review Board Statement: Not applicable.

Informed Consent Statement: Not applicable.

Data Availability Statement: Not applicable.

Acknowledgments: Our deepest gratitude goes to the anonymous reviewers for their careful work and thoughtful suggestions that have helped improve this paper substantially.

Conflicts of Interest: The authors declare no conflict of interest.

Abbreviations

The following abbreviations are used in this manuscript:

ADL*	Alternating-time dynamic strategic logic
AMC	Alternating-time mu-calculus
ATL/ATL*	(Flat) alternating-time temporal logic
BSL	Branching version of Strategy Logic
CDL*	Computational-tree dynamic logic
CGS	Concurrent game structure
CL	Coalition logic
CMPG	Concurrent multi-player parity game
CTL/CTL*	(Flat) computational tree logic
LDL	Linear dynamic logic
LDL-SL	LDL-based Strategy Logic
LTL	Linear-time temporal logic
MCP	Model checking problem
PDL	Propositional Dynamic Logic
QCTL*	Quantified computational tree logic
sf	Star-free
SL	Strategy Logic

References

1. Pnueli, A. The temporal semantics of concurrent programs. *Theor. Comput. Sci.* **1981**, *13*, 45–60. [CrossRef]
2. Clarke, E.M.; Emerson, A. Design and Synthesis of Synchronization Skeletons Using Branching-time Temporal Logic. In *Logic of Programs: Workshop on Logic of Programs*; Kozen, D.C., Ed.; Springer: Berlin/Heidelberg, Germany, 1982; Volume 131, pp. 45–60.
3. Emerson, E.A.; Halpern, J.Y. "Sometimes" and "Not Never" revisited: On branching versus linear time temporal logic. *J. ACM* **1986**, *33*, *1*, 151–178. [CrossRef]
4. Bouyer, P.; Kupferman, O.; Markey, N.; Maubert, B.; Murano, A.; Perelli, G. Reasoning about Quality and Fuzziness of Strategic Behaviours. In Proceedings of the Twenty-Eighth International Joint Conference on Artificial Intelligence Main Track, Macao, China, 10–16 August 2019; pp. 1588–1594.
5. Alur, R.; Henzinger, T.A. Alternating-time temporal logic. *J. ACM* **2002**, *49*, *5*, 672–713. [CrossRef]
6. Chatterjee, K.; Henzinger, T.A.; Piterman, N. Strategy logic. *Inf. Comput.* **2010**, *208*, *6*, 677–693. [CrossRef]
7. Mogavero, F.; Murano, A.; Vardi, M.Y. Reasoning About Strategies. In Proceedings of the IARCS Annual Conference on Foundations of Software Technology and Theoretical Computer Science, (FSTTCS-2010), Chennai, India, 15–18 December 2010; pp. 133–144.
8. Aminof, B.; Malvone, V.; Murano, A.; Rubin, S. Graded Strategy Logic: Reasoning about Uniqueness of Nash Equilibria. In Proceedings of the AAMAS 2016, Singapore, 9–13 May 2016; pp. 133–144.
9. Bozzelli, L.; Murano, A.; Sorrentino, L. Alternating-time temporal logics with linear past. *Theor. Comput. Sci.* **2020**, *813*, 199–217. [CrossRef]
10. Belardinelli, F.; Knight, S.; Lomuscio, A.; Maubert, B.; Murano, A.; Rubin, S. Reasoning About Agents That May Know Other Agents' Strategies. In Proceedings of the IJCAI 2021, Montreal, QC, Canada, 19–27 August 2021; pp. 1787–1793.
11. Pnueli, A. The Temporal Logic of Programs. In Proceedings of 18th Annual Symposium on Foundations of Computer Science, Providence, RI, USA, 31 October–1 November 1977; pp. 46–57.

12. Emerson, E.A.; Halpern, J.Y. Decision Procedures and Expressiveness in the Temporal Logic of Branching Time. In Proceedings of the 14th Annual ACM Symposium on Theory of Computing, San Francisco, CA, USA, 5–7 May 1982; pp. 169–180.
13. Kozen, D. Results on the propositional mu-calculus. *Theor. Comput. Sci.* **1983**, *27*, 333–354. [CrossRef]
14. Wolper, P. Temporal logic can be more expressive. *Inf. Control* **1983**, *56*, 72–99. [CrossRef]
15. Armoni, R; Fix, L.; Flaisher, A.; Gerth, R.; Ginsburg, B.; Kanza, T.; Landver, A.; Mador-Haim, S.; Singerman, E.; Tiemeyer, A.; et al. The ForSpec Temporal Logic: A New Temporal Property-Specification Language. In *Tools and Algorithms for the Construction and Analysis of Systems, Proceedings of the 8th International Conference, TACAS 2002, Held as Part of the Joint European Conference on Theory and Practice of Software, ETAPS 2002, Grenoble, France, 8–12 April 2002*; Springer: Berlin, Heidelberg, 2002; pp. 296–211.
16. Henriksen, J.G.; Thiagarajan, P.S. Dynamic linear time temporal logic. *Ann. Pure Appl. Logic* **1999**, *96*, 187–207. [CrossRef]
17. Vardi, M.Y. The Rise and Fall of Linear Time Logic. In Proceedings of the Second International Symposium on Games, Automata, Logics and Formal Verification, GandALF 2011, Minori, Italy, 15–17 June 2011.
18. Fischer, M.J.; Ladner, R.E. Propositional dynamic logic of regular programs. *J. Comput. Syst. Sci.* **1979**, *18*, 194–211. [CrossRef]
19. Büchi, J.R.; Landweber, L.H. Definability in the monadic second-order theory of successor. *J. Symb. Log.* **1969**, *34*, 166–170. [CrossRef]
20. De Giacomo, G.; Vardi, M.Y. Linear Temporal Logic and Linear Dynamic Logic on Finite Traces. In Proceedings of the IJCAI, Beijing, China, 3–9 August 2013; pp. 854–860.
21. Faymonville, P.; Zimmermann, M. Parametric linear dynamic logic. *Inf. Comput.* **2017**, *253*, 237–256. [CrossRef]
22. Liu, Z.; Xiong, L.; Liu, Y.; Lespérance, Y.; Xu, R.; Shi, H. A Modal Logic for Joint Abilities under Strategy Commitments. In Proceedings of IJCAI, Yokohama, Japan, 7–15 January 2020; pp. 1805–1812.
23. Belardinelli, F.; Lomuscio, A.; Murano, A.; Rubin, S. Decidable Verification of Multi-agent Systems with Bounded Private Actions. In Proceedings of the 17th International Conference on Autonomous Agents and MultiAgent Systems, AAMAS, Stockholm, Sweden, 10–15 July 2018; pp. 1865–1867.
24. Mogavero, F.; Murano, A.; Perelli, G.; Vardi, M.Y. Reasoning about strategies: On the model-checking problem. *ACM Trans. Comput. Log.* **2014**, *34*, 1–47. [CrossRef]
25. Kong, J. MCMAS-Dynamic: Symbolic Model Checking for Linear Dynamic Logic and Several Temporal and Epistemic Extensions. Ph.D. Thesis, Imperial College London, London, UK, 2016.
26. Knight, S.; Maubert, B. Dealing with Imperfect Information in Strategy Logic. Available online: https://arxiv.org/abs/1908.02488 (accessed on 7 August 2019).
27. Thomas, W. Star-free regular sets of ω-sequences. *Inf. Control* **1979**, *42*, 148–156. [CrossRef]
28. Gabbay, D.M.; Pnueli, A.; Shelaho, S.; Shelah, J. On the Temporal Basis of Fairness. In Proceedings of the Conference Record of the Seventh Annual ACM Symposium on Principles of Programming Languages, Las Vegas, NV, USA, 28–30 January 1980; pp. 163–173.
29. Pauly, M. A modal logic for coalitional power in games. *J. Log. Comput.* **2002**, *12*, 149–166. [CrossRef]
30. Mogavero, F. *Logics in Computer Science—A Study on Extensions of Temporal and Strategic Logics*; Atlantis Studies in Computing 3; Atlantis Press: Paris, France, 2013; pp. 85–101.
31. Thomas, W. Automata on infinite objects. In *Handbook of Theoretical Computer Science, Volume B: Formal Models and Semantics*; MIT Press: Cambridge, MA, USA, 1990; pp. 133–191.
32. Miyano, S.; Hayashi, T. Alternating finite automata on omega-words. *Theor. Comput. Sci.* **1984**, *32*, 321–330. [CrossRef]
33. Schewe, S. Tighter Bounds for the Determinisation of Büchi Automata. In Proceedings of the Foundations of Software Science and Computational Structures, 12th International Conference, York, UK, 22–29 March 2009; pp. 167–181.
34. Emerson, E.A.; Jutla, C.S. The Complexity of Tree Automata and Logics of Programs (Extended Abstract). In Proceedings of the 29th Annual Symposium on Foundations of Computer Science, White Plains, New York, NY, USA, 24–26 October 1988; pp. 328–337.
35. Pnueli, A.; Rosner, R. On the Synthesis of a Reactive Module. In Proceedings of the Conference Record of the Sixteenth Annual ACM Symposium on Principles of Programming Languages, Austin, TX, USA, 11–13 January 1989; pp. 179–190.
36. Emerson, E.A. Temporal and modal logic. In *Handbook of Theoretical Computer Science, Volume B: Formal Models and Semantics*; MIT Press: Cambridge, MA, USA, 1990; pp. 995–1072.
37. Kupferman, O.; Vardi, M.Y.; Wolper, W. Module checking. *Inf. Comput.* **2001**, *164*, *2*, 322–344. [CrossRef]
38. Malvone, V.; Murano, A.; Sorrentino, L. Concurrent Multi-Player Parity Games. In Proceedings of the 2016 International Conference on Autonomous Agents & Multiagent Systems, Singapore, 9–13 May 2016; pp. 689–697.
39. Piterman, N. From nondeterministic Büchi and Streett automata to deterministic parity automata. *Log. Methods Comput. Sci.* **2007**, *3*, 1–21. [CrossRef]
40. Laroussinie, F.; Markey, N. Quantified CTL: Expressiveness and complexity. *Log. Methods Comput. Sci.* **2014**, *10*, 1–45.
41. Laroussinie, F.; Markey, N. Augmenting ATL with strategy contexts. *Inf. Comput.* **2015**, *245*, 98–123. [CrossRef]
42. Bulling, N.; Dix, J.; Jamroga W. Model checking logics of strategic ability: Complexity. In *Specification and Verification of Multi-Agent Systems*; Springer: Berlin, Heidelberg, 2010; pp. 125–159.
43. Alur, R.; Henzinger, T.A.; Mang, F.Y.C.; Qadeer, S.; Rajamani, S.; Tasiran, S. MOCHA: Modularity in Model Checking. In Computer Aided Verification. In Proceedings of CAV, Vancouver, BC, Canada, 28 June–2 July 1998; pp. 521–525.

44. Lomuscio, A.; Qu, H.; Raimondi, F. MCMAS: An open-source model checker for the verification of multi-agent systems. *Int. J. Softw. Tools Technol. Transf.* **2017**, *19*, 9–30. [CrossRef]
45. van der Hoek, W.; Wooldridge, M.J. Cooperation, knowledge, and time: Alternating-time temporal epistemic logic and its applications. *Stud. Log.* **2003**, *75*, 125–157. [CrossRef]
46. Jamroga, W.; Ågotnes, T. What Agents Can Achieve Under Incomplete Information. In Proceedings of the AAMAS, Hakodate, Japan, 8–12 May 2006; pp. 232–234.
47. Belardinelli, F.; Lomuscio, A.; Malvone, V. An Abstraction-Based Method for Verifying Strategic Properties in Multi-Agent Systems with Imperfect Information. In Proceedings of the AAAI, Honolulu, HI, USA, 27 January–1 February 2019; pp. 6030–6037.
48. Xiong, L.; Guo, S. Model Checking Dynamic Strategy Logic with Memoryless Strategies. In Proceedings of the CSAE 2020, Sanya, China, 20–22 October 2020; pp. 68:1–68:5.
49. Jamroga, W.; Tabatabaei, M. Information Security as Strategic (In)effectivity. In Proceedings of the STM 2016, Heraklion, Greece, l26–27 September 2016; pp. 154–169.
50. Wu, K.; Fang, L.; Xiong, L.; Lai, Z.; Qiao, Y.; Rong, F. Automatic Synthesis of Generalized Winning Strategies of Impartial Combinatorial Games Using SMT Solvers. In Proceedings of the IJCAI, Yokohama, Japan, 7–15 January 2020; pp. 1703–1711.
51. Belardinelli, F.; Condurache, R.; Dima, C.; Jamroga, W.; Knapik, M. Bisimulations for verifying strategic abilities with an application to the ThreeBallot voting protocol. *Inf. Comput.* **2021**, *276*, 104552. [CrossRef]

Article

Supervised Learning Perspective in Logic Mining

Mohd Shareduwan Mohd Kasihmuddin [1], Siti Zulaikha Mohd Jamaludin [1], Mohd. Asyraf Mansor [2,*], Habibah A. Wahab [3] and Siti Maisharah Sheikh Ghadzi [3]

[1] School of Mathematical Sciences, Universiti Sains Malaysia, George Town 11800, Malaysia; shareduwan@usm.my (M.S.M.K.); szulaikha.szmj@usm.my (S.Z.M.J.)
[2] School of Distance Education, Universiti Sains Malaysia, George Town 11800, Malaysia
[3] School of Pharmaceutical Sciences, Universiti Sains Malaysia, George Town 11800, Malaysia; habibahw@usm.my (H.A.W.); maisharah@usm.my (S.M.S.G.)
* Correspondence: asyrafman@usm.my; Tel.: +60-4-6533-935

Abstract: Creating optimal logic mining is strongly dependent on how the learning data are structured. Without optimal data structure, intelligence systems integrated into logic mining, such as an artificial neural network, tend to converge to suboptimal solution. This paper proposed a novel logic mining that integrates supervised learning via association analysis to identify the most optimal arrangement with respect to the given logical rule. By utilizing Hopfield neural network as an associative memory to store information of the logical rule, the optimal logical rule from the correlation analysis will be learned and the corresponding optimal induced logical rule can be obtained. In other words, the optimal logical rule increases the chances for the logic mining to locate the optimal induced logic that generalize the datasets. The proposed work is extensively tested on a variety of benchmark datasets with various performance metrics. Based on the experimental results, the proposed supervised logic mining demonstrated superiority and the least competitiveness compared to the existing method.

Keywords: supervised learning; Hopfield neural network; logic mining; artificial neural network

MSC: 68T07

1. Introduction

In the area of artificial intelligence (AI), two important perspectives stand out. The first is the applied rule that represents the given problem. The applied rule is vital in decision making in order to explain the nature of the problem. The second perspective is the automation process based on the rule which leads to neuro symbolic integration. These two perspectives rely heavily on the practicality of the symbolic rule that governs the AI system. The use of a satisfiability (SAT) perspective in software and hardware system theories is currently one of the most effective methods in bridging the two perspectives. SAT offers the promise, and often even the reality, that the model checks efforts with feasible industrial application. There were several practical applications of SAT that can be mentioned in this section. Ref. [1] utilized Boolean SAT by integrating satisfiability modulo theories (SMT) in tackling the scheduling problem. The proposed SMT method was reported to outperform other existing methods. Ref. [2] discovered vesicle traffic network by model checking that incorporates Boolean SAT. The proposed SAT model established a connection between vesicle transport graph connectedness and underlying rules of SNARE protein. In another development, [3] developed several SAT formulations to deal with the resource-constrained project scheduling problem (RCPSP). The proposed method is reported to solve various benchmark instances and outperform the existing work in terms of computation time and optimality. SAT formulation is a dynamic language that can be used in representing problem in hand. Ref. [4] proposed a special SAT in modelling the circuit. The proposed method reconstructed the accurate circuit configuration up to 90%. The application of SAT in very-large-scale integration (VLSI) inspires the authors to extend the application of SAT into pattern reconstruction [5] where they used the variable in SAT as a building block of the desired pattern. The practicality of SAT motivates researchers to implement SAT in navigating the structure in an artificial neural network (ANN).

Logic programming in ANN has been initially proposed by [6]. In his work, logic programming can be embedded into the Hopfield neural network (HNN) by minimizing the logical inconsistencies. This is also a pioneer to the Wan Abdullah method which obtains the synaptic weight by comparing cost function with Lyapunov energy function. Ref. [7] further developed the idea of the logic programming in HNN by implementing Horn satisfiability (HornSAT) as a logical structure of HNN. The proposed network achieved more than 80% global minima ratio but high computation time due to the complexity of the learning phase. Since then, logic programming in ANN was extended to another type of ANN. Ref. [8] initially proposed logic programming in radial basis function neural network (RBFNN) by calculating the centre and width of the hidden neurons that corresponds to the logical rule. In the proposed method, the dimensionality of the logical rule from input to output can be reduced by implementing Gaussian activation function. The further development of logic programming in RBFNN were proposed in [9] where the centre and the width of the RBFNN are systematically calculated. In another development, [10] proposed a systematic logical rule by implementing a 2-satisfiability logical rule (2SAT) in HNN. The proposed hybrid network is incorporated with effective learning methods, such as genetic algorithm [11] and artificial bee colony [12]. The proposed network managed to achieve more than 95% of global minima ratio and can sustain a high number of neurons. In another development, [13] proposed the higher order non-systematic logical rule, namely random k satisfiability (RANkSAT) that consists of random first-, second-, and third-order logical rule. The proposed works run a critical comparison among a combination of RANkSAT and demonstrate the capability of non-systematic logical rule to achieve optimal final state. The practicality of the SAT in HNN was explored in pattern satisfiability [5] and circuit satisfiability [4] where the user can capture the visual interpretation of logic programming in HNN. However, up to this point, the choice of SAT structure in HNN has received very little research attention, despite its practical importance.

Current data mining were reported to achieve good accuracy but the interpretability of the output is poorly understood due to emphasize of the black box model. In other words, the output makes sense for the AI but not for the user. One of the most useful applications of logic programming in HNN is logic mining. Logic mining is a relatively new perspective in extracting the behaviour of the dataset via logical rule. This method is a pioneer work of [14]. In this work, the proposed RA extracted individual logical rule that represents the performance of the students. The logical rule extracted from the datasets is based on the number of induced Horn logics produced by HNN. Thus, there is very limited effort to identify the "best" induced logical rule that represent the datasets. To complement the limitation of the previous RA, several studies include specific SAT logical rules to be embedded into HNN. Ref. [15] introduced 3-satisfiability (3SAT) as a logical rule in HNN, thus creating the first systematic logic mining technique, i.e., the k satisfiability reverse analysis method (kSATRA). The proposed hybrid logic mining is used to extract logical rule in several fields of studies, such as social media analysis [15] and cardiovascular disease [16]. In another development, different types of logical rule (2SAT) have been implemented by [17]. They proposed 2SATRA by incorporating the 2SAT logical rule in extracting a diabetes dataset [17] and student's performance dataset [18]. Ref. [19] utilized 2SATRA by extracting logical rule for football datasets in several established football league in the world. Pursuing that, the ability of 2SATRA is further tested when the proposed method is implemented in e-games. The 2SATRA has been proposed to extract the logical rule that explains the simulation game of the League of Legend (LOL) [20]. The proposed method achieved an acceptable range of logical accuracy. The application of logic mining was extended to several prominent areas, such as extracting the price information from commodities [21]. Another interesting development for *k*SATRA is by incorporating energy in induced logic. Ref. [22] proposed an energy-based 2-satisfiability-based reverse analysis method (E2SATRA) for e-recruitment. The proposed method reduced the suboptimal induced logic and increased the classification accuracy of the network. Despite the increase in application in data mining, the existing logic mining endured a significant drawback. The induced logic produced by the proposed method suffers from a limited amount of search space. This is due to the positioning of the neurons in *k*SAT formulation which affects the classification ability of 2SATRA. In this case, the optimal choice of the neuron pair in the *k*SAT clause in logic mining is crucial to avoid possible overfitting.

There were various studies that implemented regression analysis in ANN. Standalone regression analysis was prone to data overfitting [23], easily affected by outlier [24], and mostly limited to a linear relationship [25]. Due to the above weaknesses, regression analysis was implemented to complement the intelligent system. In most studies, regression analysis will be utilized in the pre-processing layer before it can be processed by the ANN. Ref. [26] proposed a combination of regression analysis with a RBFNN. The proposed method formed a prediction model for national economic data. Ref. [27] proposed an ANN that combines with regression analysis via a mean impact value. The proposed hybrid network identifies and extracts input variables that deal with irregularity and vitality of Beijing International Airport's passenger flow dataset. In [28], ANN is used to predict the water turbidity level by using optical tomography. The proposed ANN utilized the regression analysis value as an objective function of the network. Ref. [29] fully utilized logistic regression to identify significant microseismic parameters. The significant parameters will be trained by a simple neural network which results in the highly accurate seismic model. By nature, ANN is purely unsupervised learning and logistic regression analysis displays a major improvement to the overall performance. Although there were many studies conducted to confirm the benefit logistic regression analysis in classification and prediction paradigm, regression analysis has never been implemented in classifying the SAT logical rule. Regression analysis has the ability to restructure the logical rule based on the strength of relationship for each *k* variables in the *k*SAT clause. In that regard, the ANN will learn the correct logical structure and the probability to achieve highly accurate induced logical rule will increase dramatically. In that regard, relatively few studies have examined the effectiveness of regression in analysing data features that correspond to the *k*SAT. The choice of variable pair in the 2SAT clause can be made optimally by implementing regression analysis without interrupting the value of the cost function.

Unfortunately, there is no recent effort to discover the optimal choice that leads to the true outcome of the *k*SAT. The closest work that addresses this issue is shown by [30]. This work [30] utilized neuron permutation to obtain the most accurate induced logical rule by considering $n(n-1)!$ neuron arrangement in *k*SAT. Hence, the aim of this paper is to effectively explore the various possible logical structures in 2SATRA. The proposed logic mining model identifies the optimal neuron pair for 2SAT clause forming a new logical formula. Pearson chi-square association analysis will be conducted to examine the connectedness of the neuron with respect to the outcome. By doing so, the new 2SAT formula learned by HNN as an input logic and the new induced logical rule can be obtained. Thus, the contributions of this paper are:

(a) To formulate a novel supervised learning that capitalize correlation filter among variables in the logical rule with respect to the logical outcome;
(b) To implement the obtained supervised logical rule into HNN by minimizing the cost function which minimizes the final energy;
(c) To develop a novel logic mining based on the hybrid HNN integrated with the 2-satisfiability logical rule;
(d) To construct the extensive analysis for the proposed logic mining in doing various datasets. The proposed logic mining will be compared to the existing state of the art logic mining.

An effective 2SATRA model incorporating a new supervised model will be compared with the existing 2SATRA model for several established datasets. In Section 2, we describe satisfiability programming in HNN in detail. In Section 3, we describe some simulation of HNN by using simulated result. Discussion follows in Section 4. The concluding remarks in Section 5 complete the paper.

2. Motivation
2.1. Optimal Attribute Selection Strategy

Optimal attribute selection is vital to ensure HNN learn the correct logical rule during the learning phase. Ref. [30] proposed logic mining that capitalize random attribute combination that leads to creation of 2SAT logic. In this study, the synaptic weight connection obtained from 2SAT is purely based on the most frequent logical incidence in the datasets. The main question to ask: what happen if the 2SAT logical rule selected the wrong attribute? Hence, there is a huge possibility of the logic mining to learn the wrong synaptic which leads to suboptimal induced logic. A similar observation was made in the study by [31] which proposed 3SAT for induced logic, with a heavy focus on the random attribute selection. It is agreeable that the induced logic might produce accurate induced logic, but this issue leads logic mining to choose the random attributes that reduce the interpretability of induced logic. To solve this issue, the latest study by [30] proposed permutation operator to optimize the random selection proposed by [20]. The permutation operator will increase the accuracy of the induced logic when we change the attribute in the logical formula. Despite the increase in the accuracy and other metrics, the interpretability issue remains unsolvable. This is due to the random selection that contributes to a lack of interpretability of the learned logic in HNN. In this paper, we capitalize the work of [20,30] by constructing the dataset in the form of 2SAT logical rule and permutation operator. By selecting the optimal attribute combination of 2SAT, we can obtain more search space which leads to optimal induced logic.

2.2. Energy Optimization Strategy

Energy optimization in HNN is vital to ensure that every induced logic produced during retrieval phase is always achieved by global minimum energy. This creates an important question is: why HNN must achieve global minimum energy? Global minimum energy indicates a good agreement between the learned logic during pre-processing stage with the induced logic during retrieval phase. Induced logic that achieved global minimum energy can be interpreted. In contrast, induced logic that can achieve local minimum energy might achieve good accuracy, but this is difficult to interpret. In [22], the proposed logic mining is mainly the focus on the energy stability. The main issue when the induced logic is solely focusing on global minimum energy is limit on the possible search space of the HNN. The proposed HNN tends to overfit and produce more redundant induced logic. This will worsen when the proposed HNN selects the wrong attribute to learn. Non-optimal induced logic obtained a lack of interpretability and generalization during the retrieval phase. We tend to achieve similar induced logic which will lead to lower accuracy. Another factor that might affect overfitting of the induced logic structure is the monotonous behaviour of HNN that always converges to the nearest minimum energy. Hence, the feature of energy optimization with the optimal attributes selection will lead to a result that is optimal and easy to interpret.

2.3. Lack of Effective Metric to Assess the Performance of Logic Mining

Effective metric in logic mining is crucial to ensure the actual performance of the induced logic in doing clustering and classification. According to the previous studies, the point of assessment and type of metric are still shallow and do not represent the performance of the logic mining. For instance, the work of [21] reported the error analysis learning phase of HNN but a failure to provide metrics that are related to the contingency table. As a result, the actual performance of the induced logic is still not well understood.

Similar limitation reported in [14] where only metric of global minima ratio is used to demonstrate the connection between neurons. The local minimum solution signifies the induced logic rule does not correspond to the learned logic which contribute to the lack of generalization capability. In this case, if the measurement is solely based on the energy metric, then quantifying each element, in terms of confusion metric, is necessary so that the induced logic can carry out the classification task. In addition, the building block that leads to intermediate logics is solely based on the obtained synaptic weight. In this context, without synaptic weight analysis, the connection of the induced logic is poorly understood. For instance, logic mining [20] does not report the result of the strength of connection between variables in the induced logic. As a result, there is no method to assess the logical pattern stored in the content addressable memory (CAM). In this paper, comprehensive analysis, such as error analysis, synaptic weight analysis, and statistical analysis will be employed to get an overall view on the actual performance of all the logic mining models.

3. Satisfiability Representation

SAT is a representation of determining the interpretation that satisfies the given Boolean formula. According to [32], SAT is proven to be an NP-complete problem and is included to cover wide range of optimization problem. Extensive research on SAT leads to the creation of variant SAT which is 2SAT. In this paper, the choice of $k = 2$ is due to the two-dimensional decision-making system. Generally, 2SAT consist of the following properties [19]:

(a) A set of defined x variables, $q_1, q_2, q_3, \ldots, q_x$ where $q_i \in \{-1, 1\}$ that exemplify false and true, respectively.
(b) A set of literals. A literal can be variable or the negation of variable such that $q_i \in \{q_i, \neg q_i\}$.
(c) A set of x definite clauses, $C_1, C_2, C_3, \ldots, C_y$. Every consecutive C_i is connected to logical AND ($\wedge$). Each two literals in (b) are connected by logical OR ($\vee$).

By taking property (a) into account until (c), one can define the explicit definition of Q_{2SAT} as follows:

$$Q_{2SAT} = \bigwedge_{i=1}^{y} C_i \qquad (1)$$

where C_i is a list of clause with two variables each

$$C_i = \bigvee_{i=1}^{x} (m_i, n_i) \qquad (2)$$

By considering the Equations (1) and (2), a simple example of Q_{2SAT} can be written as

$$Q_{2SAT} = (A \vee \neg B) \wedge (\neg M \vee D) \wedge (\neg E \vee \neg F) \qquad (3)$$

where the clauses in Equation (3) are $C_1 = (A \vee \neg B)$, $C_2 = (\neg M \vee D)$, and $C_3 = (\neg E \vee \neg F)$. Note that each clauses mentioned above must be satisfied with specific interpretations [10]. For example, if the interpretation reads $(M, D) = (1, -1)$, Q_{2SAT} will evaluate false or -1. Since Q_{2SAT} contains an information storage mechanism and is easy to classify, we implemented Q_{2SAT} into ANN as a logical system.

4. Satisfiability in Discrete Hopfield Neural Network

HNN [33] consists of interconnected neurons without a hidden layer. Each neuron in HNN is defined in bipolar state $S_i \in \{1, -1\}$ that represents true and false, respectively. An interesting feature about HNN is the ability to restructure the neuron state until the network reached its minimum state. Hence, the proposed HNN achieved the optimal final state if the collection of neurons in the network reached the lowest value of the minimum energy. The general definition of HNN with the i-th activation is given as follows

$$S_i = \begin{cases} 1, & \text{if } \sum_{i=0}^{N} W_{ij}S_j \geq \theta \\ -1, & \text{otherwise} \end{cases} \quad (4)$$

where θ and W_{ij} represent a threshold and synaptic weight of the network, respectively. Without compromising the generality of HNN, some study used $\theta = 0$ as the threshold value. Note that N is the number of 2SAT variables. W_{ij} is also defined as the connection between neuron S_i and S_j. The idea of implementing Q_{2SAT} in HNN (HNN-2SAT) is due to the need of some symbolic rule that can govern the output of the network. The cost function $E_{Q_{2SAT}}$ of the proposed Q_{2SAT} in HNN is given as follows:

$$E_{Q_{2SAT}} = \sum_{i=1}^{NC} \prod_{j=1}^{2} M_{ij} \quad (5)$$

where NC is the number of $E_{Q_{2SAT}}$ clause. The definition of the clause M_{ij} is given as follows [9]

$$M_{ij} = \begin{cases} \frac{1}{2}(1 - S_y), & \text{if } \neg y \\ \frac{1}{2}(1 + S_y), & \text{otherwise} \end{cases} \quad (6)$$

where y is the negation of literal in Q_{2SAT}. It is also worth mentioning that $E_{Q_{2SAT}} = 0$ if the $\frac{1}{4}(1 \pm S_y) = 0$ is because the neuron state S_y associated to Q_{2SAT} is fully satisfied. Each variable inside a particular M_{ij} will be connected by W_{ij}. Structurally, the synaptic weight of Q_{2SAT} is always symmetrical for both the second- and third-order logical rule:

$$W_{AB}^{(2)} = W_{BA}^{(2)} \quad (7)$$

with no self-connection between neurons:

$$W_{AA}^{(2)} = W_{BB}^{(2)} = 0 \quad (8)$$

Note that Equations (5)–(8) only account for a non-redundant logical rule because the logical redundancies will result in the diminishing effect of the synaptic weight. The goal of the learning in HNN is to minimize the logical inconsistency that leads to $Q_{2SAT} = -1$ or $\neg Q_{2SAT} = 1$. Although synaptic weight of the HNN can be properly trained by using conventional method, such as Hebbian learning [33], ref. [14] demonstrated that the Wan Abdullah method can obtain the optimal synaptic weight with minimal neuron oscillation compared to Hebbian learning. For example, if the embedded logical clause is $C_1 = (A \vee \neg B)$, the synaptic weights will read $(W_A, W_B, W_{AB}) = (0.25, 0.25, -0.25)$. During retrieval phase of HNN-2SAT, the neuron state will be updated asynchronously based on the following equation.

$$S_i = \begin{cases} 1, & \sum_{j=1, i \neq j}^{N} W_{ij}^{(2)} S_j + W_i^{(1)} \geq \xi \\ -1, & \sum_{j=1, i \neq j}^{N} W_{ij}^{(2)} S_j + W_i^{(1)} < \xi \end{cases} \quad (9)$$

where S_i is a final neuron state with pre-defined threshold ξ. In terms of output squashing, the Sigmoid function can be used to provide non-linearity effects during neuron classification. Potentially, the final state of the neuron must contain information that lead to

$E_{Q_{2SAT}} = 0$, and the quality of the obtained state can be computed by using Lyapunov energy function:

$$H_{Q_{2SAT}} = -\frac{1}{2}\sum_{i=0,i\neq j}^{N}\sum_{j=0,j\neq i}^{N} W_{ij}^{(2)} S_i S_j - \sum_{i=0}^{N} W_i^{(1)} S_i \qquad (10)$$

According to [33], the symmetry of the synaptic weight is sufficient condition for the existence of the Lyapunov function. Hence, the value of $H_{Q_{2SAT}}$ in Equation (10) decreases monotonically with network. The absolute minimum energy $H_{Q_{2SAT}}^{min}$ can pre-determined by substituting interpretation that leads to $E_{Q_{2SAT}} = 0$. In this case, if the obtained neuron state can satisfy $\left|H_{Q_{2SAT}} - H_{Q_{2SAT}}^{min}\right| \leq Tol$, the final neuron state achieved global minimum energy. Note that the current conventions of $S_i \in \{1, -1\}$ can be converted to binary by implementing different a Lyapunov function coined by [6].

5. Proposed Method

2SATRA is a logic mining method that can extract a logical rule from the dataset. The philosophy of the 2SATRA is to find the most optimal logical rule of Equation (1), which corresponds to the dynamic system of Equation (9). In the conventional 2SATRA proposed by [20], the choice of variable in 2SATRA will be determined randomly which leads to poor quality of the induced logic. The choices of the neurons are arranged randomly before the learning of HNN can take place. In this section, chi-square analysis will be used during the pre-processing stage. The aim of the association method is to assign the two best neurons/clauses that correspond to the outcome Q_{2SAT}. These neurons will take part during the learning phase of HNN-2SAT which leads to better induced logic. In other words, the additional optimization layer is added to reduce the pre-training effort for 2SATRA to find the best logical rule.

Let N the number of neurons represent the attribute of the datasets $S_i = (S_1, S_2, S_3, \ldots, S_N)$ where each neuron is converted into bipolar interpretation $S_i = \{-1, 1\}$. Necessarily, 2SATRA is required to select d neurons that will be learned by HNN-2SAT. In this case, the number of possible neuron permutation after considering the learning logic Q_i^l structure is $\frac{N!}{2(N-d)!}$. By considering the relationship between Q_i^l and neuron S_i, we can optimally select the pair of S_i for each clause C_i. The S_i selection for each C_i is given as follows:

$$Q_i^l = \bigwedge_{i=0,i\neq j}^{NC} \left(S_i^{min|P_i|} \vee S_j^{min|P_j|}\right), \quad i \neq j, \quad 0 \leq P_i \leq \alpha, \quad 0 \leq P_j \leq \alpha \qquad (11)$$

where P_i is the P value between Q_i^l and the neuron S_i. $min|P_i|$ signifies the minimized value of P_i recorded between Q_i^l and S_i, and the value of α is pre-defined by the network. Note that $i \neq j$ does not significy a self-connection between the same neurons. By considering the best- and worst-case scenario, the neuron will be chosen at random if $min|P_i| = min|P_j|$. If the examined neurons do not achieve the pre-determined association, HNN-2SAT will reset the search space, which fulfils the threshold association value. Hence, by using Equation (11), the proposed 2SATRA is able to learn the early feature of the dataset. After obtaining the right set of neurons for Q_i^l, the dataset will be converted into bipolar representation:

$$S_i = \begin{cases} 1, & S_i = 1 \\ -1, & otherwise \end{cases} \qquad (12)$$

Note that we only consider the second-order clause or $C_i^{(2)}$ for each clause in Q_i^l. Hence, the collection of S_i that leads to positive outcome of the learning data or $Q_i^l = 1$ will be segregated. By calculating the collection of $C_i^{(2)}$ that leads to $Q_i^l = 1$, the optimum logic Q_{best} is given as follows:

$$Q_{best} = \max\left[n\left(C_i^{(2)}\right)\right], \quad Q_i^l = 1 \qquad (13)$$

where $n\left(C_i^{(2)}\right)$ is the number of Q_i^l that leads to $Q_i^l = 1$. Hence, the logical feature of the Q_{best} can be learned by obtaining the synaptic weight of the HNN. In this case, the cost function in Equation (11) which corresponds to Q_{best} will be compared to Equation (5). By using Equation (9), we obtain the final neuron state S_i^B.

$$S_i^{induced} = \begin{cases} S_i, & S_i^B = 1 \\ \neg S_i, & S_i^B = -1 \end{cases} \quad (14)$$

Since the proposed HNN-2SAT only allows an optimal final neuron state, the quality of the S_i^B will be verified by using $\left|H_{Q_{2SAT}} - H_{Q_{2SAT}}^{min}\right| \leq Tol$. In this case, S_i^B that leads to local minima will not be considered. Hence, the classification of the induced Q_i^B is as follows:

$$Q_i^B = \begin{cases} Q_i^B, & \left|H_{Q_i^B} - H_{Q_i^B}^{min}\right| \leq \partial \\ 0, & otherwise \end{cases} \quad (15)$$

where $H_{Q_i^B}^{min}$ can be obtained from Equation (10). It is worth mentioning that if the two neurons do not have the strong association, the neurons will not be considered. Thus, if the association value for all neurons does not achieve the threshold variable $0 \leq \rho_i \leq \alpha$, the proposed network will be reduced to conventional kSATRA proposed by [21,31]. Figure 1 shows the implementation of the proposed supervised logic mining or (S2SATRA). Algorithm 1 shows Pseudo code of the Proposed S2SATRA.

Algorithm 1. Pseudo code of the Proposed S2SATRA.

Input: Set all attributes $A_1, A_2, A_3, \ldots, A_N$ with respect to Q_{learn}.
Output: The best induced logic Q_i^B.

1. **Begin**
2. Initialize algorithm parameters;
3. Define the Attribute for $A_1, A_2, A_3, \ldots, A_N$ with respect to Q_i^l;
4. Find the correlation value between A_i with Q_i^l;
5. **for** $\left(Q_i^l \leq Q_{N_{data}}^l\right)$ **do**
6.   **if** Equation (11) is satisfied **then**
7.   Assign A_i as S_i, and **continue**;
8.   **while** $(i \leq Per)$ **do**
9.   Using the found attributes, find Q_{best} using Equation (13);
10.   Check the clause satisfaction for Q_{best};
11.   Compute $H_{Q_{best}}^{min}$ using Equation (10);
12.   Compute the synaptic weight associated with Q_{best} using the WA method;
13.   Initialize the neuron state;
14.   **for** $(g \leq trial)$
15.   Compute h_i using Equation (9);
16.   Convert S_i^B to the logical form using Equation (14);
17.   Evaluate the $H_{Q_i^B}$ by using Equation (10);
18.   **If** Condition (15) is satisfied **then**
19.   Convert to induced logic Q_i^B;
20.   Compare the outcome of the Q_i^B with Q_{test} and **continue**;
21. $g \leftarrow g + 1$;
22.   **end for**
23. $i \leftarrow i + 1$;
24.   **end while**
25. **end for**
26. **End**

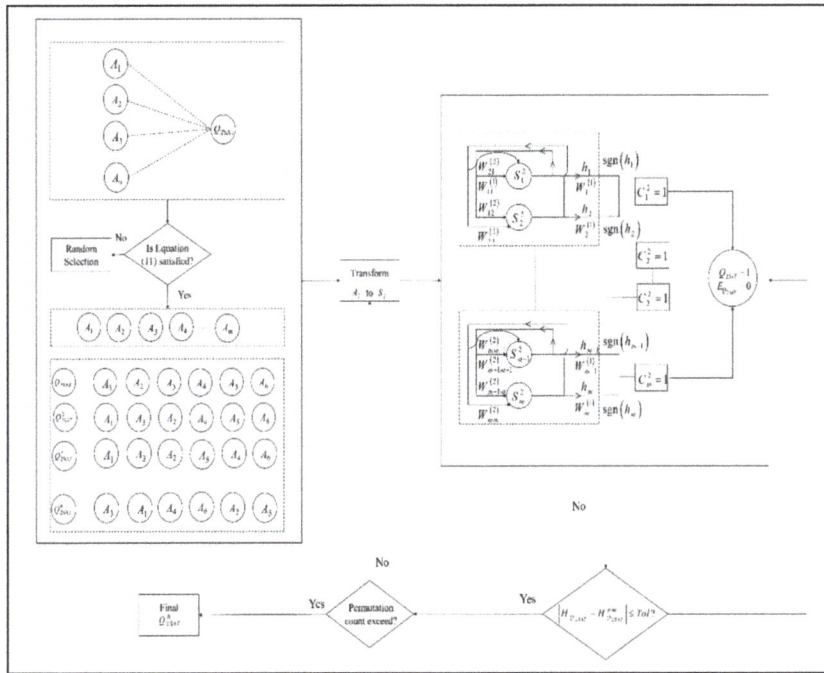

Figure 1. The implementation of the proposed S2SATRA.

6. Experiment and Discussion

6.1. Experiment Setup

In this section, we describe the components of the experiments carried out here. The purpose of this experiment is to elucidate the different logic mining mechanism that leads to Q_{best} before it can be learned by HNN. To guarantee the reproducibility of the experiment, we set up our experiment as follows.

6.1.1. Benchmark Datasets

In this experiment, 12 publicly available datasets are obtained from UCI repository https://archive.ics.uci.edu/mL/datasets.php (accessed on 10 December 2021). These datasets are widely used in the classification field and are representative of practical classification problem. The details of the datasets are summarized in Table 1.

Table 1. List of datasets.

ID	Data	Instances	Attributes	Area	Outcome $Q_{2SAT}^{k_i}$
F1	Pageblocks	5473	10	Computer	Class
F2	Australian	690	14	Financial	Class
F3	Zoo	101	17	Life	Class
F4	Wisconsin	569	32	Life	Class
F5	Speaker	329	12	Social	Language
F6	Shuttle	58,000	9	Physical	Class
F7	Facebook	500	19	Business	Status
F8	Wine	178	13	Physical	Class
F9	Computer	209	9	Computer	ERP
F10	Energy Y1	768	8	Computer	Heating Load
F11	Ionosphere	351	34	Physical	Class
F12	Energy Y2	768	8	Computer	Cooling Load

To avoid possible field bias, the area of interest in the dataset varies from science to social datasets. The choice of datasets is based on two aspects. First, we only select a dataset that contains more than 100 instances to preserve the statistical property of a distribution. For example, we avoid choosing balloon datasets because the number of instances is statistically too small to assess the capability learning phase of the proposed model. Second, we only select a dataset that contains more than six attributes. The choice of having more than six attributes is to check the effectiveness of the proposed model in adapting the concept of an optimal attribute selection. In other words, this experiment is unable to assess the effectiveness of the proposed model using association analysis and permutation if the number of attributes is low. Note that the state of the data will be stored in neuron by using bipolar representation $S_i \in \{-1, 1\}$ and each state can represent the behaviour of the dataset with respect to Q_{best}. In terms of data normalization, k-mean clustering [34] will be used to normalize the continuous datasets into 1 and -1. For a dataset that contains categorical data, the proposed model and the existing model will randomly select $Q_{2SAT}^{k_i}$. Since the number of missing values for all datasets is very small and negligible, we replaced the missing value with a random neuron state. The experiment employs a train-split method where 60% of the dataset will be trained and 40% of the dataset will be tested [31]. Note that multi-fold validation was not implemented in this paper because we wanted to ensure that Q_{best} learned by HNN has a similar starting point for all logic mining models. A multi-fold validation method will eliminate the original point of assessment during the training phase of logic mining. Hence, the comparison among logic mining is not possible.

6.1.2. Performance Metrics

In terms of metric evaluation performance, several performance metrics were selected to measure the robustness of the proposed method compared to the other existing work. We divided performance metrics into a few parts. Error evaluations consist of a standard error metric, such as a root mean square error (RMSE) and a mean absolute error (MAE). The formulation for both errors are as follows:

$$RMSE = \sum_{i=1}^{n} \frac{1}{n} \left(Q_i^{test} - Q_i^{B} \right)^2 \tag{16}$$

$$MAE = \sum_{i=1}^{n} \frac{1}{n} \left| Q_i^{test} - Q_i^{B} \right| \tag{17}$$

where Q_i^{test} is the state of the data $Q_i^{test} \in \{-1, 1\}$. In detail, the best logic mining model will produce the Q_i^{B} with the lowest error evaluation. Next, standard classification metrics, such as accuracy, F-score, precision, and sensitivity will be utilized in the experiment. According to [35], the sensitivity metric Se analyses how well a case correctly produces a positive result for an instance that has a specific condition. Note that, TP (true positive) is the number of positive instances that correctly classified, FN (false negative) is the number of positive instances that incorrectly classified, TN (true negative) is the number of negative instances that correctly classified, and FP (false positive) is the number of incorrectly classified positive instances.

$$Se = \frac{TP}{TP + FN} \tag{18}$$

Meanwhile, precision is utilized to measure the algorithm's predictive ability. Precision refers to how precise the prediction is from those positively predicted with how many of them are actually positive. The calculation for precision (Pr) is defined as follows:

$$Pr = \frac{TP}{TP + FP} \tag{19}$$

Accuracy (*Acc*) is generally the common metric for determining the performance of the classification. This metric measures the percentage of instances categorized correctly:

$$Acc = \frac{TP + TN}{TP + TN + FP + FN} \tag{20}$$

As stated by [36], *F-score* is a significant necessity that reflects the highest probability of correct result, explicitly representing the ability of the algorithm. Additionally, F1-score is described as the harmonic mean of precision and sensitivity. Next, the Matthews correlation coefficient (*MCC*) will be used to examine the performance of the logic mining based on the eight major derived ratios from the combination of all components of a confusion matrix. *MCC* is regarded as a good metric that represents the global model quality and can be used for classes of a different size [37].

$$F\ Score = \frac{2TP}{2TP + FP + FN} \tag{21}$$

$$MCC = \frac{TP\ TN\ -\ FP\ FN}{\sqrt{(TP+FP)(TP+FN)(TN+FP)(TN+FN)}} \tag{22}$$

It is worth mentioning that this is our first encounter to approach logic mining with various performance metrics. In [20,22], the only metric used is only accuracy and testing error.

6.1.3. Baseline Methods

Since the main focus of this paper is to examine the performance of the induced logic produced by S2SATRA, we limit our comparison to only method that produce induced logic. Despite the fact that we respect the capability of the existing model in classifying the dataset, we will not compare S2SATRA with the existing classification model, such as random forest, decision tree, etc., because these models do not produce any logical rule that classifies the dataset. For consistency purposes, all the experiments will employ the same type of logical rule, i.e., Q_{2SAT}. For comparison purposes, the proposed S2SATRA will be compared with all the existing logic mining models, such as 2SATRA [20], the energy-based 2-satisfiability reverse analysis method (E2SATRA) [22], the 2-satisfiability reverse analysis method with permutation element (P2SATRA) [30], and the state-of-the-art reverse analysis method (RA) [14]. This section will discuss the implementation of each logic mining models.

(a) The conventional 2SATRA model proposed by [20] utilizes Q_{2SAT} integrated with the Wan Abdullah method. The determination of Q_{best} follows the Equation (13) and the selected attributes are randomized. During the retrieval phase, HNN-2SAT will retrieve the optimal S_i^B that leads to optimal induced logic which then leads to the potential generalization of the datasets. There is no layer of verification around whether the final state S_i^B produced is the global minimum energy.

(b) In E2SATRA [22], Lyapunov energy function in Equation (10) will be used to verify the Q_i^B. The final state of the HNN will converge to the nearest minimum solution. In this case, Q_i^B that achieve local minimum energy will be filtered out during retrieval phase of HNN-2SAT. The dataset generalization of E2SATRA does not consider the optimal attribute selection.

(c) In P2SATRA [30], the permutation operator will be used to permutate the attribute in $C_i^{(2)}$. The permutation operator will explore the possibility of search space related to the chosen attributes. Note that redundant permutation will not be considered during the attribute selection. The retrieval property of the P2SATRA will have the same property as conventional 2SATRA.

(d) As for RA proposed by [14], we introduced RA that can only produce HornSAT property [7] while still maintaining the two attributes per $C_i^{(2)}$. To make the proposed RA comparable with our proposed method, calibration is required. The main calibration from the previous RA is the number of Q_i^B produced by the datasets. Instead of assigning neuron for each instance, we assign each neuron with attributes. The neuron redundancy is also introduced to avoid the net-zero effect of the synaptic weight.

During the learning phase, learning optimization is implemented to ensure that the synaptic weight obtained is purely due to the HNN. Note that the effective synaptic weight management will change the final state of HNN, leading to different Q_i^B. Since the HNN has a recurrent learning property [33], the neuron will change states until $Q_i^{learn} = 1$ and until the learning threshold NH is reached. According to [14], if the learning of Q_{2SAT} exceeds the proposed NH, the HNN will use the current optimal synaptic weight for the retrieval phase. During the retrieval phase of HNN, the neuron state will be initially randomized to reduce the possible bias. Noise function is not added, such as in [22,31], because the main objective of this experiment is to investigate the type of attributes that retrieve the most optimal final Q_i^B. To obtain consistent results throughout all 2SATRA models, the only squashing function employed by the neurons in 2SATRA models is the hyperbolic activation function in [38]. By considering only one fixed learning rule, we can examine the effect of supervised learning towards the 2SATRA model. Tables 1–5 illustrate the list of parameters involved in the experiment.

Table 2. List of parameters in S2SATRA.

Parameter	Parameter Value
Neuron Combination	100
Number of Trial	100
Number of Learning (Ω)	100
P-Value (P)	0.05
Logical Rule	Q_{2SAT}
Tolerance Value (∂)	0.001
No_Neuron String	100
Maximum Permutation (Per)	100

Table 3. List of parameters in E2SATRA [22].

Parameter	Parameter Value
Neuron Combination	100
Attribute Selection	Random
Number of Learning (Ω)	100
Logical Rule	Q_{2SAT}
Tolerance Value (∂)	0.001
No_Neuron String	100
Selection_Rate	0.1
Neuron Combination	100

Table 4. List of parameters in 2SATRA [20].

Parameter	Parameter Value
Neuron Combination	100
Attribute Selection	Random
Number of Learning (Ω)	100
Logical Rule	Q_{2SAT}
No_Neuron String	100
Selection_Rate	0.1

Table 5. List of parameters in P2SATRA [30].

Parameter	Parameter Value
Neuron Combination	100
Attribute Selection	Random
Number of Learning (Ω)	100
Logical Rule	Q_{2SAT}
No_Neuron String	100
Selection_Rate	0.1
Maximum Permutation	100

6.1.4. Experimental Design

The simulations were all implemented using Dev C++ Version 5.11 (manufactured by Bloodshed Company from USA) for Windows 10 (Microsoft from USA) in 2 GB RAM with Intel Core I3 (Intel from USA) as a workstation. As for association analysis, Q_{best} will be obtained by using IBM SPSS Statistics Version 27 (manufactured by IBM from New York, NY, USA). All the experiments were implemented in the same device to avoid a possibly bad sector during the simulation. Each 2SATRA model will undergo 10 independent runs to reduce the impact of bias caused by the random initialization of a neuron state.

7. Results and Discussion

7.1. Synaptic Weight Analysis

Figure 1 demonstrates that the optimal 2SATRA model requires pre-processing structure for neurons before the Q_{best} can be learned by HNN. The currently available 2SATRA model specifically optimizes the logic extraction from the dataset without considering the optimal Q_{best}. Hence, the mechanism that optimizes the optimal neuron relationship before the learning can occur remains unclear. Identifying a specific pair of neurons for Q_{2SAT} will facilitate the logic mining to obtain the optimal induced logic.

Figures 2–13 demonstrate the synaptic weight for all logic mining models in extracting logical information for F1–F12. Note that $W_i^{(1)}$ and $W_{ij}^{(2)}$ represent the first- and second-order connection in the $C_i^{(2)}$ clause. In this section, we will check the optimality of the synaptic weight with respect to the obtained accuracy value. Several interesting points can be made from Figures 2–13.

(a) Despite different attribute selection for S2SATRA compared to the other logic mining model, the induced logic for S2SATRA shows more logical variation compared to other existing work. For instance, the synaptic weight for S2SATRA has a bias towards a positive literal for only four datasets while maintaining high accuracy.

(b) RA demonstrates logical rigidness because the synaptic weight must produce a final state with at least one positive literal. According to Figures 2–13, the induced logic tends to overfit with the datasets. The structure of the induced logic obtained in RA might exhibit some diversity compared to S2SATRA but remains suboptimal, leading to a lower accuracy value. Hence, great diversity with wrong attribute selection reduces the effectiveness of logic mining model.

(c) In terms of energy optimization strategy, the energy filter in S2SATRA is able to retrieve global induced logic that contains more negated neurons compared to E2SATRA. This shows that the choice of attribute will definitely influence the choice of synaptic weight learning. For example, E2SATRA managed to achieve 10 similar global induced logic as an optimal logic for F1, F2, F3, F4, F5, F6, F7, F9, F10, and F12 compared to S2SATRA which can only retrieve 4 similar induced logic for F3, F4, F8, and F9. Despite having similar global induced logic, S2SATRA can still obtain a high accuracy level.

(d) Another interesting insight is that permutation operators improve P2SATRA in learning optimal synaptic weight, but the improvement seems more obvious in S2SATRA. For instance, with the same synaptic weight for neuron A and D but a different attribute representation, S2SATRA is able to achieve higher accuracy. A similar observation is made for other neurons from A to E. This implies the need of the optimal attribute selection before learning of HNN can take place.

7.2. Correlation Analysis for S2SATRA

Tables 6 and 7 demonstrate the correlation value between the attribute A_i for F1 until F12 with respect to $Q_{2SAT}^{k_i}$. For a clear illustration, H_0 signifies that there is no correlation between the attribute A_i with $Q_{2SAT}^{k_i}$. Hence, if the correlation exists between the attributes and the outcome, we will "reject" the decision of H_0 and the connotation of "Accept" means the otherwise [39]. In other words, the aim of this analysis is to verify which A_i will be chosen to represent the C_i in $Q_{2SAT}^{k_i}$. Based on Table 8, most of the attributes selected in S2SATRA have a high correlation with $Q_{2SAT}^{k_i}$. The non-correlated attributes will be disregarded in the right way before it can be introduced in the learning phase of HNN. The main concern in the conventional logic mining model is the possible choice of A_i that construct C_i purely based on the random selection. For example, in F12, the logic mining model without a supervised layer might choose A_6 and A_8 to construct C_i and will have to learn unnecessary attributes that lead to $Q_{2SAT}^{k_i} = 1$. In this context, HNN-2SAT will learn non-optimal $Q_{2SAT}^{k_i}$ that corresponds to the datasets which has no correlation with the final outcome. Hence, the effectiveness of knowledge extraction for logic mining will be reduced dramatically because one of the C_i is not correlated to the desired outcome. Based on the result, the correlation layer is vital to avoid S2SATRA from choosing the wrong attributes.

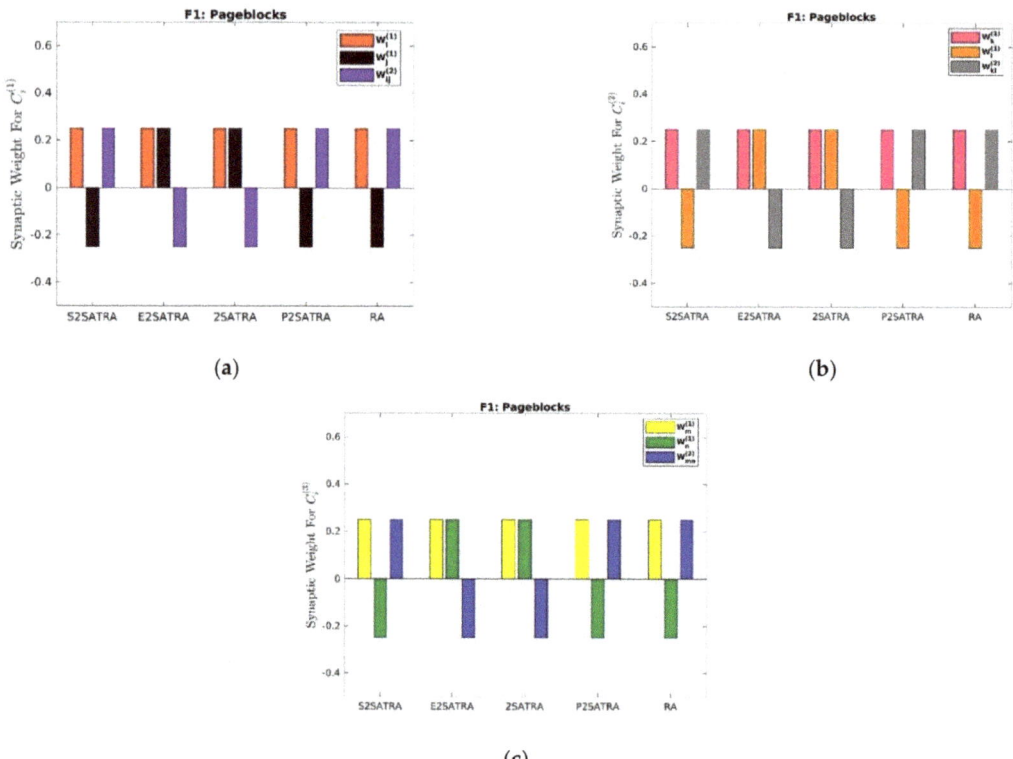

Figure 2. Synaptic weight analysis for F1: (a) $C_i^{(1)}$; (b) $C_i^{(2)}$ and (c) $C_i^{(3)}$.

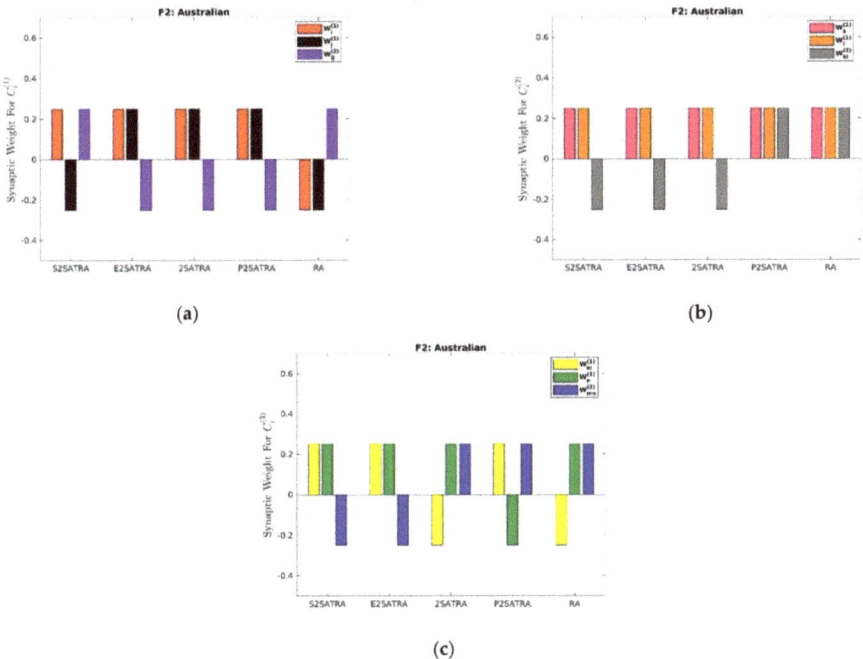

Figure 3. Synaptic weight analysis for F2: (**a**) $C_i^{(1)}$; (**b**) $C_i^{(2)}$ and (**c**) $C_i^{(3)}$.

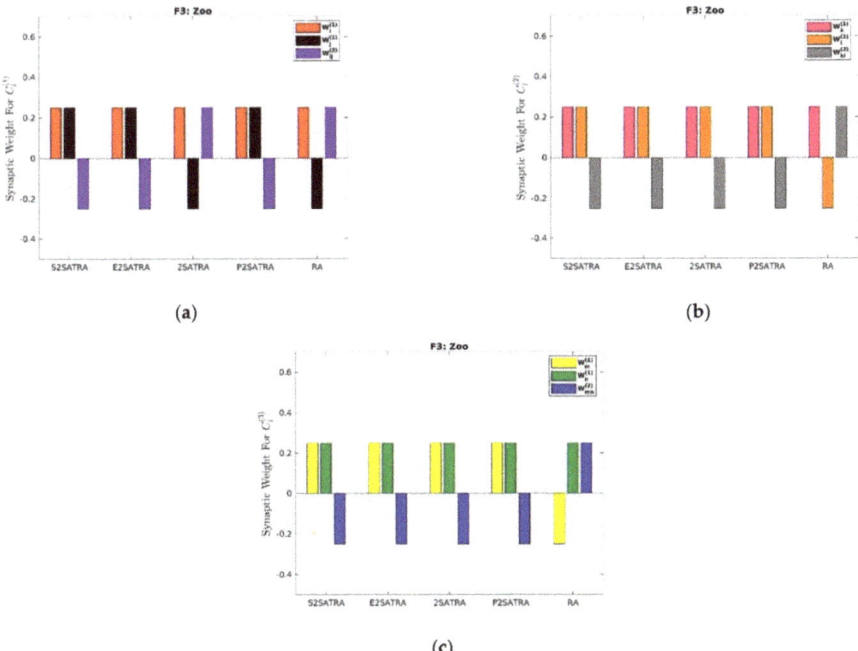

Figure 4. Synaptic weight analysis for F3: (**a**) $C_i^{(1)}$; (**b**) $C_i^{(2)}$ and (**c**) $C_i^{(3)}$.

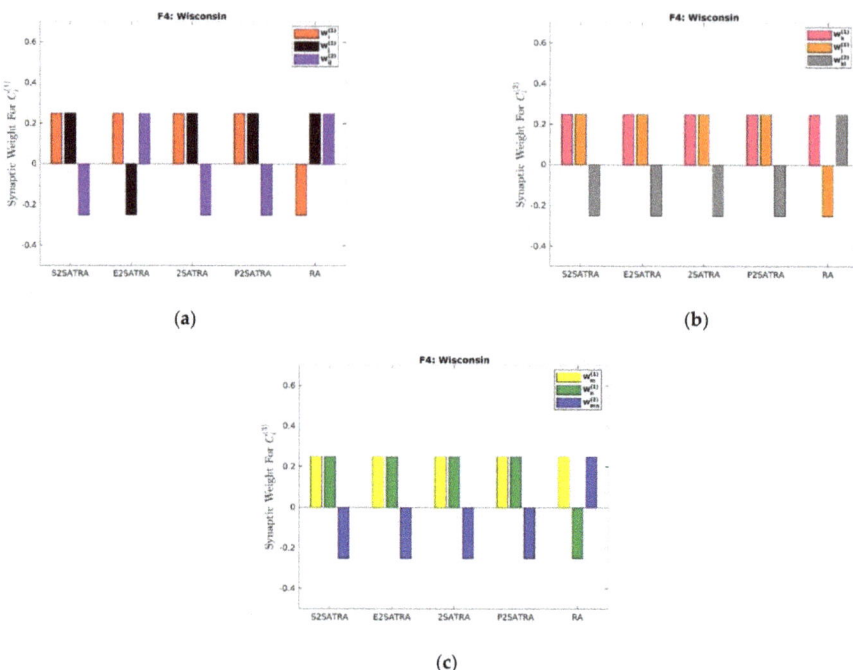

Figure 5. Synaptic weight analysis for F4: (**a**) $C_i^{(1)}$; (**b**) $C_i^{(2)}$ and (**c**) $C_i^{(3)}$.

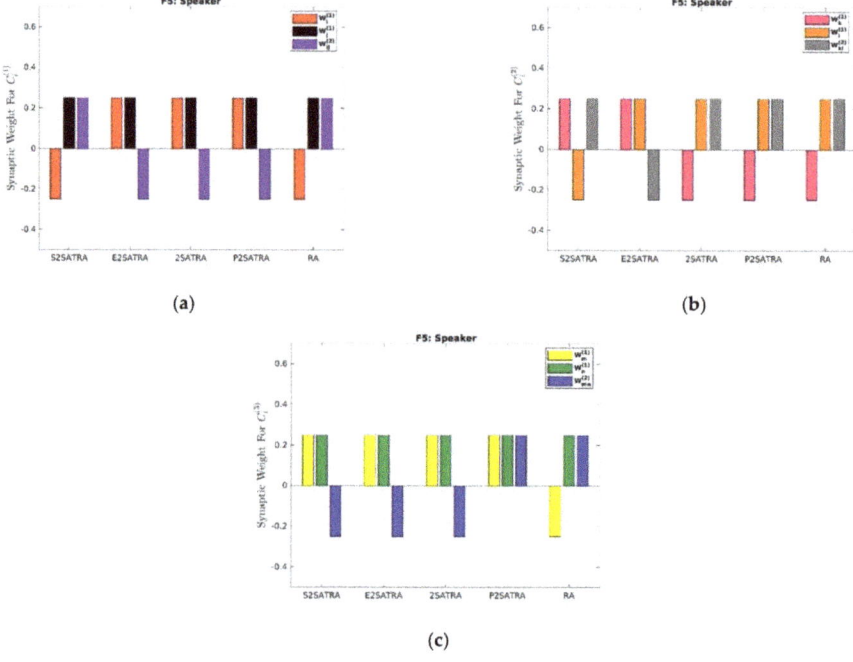

Figure 6. Synaptic weight analysis for F5: (**a**) $C_i^{(1)}$; (**b**) $C_i^{(2)}$ and (**c**) $C_i^{(3)}$.

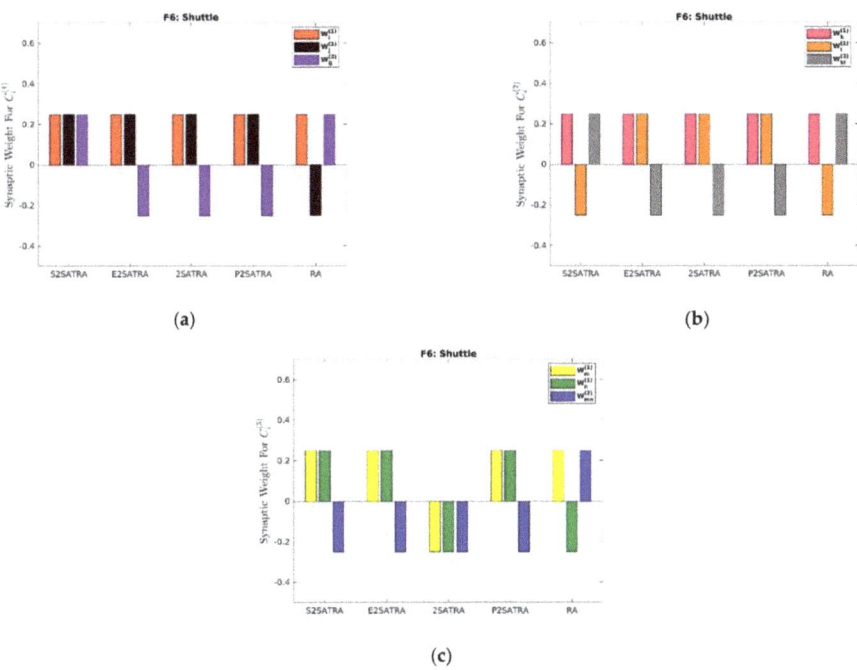

Figure 7. Synaptic weight analysis for F6: (**a**) $C_i^{(1)}$; (**b**) $C_i^{(2)}$ and (**c**) $C_i^{(3)}$.

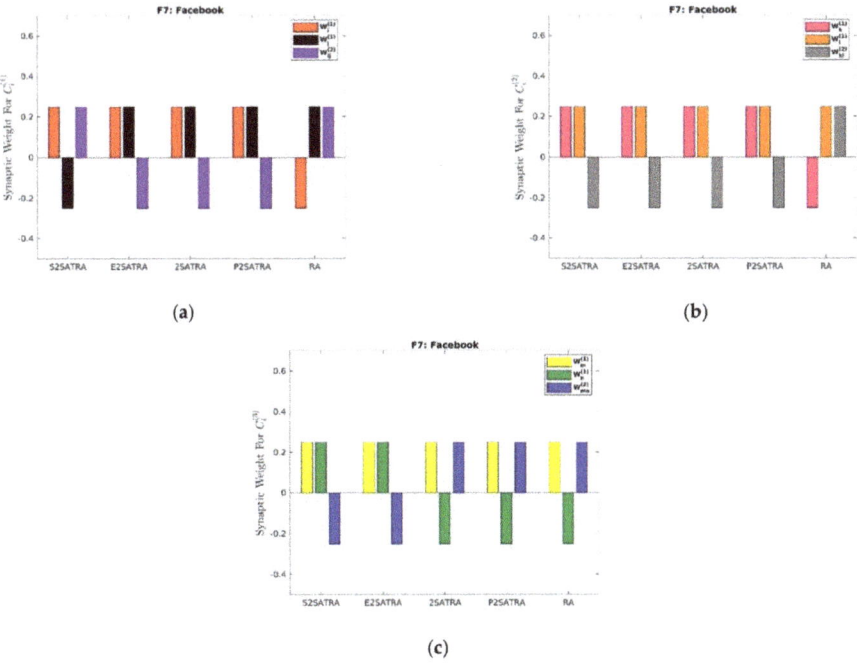

Figure 8. Synaptic weight analysis for F7: (**a**) $C_i^{(1)}$; (**b**) $C_i^{(2)}$ and (**c**) $C_i^{(3)}$.

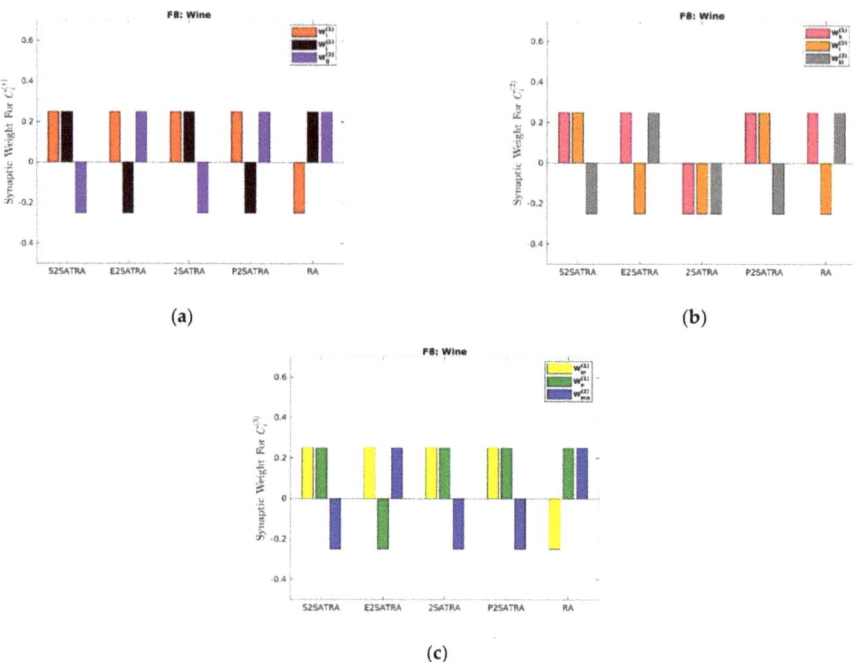

Figure 9. Synaptic weight analysis for F8: (**a**) $C_i^{(1)}$; (**b**) $C_i^{(2)}$ and (**c**) $C_i^{(3)}$.

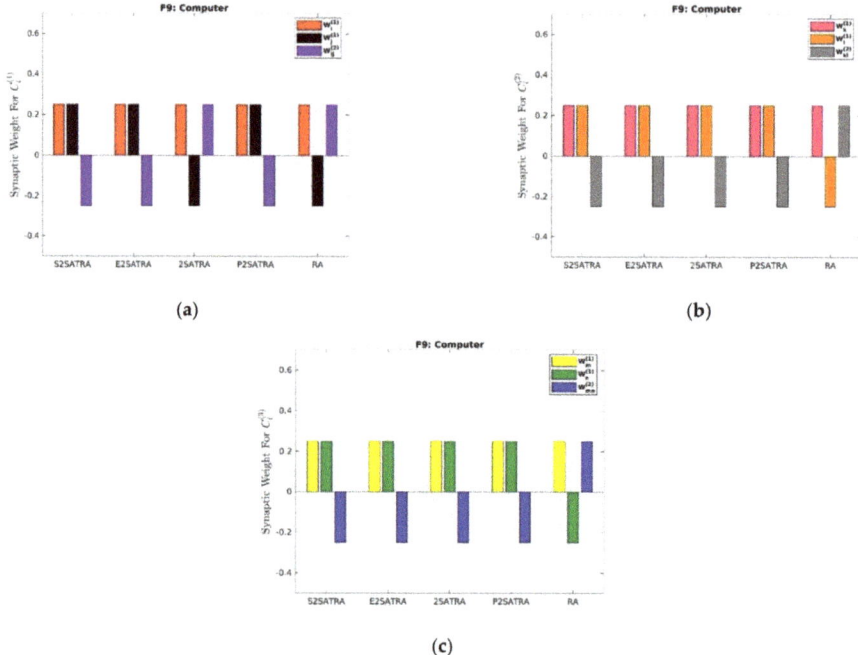

Figure 10. Synaptic weight analysis for F9: (**a**) $C_i^{(1)}$; (**b**) $C_i^{(2)}$ and (**c**) $C_i^{(3)}$.

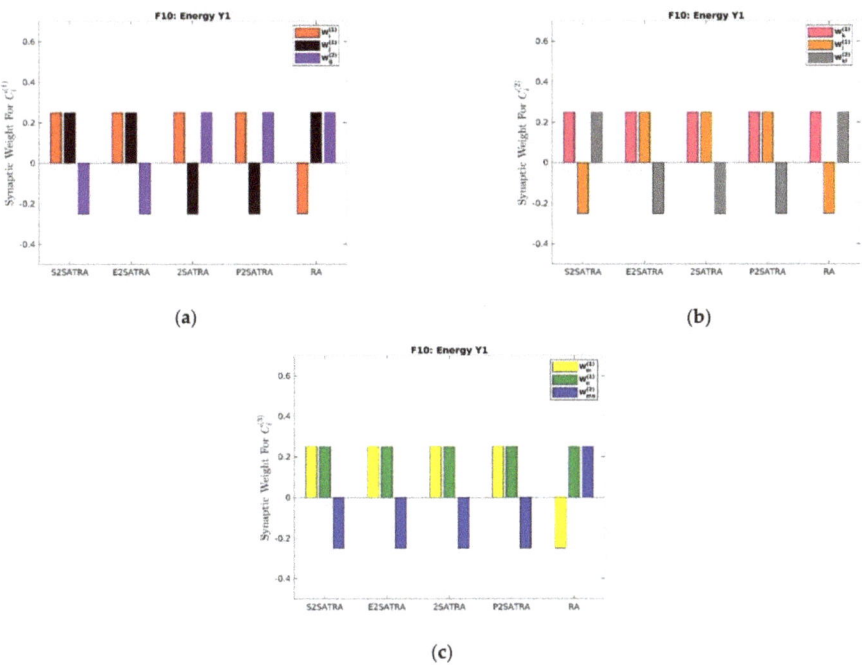

Figure 11. Synaptic weight analysis for F10: (**a**) $C_i^{(1)}$; (**b**) $C_i^{(2)}$ and (**c**) $C_i^{(3)}$.

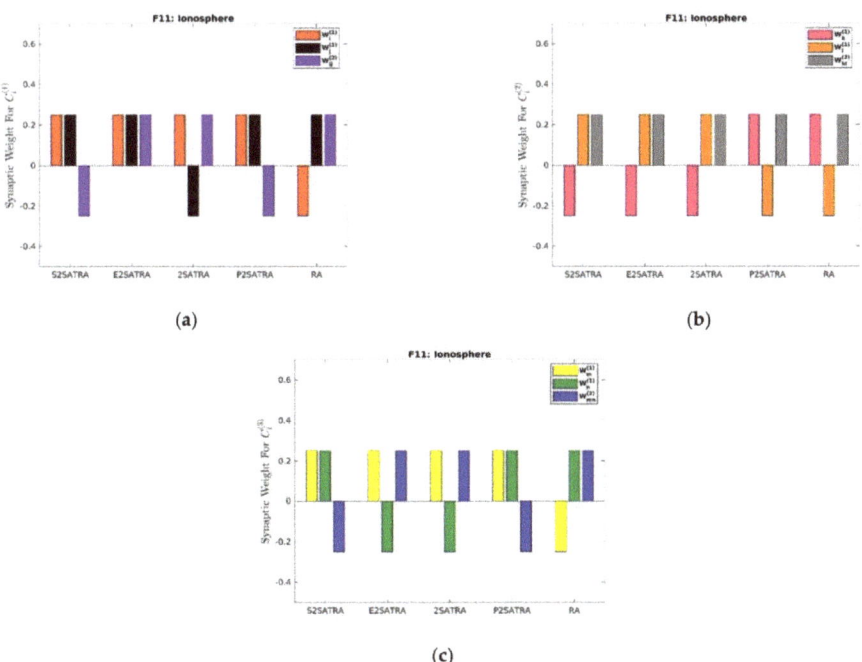

Figure 12. Synaptic weight analysis for F11: (**a**) $C_i^{(1)}$; (**b**) $C_i^{(2)}$ and (**c**) $C_i^{(3)}$.

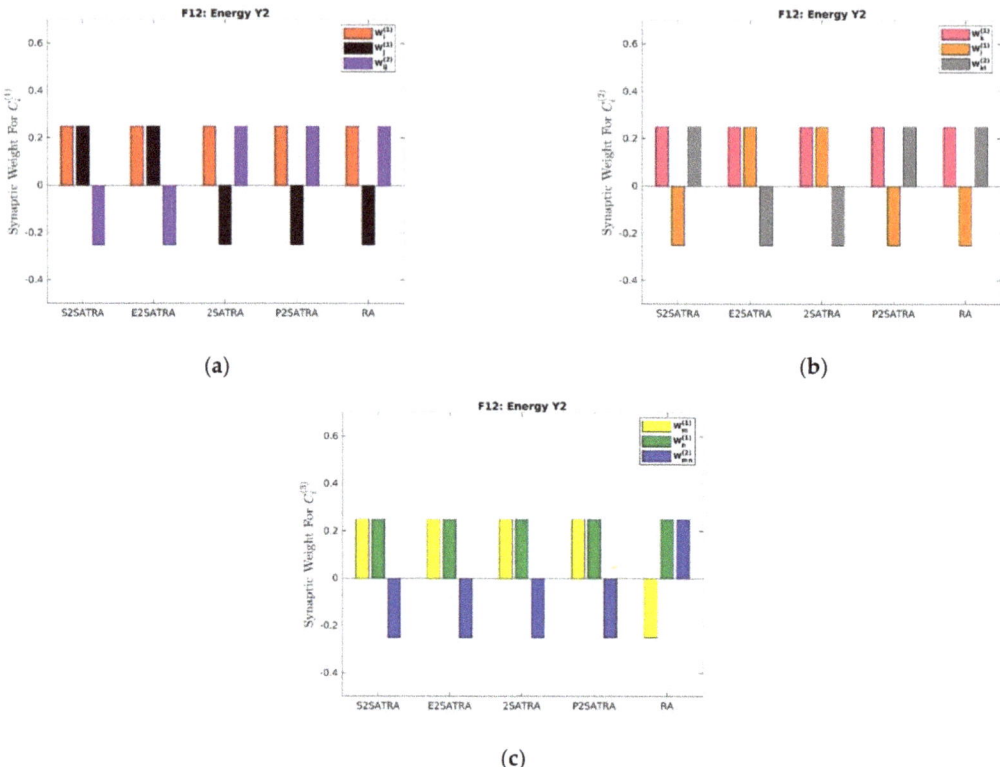

Figure 13. Synaptic weight analysis for F13: (**a**) $C_i^{(1)}$; (**b**) $C_i^{(2)}$ and (**c**) $C_i^{(3)}$.

(a) According to Tables 7 and 8, the worst performing correlation values which account for most of the weakly correlated values are F1, F5, F7, and F11. The weak correlation is determined after considering the absolute value of the correlation. Despite the low correlation value, S2SATRA is still able to avoid attributes with no correlation at all.

(b) The best performing correlation datasets are F4, F9, F10, and F12 where all the attributes of interest are selected for learning. The optimal selection by S2SATRA has a good agreement with high accuracy of the induced logic compared to the existing model.

(c) F6 and F8 are the only datasets that partially achieve the optimal number of attributes with a high correlation with $Q_{2SAT}^{k_i}$. These datasets are reported to be highly correlated and the results have slightly low accuracy in terms of induced logic.

(d) Overall, we can also conclude that S2SATRA does not require any randomized attribute selection because all correlation values agree with the association threshold value.

7.3. Error Analysis

Tables 9 and 10 demonstrate the error evaluation for all the logic mining models. The S2SATRA model outperforms all logic mining models in terms of $RMSE$ and MAE. Note that the improvement ratio is considered by taking into account the differences between the error value divided with the error produced by logic mining.

Table 6. Correlation analysis (ρ) for 8 sampled attributes for F1–F6.

	A_1	A_2	A_3	A_4	A_5	A_6	A_7	A_8
F1								
Correlation	0.352	−0.004	0.335	0.097	0.211	−0.178	0.166	0.157
P	5.4×10^{-159}	7.7×10^{-1}	2.1×10^{-69}	7.8×10^{-13}	4.3×10^{-56}	2.7×10^{-40}	3.9×10^{-35}	1.6×10^{-31}
Decision H_0	**Reject**	Accept	**Reject**	**Reject**	**Reject**	**Reject**	**Reject**	**Reject**
F2								
Correlation	−0.014	0.374	0.247	0.720	0.458	0.406	0.032	0.115
P	7.2×10^{-1}	2.7×10^{-24}	5.1×10^{-11}	1.9×10^{-111}	3.9×10^{-37}	7.9×10^{-29}	4.1×10^{-1}	2.0×10^{-3}
Decision H_0	Accept	**Reject**	**Reject**	**Reject**	**Reject**	**Reject**	Accept	**Reject**
F3								
Correlation	0.366	0.202	0.344	0.230	0.376	0.581	−0.338	0.432
P	2.0×10^{-3}	1.0×10^{-1}	4.0×10^{-3}	6.2×10^{-2}	2.0×10^{-3}	2.4×10^{-7}	5.0×10^{-3}	3.0×10^{-4}
Decision H_0	**Reject**	Accept	**Reject**	Accept	**Reject**	**Reject**	**Reject**	**Reject**
F4								
Correlation	0.687	0.678	0.686	0.580	0.752	0.636	0.604	0.284
P	9.3×10^{-99}	4.2×10^{-95}	2.3×10^{-98}	5.4×10^{-64}	1×10^{-127}	1.4×10^{-80}	1.1×10^{-70}	2.1×10^{-14}
Decision H_0	**Reject**	**Reject**	**Reject**	Reject	**Reject**	**Reject**	Reject	Reject
F5								
Correlation	0.081	−0.278	0.250	0.269	0.077	0.189	−0.271	0.214
P	1.4×10^{-1}	2.8×10^{-7}	4.4×10^{-6}	7.5×10^{-7}	1.6×10^{-1}	5×10^{-4}	5.8×10^{-7}	0.0×10^{-1}
Decision H_0	Accept	**Reject**	**Reject**	**Reject**	Accept	**Reject**	**Reject**	**Reject**
F6								
Correlation	0.737	0.144	−0.010	−0.447	−0.016	−0.595	0.521	0.735
P	0.0×10^{-1}	8.8×10^{-68}	2.3×10^{-1}	0.0×10^{-1}	5.5×10^{-2}	0.0×10^{-1}	0.0×10^{-1}	0.0×10^{-1}
Decision H_0	**Reject**	**Reject**	Accept	**Reject**	Accept	**Reject**	**Reject**	**Reject**

Table 7. Correlation analysis (ρ) for 8 sampled attributes for F7–F12.

	A_1	A_2	A_3	A_4	A_5	A_6	A_7	A_8
F7								
Correlation	−0.086	−0.0324	−0.397	0.393	−0.091	−0.180	−0.072	−0.133
P	4.1×10^{-13}	7.9×10^{-172}	2.0×10^{-264}	4.3×10^{-259}	2.7×10^{-14}	1.4×10^{-52}	1.8×10^{-9}	5.4×10^{-29}
Decision H_0	**Reject**	Reject	**Reject**	**Reject**	**Reject**	**Reject**	Reject	**Reject**
F8								
Correlation	0.518	−0.847	0.489	−0.499	0.266	−0.617	−0.788	−0.634
P	1.3×10^{-13}	2.7×10^{-50}	4.3×10^{-12}	1.3×10^{-12}	3.0×10^{-4}	4.4×10^{-20}	5.9×10^{-39}	2.2×10^{-21}
Decision H_0	**Reject**	**Reject**	Reject	**Reject**	Reject	**Reject**	**Reject**	**Reject**
F9								
Correlation	0.178	0.009	0.819	0.901	0.649	0.611	0.592	0.966
P	1.0×10^{-2}	8.9×10^{-1}	6.7×10^{-52}	4.2×10^{-77}	2.5×10^{-26}	9.7×10^{-23}	3.6×10^{-21}	3.4×10^{-124}
Decision H_0	**Reject**	Accept	**Reject**	**Reject**	**Reject**	**Reject**	**Reject**	**Reject**
F10								
Correlation	0.671	−0.704	0.473	−0.914	0.933	0.995	0.156	−0.055
P	4.4×10^{-50}	4.2×10^{-57}	3.3×10^{-22}	3.8×10^{-147}	2.2×10^{-166}	0.0×10^{-1}	3.0×10^{-3}	2.9×10^{-1}
Decision H_0	**Reject**	**Reject**	**Reject**	**Reject**	**Reject**	**Reject**	Reject	Reject
F11								
Correlation	0.011	0.072	0.310	0.315	0.345	0.581	0.336	0.306
P	8.4×10^{-1}	1.8×10^{-1}	3.0×10^{-9}	1.6×10^{-9}	3.1×10^{-11}	5.0×10^{-33}	9.9×10^{-11}	4.9×10^{-9}
Decision H_0	Accept	Accept	**Reject**	**Reject**	**Reject**	**Reject**	**Reject**	**Reject**
F12								
Correlation	0.674	−0.710	0.435	−0.900	0.924	0.022	0.136	−0.051
P	8.4×10^{-51}	2.1×10^{-58}	1.2×10^{-18}	3.7×10^{-136}	6.2×10^{-157}	6.8×10^{-1}	9.0×10^{-3}	3.3×10^{-1}
Decision H_0	**Reject**	**Reject**	**Reject**	**Reject**	**Reject**	Accept	**Reject**	Accept

Table 8. Improved RA [14].

Parameter	Parameter Value
Neuron Combination	100
Number of Learning (Ω)	100
Logical Rule	Q_{2SAT}
No_Neuron String	100
Selection_Rate	0.1

Table 9. RMSE for all logic mining models. The bracket indicates the ratio of improvement and * indicates division by zero. A negative ratio implies the method outperform the proposed method. P is obtained from the paired Wilcoxon rank test and ** indicates the model with significant inferiority compared to the superiority model.

Dataset	S2SATRA	E2SATRA	2SATRA	P2SATRA	RA
F1	18.125	**18.125 (0)**	31.034 (0.416)	31.034 (0.416)	676.174 (0.973)
F2	5.417	15.289 (0.646)	17.215 (0.685)	15.891 (0.659)	76.601 (0.929)
F3	0.000	0.920 (1.000)	3.849 (1.000)	0.770 (1.000)	49.267 (1.000)
F4	0.569	3.695 (0.846)	1.563 (0.636)	**0.569 (0.000)**	1.563 (0.636)
F5	1.572	11.708 (0.866)	14.329 (0.890)	7.514 (0.791)	20.794 (0.9244)
F6	25.134	32.199 (0.219)	106.945 (0.765)	30.124 (0.166)	958.121 (0.974)
F7	18.839	34.874 (0.460)	46.760 (0.597)	20.745 (0.092)	98.791 (0.809)
F8	1.179	10.371 (0.886)	11.078 (0.894)	1.414 (0.166)	10.371 (0.886)
F9	0.655	2.619 (0.749)	8.510 (0.923)	**0.655 (0.000)**	12.001 (0.945)
F10	0.000	3.932 (1.000)	24.413 (1.000)	**0.000 (*)**	54.367 (1.000)
F11	2.556	5.112 (0.500)	19.369 (0.868)	2.695 (0.052)	59.337 (0.957)
F12	0.000	0.000 (*)	10.650 (1.000)	**0.000 (*)**	7.865(1.000)
(+/=/−)	-	11/1/0	12/0/0	8/4/0	12/0/0
Avg	6.170	11.814	24.643	9.284	168.761
Std	9.039	11.528	28.760	12.008	4.662
min	0.000	0.000	1.563	0.000	1.563
max	18.839	34.874	106.945	31.034	958.121
Avg Rank	**1.250**	2.917	4.083	2.083	4.667
P		0.005 **	0.002 **	0.012 **	0.002 **

Table 10. MAE for all logic mining models. The bracket indicates the ratio of improvement and * indicates division by zero. A negative ratio implies the method outperform the proposed method. P is obtained from the paired Wilcoxon rank test and ** indicates the model with significant inferiority compared to the superiority model.

Dataset	S2SATRA	E2SATRA	2SATRA	P2SATRA	RA
F1	0.387	**0.387 (0.000)**	0.663 (0.416)	0.663 (0.416)	12.452 (0.973)
F2	0.326	0.920 (0.646)	1.109 (0.706)	0.957 (0.659)	4.601 (0.929)
F3	0.000	0.741 (1.000)	0.741 (1.000)	0.148 (1.000)	9.481 (1.000)
F4	0.040	0.263 (0.848)	0.111 (0.640)	0.040 (0.000)	0.111 (0.640)
F5	0.137	1.023 (0.866)	1.252 (0.891)	0.656 (0.791)	1.817 (0.925)
F6	0.330	0.423 (0.220)	1.404 (0.765)	0.396 (0.167)	12.582 (0.974)
F7	0.352	0.652 (0.460)	0.874 (0.597)	0.388 (0.093)	1.846 (0.809)
F8	0.139	1.222 (0.886)	1.306 (0.894)	0.167 (0.168)	1.222 (0.886)
F9	0.071	0.286 (0.752)	0.929 (0.924)	**0.071 (0.000)**	1.310 (0.946)
F10	0.000	0.322 (1.000)	2.000 (1.000)	**0.000 (*)**	4.456 (1.000)
F11	0.233	0.467 (0.501)	1.631 (0.857)	0.227 (−0.026)	5.417 (0.957)
F12	0.000	**0.000 (*)**	0.872 (1.000)	**0.000 (*)**	0.644 (1.000)
(+/=/−)	-	10/2/0	12/0/0	7/4/1	12/0/0
Avg	0.168	0.559	1.074	0.309	310.235
Std	0.151	0.359	0.493	0.309	4.505
min	0.000	0.000	0.111	0.000	0.111
max	0.387	1.222	2.000	0.957	12.582
Avg Rank	**1.333**	2.958	4.041	2.000	4.667
P		0.002 **	0.002 **	0.003 **	0.003 **

A high value of RMSE demonstrates the high deviation of the error compared with the $Q_{2SAT}^{k_i}$. S2SATRA ranks first on 12 datasets. The "+", "−", and "=" in the results column indicate that S2SATRA is superior, inferior, and equal to the comparison algorithm, respectively. The "Avg" indicates the corresponding algorithm's average of the Friedman test for 12 datasets. The rank represents the ranking of the "Avg Rank". Although the value S2SATRA is the lowest compared to other logic mining model, the RMSE value is high, which shows that the error is deviated from the mean of the error for the whole $Q_{2SAT}^{k_i}$. According to Tables 9 and 10, there are several winning points for S2SATRA, which are as follows.

(a) In terms of individual *RMSE* and *MAE*, S2SATRA outperforms all the existing logic mining models which extract the logical rule from the datasets.

(b) There were several datasets that recorded zero error, such as in F3 and F10. In terms of *MAE*, S2SATRA achieved less than 0.5 for all the datasets, resulting in a lower mean *MAE* (0.168).

(c) Despite showing the best performance compared to all existing methods, the *RMSE* value for S2SATRA is still high for several datasets, such as in F1, F6, and F7. Although a high value of *RMSE* is recorded, the value is much lower compared to the other existing work.

(d) The Friedman test rank is conducted for all the datasets with $\alpha = 0.05$ and a degree of freedom of $df = 4$. The *P* for both *RMSE* and *MAE* are 1.27×10^{-7} ($\chi^2 = 37.33$) and 2.09×10^{-7} ($\chi^2 = 36.68$), respectively. Hence, the null hypothesis of equal performance for all the logic mining models is rejected. According to Tables 9 and 10 for all the datasets, S2SATRA has an average rank of 1.25 and 1.333 for *RMSE*, respectively, which is highest compared to other existing methods. The closest method that competes with S2SATRA is P2SATRA with an average rank of 2.083 and 2.000, respectively.

(e) Overall, the average *RMSE* and *MAE* for S2SATRA shows an improvement by 83.9% compared to the second best method which is P2SATRA. In this case, the optimal attribute selection contributes towards a lower value of *RMSE* and *MAE*.

(f) In addition, the Wilcoxon rank test is conducted to statistically validate the superiority of S2SATRA [40]. From the table, we observe that S2SATRA is the top-ranked logic mining model in terms of error analysis followed by P2SATRA, E2SATRA, 2SATRA, and RA.

P2SATRA is observed to achieve a competitive result where the 5 out of 12 datasets have the same error during the retrieval phase. This indicates that the conventional 2SATRA model can be further improved with a permutation operator. Despite the high permutation value (up to 1000 permutation/run) implemented in each dataset, most of the attributes in the P2SATRA are insignificant with respect to the final output. Hence, the accumulated testing error will be higher than the proposed S2SATRA. It is also worth noting that implementation of the permutation operator from P2SATRA benefits S2SATRA in terms of search space. In another perspective, an energy-based approach, E2SATRA, is able to obtain $Q_{2SAT}^{k_i}$ which can achieve the global minima energy but tends to get trapped in suboptimal solution. According to Tables 9 and 10, E2SATRA showed improvement in terms of error compared to the conventional 2SATRA but the induced logic only explores a limited search space. For example, the high accumulation error in F2–F8 were due to small number of $Q_{2SAT}^{k_i}$ produced by E2SATRA. The only advantage for E2SATRA compared to RA is the stability of the $Q_{2SAT}^{k_i}$ in finding the correction dataset generalisation. E2SATRA is reported to be slightly worse compared to P2SATRA, except for F8 and F10 where the error difference is 86.3% and 47.2%, respectively. Conventional 2SATRA and RA were reported to produce $Q_{2SAT}^{k_i}$ with the worst quality due to the wrong choice of attribute selection. Another interesting insight is that the modified RA from [14] tends to overlearn, which results in an accumulation of error. For instance, RA accumulates a large *RMSE* value in F1, F6, and F7, due to the rigid structure of $Q_{2SAT}^{k_i}$ during the learning phase and the testing phase of RA. Additionally, the rigid structure for $Q_{2SAT}^{k_i}$ in RA does not contribute to effective attribute representation. Overall, it can be seen that, compared with each comparison algorithm, S2SATRA has the greatest advantages on more than 10 datasets in terms of *RMSE* and *MAE*.

7.4. Accuracy, Precision, Sensitivity, F1-Score, and MCC

Figures 14 and 15 demonstrate the result for *F-score* and *Acc* for all the logic mining models. There are several winning points for S2SATRA according to both figures, which are as follows.

(a) In terms of *Acc*, S2SATRA achieved the highest *Acc* value in 11 out of 12 datasets. The closest model that competes with S2SATRA is P2SATRA. A similar observation in *F-score* is that S2SATRA achieves the highest value in 8 out of 12 datasets, while the closest model that competes with S2SATRA is P2SATRA.

(b) There were three datasets (F3, F10, and F12) that achieve $Acc = 1$, which means that S2SATRA can correctly predict the $Q_{test} = 1$ for all values of TP and TN. For the *F-score* value, there were three datasets that achieved $F = 1$ value, meaning that S2SATRA can correctly produce TP during the retrieval phase of HNN. In this context, $F = 1$ indicates the perfect precision and recall.

(c) There is no value for *F-score* for F5 for all the logic mining models because there is no TP in the testing data.

(d) According to the Figures 14 and 15, no value for $Acc < 0.8$ is reported and only F11 reports the lowest value of *F-score*. No *F-score* value in F5 indicates that there is no value of TP during the testing data. This justifies the superiority of the S2SATRA in differentiating TP and TN cases which is very crucial in logic mining.

(e) S2SATRA shows an average improvement in the *Acc* value ranging from 27.1% to 97.9%. This shows that the clustering capability of S2SATRA significantly improved while the error value remains low (refer Table 7 (A)). A similar observation is reported in *F-score*. S2SATRA shows an average improvement ranging from 30.1% until 75.7%. This also shows that the clustering capability of S2SATRA significantly improved while the error value remains low.

(f) The Friedman test rank is conducted for all the datasets with $\alpha = 0.05$ and a degree of freedom of $df = 4$. The *P* both for *Acc* and *F-score* are 4.26×10^{-7} ($\chi^2 = 35.18$) and 8.00×10^{-6} ($\chi^2 = 29.03$), respectively. Hence, the null hypothesis of equal performance for all the logic mining models is rejected. S2SATRA has an average rank of 1.375 which is the highest compared to other existing method for *Acc*. The closest method that competes with S2SATRA is P2SATRA with an average rank of 2.083. On the other hand, S2SATRA has an average rank of 1.458 which is the highest compared to other existing logic mining models for *F-score*. The closest method that competes with S2SATRA is P2SATRA with an average rank of 2.333. Both results statistically validate the superiority of S2SATRA compared to the existing work.

(g) In addition, the paired Wilcoxon rank test is conducted to statistically validate the superiority of the S2SATRA. From the table, we observed that S2SATRA is the top-ranked logic mining model in terms of *Acc* and *F-score* followed by P2SATRA, E2SATRA, 2SATRA, and RA.

Tables 11 and 12 demonstrate the result for *Pr* and *Se* for all the 2SATRA models. According to Table 7 (A), there are several winning points for S2SATRA, which are as follows.

(a) In terms of *Pr*, S2SATRA outperforms other logic mining model in 6 out of 12 datasets. The closest model that competes with S2SATRA is P2SATRA. For *Se*, S2SATRA outperforms other 2SATRA models in 7 out of 12 datasets. Similar to the *Pr* value, the closest model that competes with S2SATRA is P2SATRA.

(b) There were three datasets that achieve *Pr* = 1 value, which means that S2SATRA can correctly predict the $Q_{test} = 1$ in comparison with all the positive outcomes. For the *Se* value, four datasets achieved an $Se = 1$ value, which means that S2SATRA can correctly produce a positive result during the retrieval phase of HNN.

(c) No value for both *Pr* and *Se* is reported for F5 because there is no positive outcome for these datasets.

(d) The only datasets that achieved *Pr* < 0.8 were F8 and F11. This shows that 2SATRA has good capability in differentiating a positive result with a negative result. A similar observation is reported in *Se* where the only datasets that achieved $Se < 0.8$ were F8 and F11. Hence, S2SATRA has a competitive capability to produce a positive result $Q_{test} = 1$ compared to other existing 2SATRA model.

(e) S2SATRA shows an average improvement in the *Pr* value, ranging from 12.3% to 61.2%. This shows that the clustering capability of S2SATRA significantly improved while the error value remained low (refer Table 11). A similar observation is reported in the *Se* result. S2SATRA shows an average improvement ranging from 1.8% to 63.9%. This also shows that the clustering capability of S2SATRA significantly improved while the error value remained low.

(f) According to the Friedman test rank for all the datasets, S2SATRA has an average rank of 1.458 which is the highest compared to other existing methods for *Pr*. The closest method that competes with S2SATRA is P2SATRA, with an average rank of 2.333. On the other hand, S2SATRA has an average rank of 1.375 which is the highest compared to other existing method for *Se*. The closest method that competes with S2SATRA is P2SATRA, with an average rank of 2.083. Both results statistically validate the superiority of S2SATRA compared to the other logic mining.

(g) In addition, the paired Wilcoxon rank test is conducted to statistically validate the superiority of S2SATRA. From the table, we observed that S2SATRA is the top-ranked logic mining model in terms of *Pr* and *Se*, as compared to most of the existing work.

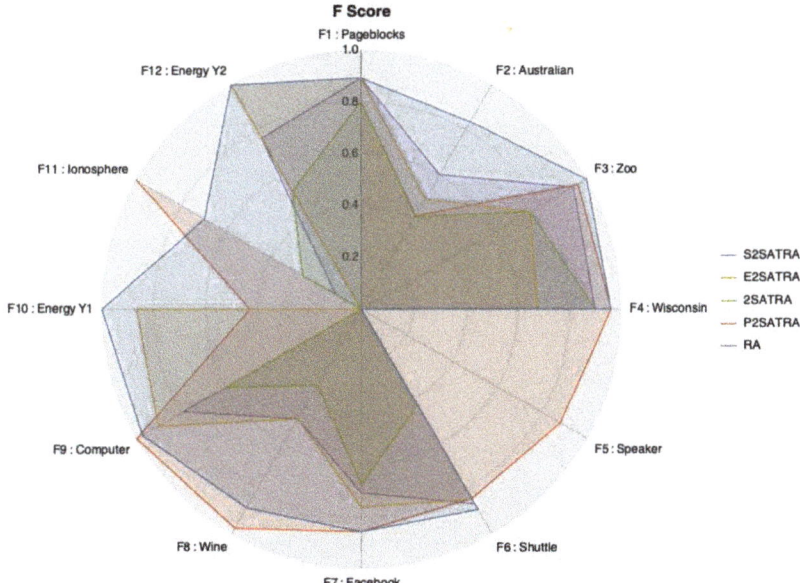

Figure 14. *F-score* for all logic mining models.

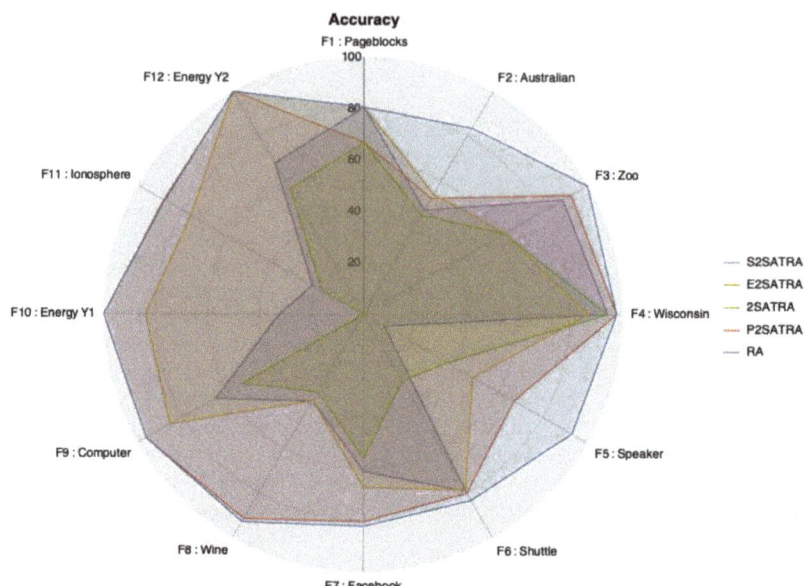

Figure 15. Accuracy for all the logic mining models.

Table 11. Precision (Pr) for all models. The bracket indicates the ratio of improvement and * indicates division by zero. A negative ratio implies the method outperform the proposed method. P is obtained from the paired Wilcoxon rank test and ** indicates the model with significant inferiority compared to the superiority model.

Dataset	S2SATRA	E2SATRA	2SATRA	P2SATRA	RA
F1	0.826	**0.826** (0)	0.685 (0.205)	0.685 (0.206)	**0.826** (0)
F2	0.934	**0.984** (−0.051)	0.443 (1.108)	0.385 (1.426)	0.902 (0.035)
F3	**1.000**	0.600 (0.667)	0.6 (0.667)	**1.000** (0)	0.960 (0.042)
F4	**0.942**	0.519 (0.815)	0.923 (0.021)	**0.942** (0)	0.923 (0.021)
F5	-	-	-	-	-
F6	0.854	0.737 (0.159)	0.330 (1.588)	**0.922** (−0.074)	0.875 (−0.024)
F7	**0.992**	0.980 (0.012)	0.850 (0.167)	0.979 (0.013)	0.880 (0.127)
F8	0.792	**0.875** (−0.095)	0.500 (0.584)	0.750 (0.056)	**0.875** (0.095)
F9	0.966	**0.983** (−0.017)	0.500 (0.932)	0.966 (0)	0.948 (0.019)
F10	**1.000**	**1.000** (0)	0.000 (*)	**1.000** (0)	0.000 (*)
F11	0.696	0.000 (-)	**0.909** (−0.2343)	0.273 (1.549)	0.261 (1.667)
F12	**1.000**	**1.000** (0)	0.468 (1.137)	**1.000** (0)	**1.000** (0)
(+/=/−)	-	6/5/2	10/1/1	5/6/1	7/4/1
Avg	**0.909**	0.773 (0.175)	0.564 (0.612)	0.809 (0.123)	0.765 (0.188)
Std	0.103	0.307	0.274	0.261	0.324
Min	**0.696**	0.000	0.000	0.273	0.000
Max	**1.000**	**1.000**	0.923	1.000	**1.000**
Avg Rank	**1.458**	3.417	4.417	2.333	3.375
P		0.003 **	0.003 **	0.003 **	0.003 **

Table 12. Sensitivity (*Se*) for all logic mining models. The bracket indicates the ratio of improvement and * indicates division by zero. A negative ratio implies the method that outperforms the proposed method. ** due to no positive outcome in the dataset. *P* is obtained from the paired Wilcoxon rank test and ** indicates a model with significant inferiority compared to the superiority model.

Dataset	S2SATRA	E2SATRA	2SATRA	P2SATRA	RA
F1	0.971	0.971 (0)	0.966 (0.0052)	0.966 (0.005)	0.971 (0)
F2	0.755	0.490 (0.541)	0.388 (0.946)	0.452 (0.670)	0.449 (−0.682)
F3	1.000	1.000 (0)	1.000 (0)	0.926 (0.080)	0.923 (0.083)
F4	0.980	0.964 (0.017)	0.8723 (0.123)	0.980 (0)	0.873 (0.123)
F5	0.000 **	0.000 (**)	0.000 (**)	0.000 (**)	0.000 (**)
F6	0.934	0.997 (−0.063)	0.611 (0.528)	0.844 (0.107)	0.867 (0.078)
F7	0.755	0.624 (0.210)	0.560 (0.348)	0.741 (0.019)	0.592 (0.275)
F8	1.000	0.339 (1.950)	0.255 (2.922)	1.000 (0)	0.339 (1.950)
F9	0.982	0.838 (0.171)	0.744 (0.320)	0.982 (0)	0.679 (0.446)
F10	1.000	0.762 (0.312)	0.000 (*)	1.000 (0)	0.000 (*)
F11	0.696	0.000 (*)	0.150 (3.64)	1.000 (−0.304)	0.073 (8.534)
F12	1.000	1.000 (0)	0.600 (0.667)	1.000 (0)	0.616 (0.6234)
(+/=/−)		7/4/1	10/2/0	5/6/1	10/2/0
Avg	0.839	0.666	0.512	0.824	0.532
Std	0.287	0.379	0.355	0.306	0.360
Min	0.000 **	0.000 **	0.000 **	0.000 **	0.000 **
Max	1.000	1.000	1.000	1.000	0.923
Avg Rank	1.375	3.167	4.708	2.083	3.667
P		0.612	0.086	0.003 **	0.084

Table 13 demonstrates MCC analysis for all logic mining models. According to Table 13, several winning points for S2SATRA are as follows.

(a) In terms of MCC, S2SATRA achieved the most optimal MCC value for 7 out of 12 datasets. The closest model that competes with S2SATRA is P2SATRA. On average, the logic mining model is reported to obtain the worst result where the MCC value approaches zero.

(b) There were three datasets (F3, F10, and F12) that achieve an $MCC = 1$ value which means that S2SATRA which produced Q_{test} represents perfect prediction.

(c) No value for MCC is reported for F5 because there is no positive outcome for this dataset.

(d) The only dataset that approaches zero MCC is F1. This shows that S2SATRA has good capability in differentiating all domain of the confusion matrix (TP, FP, TN, and FN).

(e) By taking into account the absolute value of MCC, S2SATRA shows an average improvement in the MCC value ranging from 35.9% until 3839%. This shows that the clustering capability of S2SATRA significantly improved while the error value remained low (refer Table 13).

(f) The Friedman test rank is conducted for all the datasets with $\alpha = 0.05$ and a degree of freedom of $df = 4$. The *P* for MCC is 1.09×10^{-11} ($\chi^2 = 57.26$). Hence, the null hypothesis of equal performance for all the logic mining models was rejected. S2SATRA has an average rank of 1.363 which is the highest compared to other existing logic mining for MCC. The closest method that competes with S2SATRA is P2SATRA with an average rank of 2.955. This result statistically validates the superiority of S2SATRA compared to the existing work.

(g) In addition, the paired Wilcoxon rank test is conducted to statistically validate the superiority of S2SATRA. From the table, we observed that S2SATRA is the top-ranked logic mining model in terms of MCC compared to most existing work.

Table 13. MCC for all logic mining models. P is obtained from the paired Wilcoxon rank test and ** indicates the models with significant inferiority compared to the superiority model.

Dataset	S2SATRA	E2SATRA	2SATRA	P2SATRA	RA
F1	−0.070	−0.071	−0.104	−0.104	−0.071
F2	**0.693**	0.270	−0.109	0.015	0.039
F3	**1.000**	0.316	0.316	-	−0.055
F4	**0.948**	0.647	0.860	**0.948**	0.859
F5	-	-	-	-	-
F6	0.556	**0.595**	−0.406	0.301	0.489
F7	**0.679**	0.411	0.106	0.642	0.226
F8	**0.847**	0.028	0.365	0.816	0.028
F9	**0.918**	0.659	0.107	**0.918**	−0.129
F10	**1.000**	0.713	−1.000	**1.000**	−0.453
F11	**0.623**	−0.101	−0.064	0.490	−0.442
F12	**1.000**	**1.000**	0.137	**1.000**	0.453
Avg Rank	**1.363**	3.045	3.818	2.955	3.818
Mean	**0.745**	0.406	0.019	0.548	0.086
Std	0.316	0.355	0.469	0.412	0.397
(+/=/−)		9/2/1	10/1/1	6/5/1	10/1/1
P		0.011 **	0.003 **	0.018 **	0.005 **

7.5. McNemar's Statistical Test

To evaluate whether there is any significant difference between the performance of the two logic mining models, McNemar's test is performed. According to [38], McNemar is the only test that has acceptable Type 1 error and can validate the performance of the 2SATRA model. The normal test statistics are as follows:

$$Z_{ij} = \frac{f_{ij} - f_{ji}}{\sqrt{f_{ij} + f_{ji}}} \tag{23}$$

where Z_{ij} is a measure of significance of the accuracy obtained by model i and j, while f_{ij} is the number of cases where logic mining is correctly classified by model i but incorrectly classified by model j. A similar description is given for the notation f_{ij}. In this experiment, a 5% level of significance is used. The null hypothesis dictates a pair from the logic mining model with no difference in disagreement. The performance of classification accuracy is said to differ significantly if $|Z_{ij}| > 1.96$. Note that, a positive value of Z_{ij} means the model i performs better than model j. Tables 14 and 15 presents the result of the McNemar's test for all the logic mining models. Several winning points for S2SATRA are discussed below.

(a) S2SATRA is reported to be statistically significant (in bold) in more than half of the datasets. The only dataset that has no statistical significance is F4 where S2SATRA only significantly differs with E2SATRA.
(b) In terms of statistical performance, S2SATRA is shown to be significantly better compared to other logic mining model. For instance, there is no negative test regarding the statistics found for S2SATRA (refer row) in comparison to the other 2SATRA model. The lowest test statistics value for S2SATRA is zero.
(c) The best statistical performance for S2SATRA is in F2, F5, and F6 where all the existing methods are significantly different and worse (indicated in the positive value). The second best statistical performances are F7 and F8 where at least one logic mining model is statistically insignificant but with a statistically better result.
(d) In addition, results from the McNemar test indicates the superiority of S2SATRA in distinguishing both correct and incorrect outcomes compared to the existing method.

Table 14. McNemar's statistical test for F1–F5.

		S2SATRA	E2SATRA	2SATRA	P2SATRA	RA
F1	S2SATRA	-	0.000	9.128	9.128	0.000
	ES2SATRA		-	9.128	9.128	0.000
	2SATRA			-	0.000	−9.128
	P2SATRA				-	−9.128
	RA					-
F2	S2SATRA	-	6.980	9.194	7.406	−23.263
	ES2SATRA		-	2.213	0.426	−26.567
	2SATRA			-	−15.449	78.536
	P2SATRA				-	1.277
	RA					-
F3	S2SATRA	-	3.051	2.722	0.544	0.816
	ES2SATRA		-	−0.278	−2.496	−2.219
	2SATRA			-	−2.177	−1.905
	P2SATRA				-	0.272
	RA					-
F4	S2SATRA	-	2.211	0.704	0.000	0.704
	ES2SATRA		-	−1.508	−2.211	−1.508
	2SATRA			-	−0.704	0.000
	P2SATRA				-	0.704
	RA					-
F5	S2SATRA	-	7.264	9.020	4.201	13.592
	ES2SATRA		-	1.723	−3.077	6.278
	2SATRA			-	−4.819	4.572
	P2SATRA				-	9.391
	RA					-

Table 15. McNemar's statistical test for F6–F11.

		S2SATRA	E2SATRA	2SATRA	P2SATRA	RA
F6	S2SATRA	-	4.996	57.849	3.529	4.457
	ES2SATRA		-	52.853	−1.467	−0.539
	2SATRA			-	−54.321	−53.392
	P2SATRA				-	0.929
	RA					-
F7	S2SATRA	-	11.339	19.744	1.348	16.070
	ES2SATRA		-	8.405	−9.991	4.731
	2SATRA			-	−18.396	−3.674
	P2SATRA				-	14.722
	RA					-
F8	S2SATRA	-	6.500	7.000	0.167	6.500
	ES2SATRA		-	−0.500	−6.333	0.000
	2SATRA			-	−6.833	−4.157
	P2SATRA				-	6.333
	RA					-
F9	S2SATRA	-	1.389	5.555	0.000	4.012
	ES2SATRA		-	4.166	−1.389	2.623
	2SATRA			-	−5.555	−1.543
	P2SATRA				-	4.012
	RA					-
F10	S2SATRA	-	2.781	17.263	0.000	11.702
	ES2SATRA		-	14.482	−2.781	8.921
	2SATRA			-	−17.263	−5.561
	P2SATRA				-	11.702
	RA					-
F11	S2SATRA	-	1.807	11.204	−1.052	10.199
	ES2SATRA		-	9.470	−2.785	8.391
	2SATRA			-	−11.791	−1.424
	P2SATRA				-	10.832
	RA					-
F12	S2SATRA	-	0.000	7.531	0.000	5.561
	ES2SATRA		-	7.531	0.000	5.561
	2SATRA			-	−7.531	−1.970
	P2SATRA				-	5.561
	RA					-

8. Discussion

The optimal logic mining model requires pre-processing structures for neurons before the Q_{best} can be learned by HNN. Currently, the logic mining model specifically optimizes the logic extraction from the dataset without considering the optimal Q_{best}. The mechanism that optimizes the optimal neuron relationship before the learning can occur is remain unclear. In this sense, identifying a specific pair of neurons for Q_{best} will facilitate the dataset generalization and reduce computational burden.

As mentioned in the theory section, S2SATRA is not merely a modification of a conventional logic mining model, but rather it is a generalization that absorbs all the conventional models. Thus, S2SATRA not only inherits many properties from a conventional logic mining model but it adds supervised property that reduces the search space of the optimal Q_i^B. The question that we should ponder is: what is the optimal Q_{best} for the logic mining model? Therefore, it is important to discuss the properties of S2SATRA against the conventional logic mining model in extracting optimal logical rule from the dataset. According to the previous logic mining model, such as [20,21,31], the quality of attributes is not well assessed since the attributes were randomly assigned. For instance, [21] achieved high accuracy for specific combination of attributes but the quality of different combination of the attributes will result in low accuracy due to a high local minima solution. A similar neuron structure can be observed in E2SATRA, as proposed by [24], because the choice of neurons is similar during the learning phase. Practically speaking, this learning mechanism [20–22,31] is natural in real life because the neuron assignment is based on trial and error. However, the 2SATRA model needs to sacrifice the accuracy if there is no optimum neuron assignment. By adding permutation property, as carried out in Kasihmuddin et al. [30], P2SATRA is able to increase the search space of the model in the expense of higher computational complexity. To put things into perspective, 10 neurons require learning 18,900 of Q_{best} learning for each neuron combination before the model can arrive to the optimal result. Unlike our proposed model, S2SATRA can narrow down the search space by checking the degree of association among the neurons before permutation property can take place. Supervised features of S2SATRA recognized the pattern produced by the neurons and align it with the Q_{best} clause. Thus, the mutual interaction between association and permutation will optimally select the best neuron combination.

As reported in Tables 7 and 8, the number of associations for analysis required for n attributes to create optimal Q_{best} was reduced by $\frac{1}{n}{}^nC_6$. In other words, the probability of P2SATRA to extract optimal Q_{best} is lower compared to the S2SATRA. As the Q_{best} supplied to the network has changed, the retrieval property of the S2SATRA model will improve. The best logic mining model demonstrates a high value of TP and TP with a minimized value of FP and FN. P2SATRA is observed to outperform the conventional logic mining in terms of performance metrics because P2SATRA can utilize the permutation attributes. In this case, the higher the number of permutations, the higher probability for the P2SATRA to achieve correct TP and TN. Despite a robust permutation feature, P2SATRA failed to disregard the non-significant attributes which leads to $Q_i^{learn} = 1$. Despite achieving high accuracy, the retrieved final neuron state is not interpretable. E2SATRA is observed to outperform 2SATRA in terms of accuracy because the induced logic in E2SATRA is the only amount in the final state that reached global minimum energy. The dynamic of the induced logic in E2SATRA follows the convergence of the final state proposed in [22] where the final state will converge to the nearest minima. Although all the final state in E2SATRA is guaranteed to achieve global minimum energy, the choice of attribute that is embedded to the logic mining model is not well structured. Similar to 2SATRA and P2SATRA, the interpretation of the final attribute will be difficult to design. In another development, 2SATRA is observed to outperform the RA proposed by [14] in terms of all performance metric. Although the structure of RA is not similar to 2SATRA in creating the Q_i^{learn}, the induced logic Q_i^B has a general property of $Q_{HORNSAT}$. In this case, $Q_{HORNSAT}$ is observed to create a rigid induced logic (at most 1 positive literal) and can reduce the possible solution space of the RA. In this case, we only consider the dataset that satisfies the $Q_{HORNSAT}$ that will lead to $Q^{test} = 1$.

In contrast, S2SATRA employs a flexible Q_{2SAT} logic which accounts for both positive and negative literal. This structure is the main advantage over the traditional RA proposed by [14]. S2ATRA is observed to outperform the rest of the logic mining model due the optimal choice of attributes. In terms of feature, S2SATRA can capitalize the energy feature of E2SATRA and the permutation feature of P2SATRA. Hence, the induced logic obtained will always achieve global minimum energy and only relevant attribute $\rho < \alpha$ will be chosen to be learned in HNN. Another way to explain the effectiveness of logic mining is the ability to consistently find the correct logical rule to be learned by HNN. Initially, all logic mining models begin with HNN which has too many ineffective synaptic weights due to suboptimal features. In this case, S2SATRA can reduce the inconsistent logical rule that leads to suboptimal synaptic weight.

S2SATRA is reported to outperform almost all the existing logic mining models in terms of all performance metrics. S2SATRA has the capability to differentiate between $TP(Q_i^B = 1)$ and $TP(Q_i^B = -1)$, which leads to high *Acc* and *F-score* values. Since S2SATRA is able to obtain more $TP(Q_i^B = 1)$, the *Pr* and *Sen* will increase compared to the other existing methods. In terms of *Pr* and *Sen*, S2SATRA is reported to succesfully predict $Q_i^B = 1$ during the retrieval phase. In other words, the existing 2SATRA model is less sensitive to the positive outcome which leads to a lower value of *Pr* and *Se*. It is worth mentioning that the overfitting nature of the retrieval phase will lead to Q_i^B which can only produce more positive neuron states. This phenomenon was obvious in the existing method where the HNN tends to converge to only a few final states. This result has a good agreement with the McNemar's test where the performance of S2SATRA is significantly different from the existing method. The optimal arrangement of the Q_i^B signifies the importance of the association among the attributes towards the retrieval capability of the S2SATRA. Without proper arrangement, the obtained Q_i^B tends to overfit which leads to a high classification error. S2SATRA can only utilize correlation analysis during the pre-processing stage because correlation analysis provides preliminary connection between the attribute and Q_i^{learn}.

It is worth noting that although there are many developments of the supervised learning method, such as a decision tree, a support vector machine, etc., none of these methods can provide the best approximation to the logical rule. Most of the mentioned methods are numerically compatible as an individual classification task, but not as a classification via a logical rule. For instance, a decision tree is effective in classifying the outcome of the dataset but S2SATRA is more effective in generalizing the datasets in the form of induced logics. The obtained induced logic can be utilized for a similar classification task. In term of parameter settings, S2SATRA is not dependent on any free parameter. The only parameter that can improve S2SATRA is the number of *Trial*. Increasing the number of trials will increase the number of the final state that corresponds to the Q_i^B. The main problem with this modification is that increasing the number of trials will lead to an unnecessary high computation time. Hence, in this experiment, the number of *Trial* still follows the conventional settings in [38]. It is worth noting that S2SATRA achieved the lowest accuracy for F1. This is due to imbalanced data, which leads to non-optimal induced logic. Correlation analysis cannot discriminate the correct relationship between variables and Q_i^{learn}. Generally, S2SATRA improved the pre-processing phase of the logic mining which leads to an improved learning phase due to the correct combination of Q_i^{best}. The correct combination of Q_i^{best} will lead to optimal Q_i^B which can generalize the dataset.

Finally, we would like to discuss the limitations of the study. The limitation of the S2SATRA is the computation time due to the complexity of the learning phase. Since all logic mining models utilized the same learning model to maximize the fitness of the solution, computation time is not considered as a significant factor. As the number of attribute or clausal noise increases, the learning error will exponentially increase. Hence, metaheuristics and accelerating algorithms, such as in [41], are required to effectively minimize the cost function in Equation (5) within a shorter computational time. This phenomenon can be shown when the number of neurons $NN \geq 20$ in the logic mining model is trapped in a trial-and-error state. In terms of satisfiability, all the proposed 2SATRA models do not consider non-satisfiable logical structure or $E_{Q_{2SAT}} \neq 0$, such as maximum satisfiability [42] and minimum satisfiability [43]. This is due to the nature of 2SATRA that only consider data point that leads to positive outcome or $Q^{learn} = 1$. In terms of network, HNN is chosen compared to other ANN structures, such as feedforward because feedback to the input is compatible to the cost function $E_{Q_{2SAT}}$. Another problem that might arise for feedforward ANN, such as within the radial basis function neural network (RBFNN), is the training choice. For instance, the work of [9,44] can produce a single induced logic due to the RBFNN structure. This will reduce the accuracy of the S2SATRA model. A convolution neural network (CNN) is not favoured because propositional logic only deals with bipolar representation and multiple layers only increase the computational cost for the S2SATRA. In another perspective, weighted satisfiability that randomly assign the negation of the neuron will reduce the generality of the induced logic. In this case, 2SATRA model must add one additional layer during the retrieval phase to obtain which logical weight yields the best accuracy. Unlike several learning environments in HNN-2SAT [45], learning iteration will not be restricted and will be terminated when $f_i = f_{NC}$. A restricted value of the learning iteration will lead to more induced logic trapped in local minimum energy. As a worst-case scenario, a logic mining model, such as E2SATRA, will not produce any induced logic in restricted learning environment. Hence, all the 2SATRA models exhibit the same learning rule via the Wan Abdullah method [6]. In addition, all the logic mining models, except for RA and conventional logic mining, follow the condition of $\left| H_{P_{S_i^{induced}}} - H_{P_{S_i^{induced}}}^{\min} \right| \leq \partial$. In this case, only induced logic that can achieve global minimum energy will be considered during the retrieval phase. This is supported by [33] where the final state of neuron that represents the induced logic will always converge to the nearest minimum. By employing the Wan Abdullah method and HTAF [4], the number of solutions that corresponds to the local minimum solution will reduce dramatically. The neuron combination is limited to only $COMBAX = 100$ because the higher the value of $COMBAX$, the higher the learning error and HNN tends to be trapped in a trial-and-error state.

The experimental results presented above indicate that the S2SATRA improved the classification performance more than other existing logic mining model and created more solution variation. Another interesting phenomenon we discovered is that supervised learning features in S2SATRA reduce the permutation effort in finding the optimal Q_i^{learn}. As a result, HNN can retrieve the logical rule to do with acquiring higher accuracy. Additionally, we observed that when a number of clausal noise was added, S2SATRA shows a better result compared to the existing model. It is expected that our work can give inspiration to other logic mining models, such as [20,21], to extract the logical rule effectively. The robust architecture of S2SATRA provides a good platform for the application of real-life bioinformatics. For instance, the proposed S2SATRA can extract the best logical rule that classifies single-nucleotide polymorphisms (SNPs) inside known genes associated with Alzheimer's disease. This can lead to large-scale S2SATRA design, which has the ability to classify and predict.

9. Conclusions and Future Work

In this paper, we proposed a new perspective in obtaining the best induced logic from real-life datasets. As in a standard logic mining model, the attribute selection was chosen randomly which leads to non-essential attributes and reduces the capability of the HNN to represent the dataset. To address the issue of randomness, a novel supervised learning (S2SATRA) capitalized the correlation filter among variables in the logical rule with respect to the logical outcome. In this case, the only attribute that has the best association value will be chosen during the pre-processing stage of S2SATRA. After obtaining the optimal Q_{best}, HNN can obtain the synaptic weight associated with the Q_{best} which minimizes the cost function of the network. During the retrieval phase, the best combination of Q_i^B will be generated, thus creating the best Q_i^B that generalizes the logical rule of the datasets. The effectiveness of the proposed S2SATRA is illustrated by extensive experimental analysis that compares S2SATRA with several state-of-the-art logic mining methods. Experimental results demonstrate that S2SATRA can effectively produce more optimal Q_{best} which leads to the improved Q_i^B. In this case, S2SATRA was reported to outperform all the existing logic mining models in most of the performance metrics. Given the simplicity and flexibility of the S2SATRA, it is also worth implim3n5int other logical dimensions. For instance, it will be interesting to investigate the implementation of random k satisfiability proposed by [13,41] into the supervised learning-based reverse analysis method. By implementing the flexible logical rules, the generalization of the dataset will improve dramatically.

Author Contributions: Investigation, resources, funding acquisition, M.S.M.K.; conceptualization, methodology, writing—original draft preparation, S.Z.M.J.; formal analysis, writing—review and editing, M.A.M.; visualization, project administration, H.A.W.; theory analytical, validation, S.M.S.G. All authors have read and agreed to the published version of the manuscript.

Funding: This research was supported by Ministry of Higher Education Malaysia for Transdisciplinary Research Grant Scheme (TRGS) with Project Code: TRGS/1/2020/USM/02/3/2.

Institutional Review Board Statement: Not applicable.

Informed Consent Statement: Not applicable.

Data Availability Statement: Not applicable.

Acknowledgments: The authors would like to express special dedication to all of the researchers from AI Research Development Group (AIRDG) for the continuous support.

Conflicts of Interest: The authors declare no conflict of interest.

References

1. Malik, A.; Walker, C.; O'Sullivan, M.; Sinnen, O. Satisfiability modulo theory (smt) formulation for optimal scheduling of task graphs with communication delay. *Comput. Oper. Res.* **2018**, *89*, 113–126. [CrossRef]
2. Shukla, A.; Bhattacharyya, A.; Kuppusamy, L.; Srivas, M.; Thattai, M. Discovering vesicle traffic network constraints by model checking. *PLoS ONE* **2017**, *12*, e0180692. [CrossRef] [PubMed]
3. de Azevedo, G.H.I.; Pessoa, A.A.; Subramanian, A. A satisfiability and workload-based exact method for the resource constrained project scheduling problem with generalized precedence constraints. *Eur. J. Oper. Res.* **2021**, *289*, 809–824. [CrossRef]
4. Mansor, M.A.; Kasihmuddin, M.S.M.; Sathasivam, S. VLSI circuit configuration using satisfiability logic in Hopfield network. *Int. J. Intell. Syst. Appl.* **2016**, *8*, 22–29. [CrossRef]
5. Mansor, M.A.; Kasihmuddin, M.S.M.; Sathasivam, S. Enhanced Hopfield network for pattern satisfiability optimization. *Int. J. Intell. Syst. Appl.* **2016**, *8*, 27–33. [CrossRef]
6. Abdullah, W.A.T.W. Logic programming on a neural network. *Int. J. Intell. Syst.* **1992**, *7*, 513–519. [CrossRef]
7. Sathasivam, S. Upgrading logic programming in Hopfield network. *Sains Malays.* **2010**, *39*, 115–118.
8. Hamadneh, N.; Sathasivam, S.; Tilahun, S.L.; Choon, O.H. Learning logic programming in radial basis function network via genetic algorithm. *J. Appl. Sci.* **2012**, *12*, 840–847. [CrossRef]
9. Mansor, M.; Mohd Jamaludin, S.Z.; Mohd Kasihmuddin, M.S.; Alzaeemi, S.A.; Md Basir, M.F.; Sathasivam, S. Systematic boolean satisfiability programming in radial basis function neural network. *Processes* **2020**, *8*, 214. [CrossRef]
10. Kasihmuddin, M.S.M.; Mansor, M.A.; Sathasivam, S. Hybrid genetic algorithm in the Hopfield network for logic satisfiability problem. *Pertanika J. Sci. Technol.* **2017**, *25*, 139–151.
11. Bin Mohd Kasihmuddin, M.S.; Bin Mansor, M.A.; Sathasivam, S. Genetic algorithm for restricted maximum k-satisfiability in the Hopfield network. *Int. J. Interact. Multimed. Artif. Intell.* **2016**, *4*, 52–60.
12. Kasihmuddin, M.S.M.; Mansor, M.; Sathasivam, S. Robust Artificial Bee Colony in the Hopfield network for 2-satisfiability problem. *Pertanika J. Sci. Technol.* **2017**, *25*, 453–468.
13. Karim, S.A.; Zamri, N.E.; Alway, A.; Kasihmuddin, M.S.M.; Ismail, A.I.M.; Mansor, M.A.; Hassan, N.F.A. Random satisfiability: A higher-order logical approach in discrete Hopfield neural network. *IEEE Access* **2021**, *9*, 50831–50845. [CrossRef]
14. Sathasivam, S.; Abdullah, W.A.T.W. Logic mining in neural network: Reverse analysis method. *Computing* **2011**, *91*, 119–133.
15. Mansor, M.A.; Sathasivam, S.; Kasihmuddin, M.S.M. Artificial immune system algorithm with neural network approach for social media performance metrics. In Proceedings of the 25th National Symposium on Mathematical Sciences (SKSM25): Mathematical Sciences as the Core of Intellectual Excellence, Pahang, Malaysia, 27–29 August 2017.

16. Mansor, M.A.; Sathasivam, S.; Kasihmuddin, M.S.M. 3-satisfiability logic programming approach for cardiovascular diseases diagnosis. In Proceedings of the 25th National Symposium on Mathematical Sciences (SKSM25): Mathematical Sciences as the Core of Intellectual Excellence, Pahang, Malaysia, 27–29 August 2017.
17. Kasihmuddin, M.S.M.; Mansor, M.A.; Sathasivam, S. Satisfiability based reverse analysis method in diabetes detection. In Proceedings of the 25th National Symposium on Mathematical Sciences (SKSM25): Mathematical Sciences as the Core of Intellectual Excellence, Pahang, Malaysia, 27–29 August 2017.
18. Kasihmuddin, M.S.M.; Mansor, M.A.; Sathasivam, S. Students' performance via satisfiability reverse analysis method with Hopfield Neural Network. In Proceedings of the International Conference on Mathematical Sciences and Technology 2018 (MATHTECH2018): Innovative Technologies for Mathematics & Mathematics for Technological Innovation, Penang, Malaysia, 10–12 December 2018.
19. Kho, L.C.; Kasihmuddin, M.S.M.; Mansor, M.; Sathasivam, S. Logic mining in football. *Indones. J. Electr. Eng. Comput. Sci.* **2020**, *17*, 1074–1083.
20. Kho, L.C.; Kasihmuddin, M.S.M.; Mansor, M.; Sathasivam, S. Logic mining in league of legends. *Pertanika J. Sci. Technol.* **2020**, *28*, 211–225.
21. Alway, A.; Zamri, N.E.; Mohd Kasihmuddin, M.S.; Mansor, A.; Sathasivam, S. Palm oil trend analysis via logic mining with discrete Hopfield neural network. *Pertanika J. Sci. Technol.* **2020**, *28*, 967–981.
22. Mohd Jamaludin, S.Z.; Mohd Kasihmuddin, M.S.; Md Ismail, A.I.; Mansor, M.; Md Basir, M.F. Energy based logic mining analysis with Hopfield neural network for recruitment evaluation. *Entropy* **2021**, *23*, 40.
23. Peng, Y.L.; Lee, W.P. Data selection to avoid overfitting for foreign exchange intraday trading with machine learning. *Appl. Soft Comput.* **2021**, *108*, 107461.
24. Bottmer, L.; Croux, C.; Wilms, I. Sparse regression for large data sets with outliers. *Eur. J. Oper. Res.* **2022**, *297*, 782–794.
25. Tripepi, G.; Jager, K.J.; Dekker, F.W.; Zoccali, C. Linear and logistic regression analysis. *Kidney Int.* **2008**, *73*, 806–810. [CrossRef] [PubMed]
26. Yan, X.; Zhao, J. Application of Neural Network in National Economic Forecast. In Proceedings of the 2018 IEEE 3rd International Conference on Image, Vision and Computing (ICIVC), Chongqing, China, 27–29 June 2018.
27. Sun, S.; Lu, H.; Tsui, K.L.; Wang, S. Nonlinear vector auto-regression neural network for forecasting air passenger flow. *J. Air Transp. Manag.* **2019**, *78*, 54–62. [CrossRef]
28. Khairi, M.T.M.; Ibrahim, S.; Yunus, M.A.M.; Faramarzi, M.; Yusuf, Z. Artificial neural network approach for predicting the water turbidity level using optical tomography. *Arab. J. Sci. Eng.* **2016**, *41*, 3369–3379. [CrossRef]
29. Vallejos, J.A.; McKinnon, S.D. Logistic regression and neural network classification of seismic records. *Int. J. Rock Mech. Min. Sci.* **2013**, *62*, 86–95. [CrossRef]
30. Kasihmuddin, M.S.M.; Mansor, M.A.; Basir, M.F.M.; Jamaludin, S.Z.M.; Sathasivam, S. The Effect of logical Permutation in 2 Satisfiability Reverse Analysis Method. In Proceedings of the 27th National Symposium on Mathematical Sciences (SKSM27), Bangi, Malaysia, 26–27 November 2019.
31. Zamri, N.E.; Mansor, M.; Mohd Kasihmuddin, M.S.; Alway, A.; Mohd Jamaludin, S.Z.; Alzaeemi, S.A. Amazon employees resources access data extraction via clonal selection algorithm and logic mining approach. *Entropy* **2020**, *22*, 596. [CrossRef]
32. Karp, R.M. Reducibility among combinatorial problems. In *Complexity of Computer Computations*; Raymond, E.M., James, W.T., Jean, D.B., Eds.; Springer: Boston, MA, USA, 1972; pp. 85–103.
33. Hopfield, J.J.; Tank, D.W. "Neural" computation of decisions in optimization problems. *Biol. Cybern.* **1985**, *52*, 141–152. [CrossRef] [PubMed]
34. Sejnowski, T.J.; Tesauro, G. The Hebb rule for synaptic plasticity: Algorithms and implementations. In *Neural Models of Plasticity*; Academic Press: Cambridge, MA, USA, 1989; pp. 94–103.
35. Jha, K.; Saha, S. Incorporation of multimodal multiobjective optimization in designing a filter based feature selection technique. *Appl. Soft Comput.* **2021**, *98*, 106823. [CrossRef]
36. Singh, N.; Singh, P. A hybrid ensemble-filter wrapper feature selection approach for medical data classification. *Chemom. Intell. Lab. Syst.* **2021**, *217*, 104396. [CrossRef]
37. Zhu, Q. On the performance of Matthews correlation coefficient (MCC) for imbalanced dataset. *Pattern Recognit. Lett.* **2020**, *136*, 71–80. [CrossRef]
38. Mohd Kasihmuddin, M.S.; Mansor, M.; Md Basir, M.F.; Sathasivam, S. Discrete mutation Hopfield neural network in propositional satisfiability. *Mathematics* **2019**, *7*, 1133. [CrossRef]
39. Dietterich, T.G. Approximate statistical tests for comparing supervised classification learning algorithms. *Neural Comput.* **1998**, *10*, 1895–1923. [CrossRef] [PubMed]
40. Demšar, J. Statistical comparisons of classifiers over multiple data sets. *J. Mach. Learn. Res.* **2006**, *7*, 1–30.
41. Bazuhair, M.M.; Jamaludin, S.Z.M.; Zamri, N.E.; Kasihmuddin, M.S.M.; Mansor, M.; Alway, A.; Karim, S.A. Novel Hopfield neural network model with election algorithm for random 3 satisfiability. *Processes* **2021**, *9*, 1292. [CrossRef]
42. Bonet, M.L.; Buss, S.; Ignatiev, A.; Morgado, A.; Marques-Silva, J. Propositional proof systems based on maximum satisfiability. *Artif. Intell.* **2021**, *300*, 103552. [CrossRef]
43. Li, C.M.; Zhu, Z.; Manyà, F.; Simon, L. Optimizing with minimum satisfiability. *Artif. Intell.* **2012**, *190*, 32–44. [CrossRef]

44. Alzaeemi, S.A.S.; Sathasivam, S. Examining the forecasting movement of palm oil price using RBFNN-2SATRA Metaheuristic algorithms for logic mining. *IEEE Access* **2021**, *9*, 22542–22557. [CrossRef]
45. Sathasivam, S.; Mamat, M.; Kasihmuddin, M.S.M.; Mansor, M.A. Metaheuristics approach for maximum k satisfiability in restricted neural symbolic integration. *Pertanika J. Sci. Technol.* **2020**, *28*, 545–564.

Article

Logics of Statements in Context-Category Independent Basics

Uwe Wolter

Department of Informatics, University of Bergen, 5020 Bergen, Norway; uwe.wolter@uib.no

Abstract: Based on a formalization of open formulas as statements in context, the paper presents a freshly new and abstract view of logics and specification formalisms. Generalizing concepts like sets of generators in Group Theory, underlying graph of a sketch in Category Theory, sets of individual names in Description Logic and underlying graph-based structure of a software model in Software Engineering, we coin an abstract concept of context. We show how to define, in a category independent way, arbitrary first-order statements in arbitrary contexts. Examples of those statements are defining relations in Group Theory, commutative, limit and colimit diagrams in Category Theory, assertional axioms in Description Logic and constraints in Software Engineering. To validate the appropriateness of the newly proposed abstract framework, we prove that our category independent definitions and constructions give us a very broad spectrum of Institutions of Statements at hand. For any Institution of Statements, a specification (presentation) is given by a context together with a set of first-order statements in that context. Since many of our motivating examples are variants of sketches, we will simply use the term sketch for those specifications. We investigate exhaustively different kinds of arrows between sketches and their interrelations. To pave the way for a future development of category independent deduction calculi for sketches, we define arbitrary first-order sketch conditions and corresponding sketch constraints as a generalization of graph conditions and graph constraints, respectively. Sketch constraints are the crucial conceptual tool to describe and reason about the structure of sketches. We close the paper with some vital observations, insights and ideas related to future deduction calculi for sketches. Moreover, we outline that our universal method to define sketch constraints enables us to establish and to work with conceptual hierarchies of sketches.

Keywords: first-order logic; abstract model theory; institution; sketch; algebraic specification; description logic; graph conditions; graph constraints; diagram predicate framework

MSC: 03B70; 03C95; 18C30; 68N30; 68Q65

1. Introduction

The impetus towards abstraction is often triggered by the feeling that we do, again and again, the "same thing"—that there are structural similarities between concepts and problems in various areas and on different conceptual levels. We experience facing "similar patterns" when formalizing and reasoning about certain kinds of concepts and problems.

Once we obtain the strong impression that concepts, constructions, proofs and results in various areas and on different conceptual levels are somehow related, we may feel the urge to find out what the commonalities really are and to formalize them in an adequate mathematical language. Naturally, such a formalization will be a pretty abstract one if it should cover a broader range of areas.

In light of these remarks, the paper presents the first stage of expansion of a conceptual framework intended to provide a unified view to a broad range of concepts, constructions and problems we dealt with in our long-standing research in various areas and on different conceptual levels in formal specification. The framework should enable us to describe a wide range of specification formalisms (modelling techniques) in a uniform way and thus to relate them. Since category theory is the mathematical language of choice to describe and study relations between structures and constructions, we utilize categorical concepts to describe our framework.

1.1. Background, Motivations, Challenges and Principles

In this subsection, we outline different lines of motivation and challenges encouraging us to develop our abstract conceptual framework. In particular, we discuss and try to justify the methodological principles upon which the development of the framework is based.

1.1.1. Universal Algebra and Algebraic Specifications:

We consider a morphism $\varphi : (\Sigma, E) \to (\Sigma', E')$ between two equational specifications, i.e., a signature morphism $\varphi : \Sigma \to \Sigma'$ such that the set E' of Σ'-equations entails the set $\varphi(E)$ of translated Σ-equations. For any (Σ, E)-algebra $\mathcal{A}$ there is a (Σ', E')-algebra $\mathcal{F}_\varphi(\mathcal{A})$ freely generated by $\mathcal{A}$ along φ. The construction of $\mathcal{F}_\varphi(\mathcal{A})$ can be described in four steps: (1) Construct a "syntactic encoding" of $\mathcal{A}$; (2) Translate this syntactic encoding along the signature morphism φ; (3) Use semantic entailment or a deduction calculus to extend the translated encoding of $\mathcal{A}$ to a syntactic encoding of a (Σ', E')-algebra; and (4) Transform the extended encoding into a (Σ', E')-algebra $\mathcal{F}_\varphi(\mathcal{A})$.

There is a widely-used technique to encode a Σ-algebra $\mathcal{A}$ syntactically (see, for example, [1]): The elements of the carrier A of $\mathcal{A}$ are added as auxiliary constants to the signature Σ and the complete behaviour of the operations in $\mathcal{A}$ is encoded by a set $R_\mathcal{A}$ of ground $(\Sigma + A)$-equations. To make the construction of free algebras work, we have to extend (Σ', E') and φ, in such a way that we obtain a signature morphisms $\varphi_\mathcal{A} : (\Sigma + A, E + R_\mathcal{A}) \to (\Sigma' + \varphi(A), E' + \varphi(R_\mathcal{A}))$ and $\mathcal{F}_\varphi(\mathcal{A})$ is constructed as a quotient of the ground $(\Sigma' + \varphi(A))$-term algebra $\mathcal{T}_{\Sigma' + \varphi(A)}(\emptyset)$.

In abstract model theory, this technique is reflected by the idea to define variables by means of signature extensions. (In this paper, we use the term "model" in two conflicting meanings: A "software model", e.g., is a syntactic representation of (certain properties) of a software system (semantic structure) while a "model" in logic is a semantic structure conforming to a formal syntactic description). This is the traditional approach in the theory of institutions (compare [2]). Note that this only works if the signatures in question comprise the concept of operation!

We perceive the above outlined technique in Universal Algebra as not fully adequate. The construction of free algebras becomes unnecessarily involved and we are, unfortunately, forced to work with infinite signatures since there is a kind of circularity in the sense that signatures have to be defined in such a way that the carrier of any potential Σ-algebra for any signature Σ can be encoded by a signature extension of Σ. Somehow, the concept of signature is not a "syntactic" one anymore. In our humble opinion, signatures are (or should be) located on a conceptual level above carriers of algebras. Following the principle of separation of concerns, we would therefore formulate the following first requirement for our framework.

| Requirement 1: Define signatures independent of and prior to carriers of algebras. |

Adhering to Requirement 1, we will be allowed, for example, to base a specification formalism on finite or enumerable signatures only! Another observation is that signatures are always given by sets, thus we have to adhere to Requirement 1 if we want to work with algebras where the carriers are graphs instead of sets, for example [3].

Generalizing the concept of a group generated by a set of generators and a set of defining relations the small school on Partial Algebraic Specifications in former East-Germany [4–7] developed the concept of a partial (Σ, CEE)-algebra $\mathcal{F}(\Sigma, CEE, X, R)$ freely generated by a set X of variables (generators) and a set R of Σ-equations on X where CEE is a set of conditional existence Σ-equations. Based on this concept, a fully-fledged theory of Partial Algebraic Specifications, including free functor semantics as well as limits and colimits of signatures, specifications and partial algebras, resp., has been developed [6].

We consider here the case of total algebras. Any (Σ, CE)-algebra $\mathcal{A}$ is isomorphic to $\mathcal{F}(\Sigma, CE, A, R_A)$, which, in turn, is isomorphic to $\mathcal{F}(\Sigma, \emptyset, A, R_A)$ since R_A also encodes the fact that $\mathcal{A}$ satisfies all the conditional equations in CE. However, there may be other, hopefully finite, sets X and R such that $\mathcal{A} \cong \mathcal{F}(\Sigma, CE, X, R)$. For any such syntactic representation (X, R) of a (Σ, CE)-algebra $\mathcal{A}$ and any specification morphism $\varphi : (\Sigma, CE) \rightarrow (\Sigma', CE')$, we can construct the free algebra $\mathcal{F}_\varphi(\mathcal{A})$ as the Σ'-algebra $\mathcal{F}(\Sigma', CE', \varphi(X), \varphi(R))$, which is a quotient of the Σ'-term algebra $\mathcal{T}_{\Sigma'}(\varphi(X))$.

Freely generated algebras also play a crucial role in proving the completeness of the deduction calculus for conditional equations [6,7]: A deduction rule generates new equations from a set of given equations. Any conditional equation can be transformed into a deduction rule and vice versa. Given (X, R), the deduction calculus generates the smallest Σ-congruence $C(\Sigma, CE, X, R)$ in $\mathcal{T}_\Sigma(X)$ which contains (X, R) and is closed w.r.t. the rules arising from CE. We consider the quotient Σ-term algebra $\mathcal{F}(\Sigma, CE, X, R) = \mathcal{T}_\Sigma(X)/C(\Sigma, CE, X, R)$. For any Σ-algebra $\mathcal{A}$ we have $\mathcal{A} \cong \mathcal{T}_\Sigma(A)/ker(id_A^*)$ for the Σ-homomorphism $id_A^* : \mathcal{T}_\Sigma(A) \rightarrow \mathcal{A}$, and it can be shown that $\mathcal{A}$ satisfies a set CE of conditional equations if, and only if, the kernel $ker(id_A^*)$ is closed under the deduction rules arising from CE. This insures that $\mathcal{F}(\Sigma, CE, X, R)$ is a (Σ, CE)-algebra. To show the completeness of the deduction calculus, we only have to prove that $\mathcal{F}(\Sigma, CE, X, R)$ is indeed freely generated by (X, R). Note that we work here with a kind of semantic deduction theorem: A set CE of conditional equations entails a conditional equation $(X : R \rightarrow t = t')$ if, and only if, $(t, t') \in C(\Sigma, CE, X, R)$.

In the East-German school of Algebraic Specifications, we do have syntactic representations (A, R_A), (X, R) of Σ-algebras which are well distinguished from signatures and algebras, respectively. At the same time, deduction means the step-wise generation of the congruence relations $C(\Sigma, CE, X, R)$ starting with (X, R). In [7], we describe these congruence relations, for example, as fixed points of so-called derivation operators describing the effect of parallel one-step applications of deduction rules. We are convinced that the definition of any specification formalism would benefit if it includes a separated "technological layer" where the syntactic representations of semantic structures live and where we can describe the effects of deduction explicitly and in detail.

> Requirement 2: Define a separated technological layer where the syntactic representations of semantic structures live and where deduction takes place.

Looking back, we have been left, after all the years, with two related questions:

> Question 1: Is there a general principle behind the one-to-one correspondence between conditional equations and deduction rules?

> Question 2: Is there indeed a kind of general semantic deduction theorem behind the equivalence between entailment of conditional equations and entailment of equations?

We hope that our framework will enable us to give satisfactory answers.

1.1.2. Categorical Algebra

Due to Lawvere [8], one can construct for any specification (Σ, E) with E a set of Σ-equations a category $FP_{(\Sigma,E)}$ with finite products such that the category of all (Σ, E)-algebras is equivalent to the category of all product preserving functors from $FP_{(\Sigma,E)}$ into Set. Analogously, one can construct for any specification (Σ, CE) with CE a set of conditional Σ-equations a category $FL_{(\Sigma,CE)}$ with finite limits such that the category of all (Σ, CE)-algebras is equivalent to the category of all finite limit preserving functors from $FL_{(\Sigma,CE)}$ into Set.

In [9], we generalized this result to many-sorted signatures and partial algebras. We showed how to construct for any specification (Σ, CEE), with Σ a many-sorted signature and CEE a set of conditional existence Σ-equations, a category $\mathsf{FL}_{(\Sigma, CEE)}$ with finite limits such that the category of all partial (Σ, CEE)-algebras is equivalent to the category of all limit preserving functors from $\mathsf{FL}_{(\Sigma, CEE)}$ into the functor category Set^S with S the corresponding discrete category, i.e., set, of sorts declared in Σ.

The construction of those syntactic categories starts by introducing objects that correspond to declarations of finite sets of variables. After adding for each operation symbol in Σ a morphism between the appropriate objects, one continues by constructing new morphisms and an equivalence relation between morphisms. In case of finite product categories $\mathsf{FP}_{(\Sigma, E)}$, no other objects are generated while in case of the finite limit categories $\mathsf{FL}_{(\Sigma, CE)}$ and $\mathsf{FL}_{(\Sigma, CEE)}$, resp., we have to introduce new objects (X, R) representing the set of "solutions" of the set R of (existential) Σ-equations on X, i.e., a corresponding equalizer. Triggered by this example and supported by later experiences, especially with diagrammatic specification techniques, we vote for:

> Requirement 3: Define variables prior to operation and predicate symbols and use variables to define the arities of operations and predicates.

In [9], we specified finite limit categories as partial Σ_{FL}-algebras (with Σ_{FL} a signature declaring two sorts Ob, Mor and operations like source, target, composition, product, equalizer, subobject, ...) satisfying a corresponding set CEE_{FL} of conditional existence equations. The category $\mathsf{FL}_{(\Sigma, CEE)}$ was then constructed as the freely generated partial (Σ_{FL}, CEE_{FL})-algebra $\mathcal{F}(\Sigma_{FL}, CEE_{FL}, OP + CEE, R)$ with $OP + CEE$ declaring one variable of sort Mor for each operation symbol in Σ and one variable of sort Mor for each conditional existence equation in CEE. R describes source and target of the variables in $OP + CEE$ as well as the subobject property of the variables in CEE.

Thus, what we did is to reuse the formalism of partial algebras and conditional existence equations on the higher conceptual level of formalisms to coin a (meta) specification of the specification formalism "finite limits". In the process, we downgraded operations and conditional equations, playing the leading part in Section 1.1.1, to simple variables (generators). It seems quite natural to require a similar flexibility from our conceptual framework:

> Objective 1: The framework should enable us to describe and to work with specification formalisms on different conceptual levels in a uniform way.

1.1.3. Sketches in Category Theory

Categories are graphs equipped with identities and composition; thus, a string-based formalism like algebraic specifications, for example, may be not always the most adequate tool to describe and reason about categorical structures.

In the 1960s, Charles Ehresmann invented a graph-based specification formalism–the so-called sketches. Later sketches were promoted for applications in computer science by Barr and Wells [10] and applied to data modeling problems by Johnson and Rosebrugh [11] (see [12] for a survey).

A sketch $\mathbb{S} = (G, D, L, K)$ consists of a graph G and sets D, L and K of diagrams in G. In Category Theory, a diagram in a graph G of shape I is a graph homomorphism $\delta : I \to G$. A model $\mathcal{M}$ of a sketch $\mathbb{S}$ in a category C is a graph homomorphism from G to the underlying graph of C that takes every diagram in D to a commutative diagram, every diagram in L to a limit diagram and every diagram in K to a colimit diagram [10].

We use in this paper the term "diagrammatic" as a synonym for "graph-based" in a broad sense. We consider, for example, any functor (presheaf) $\mathsf{F} : \mathsf{C} \to \mathsf{Set}$ with C a small category as a "graph-based" structure. Sketches give us a diagrammatic pendant to algebraic specifications at hand and are, at the same time, more expressive. Equational specifications can be equivalently described by finite product sketches, i.e., sketches where

K is empty and L contains only finite product diagrams, while algebraic specification with conditional equations can be transformed into equivalent finite limit sketches with K empty and L containing only finite limit diagrams.

Analogous to Section 1.1.2, we can construct for any finite product sketch $\mathbb{S} = (G, D, L)$, for example, a corresponding finite product category freely generated by $\mathbb{S}$. The methodologically important observation is that the items in the graph G now play the role of "variables (generators)" while the diagrams in D and L are the "defining relations".

1.1.4. Generalized Sketches

Sketches are a very expressive specification formalism but reveal some essential deficiencies when it comes to the formalization of diagrammatic specification techniques in Software Engineering, for example (see the discussion in [13]).

We have to deal with other properties than just commutativity, limit or colimit. In addition, we meet structures that go beyond plain graphs like typed graphs or E-graphs [14], for example.

Extending the sketch formalism along the two dimensions–properties and/or structures–we arrive at generalized sketches. Generalized sketches were developed in the 1990s independently by Makkai, motivated by his work on an abstract formulation of Completeness Theorems in Logic [15], and a group in Latvia around Diskin, triggered by their work on data modeling [16,17].

To define a certain generalized sketch formalism, we chose a category Base which may differ from the category Graph of graphs. We coin for each property we want to deal with in our formalism a predicate symbol P and define, analogous to the shape graphs in traditional sketches, the arity of this predicate by an object αP in Base. Analogous to a diagram in a sketch, we define an atomic statement about an object K in Base by a morphism $\delta : \alpha P \to K$ in Base. A generalized sketch $\mathbb{K} = (K, St^{\mathbb{K}})$ is then nothing but an object K in Base together with a set $St^{\mathbb{K}}$ of atomic statements about K (see [13]).

1.1.5. Diagram Predicate Framework (DPF)

Software models and a plethora of modeling artifacts in various scientific and industrial areas are essentially diagrammatic. Traditional string-based formalisms turn out to be unwieldy and inadequate to define syntax and semantics of diagrammatic modeling techniques and to formalize diagrammatic reasoning. Instead of trying to emulate diagrammatic models and reasoning by means of traditional string-based formalisms, we adapted therefore generalized sketches when we started, around fifteen years ago, to work with Model Driven Software Engineering (MDSE).

Software models are (or, at least, appear as) graph-based structures complemented with constraints the modeled software system has to comply with. For us, it was striking that generalized sketches are the most adequate concept to formalize those artifacts. A software model can be formalized as a generalized sketch $\mathbb{K} = (K, St^{\mathbb{K}})$, where K represents the underlying graph-based structure of the model and $St^{\mathbb{K}}$ the set of constraints in the model. We further developed the generalized sketch approach as a theoretical foundation of MDSE [13,18–20] and called it, after a while, the Diagram Predicate Framework (DPF) since it turned out to be nearly impossible to convince software engineers that a "sketch" is something precise with a well-defined syntax and semantics. For the same reason, generalized sketches are called diagrammatic specifications in DPF.

DPF has been applied to a wide range of problems in MDSE with a special focus on model transformations and meta-modeling [18,21]. Thereby, we restricted ourselves to categories of graphs or typed graphs, respectively, as the base categories. (To reduce self citation, we followed the suggestion of the editors and dropped all references to papers just illustrating applications of DPF but not being relevant for the content of the paper).

While sketches and companions are relegated to a niche existence in all the traditional formalisms we discussed so far, they take center stage in DPF. The framework, presented in this paper, arose to a big extent from the attempt to lift ideas and insights from the development of the theoretical foundations of DPF to a more general level.

> Objective 2: The framework provides a formalization of the general idea of sketches as syntactic descriptions and/or representations of semantic entities.

Our hope is that this sketch-centered approach enables us to achieve another goal.

> Objective 3: The framework allows us to describe, in a uniform way, not only string-based formalisms, like Algebraic Specifications and First-Order Logic, but also a wide variety of diagrammatic specification formalisms/techniques.

At present, DPF does have some deficiencies that we will discuss shortly.

Expressiveness of Statements

We utilize in DPF only atomic statements, called "atomic constraints", i.e., statements like parent(*Anna*, *Uwe*, *Gabi*) in predicate logic stating that *Uwe* and *Gabi* are the parents of *Anna*. With those statements, we can not express all relevant constraints for software systems. String-based languages like the Object Constraint Language (OCL), for example, are traditionally used to express those constraints. OCL is built upon a fragment of first-order predicate logic and we want to extend the diagrammatic language of sketches in such a way that we can work with statements incorporating the usual logical connectives as well as universal and existential quantification. We want to be able to formulate statements like $(\exists x_1 \exists x_2 \exists x_3 : \text{parent}(Anna, x_2, x_3) \wedge \text{parent}(x_1, x_2, x_3))$ in traditional first-order predicate logic stating that *Anna* is the sibling of someone.

Our framework obtained its abstract appearance after we realized that our initial ideas to define such an extension for graph-based sketches would work in arbitrary categories!

Structure of Software Models

There are plenty of different kinds of software models. For each kind, there is a corresponding description of the required structure of software models of this kind. Those descriptions are often called meta-models. Adapting the concepts sketch-axiom [15] and graph constraint [14], we introduced "universal constraints" and "negative universal constraints", respectively, to specify the structure of software models (sketches) [18,21].

Universal constraints are, however, not expressive enough to specify all the restrictions we want or have to impose on software models. Analogous to arbitrary first-order statements, to be used as components of sketches, we want to also define therefore arbitrary first-order sketch constraints to be used to specify the structure of sketches.

To achieve this goal, we have been choosing a more unconventional approach. We neither wanted to encode traditional first-order logic of binary predicates by graphs [22] nor to emulate nested graph conditions by traditional first-order formulas [23]. We instead developed a method to define, in a conservative way, first-order constraints in arbitrary categories of sketches. By conservative, we mean that the application of our universal method to different categories of graphs, as in [22–25], for example, allows us to describe the various corresponding variants of (nested) graph constraints.

To validate the use of the term "first-order", we have to ensure, in addition, that the application of our method to the category Set results in constraints comprising essential features of traditional first-order predicate logic.

Semantics of Diagrammatic Predicates

The advantage of the traditional Ehresmann sketches in Category Theory is that there are fixed universal definitions (formulated in a language based on the concepts graph, composition and identity) of the properties commutative, limit and colimit, respectively. Since these definitions axiomatize the concepts limit and colimit "up to isomorphism", we can presuppose a fixed semantics of all corresponding diagrammatic predicates in any category, i.e., for any fixed interpretation of the concepts graph, composition and identity complying to the axioms of a category.

A price we have to pay, moving from Ehresmann sketches to generalized sketches, is that we have to describe the intended semantics of the predicates we want to include in a formalism on our own. In some cases, a complete axiomatization of the semantics of predicates will be not feasible but we should provide, at least, a partial axiomatization.

At present, we do have in DPF only the very simple notion of sketch entailment at hand to express properties of predicates. We have to extend this notion or find other notions of "arrows" between sketches that provide more appropriate tools for the axiomatization of the semantics of predicates.

On the other side, if we find a way to define arbitrary first-order diagrammatic statements, we will also have closed formulas, like $(\forall x_1 \exists x_2 \exists x_3 : \mathtt{parent}(x_1, x_2, x_3))$, available for axiomatization purposes.

We intend to develop necessary tools to describe the semantics of diagrammatic predicates. We want to understand how these tools are related and, especially, find an answer to the question:

> Question 3: How are the concepts specification morphism, universal constraint and specification entailment in DPF actually related?

Operations and Substitutions

One of the crucial motivations to write this paper was to find an answer to the:

> General Question: What mathematical infrastructure we need to define a formalism enabling us to specify semantic structures with the full expressive power of first-order predicate logic?

Our answer will be: We need nothing but a category!

We are able to give such a general answer since we use only predicate symbols and no operation symbols to construct first-order statements in context. This restriction allows us to realize the translation of first-order statements along context morphisms by simple composition. In particular, there is no need for any kind of "substitution" to define those translations and thus to construct first-order formalisms for specification purposes.

For a future development of reasonable deduction calculi within our framework, we have to rely, however, on "substitutions" and, to have substitutions at hand, we need more infrastructure than just a simple category. In particular, we will need well-behaved pushout constructions as it will be shortly demonstrated in the paper.

Makkai's work [15,26] exemplifies that predicates may be, in principal, quite sufficient to build reasonable specification formalisms.

However, for applications in Software Engineering, for example, operations are sadly missed. Therefore, we are also interested in finding out if and how we can define operations in arbitrary categories. As an initial step, we started to develop a theory of graph operations [3]. It turns out that the step from traditional set operations to graph operations is not trivial at all. We are, however, optimistic that it will be possible to lift the concepts and results of a future comprehensive theory of graph operations, at least, to the level of arbitrary presheaf topoi.

Deduction

To keep software models readable and feasible, we should not overload them with unnecessary items and/or information. In particular, we should drop information that can be derived from the already given information.

To put this principle into practice, we have, however, to rely on mechanisms to derive information. Applied to DPF, this means, especially, that we need rules enabling us to deduce statements from given statements and those deduction rules should be sound.

In the paper, we introduce the concept sketch arrow and discuss the utilization of sketch arrows as deduction rules. The development of a fully fledged deduction calculus for Logics of Statements has, however, to be left as a topic of future research. We will, nevertheless, present and discuss some vital observations, insights and ideas for this future expansion of our framework.

Category Theory can be seen as a diagrammatic specification formalism since it is based on the concepts graph, composition and identity. The development of our abstract framework is also triggered and guided by the quest to put this understanding on a precise formal ground and to develop a purely diagrammatic presentation of Category Theory where the properties commutative, limit and colimit are described by first-order statements on graphs. Most of the diagrammatic pictures in textbooks on Category Theory are nothing but sketches. The vision is to define concepts and to prove results in Category Theory based on pure "diagrammatic reasoning"–or, to formulate it differently: Let us present Category Theory in such a way that "diagram chasing" becomes a precise and well-founded proof technique. As result of such a project, one would probably end up with something very much related to the language of diagrams introduced in [27] and used in [28] to present and define categorical concepts and carry out proofs in a diagrammatic manner. We became acquainted with this language only in the final stage of writing this paper and will include a discussion of this language in the future development of a fully fledged deduction calculus for Logics of Statements.

Meta-Modeling

In DPF, we utilize categories of typed graphs, i.e., slice categories, to define the semantics of sketches. This enabled us to formalize arbitrary deep modeling hierarchies in a quite straightforward way. In this paper, we follow the tradition in logic and work with a Tarskian semantics of sketches, i.e., we work with functor categories instead of slice categories. This makes the formalization of modeling hierarchies rather involved.

Meta-modeling is a big topic on its own and, at the present stage, we are not capable of providing a detailed analysis and treatment of meta-modeling in Logics of Statements. The examples are, however, designed in such a way that we can, at least, point at the meta-modeling issue. We have to include, nevertheless, meta-modeling is an important item on our overall wish list:

> Objective 4: The framework enables us to address and formalize meta-modeling.

1.1.6. Abstract Model Theory

From our various studies in Abstract Model Theory, the technical report [29] is particularly relevant for the present paper. That time, we proved in detail and in a systematic way that four specification formalisms are indeed institutions. Our main finding was that the proof of the satisfaction condition always boiled down to the existence of what we called corresponding assignments and corresponding evaluations, respectively. This finding has been integrated later by Pawlowski in his concept of context institutions [30]. One of the main motivations for context institutions was to incorporate open formulas in the abstract description of specification formalisms and the term context has been coined as an abstract pendant for a "set of variables".

What we call feature expressions in our framework are nothing but a generalization of open formulas. We differentiate, however, conceptually between variable declarations and contexts. In some specification formalisms, both concepts may denote the same thing. In other formalisms, any variable declaration will be also a context but not vice versa. In addition, there can be formalisms where variable declarations and contexts are kept apart, as in Description Logic for example. We use the term context as an abstract pendant for things like a set of generators in Group Theory, an underlying graph of a sketch in Category Theory, an underlying graph of a software model in Software Engineering, a set of literals (atomic values) in Logic Programming and a set of individual names in Description Logic, for example.

1.2. Content and Structure of the Paper

Section 2 recapitulates some basic concepts and corresponding notational conventions. We include a short discussion concerning foundations and outline how the tuple notation is used in this paper to represent (partial) finite maps.

In Section 3, we present a universal mechanism to define first-order statements and their semantics in arbitrary categories. We show that any choice of the seven parameters we are going to introduce (see Figure 1) gives us a corresponding Institution of Statements at hand. The concept of institution [2,31] is a very simple one and lives on the same abstraction level as categories and functors. We utilize institutions as a very convenient guideline to present logical formalisms in a uniform and well-organized way. The satisfaction condition is the only more complicated thing and simply tells us that we designed syntax and semantics compatible in the way that the translation of sentences corresponds exactly to model extensions (see [32–34]). Thus, validating the satisfaction condition is a kind of sanity check for the design of our formalism. At the beginning of the section, we introduce the five running examples we have chosen to illustrate and validate our definitions and constructions.

At the present stage, Institutions of Statements do not incorporate operations since we have not found yet a way to define operations in arbitrary categories. To close, nevertheless, the circle to the ideas and motivations discussed in the Introduction Section 1.1.1, we recapitulate in Section 4 the traditional concepts of operations on sets and many-sorted equations. We show that the procedure we developed in Section 3 to construct Institutions of Statements enables us also to construct corresponding Institutions of Equational Statements. Substitutions play a central role in Universal Algebra, and this section may also provide some hints and guidelines for the future development of a more abstract and general account of substitutions in Logics of Statements.

Any institution gives us a corresponding category of presentations and an extension of the model functor of the institution to the category of presentations at hand [2,31]. In Section 5, we outline this construction for Institutions of Statements and Institutions of Equations, respectively. To distinguish presentations for Institutions of Statements (Equations) from presentations in general, we will use the term sketch for these specific presentations. The general theory of institutions [2,31] also provides us with a standard notion of morphism between sketches (presentations). Those morphisms are of minor importance in this paper. We introduce and investigate, in addition, sketch arrows and sketch implications as well as the relationships between these three concepts. As a pendant to elementary diagrams in traditional first-order logic, we define sketch encodings of semantic structures and will give a kind of positive answer to Question 4 (p. 39): Is there any justification to ignore completely the concept of semantic structure (model)?

To describe the syntactic structure of software models and, more generally, the structure of sketch encodings of semantic structures, we introduce and study in Section 6 arbitrary first-order sketch conditions and sketch constraints, thereby unifying and generalizing the different concepts of graph conditions and graph constraints in the area of Graph Transformations. We outline that we can, analogous to the hierarchy of generalized sketches in [15], also establish a conceptual hierarchy of sketches and sketch constraints. Moreover, we present some vital observations, insights, concepts and ideas to establish a basis for the future development of deduction calculi for Institutions of Statements.

We conclude the paper with a discussion of the results, findings and shortcomings of the paper and highlight future research directions.

The only categorical concepts we actually use in this paper are category, functor, product, functor category and slice category, and a basic understanding of these concepts is recommended. Looking up the definition of institutions may not be necessary but helpful.

2. Notations and Preliminaries

C_{Obj} denotes the collection of objects of a category C and C_{Mor} the collection of morphisms of C, respectively. $C(a, b)$ is the collection of all morphisms from object a to object b in C. We use the diagrammatic notation $f;g : a \to c$ for the composition of morphisms $f : a \to b$ and $g : b \to c$ in C. $C \sqsubseteq D$ states that category C is a subcategory of category D. A category C is *small* if the collection C_{Mor}, and thus also the collection C_{Obj}, is a set. Cat is the category of all small categories. Set denotes the category of all sets and all (total) maps, while Par is the category of all sets and partial maps. We consider Set as a subcategory of Par. Cat, Set and Par are not small!

A (directed multi) graph $G = (G_V, G_E, sc^G, tg^G)$ is given by a collection G_V of vertices, a collection G_E of edges and maps $sc^G : G_E \to G_V$, $tg^G : G_E \to G_V$ assigning to each edge its source and target vertex, respectively. $gr(C)$ denotes the underlying graph of a category C, i.e., we have $gr(C)_V := C_{Obj}$ and $gr(C)_E := C_{Mor}$. A graph G is small if G_V and G_E are sets. A homomorphism $\varphi : G \to H$ between two graphs is given by a pair of maps $\varphi_V : G_V \to H_V$, $\varphi_E : G_E \to H_E$ such that $sc^G;\varphi_V = \varphi_E;sc^H$ and $tg^G;\varphi_V = \varphi_E;tg^H$. Graph is the category of all small graphs and all graph homomorphims between them.

The category comprising as well finite and small graphs as the underlying graphs of categories like Cat, Set, Par and Graph, for example, is denoted by GRAPH, while SET is the category containing all the corresponding collections of vertices and edges, respectively. Correspondingly, we denote the category with all small categories and categories like Cat, Set, Par and Graph as objects by CAT.

Remark 1 (Foundations). *We rely on Tarski–Grothendieck set theory, which is based on the concept of Grothendieck universes. That is, we allow ourselves to work, in principal, with open hierarchies of sets, graphs and categories, respectively. In contrast, many expositions of set theory and category theory, respectively, rely on a strict two level approach. We cite from [35], page 5:*

> Is CAT a category in itself? Our answer here is to treat CAT as a regulative idea; which is an inevitable way of thinking about categories and functors, but not a strictly legitimate entity. (Compare the self, the universe, and God in Kant "Kritik der Reinen Vernunft".)

Here, we work with a three-level hierarchy. That is, we also consider SET, GRAPH and CAT as legitimate entities but take the level above as a "regulative level".

In view of CAT the category Cat appears in two different roles: First, Cat is an object in CAT. Second, Cat is a subcategory of CAT. We consider the inclusion functor Cat $\sqsubseteq$ CAT as an anonymous coercion functor which embeds any object C in Cat into the bigger context of CAT where we can even consider functors between C and Cat, for example. (We use the term coercion analogous to programming languages where coercion describes the implicit conversion of a value into another equivalent value of a different data type). If necessary, we will indicate in what role a small category C appears in a certain situation in CAT, namely as an object in Cat $\in$ CAT$_{Obj}$ (the default case) or as an element in CAT$_{Obj}$, respectively.

Analogously, we assume corresponding anonymous coercion functors Set $\sqsubseteq$ SET and Graph $\sqsubseteq$ GRAPH, respectively. Note that the isomorphisms between small categories C and the corresponding objects in CAT as well as the anonymous coercion functors are not living in CAT! They are located on our third regulative level. Finally, we assume also implicit coercion from the categories SET, GRAPH and CAT, respectively, to the regulative level.

In other words, we comply with the following principles: (1) Any item on a certain level of the hierarchy can be used at any level above but it can not be used at any level below the level where it has been declared or constructed. (2) Located on a certain level of the hierarchy, we can see, declare and construct items on this level and on all levels below. (3) We are, however, not allowed to push an item to a lower level! Instead, we have to declare or construct a "new" item on the lower level and establish an isomorphism between the given item and the new item. The lowest level, where the isomorphism could be established, is the level of the given item but sometimes we will be only able to establish the isomorphism on an even higher level.

To achieve Objective 3 (p. 6), we have to pay a small price. In addition to the conventional interpretation of an n-tuple $(a_1, \ldots, a_n)$ as a "list of values of length n", we will also work with a more unconventional interpretation. We interpret an n-tuple $\mathbf{a} = (a_1, \ldots, a_n)$ with $n \geq 1$ and $a_1, \ldots, a_n \in A$ as a convenient shorthand notation for an "indexed array" of length n, i.e., for a set of assignments $\{1 \mapsto a_1, \ldots, n \mapsto a_n\}$ representing a map $\mathbf{a} : [n] \to A$ with $[n] := \{1, \ldots, n\}$ and $\mathbf{a}(i) = a_i$. That is, the numbers in $[n]$ indicate the corresponding *position* in the tuple. The empty tuple () represents, in such a way, the only map from $[0] := \emptyset$ into A.

Given an $[n]$-indexed family $A_1, \ldots, A_n, n \geq 1$ of sets, i.e., a map $A : [n] \to \text{Set}_{Obj}$, we denote the set of all maps $\mathbf{a} : [n] \to \bigcup_{i \in [n]} A_i$ with $\mathbf{a}(i) \in A_i$ for all $i \in [n]$ by $A_1 \otimes \ldots \otimes A_n$, $\bigotimes_{i \in [n]} A_i$ or simply $\bigotimes A$, respectively. Relying on the assumption that $[n]$ is (implicitly) equipped with the total irreflexive order $1 < 2 < \ldots < n$, we can still use the traditional tuple notation to represent those maps, as discussed in the last paragraph. The traditional Cartesian product $A_1 \times \ldots \times A_n$ and $\bigotimes A$ are isomorphic and both give us a categorical product of the family $A_1, \ldots, A_n$ of objects in Set at hand. If necessary, we will use the term traditional tuple to indicate the traditional interpretation of a tuple as a simple "list of values".

To describe, for example, the concept of a row in Relational Databases (see Section 3.1.5), we also take the step from indexed arrays to "associative arrays".

Instead of the standard sets $[n]$ of indexes, we consider arbitrary finite sets I of indexes (identifiers, names) with n elements. For an I-indexed set $A = (A(i) \mid i \in I)$, i.e., a map $A : I \to \text{Set}_{Obj}$, we denote by $\bigotimes_{i \in I} A(i)$, or simply $\bigotimes A$, the set of all maps $\mathbf{a} : I \to \bigcup_{i \in I} A(i)$ with $\mathbf{a}(i) \in A(i)$ for all $i \in I$. $\bigotimes A$ is a categorical product of the I-indexed family A of objects in Set where for any $i \in I$ the corresponding *projection map* $\pi_i : \bigotimes A \to A(i)$ is simply defined by $\pi_i(\mathbf{a}) := \mathbf{a}(i)$ for all $\mathbf{a} \in \bigotimes A$.

Each element $\mathbf{a}$ in $\bigotimes A$ can be represented by a corresponding *associative array*, i.e., by the set $\{i \mapsto \mathbf{a}(i) \mid i \in I\}$ of assignments. To be able, however, to utilize the tuple notation to represent the elements in $\bigotimes A$, we have to equip the set I, explicitly, with a fixed (!) total order $i_1 < i_2 < \ldots < i_n$. Under this assumption, we can then represent each $\mathbf{a}$ in $\bigotimes A$ by the tuple $(a_1, \ldots, a_n)$ with $a_j = \mathbf{a}(i_j)$ for all $1 \leq j \leq n$.

In practice, it is often more convenient to work with interpretation categories instead of functor categories. An interpretation of a graph G in a category C is a graph homomorphism φ from G to $gr(C)$ denoted by $\varphi : G \to C$. A natural transformation $\mu : \varphi \Rightarrow \psi$ between two interpretations $\varphi : G \to C$ and $\psi : G \to C$ is a family $\mu_v : \varphi_V(v) \to \psi_V(v), v \in G_V$ of morphism in C such that $\varphi_E(f); \mu_u = \mu_v; \psi_E(f)$ for all edges $f : v \to u$ in G. All interpretations of G in C and all natural transformations between them constitute the interpretation category $[G \to C]$ with composition–the vertical composition of natural transformations. (In [10], interpretations $\varphi : G \to C$ are called "models of G in C", and the notation $\mathbf{Mod}(G, C)$ is used instead of $[G \to C]$. For our purposes, the more neutral and general term "interpretation" is more convenient, and we do not want to overload the term "model" too heavily). For convenience and uniformity reasons, we will often consider a set A as a graph without edges and use the interpretation category $[A \to C]$ to represent all maps from A into C_{Obj}. Moreover, we will also use the more compact notations C^G and C^A instead of $[G \to C]$ or $[A \to C]$, respectively.

3. Institutions of Statements

Before we are going to define Institutions of Statements, we outline the running examples we have chosen to illustrate and validate our definitions. The reader should be aware that our framework is very abstract and thus also very flexible. It enables us to present one and the same specification formalism in various ways. Thus, the way we have chosen for each single sample formalism may be not the most adequate one and, especially, not the one preferred by the reader.

3.1. Examples
3.1.1. First-Order Predicate Logic (FOL)

Our category independent framework does not incorporate operations. Therefore, we examine many-sorted first-order predicate logic without functions. We consider many-sorted signatures $\Sigma = (S, P, ar : P \to S^*)$ with S a set of sort symbols, P a set of predicate symbols and a map $ar : P \to S^*$ assigning to each predicate symbol its arity. We may sometimes omit the word 'symbol' and simply refer to sort symbols as sorts and to predicate symbols as predicates. We show that any many-sorted signature can be represented quite naturally within our framework and therefore gives rise to different institutions of statements. We will demonstrate this by means of a sample signature.

3.1.2. Description Logic (ALC)

Description logics are a family of formal knowledge representation languages. We discuss the prototypical description logic Attributive Concept Language with Complements (ALC) which can be seen as a fragment of unsorted FOL without functions (see [36]). We include this non-classical example to illustrate that our framework may be indeed suitable to describe a wide variety of specification formalisms.

This adaption of First-Order Logic to deal with the practical problem of knowledge representation and the example of DPF demonstrate that contexts and sketches, as they are defined in our framework, appear quite natural as conceptual building blocks in practical specification formalisms.

3.1.3. The Formalism "First-Order Predicate Logic" (mFOL)

This example is meant to provide some evidence that our framework lives up to Objective 1 (p. 4). In the FOL-example, we work within the formalism many-sorted first-order logic without functions. Here, we move one abstraction level up and intend to describe this formalism as such. The "m" in "mFOL" stands for meta.

The sketches in the FOL-example are related to concepts like generators and defining relations in Group Theory and literals and facts in Logic Programming but are not a common ingredient in traditional expositions of First-Order Logic. The sketches that appear in this example, however, reconstruct the concept many-sorted signature as we meet it in the FOL-example. As an example, we reconstruct the sample signature we will work with in the FOL-example. Thus, the FOL-example and the mFOL-example together exemplify the topic of meta-modeling.

3.1.4. Category Theory (CT)

Together with the DPF-example, this example should demonstrate the potential of our framework to support a shift of paradigm from string-based to diagrammatic specification formalisms.

Located on the same abstraction (modeling) level as the examples FOL and ALC and reflecting the viewpoint that a category is a graph equipped with composition and identities, we outline a diagrammatic version of the theory of small categories.

In fact, we take a step back from Ehresmann's sketches. We restrict ourselves to the language of graphs, composition and identities and reconstruct the concepts commutative diagram, limit and colimit, respectively, by means of diagrammatic first-order statements formulated in this restricted language. The universal properties defining the different kinds of limits and colimits, respectively, do have a uniform and very simple logical structure; thus, we need only a very restricted form of first-order statements to express them. In the light of this observation, our envisioned diagrammatic version of the theory of small categories goes beyond Ehresmann's sketches in the sense that we allow for utilizing arbitrary first-order statements. Even if we do not need the full "first-order power" to define limits and colimits, this power will be probably useful (or even necessary) to formulate category theoretic statements and to prove them.

3.1.5. Diagram Predicate Framework (DPF)

Now, we arrive indeed at generalized sketches since we will utilize typed graphs instead of just plain graphs as in the CT-example. We are on the same abstraction level as the mFOL-example.

DPF has been developed to describe and relate, in a uniform and precise formal way, a wide variety of diagrammatic modeling techniques in Software Engineering. Each diagrammatic modeling technique, like database schemata, ER diagrams, class diagrams, workflow diagrams, for example, is characterized by a certain footprint. A sketch for such a footprint formalizes then nothing but a single software model. As an example, we outline in this paper a revised and extended version of our diagrammatic Relational Data Model (RM) [18,21].

In Relational Databases, we do have data types and tables with rows and columns. In addition, we can declare different kinds of constraints. A table is identified by a name, and each table has a fixed non-empty set of columns. All columns in a certain table are identified by a unique name; thus, the order of columns is immaterial. It is allowed to use the same column name in different tables. All values in a certain column have to be of the same data type. A table is considered as a set of rows with one cell for each column. In some cells of a table, there may be no values. A row with no values at all is not allowed! Let us declare a table with name T, a corresponding set $C = \{cn_1, \ldots, cn_m\}$ of column names and a declaration of a data type name dn_j for each column name cn_j.

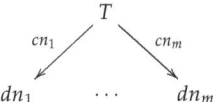

We represent this declaration by the graph shown above. To define the semantics of table T, we first have to fix the semantics of the data type names dn_j by assigning to each data type name dn_j a fixed set D_{dn_j} of data values. This gives us an C-indexed set $D = (D_{dn_j} \mid cn_j \in C)$ at hand.

Since there may be no values in some of the cells in a row, we generalize the definitions in Section 2 and describe a row $\mathbf{r}$ in table T as a partial map $\mathbf{r} : C \dashrightarrow \bigcup D$ with $\mathbf{r}(cn_j) \in D_{dn_j}$ as long as $\mathbf{r}(cn_j)$ is defined. We denote by $\bigotimes_{j \in I}^p D_{dn_j}$, or simply $\otimes^p D$, the set of all those partial maps except the completely undefined map (empty row). For any $cn_j \in C$, we obtain as projection a partial map $\pi_{cn_j} : \otimes^p D \dashrightarrow D_{dn_j}$ defined for all $\mathbf{r} \in \otimes^p D$ by $\pi_{cn_j}(\mathbf{r}) := \mathbf{r}(cn_j)$ if $\mathbf{r}(cn_j)$ is defined. These projections turn $\otimes^p D$ into a categorical product of the C-indexed set $D = (D_{dn_j} \mid cn_j \in C)$ in the category Par of all sets and partial maps.

Reflecting the idea of a row in a table, we can still utilize the tuple notation, discussed in Section 2, to denote the elements in $\otimes^p D$. We fix a total order $cn_1 < cn_2 < \ldots < cn_n$ on C and represent a partial map $\mathbf{r} : C \dashrightarrow \bigcup D$ by the tuple $(r_1, \ldots, r_n)$ with $r_j = \mathbf{r}(cn_j)$ if $\mathbf{r}(cn_j)$ is defined and r_j an anonymous indicator "$\_$" for *nothing* in all other cases.

The content of table T may change. At any point in time, however, the content (semantics) of table T is a finite subset of $\otimes^p D$ and the semantics of the edges cn_j are the corresponding restrictions of the projections $\pi_{cn_j} : \otimes^p D \dashrightarrow D_{dn_j}$.

```
       Empl                    Addr
        / \   name      ssn    / \
    eid(   )ssn*     town(   )street
        ↓       ⨯        ↓
       Int              String
```

To discuss constraints, let us consider a database schema declaring two data types Int(eger), String and two tables Empl(oyee), Addr(ess) with columns as depicted in the diagram above.

Since a table is a set (!) of rows, we need a mechanism to identify rows uniquely. These are the so-called primary keys (pk). For each table, one of the columns has to be declared as a primary key. In the example, we declare the primary keys *eid* (employee identity) in table *Empl* and *ssn* (social security number) in table *Addr* indicated by underlined names. All values in a primary key have to be distinct and empty cells are not allowed. This means that the corresponding projection has to be injective and total. To require only injectivity, we declare a unique constraint and a not null constraint will enforce a total projection. We may put both constraints on the column *ssn* in *Empl*. This will, however, not turn *ssn* into a primary key but only into a candidate key. A primary key is the one of the candidate keys we have chosen to serve as a primary key!

To store and retrieve information, the tables in a database have to be somehow connected. To find, for example, the address of an employee, we have to consult Table *Addr*. *Foreign key (fk)* constraints are the mechanism to connect tables. In the example, we declare a foreign key from column *ssn* in *Empl* to column *ssn* in *Addr* indicated by a star *ssn**. A column declared as a foreign key may contain empty cells but any value appearing in this column has to also appear in the column the key refers to. This means, especially, that both columns are required to have the same data type!

The Blueprint for Constructing Institutions of Statements

In the following subsections, we define Institutions of Statements (IoS). Each Institution of Statements is characterized by seven parameters that we will introduce step by step. The reader can keep track of the development consulting the scheme in Figure 1.

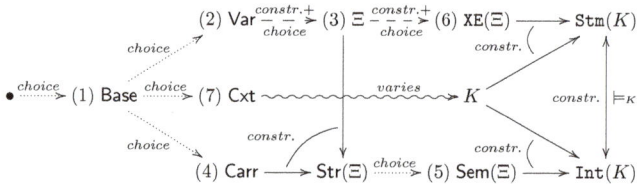

Figure 1. Stepwise construction of an Institution of Statements (IoS).

3.2. Base Category

To define a certain Institution of Statements, we first have to choose a base category comprising as well the basic syntactic entities as the semantic domains. The base category fixes, somehow, the linguistic and conceptual universe we intend to work within.

Definition 1 (First parameter: Base Category). *The first parameter of an Institution of Statements is a chosen **base category** Base.*

Remark 2 (Uniformity). *All components of a logic are related with each other; thus, it seems to be natural to require that they all live in the same category (universe). It turns out, however, that this uniformity requirement is not as trivial, as it looks like at a first glance. Some effort may be needed to present known logic's and formalisms in such a uniform way. One underlying cause for this kind of additional effort is that we follow the tradition in logic and work here with the semantics-as-interpretation paradigm (Tarskian semantics) (see Section* 3.3.2*).*

One problem could be that we become obliged to reflect a distinction between different syntactic entities, like predicate symbols and sort symbols, for example, already on the semantic level. In the more practical relational data model example, this is quite appropriate while it needs getting used to in the mFOL-example.

In other words: We take the chance to present the mFOL-example in a more unconventional way also with the intention to illustrate the flexibility of our framework.

Example 1 (FOL: Base category). *There is a particular dependency in many-sorted first-order signatures. We have first to establish a set of sort symbols before we can define the arity of predicates (compare Chapter 12 in [2]). We fix a set $S \in \mathsf{Set}_{Obj}$ of sort symbols and consider S as a graph (without edges) in* Graph. *Relying on the coercion* Graph $\sqsubseteq$ GRAPH *(see Remark* 1*), we choose the interpretation category* $\mathsf{Set}^S = [S \to \mathsf{Set}]$ *in* CAT *as base category* Base_{FOL}. *We call the objects in* $[S \to \mathsf{Set}]$ *S-sets and the morphisms S-maps, respectively.*

Example 2 (ALC: Base category). *The prototypical description logic Attributive Concept Language with Complements (ALC) can be seen as a fragment of unsorted FOL without functions [36], thus the category* Base$_{ALC}$:= Set *in* CAT *is our base category of choice.*

Example 3 (mFOL: Base category). *In this example, we describe the traditional formalism many-sorted first-order logic without functions as such.*

In this formalism, sorts *and* predicates *are the only concepts. Therefore, we use the set $M_{mF} := \{S, P\} \in$ Set$_{Obj}$ of concept symbols. Relying on coercion Set $\sqsubseteq$ SET, we define the base category as a slice category* Base$_{mF}$:= SET/M_{mF}. *(For any category C and any object T in C we can define the slice category C/T with objects all pairs (A, φ) of an object A and a morphism $\varphi : A \to T$ in C and morphisms $f : (A, \varphi) \to (B, \psi)$ given by morphisms $f : A \to B$ in C satisfying the condition $\varphi = f; \psi$.) We use the term M_{mF}-typed set for the objects in* SET/M_{mF}, *i.e., for pairs (A, τ_A) of a set A and a typing map $\tau_A : A \to M_{mF}$.*

Example 4 (CT: Base category). *Located on the same abstraction (modeling) level as the examples FOL and ALC and reflecting the viewpoint that a category is a graph equipped with composition and identities, we outline a diagrammatic version of the theory of small categories; thus, the category* Graph *of small graphs is chosen as the base category* Base$_{CT}$. *Note that* Graph *is isomorphic to the interpretation category $[M_{CT} \to$ Set$]$ with M_{CT} the graph $E \xrightarrow[tg]{sc} V$ thus we follow somehow the same pattern as in example FOL.*

Example 5 (RM: Base category). *The relational data model relies on the concepts* table, column *and* datatype. *Analogously to example mFOL, we use a graph $M_{RM} := (T \xrightarrow{c} D) \in$ Graph$_{Obj}$ of concept symbols and define the base category as a slice category* Base$_{RM}$:= GRAPH/M_{RM} *relying on the coercion* Graph $\sqsubseteq$ GRAPH. *We use the term M_{RM}-typed graph for the objects in* GRAPH/M_{RM}, *i.e., for pairs (G, τ_G) of a graph G and a typing morphism $\tau_G : G \to M_{RM}$.*

3.3. Variables, Features and Footprints

3.3.1. Variables, Features and Footprints: Syntax

Traditionally, the construction of syntactic entities in logic, like terms, expressions and formulas, starts by declaring what variables can be used in the language of a certain logic. Often, we assume an enumerable set of variables and then any term, expression or formula is based upon a chosen finite subset of this enumerable set of variables. Moreover, variable translations can be described by maps between finite sets of variables. Generalizing this traditional approach, we announce what kind of variables we want to use in our institution.

Definition 2 (Second parameter: Variables). *As the second parameter of an Institution of Statements, we choose a subcategory* Var *of the base category* Base. *We refer to the objects in* Var *as* **variable declarations** *while the morphisms in* Var *will be called* **variable translations**.

If Base *has initial objects, we assume that* Var *contains exactly one of them denoted by* **0**.

This is a completely different view on variables compared to the tradition in the theory of institutions [2], where variables generally depend on the notion of signature.

Example 6 (FOL: Variables). *Variable declarations are traditionally just finite S-sets of variables. We take* Var$_{FOL}$ *to be the full subcategory of* Base$_{FOL} = [S \to$ Set$]$ *given by all finite and disjoint S-sets $X = (X_s \mid s \in S)$ with X_s a subset of the set $\{x, x_1, x_2, \ldots, y, y_1, y_2, \ldots\}$ for all $s \in S$.*

Example 7 (ALC: Variables). *Officially, there are no variables in ALC. To describe ALC as a fragment of FOL we need, however, variables. As* Var$_{ALC}$, *we take the subcategory of* Set *with objects all finite subsets of the set $\{x, x_1, x_2, \ldots, y, y_1, y_2, \ldots\}$ and morphisms all injective maps.*

Example 8 (mFOL: Variables). *We choose as* Var_{mF} *the full subcategory of* $\mathsf{Set}/M_{mF} \sqsubseteq \mathsf{Base}_{mF} = \mathsf{SET}/M_{mF}$ *given by all finite M_{mF}-typed sets* $(X, \tau_X : X \to M_{mF})$ *such that the pre-image* $\tau_X^{-1}(S)$ *is a subset of the set* $\{xs, xs_1, xs_2, \ldots, ys, ys_1, ys_2, \ldots\}$ *and* $\tau_X^{-1}(P) = \{xp\}$.

Example 9 (CT: Variables). *The variable declarations are graphs of variables, i.e., we work with two kinds of variables: vertex variables and edge variables that are connecting vertex variables. We choose* Var_{CT} *to be the full subcategory of* $\mathsf{Base}_{CT} = \mathsf{Graph}$ *given by all finite graphs* $X = (X_V, X_E, sc^X, tg^X)$ *with X_V a finite subset of the set* $\{xv, xv_1, xv_2, \ldots, yv, yv_1, yv_2, \ldots\}$ *and X_E a finite subset of the set* $\{xe, xe_1, xe_2, \ldots, ye, ye_1, ye_2, \ldots\}$. *"e" stands for edge while "v" refers to vertex.*

Example 10 (RM: Variables). *As Var_{RM}, we choose the full subcategory of* $\mathsf{Graph}/M_{RM} \sqsubseteq \mathsf{Base}_{RM} = \mathsf{GRAPH}/M_{RM}$ *given by all finite M_{RM}-typed graphs* $(X, \tau_X : X \to M_{RM})$ *such that the pre-image* $\tau_X^{-1}(T)$ *is a finite subset of the set* $\{xt, xt_1, xt_2, \ldots, yt, yt_1, yt_2, \ldots\}$, $\tau_X^{-1}(D)$ *is a finite subset of* $\{xd, xd1, xd_2, \ldots, yd, yd_1, yd_2, \ldots\}$ *and* $\tau_X^{-1}(c)$ *is a finite subset of* $\{xc, xc_1, xc_2, \ldots, yc, yc_1, yc_2, \ldots\}$, *respectively.*

Guided by Requirement 3 (p. 4), we introduced variables first and can utilize them now to define arities.

Definition 3 (Third parameter: Footprint). *The third parameter of an Institution of Statements is a **footprint** $\Xi = (\Phi, \alpha)$ over Var given by a set Φ of **feature symbols** and a map $\alpha : \Phi \to \mathsf{Var}_{Obj}$. For any feature symbol $F \in \Phi$, the variable declaration $\alpha(F)$ is called the **arity of** F. We will often write αF for $\alpha(F)$.*

Remark 3 (Terminology: Footprint vs. signature). *In most of our applications of DPF, footprints occur as meta-signatures, in the sense that each specification formalism (modeling technique) is characterized by a certain footprint. Each of the formalisms Universal Algebra, Category Theory, First-Order Logic, ER diagrams, class diagrams is characterized by a certain footprint. The sketch data model in [11] corresponds to a certain footprint and so on. For the footprint of the modeling technique* class diagrams, *we refer to [18,21].*

Until today, we used in all our DPF papers the terms signature instead of footprint and predicate symbol instead of feature symbol (compare [13,21]). This turned out to be a source for serious misunderstandings and misleading perceptions; thus, we decided to coin new terms.

Remark 4 (Dependencies between features). *Extending Makkai's approach [15], we worked in [13] with categories Φ of feature symbols, instead of just sets of feature symbols, and with arity functors $\alpha : \Phi \to \mathsf{Var}$, instead of just arity maps. Arrows between feature symbols represent dependencies between features. This allows us to reflect, already on the level of feature symbols and thus prior to arities and semantics of features that certain features depend on (are based upon) other features. As examples, one may express that both concepts pullback and pushout are based upon the concept commutative square and that the categorical concept inverse image depends on the concept monomorphism.*

Any semantics of feature symbols then has to respect those dependencies. Dependency arrows are a tool to represent knowledge about and requirements on features prior to and independent of any kind of logic. Dependency arrows somehow make the framework of generalized sketches conceptual and structural round.

It may be worth mentioning that the concept of order-sorted algebra is somehow related to our idea of dependencies since it works with arrows between sort symbols [37].

In this first paper about Logics of Statements, we drop dependency arrows due to, at least, three reasons: (1) We do not want to deviate too much from the traditional first-order logic setting. (2) Dependencies trigger an additional theoretical overhead that may be not worth it at the moment. If we introduce dependencies between feature symbols, we should consequently describe, for example, to what extent and how they generate dependencies between feature expressions (introduced in

Section 3.4). On one side, this is technically not fully trivial, if possible at all. On the other side, such an effort has no relevance for our applications. (3) The requirements expressed by dependency arrows can be mimicked by the logical tools we are going to introduce later.

Example 11 (FOL: Footprint). *We show, first, how an arbitrary traditional many-sorted signature $\Sigma = (S, P, ar : P \to S^*)$ can be transformed into a footprint $\Xi_\Sigma = (\Phi_\Sigma, \alpha_\Sigma)$ and then we present a sample FOL-footprint to be used in the forthcoming parts of this example.*

The set S of sort symbols has been already transformed into the IoS-setting by choosing the base category $[S \to \mathsf{Set}]$. The set Φ_Σ of feature symbols is nothing but the set P of predicate symbols. Thus, it remains to transform each $w \in S^*$ into a corresponding S-set X^w of variables.

The empty sequence $\varepsilon \in S^*$ is simply transformed into the empty S-set $X^\varepsilon := (\emptyset \mid s \in S)$. A non-empty sequence $w = s_1 s_2 \ldots s_n$ gives rise to a list $[x_1:s_1, x_2:s_2, \ldots, x_n:s_n]$ of variable declarations, i.e., to a canonical set $\{x_1, x_2, \ldots, x_n\}$ of variables, equipped with a canonical total order $x_1 < x_2 < \ldots < x_n$, together with a map from $\{x_1, x_2, \ldots, x_n\}$ into S. X^w is defined by $X_s^w := \{x_i \mid s_i = s\}$ for all $s \in S$. In the examples, we will use lists of variable declarations to represent S-sets of variables.

To complete the definition of Ξ_Σ, we simply set $\alpha_\Sigma(\mathsf{p}) := X^{ar(\mathsf{p})}$ for all $\mathsf{p} \in \Phi_\Sigma = P$.

As an example for a FOL-footprint, we chose $S = \{prs, nat\}$ with sort symbols "prs" for person and "nat" for natural number, respectively. The sample footprint $\Xi_{FOL} = (\Phi_{FOL}, \alpha_{FOL})$ is then defined by the feature symbols $\Phi_{FOL} := \{\mathtt{parent}, \mathtt{male}, \mathtt{age}, \mathtt{less}\}$ with the following S-sets as arities: $\alpha_{FOL}(\mathtt{parent}) := (\{x_1, x_2, x_3\}, \emptyset)$ represented by $[x_1: prs, x_2: prs, x_3: prs]$, $\alpha_{FOL}(\mathtt{male}) := (\{x\}, \emptyset)$ represented by $[x: prs]$, $\alpha_{FOL}(\mathtt{age}) := (\{x_1\}, \{x_2\})$ represented by $[x_1: prs, x_2: nat]$ and $\alpha_{FOL}(\mathtt{less}) := (\emptyset, \{x_1, x_2\})$ represented by $[x_1: nat, x_2: nat]$.

Example 12 (ALC: Footprint). *A signature in ALC declares a set N_C of concept names and a disjoint set N_R of role names. In view of Definition 3, this means defining a footprint $\Xi_{ALC} = (\Phi_{ALC}, \alpha_{ALC})$ with $\Phi_{ALC} = N_C \cup N_R$, $\alpha_{ALC}(F) = \{x\}$ for all $F \in N_C$ and $\alpha_{ALC}(F) = \{x_1, x_2\}$ for all $F \in N_R$.*

A signature in ALC also declares a set N_O of individual names (nominals, objects). In our framework, those sets of individual names are considered as contexts *(see Definition 11).*

Example 13 (mFOL: Footprint). *An mFOL-footprint describes which one of the enumerable many formal tools n-ary many-sorted predicates we will have at hand. As an example, we consider an mFOL-footprint $\Xi_{mF} = (\Phi_{mF}, \alpha_{mF})$ providing the formal tools unary many-sorted predicates, binary many-sorted predicates and tertiary many-sorted predicates, respectively.*

We have $\Phi_{mF} := \{\mathtt{un}, \mathtt{bin}, \mathtt{trt}\}$ with $\alpha_{mF}(\mathtt{un}) = (X_{\mathtt{un}}, \tau_{X_{\mathtt{un}}} : X_{\mathtt{un}} \to M_{mF})$ given by $X_{\mathtt{un}} := \{xp, xs\}$ and $\tau_{X_{\mathtt{un}}}(xp) := \boldsymbol{P}$, $\tau_{X_{\mathtt{un}}}(xs) := \boldsymbol{S}$. Analogously to Example 11, we represent the M_{mF}-typed set $(X_{\mathtt{un}}, \tau_{X_{\mathtt{un}}})$ by the list $[xp: \boldsymbol{P}, xs: \boldsymbol{S}]$ of variable declarations. $(X_{\mathtt{bin}}, \tau_{X_{\mathtt{bin}}})$ is defined by $[xp: \boldsymbol{P}, xs_1: \boldsymbol{S}, xs_2: \boldsymbol{S}]$ while $(X_{\mathtt{trt}}, \tau_{X_{\mathtt{trt}}})$ is given by $[xp: \boldsymbol{P}, xs_1: \boldsymbol{S}, xs_2: \boldsymbol{S}, xs_3: \boldsymbol{S}]$, respectively. Keep in mind that, for any set M in Set the interpretation category $[M \to \mathsf{Set}]$ and the slice category Set/M are equivalent.

Example 14 (CT: Footprint). *Category Theory relies on a language based upon the concepts* object (vertex), morphism (arrow, edge), composition *and* identity. *The concept* graph *comprises already the concepts* object (vertex) *and* morphism (arrow, edge); *thus, a footprint for our diagrammatic reconstruction of the theory of small categories only needs to take care of composition and identity.*

We do not have operations in footprints; thus, we have to formalize composition and identity by means of features (predicates). Therefore, the footprint Ξ_{CT} for the formalism Category Theory declares two feature symbols $\mathtt{cmp}$ and $\mathtt{id}$. The arities of the feature symbols in $\Phi_{CT} := \{\mathtt{cmp}, \mathtt{id}\}$ are described in Table 1:

Table 1. CT Footprint.

F	Arity $\alpha_{CT}(F)$	F	Arity $\alpha_{CT}(F)$
cmp	$xv_1 \xrightarrow{xe_1} xv_2 \xrightarrow{xe_2} xv_3$, xe_3	id	$xv \circlearrowright xe$

Example 15 (RM: Footprint). *The footprint $\Xi_{RM} = (\Phi_{RM}, \alpha_{RM})$ declares features $\Phi_{RM} := \{\texttt{tb(n)}, \texttt{pk}, \texttt{fk}, \texttt{tot}, \texttt{inj}\}$ for the concepts table with n columns, primary key, foreign key, not null (total) and unique (injective), respectively. We discussed these concepts in Section 3.1.5 where we introduced the relational data model example. The arities of the feature symbols in Φ_{RM} are M_{RM}-typed graphs (G, τ_G) and are described in Table 2. Analogously to Example 13, we use the colon-notation "_:_" to represent the typing morphisms $\tau_G : G \to M_{RM}$.*

Table 2. RM Footprint.

F	Arity $\alpha_{RM}(F)$
tb(n)	$xt:\mathbf{T}$, $xc_1:\mathbf{C}$ ... $xc_n:\mathbf{C}$, $xd_1:\mathbf{D}$ • • • $xd_n:\mathbf{D}$
fk	$xt_1:\mathbf{T} \xrightarrow{xc_1:\mathbf{C}} xd:\mathbf{D} \xleftarrow{xc_2:\mathbf{C}} xt_2:\mathbf{T}$
pk	$xt:\mathbf{T} \xrightarrow{xc:\mathbf{C}} xd:\mathbf{D}$
inj	$xt:\mathbf{T} \xrightarrow{xc:\mathbf{C}} xd:\mathbf{D}$
tot	$xt:\mathbf{T} \xrightarrow{xc:\mathbf{C}} xd:\mathbf{D}$

Remark 5 (Category of footprints). *We indicated the arrow from (2) to (3) in Figure 1 as construction+choice since we could straightforwardly define a category of footprints on Var while we decided to consider only one footprint. To also explore categories of footprints goes simply beyond the scope of this first paper on Logics of Statements. In Remark 20, we will, however, outline, what has to be done if we want or need to work with a category of footprints.*

3.3.2. Variables, Features and Footprints: Semantics

To make things not too complicated and to deviate not too far from traditional logic, we work here with the semantics-as-interpretation paradigm, also called indexed or Tarskian semantics. In contrast, we spelled out in [13] the semantics-as-instance paradigm, also called fibred semantics. To define the semantics of variables and features, we first have to decide for (potential) carriers of structures.

Definition 4 (Fourth parameter: Carriers). *As the fourth parameter of an Institution of Statements, we choose a subcategory Carr of Base of (potential) **carriers** of Ξ-structures.*

Example 16 (FOL: Carriers). *In this example, we follow the traditional approach and choose simply $\mathsf{Carr}_{FOL} := \mathsf{Base}_{FOL} = \mathsf{Set}^S = [S \to \mathsf{Set}]$.*

Example 17 (ALC: Carriers). *ALC considers only non-empty sets as potential carriers and calls them domains (of an interpretation). Thus, we take as Carr_{ALC} the full subcategory of $\mathsf{Base}_{ALC} = \mathsf{Set}$ given by all non-empty sets.*

Example 18 (mFOL: Carriers). *A potential carrier of a Ξ_{mF}-structure should provide a family of sets to define the semantics of sort symbols as well as a family of sets to define the semantics of* predicate symbols. As Carr$_{mF}$, we choose therefore the full subcategory of Base$_{mF}$ = SET/M$_{mF}$ given by all M_{mF}-typed sets (C, τ_C) with $C \subseteq$ Set$_{Obj}$. Note that we consider here Set$_{Obj}$ (and thus also C) as an element in SET$_{Obj}$ and not as a subset of SET$_{Obj}$ (compare Remark 1).

Example 19 (CT: Carriers). *We could choose only those graphs that appear as underlying graphs of small categories. We will, however, not restrict ourselves and choose, analogous to Example 16,* Carr$_{CT}$:= Base$_{CT}$ = Graph.

Example 20 (RM: Carriers). *Tables are sets of rows and data types are sets of data values while columns can be formalized as maps assigning to each row in a table the value in the corresponding column. As discussed in Section 3.1.5, these maps can be partial since there may be no values in some cells of a table.*

Analogous to Example 18, we choose therefore as Carr$_{RM}$ *the full subcategory of* Base$_{RM}$ = GRAPH/M_{RM} *given by all M_{RM}-typed graphs $(G, \tau_G : G \to M_{RM})$ with G a subgraph of gr(Par). We consider here gr(Par) (and thus also G) as an element in* GRAPH$_{Obj}$ *and not as a subgraph of gr(GRAPH) (compare Remark 1). Be aware that we can have in G only maps from sets in $\tau_G^{-1}(T)$ to sets in $\tau_G^{-1}(D)$ since c is the only edge in M_{RM}!*

The semantics of a variable declaration $X \in$ Var$_{Obj}$ relative to a chosen carrier $U \in$ Carr is simply the set of all **variable assignments** (keep in mind that Var $\sqsubseteq$ Base and Carr $\sqsubseteq$ Base):

$$[\![X]\!]^U := \mathrm{Base}(X, U). \tag{1}$$

Structures for footprints are defined in full analogy to the definition of structures for signatures in traditional first-order logic.

Definition 5 (Structures). *A Ξ-structure $\mathcal{U} = (U, \Phi^{\mathcal{U}})$ is given by an object U in* Carr, *the* **carrier of** $\mathcal{U}$, *and a family* $\Phi^{\mathcal{U}} = \{[\![F]\!]^{\mathcal{U}} \mid F \in \Phi\}$ *of sets* $[\![F]\!]^{\mathcal{U}} \subseteq$ Base$(\alpha F, U)$ *of* **valid interpretations** *of feature symbols F in U.*

Homomorphisms are also defined in the usual way that "truth is preserved".

Definition 6 (Homomorphisms). *A* **homomorphism** $\varsigma : \mathcal{U} \to \mathcal{V}$ *between Ξ-structures is given by a morphism $\varsigma : U \to V$ in* Carr *such that $\iota \in [\![F]\!]^{\mathcal{U}}$ implies $\iota;\varsigma \in [\![F]\!]^{\mathcal{V}}$ for all feature symbols F in Φ and all interpretations $\iota : \alpha F \to U$.*

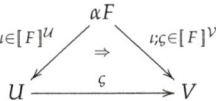

Identities of carriers define identity homomorphisms and composition of homomorphisms is inherited from composition in Carr. In such a way, we obtain a category Str(Ξ) of all available Ξ-structures. We are, however, free to choose only those structures we are interested in (see Figure 1).

Definition 7 (Fifth parameter: Semantics). *As the fifth parameter of an Institution of Statements, we choose a certain subcategory* Sem(Ξ) *of the category* Str(Ξ) *of all Ξ-structures.*

Example 21 (FOL: Semantics). *In accordance with the traditional approach* Sem(Ξ_{FOL}) := Str(Ξ_{FOL}) *comprises all Ξ_{FOL}-structures $\mathcal{U}$, given by an arbitrary S-set U, where* $S = \{prs, nat\}$ *as in Example 11, together with arbitrary subsets* $[\![\texttt{parent}]\!]^{\mathcal{U}} \subseteq$ Set$^S((\{x_1, x_2, x_3\}, \emptyset), U)$, $[\![\texttt{male}]\!]^{\mathcal{U}} \subseteq$ Set$^S((\{x\}, \emptyset), U)$, $[\![\texttt{age}]\!]^{\mathcal{U}} \subseteq$ Set$^S((\{x_1\}, \{x_2\}), U)$ *and* $[\![\texttt{less}]\!]^{\mathcal{U}} \subseteq$ Set$^S((\emptyset, \{x_1, x_2\}), U)$, *as well as all homomorphisms between those Ξ_{FOL}-structures.*

Example 22 (ALC: Semantics). *Any terminological interpretation $\mathcal{I}$ in ALC includes the choice of a non-empty set $\Delta^{\mathcal{I}}$, called* domain, *an interpretation of each concept name in N_C as a subset of $\Delta^{\mathcal{I}} \cong \mathsf{Set}(\{x\}, \Delta^{\mathcal{I}})$ and an interpretation of each role name in N_R as a subset of $\Delta^{\mathcal{I}} \times \Delta^{\mathcal{I}} \cong \mathsf{Set}(\{x_1, x_2\}, \Delta^{\mathcal{I}})$. Obviously, there is a one-to-one correspondence between a terminological interpretation and a Ξ_{FOL}-structure in the sense of Definition 5. Homomorphisms are not considered in ALC; thus, $\mathsf{Sem}(\Xi_{ALC}) := \mathsf{Str}(\Xi_{ALC})$ is a discrete category.*

Example 23 (mFOL: Semantics). *In contrast to the Examples 21 and 22, we transform any carrier (U, τ_U) in Carr_{mF} (see Example 18) into exactly one corresponding Ξ_{mF}-structure $\mathcal{U}$ with:*

$$[\![\mathtt{un}]\!]^{\mathcal{U}} := \{\iota : (X_{\mathtt{un}}, \tau_{X_{\mathtt{un}}}) \to (U, \tau_U) \mid \iota(xp) \subseteq \iota(xs)\}$$

$$[\![\mathtt{bin}]\!]^{\mathcal{U}} := \{\iota : (X_{\mathtt{bin}}, \tau_{X_{\mathtt{bin}}}) \to (U, \tau_U) \mid \iota(xp) \subseteq \iota(xs_1) \otimes \iota(xs_2)\}$$

$$[\![\mathtt{trt}]\!]^{\mathcal{U}} := \{\iota : (X_{\mathtt{trt}}, \tau_{X_{\mathtt{trt}}}) \to (U, \tau_U) \mid \iota(xp) \subseteq \iota(xs_1) \otimes \iota(xs_2) \otimes \iota(xs_3)\}$$

$\mathsf{Str}(\Xi_{mF})$ *is given by all these Ξ_{mF}-structures and all homomorphims between them according to Definition 6. Note that the homomorphisms in $\mathsf{Str}(\Xi_{mF})$ resemble the idea of functors that preserve finite products and monomorphisms (inclusions).*

To cover the traditional approach that a predicate in a first-order structure can be an arbitrary subset of a corresponding Cartesian product of sorts (compare Example 21), we choose as $\mathsf{Sem}(\Xi_{mF})$ the full subcategory of $\mathsf{Str}(\Xi_{mF})$ given by all Ξ_{mF}-structures $\mathcal{U} = ((U, \tau_U), \Phi_{mF}^{\mathcal{U}})$ such that $\tau_U^{-1}(P)$ is the union of all power sets $\wp(A)$, $\wp(A \otimes B)$, $\wp(A \otimes B \otimes C)$ with A, B, C ranging over all the sets in $\tau_U^{-1}(S)$.

Example 24 (Category Theory: Semantics). *Analogously to Example 21, $\mathsf{Sem}(\Xi_{CT}) := \mathsf{Str}(\Xi_{CT})$ comprises all Ξ_{CT}-structures $\mathcal{U} = (U, \Phi_{CT}^{\mathcal{U}})$ given by an arbitrary small graph U together with arbitrary subsets $[\![\mathtt{id}]\!]^{\mathcal{U}} \subseteq \mathsf{Graph}(\alpha_{CT}(\mathtt{id}), U)$, $[\![\mathtt{cmp}]\!]^{\mathcal{U}} \subseteq \mathsf{Graph}(\alpha_{CT}(\mathtt{cmp}), U)$, $[\![\mathtt{mon}]\!]^{\mathcal{U}} \subseteq \mathsf{Graph}(\alpha_{CT}(\mathtt{mon}), U)$ and $[\![\mathtt{fnl}]\!]^{\mathcal{U}} \subseteq \mathsf{Graph}(\alpha_{CT}(\mathtt{fnl}), U)$. That is, we also include structures like categories without identities, categories with partial composition and so on. Moreover, $\mathsf{Sem}(\Xi_{CT})$ includes all homomorphisms between those Ξ_{CT}-structures.*

Example 25 (RM: Semantics). *Analogous to Example 23, we transform any carrier (U, τ_U) in Carr_{RM} into exactly one corresponding Ξ_{RM}-structure $\mathcal{U}$. We take, however, into account that tables do have only finitely many rows:*

$[\![\mathtt{tb(n)}]\!]^{\mathcal{U}}$ *is the set of all M_{RM}-typed graph homomorphisms $\iota : \alpha_{RM}(\mathtt{tb(n)}) \to (U, \tau_U)$ such that $\iota(xt)$ is a finite (!) subset of $\bigotimes^p(\iota(xd_i) \mid 1 \leq i \leq n)$ and the partial maps $\iota(xc_i) : \iota(xt) \rightharpoonup \iota(xd_i)$ are exactly the corresponding restricted projections.*

Reflecting the usual definition of foreign keys, we define $[\![\mathtt{fk}]\!]^{\mathcal{U}}$ as the set of all M_{RM}-typed graph homomorphisms $\iota : \alpha_{RM}(\mathtt{fk}) \to (U, \tau_U)$ such that $\iota(xc_1)(\iota(xt_1)) \subseteq \iota(xc_2)(\iota(xt_2))$, i.e., each value in row xc_1 in table xt_1 has to appear in row xc_2 in table xt_2.

$[\![\mathtt{tot}]\!]^{\mathcal{U}}$ *is the set of all $\iota : \alpha_{RM}(\mathtt{tot}) \to (U, \tau_U)$ such that $\iota(xc) : \iota(xt) \rightharpoonup \iota(xd)$ is total. $[\![\mathtt{inj}]\!]^{\mathcal{U}}$ comprises, correspondingly, all cases where $\iota(xc)$ is injective and $[\![\mathtt{pk}]\!]^{\mathcal{U}}$ all cases where $\iota(xc)$ is as well total as injective.*

As $\mathsf{Sem}(\Xi_{RM})$, we can choose the full subcategory of $\mathsf{Str}(\Xi_{RM})$ given by all Ξ_{RM}-structures $\mathcal{U} = ((U, \tau_U), \Phi_{RM}^{\mathcal{U}})$ such that $\tau_U^{-1}(T)$ is the union of all power sets $\wp_{fin}(\bigotimes^p(A_i \mid 1 \leq i \leq n)$ with $1 \leq n$ and the A_i's ranging over all the sets in $\tau_U^{-1}(D)$. We could require, in addition, that the sets in $\tau_U^{-1}(D)$ are restricted to those data types that appear in a certain version of SQL, for example.

3.4. First-Order Feature Expressions

3.4.1. Syntax of Feature Expressions

By a feature expression, we mean something like a "formula with free variables" in traditional FOL. However, we do not consider them as formulas, but rather as derived anonymous features. For us, a formula is, semantically seen, the subject of being "valid or not valid" in a given structure, while the semantics of a feature expression, with respect to a given structure, is the set of all its solutions, i.e., the set of all valid interpretations of the derived feature in this structure. We experience this perspective as the most adequate one when formalizing and working with constraints in Model Driven Software Engineering. Sets of solutions have also been utilized to define the validity of conditional existence equations in [7,9], for example.

Definition 8 (Feature expressions: Syntax). *For a footprint $\Xi = (\Phi, \alpha)$ over Var we define inductively and in parallel a family $\mathrm{FE}(\Xi)$ of sets $\mathrm{FE}(\Xi, X)$ of **(first-order) feature Ξ-expressions** Ex on X, $X \triangleright Ex$ in symbols, where X varies over all the objects in Var:*

1. *Atomic expressions: $X \triangleright F(\beta)$ for any $F \in \Phi$ and any morphism $\beta : \alpha F \to X$ in Var.*
2. *Everything: $X \triangleright \top$ for any object X in Var.*
3. *Void: $X \triangleright \bot$ for any object X in Var.*
4. *Conjunction: $X \triangleright (Ex_1 \wedge Ex_2)$ for any expressions $X \triangleright Ex_1$ and $X \triangleright Ex_2$.*
5. *Disjunction: $X \triangleright (Ex_1 \vee Ex_2)$ for any expressions $X \triangleright Ex_1$ and $X \triangleright Ex_2$.*
6. *Implication: $X \triangleright (Ex_1 \to Ex_2)$ for any expressions $X \triangleright Ex_1$ and $X \triangleright Ex_2$.*
7. *Negation: $X \triangleright \neg Ex$ for any expression $X \triangleright Ex$.*
8. *Quantification: $X \triangleright \exists(\varphi, Y : Ex)$ and $X \triangleright \forall(\varphi, Y : Ex)$ for any expression $Y \triangleright Ex$ and any morphism $\varphi : X \to Y$ in Var that is not an isomorphism.*

Remark 6 (Notation for expressions). *In traditional FOL, X and Y are sets of variables and, instead of arbitrary maps $\varphi : X \to Y$, only inclusion maps $\varphi = in_{X,Y} : X \hookrightarrow Y$ are considered. Moreover, only the quantified variables $Y \setminus X$ are recorded while Y has to be (re)constructed as the union $X \cup (Y \setminus X)$. In other words, our Y lists all (!) variables that are allowed to appear as free variables in Ex! We record the whole Y for three reasons: (1) Already in Graph (not to talk about arbitrary presheaf topoi), we do not have complements; (2) We quantify actually over morphisms with source Y when we define the semantics of quantifications (compare Definition 10); (3) In contrast to traditional FOL, $\varphi : X \to Y$ is allowed to be non-monic.*

We allow non-monic morphisms $\varphi : X \to Y$ to express identifications. In such a way, we can survive, for the moment, without explicit equations even in cases where Var is a subcategory of a set-based category. We illustrate this mechanism in the Examples 26 and 29.

If Var is a subcategory of a set-based category, like Set, $[S \to Set]$, Set/M_{mF}, Graph or Graph/M_{RM}, for example, variable declarations X are constituted by single entities; thus, we can talk about individual "variables". Moreover, inclusions of sets give us corresponding inclusion morphisms at hand. In case, $\varphi = in_{X,Y} : X \hookrightarrow Y$ is such an inclusion morphism we will drop φ (see Examples 26, 28 and 29).

If $\varphi : X \to Y$ is an isomorphism, quantification is obsolete; thus, we excluded those cases.

Remark 7 (Everything and Void). *For the definition of sketch conditions in Section 6, we need another pair of symbols for "true" and "false"; thus, we decided to use for feature expressions the symbols $\top$ and $\bot$, respectively.*

We consider $\top$ and $\bot$ not as logical constants but as special feature symbols, inbuilt in any Institution of Statements (analogously to the equation symbol in Universal Algebra).

To make this statement fully precise, we have to assume that Base, and thus also Var, has an initial object $\mathbf{0}$. $\mathbf{0}$ is then the arity of $\top$ and $\bot$, while the fixed semantics for any carrier U is given by the two subsets of the singleton $\mathrm{Base}(\mathbf{0}, U) = \{!_U : \mathbf{0} \to U\}$, namely $[\![\bot]\!]^U = \varnothing$ and $[\![\top]\!]^U = \{!_U\}$. Consequently, we could use then the same notation as for atomic expressions, namely $X \triangleright \top(!_X)$ and $X \triangleright \bot(!_X)$ where $!_X : \mathbf{0} \to X$ is the unique initial morphism into X.

Remark 8 (Closed expressions: Syntax). *If Base has an initial object $\mathbf{0}$, feature expressions of the form $\mathbf{0} \triangleright Ex$ will be called **closed expressions**. Note that quantification will generate closed expressions only in case $X = \mathbf{0}$ where $\varphi = !_Y : \mathbf{0} \to Y$ is the only choice for φ, in this case.*

Example 26 (FOL: Expressions). *We intend to illustrate that and how traditional first-order formulas appear in our framework. First, we consider only those cases where the morphism φ in quantifications is an inclusion morphisms and will be therefore dropped.*

In Example 11, we proposed to represent finite S-sorted sets by lists of variable declarations. The arity $\alpha_{FOL}(\mathtt{parent}) := (\{x_1, x_2, x_3\}, \varnothing)$ for the feature symbol $\mathtt{parent} \in \Phi_{FOL}$, for example, is represented by $[x_1 \colon prs, x_2 \colon prs, x_3 \colon prs]$. Pursuing the idea to consider a tuple as a convenient notation for an "associative array", we can denote the atomic expression $\mathtt{parent}(\beta)$, with $\beta \colon \alpha_{FOL}(\mathtt{parent}) \to Y$ an $\{prs, nat\}$-map, simply as $\mathtt{parent}(\beta(x_1), \beta(x_2), \beta(x_3))$.

Relying on this notational convention, we obtain, for example, the closed Ξ_{FOL}-expression
$$\mathbf{0} \triangleright \forall([x_1 : prs, x_2 : prs, x_3 : prs, y_1 : nat, y_2 : nat] :$$
$$((\mathtt{parent}(x_1, x_2, x_3) \wedge \mathtt{age}(x_1, y_1)) \wedge \mathtt{age}(x_2, y_2)) \longrightarrow \mathtt{less}(y_1, y_2))$$
(with $\mathbf{0}$ the empty S-set) expressing that a child is always younger than a parent.

*Our main point, however, is to consider feature expressions as derived features enabling us to denote properties in an anonymous way. The following feature Ξ_{FOL}-expression younger, for example, gives us the property **younger than** at hand by hiding the exact age of a person:*

$$[y : prs, x : nat] \triangleright \exists([y : prs, x : nat, x_1 : nat] : (\mathtt{less}(x, x_1) \wedge \mathtt{age}(y, x_1)))$$

*The next feature Ξ_{FOL}-expression sbl provides the property **being a sibling of someone**:*

$$[y : prs] \triangleright \exists([y : prs, x_1 : prs, x_2 : prs, x_3 : prs] :$$
$$\mathtt{parent}(y, x_2, x_3) \wedge \mathtt{parent}(x_1, x_2, x_3) \wedge \neg \exists(\varphi, [x : prs, x_2 : prs, x_3 : prs] : \top))$$

with $\varphi : [y : prs, x_1 : prs, x_2 : prs, x_3 : prs] \to [x : prs, x_2 : prs, x_3 : prs]$ defined by the assignments $y, x_1 \mapsto x; x_2 \mapsto x_2; x_3 \mapsto x_3$. Note that the Ξ_{FOL}-expression $\neg \exists(\varphi, [x : prs, x_2 : prs, x_3 : prs] : \top)$ on $[y : prs, x_1 : prs, x_2 : prs, x_3 : prs]$ encodes the inequality $\neg(y = x_1)$.

*For convenience, we could introduce an auxiliary feature symbol $\mathtt{sibling}$ with arity $[y : prs]$ and use $\mathtt{sibling}(y)$ as a shorthand (macro) for this derived feature expression. The conjunction $(\mathtt{male}(y) \wedge \mathtt{sibling}(y))$ would then represent a unary property **being brother of someone**. To ensure that then any feature expression $X \triangleright Ex$, containing the auxiliary feature symbol $\mathtt{sibling}$, can be expanded into an equivalent feature expression $X \triangleright Ex'$, containing only the original feature symbols $\mathtt{male}$ and $\mathtt{parent}$, we need a corresponding substitution mechanism.*

Remark 9 (Substitution). *Fortunately, we do not need substitution mechanisms to define Institutions of Statements and to utilize them for specifications purposes. We need, essentially, only a category as we show and demonstrate it in this paper. To develop, however, fully fledged and practical Logics of Statements and, especially, corresponding deduction calculi, we will need appropriate substitution mechanisms.*

An exhaustive and systematic study on what additional categorical infrastructure we have to presuppose to have handy substitution mechanisms at hand is out of range for this paper. In Appendix A, we present, nevertheless, some first observations, definitions and constructions.

Example 27 (ALC: Expressions). *ALC focuses on derived concepts, i.e., in our view, on feature expressions with X a singleton. To describe, however, all derived concepts as feature expressions, we have to use arbitrary finite sets of variables and inclusions between them. We outline the standard encoding of ALC in FOL. Using our notational conventions, the ALC construct "universal restriction $\forall \mathtt{R}.\mathtt{C}$ for any role $\mathtt{R} \in N_R$, any (derived) concept $\mathtt{C}$", can be described as follows: For any role $\mathtt{R}$ in N_R, any expression $\{y\} \triangleright \mathtt{C}$ and any variables x_1, x_2, not appearing in $\mathtt{C}$, we have: $\{x_1\} \triangleright \forall(\{x_1, x_2\} : \mathtt{R}(x_1, x_2) \to \mathtt{C}_\psi(x_2))$ where $\psi : \{y\} \to \{x_1, x_2\}$ is given by $\psi(y) = x_2$ and the expression $\{x_1, x_2\} \triangleright \mathtt{C}_\psi(x_2)$ is obtained by substituting each occurrence of y in $\mathtt{C}$ by x_2 and by extending each variable declaration Y in $\mathtt{C}$ by the "fresh variable" x_1 (compare Appendix A). Analogously, the ALC construct "the existential restriction $\exists \mathtt{R}.\mathtt{C}$ of a concept $\mathtt{C}$ by a role $\mathtt{R} \in N_R$" can be described by existential quantification: For any role $\mathtt{R}$ in N_R, any expression $\{y\} \triangleright \mathtt{C}$ and any variables x_1, x_2, not appearing in $\mathtt{C}$, we have: $\{x_1\} \triangleright \exists(\{x_1, x_2\} : \mathtt{R}(x_1, x_2) \wedge \mathtt{C}_\psi(x_2))$.*

Example 28 (mFOL: Expressions). *This is an example where we do not need the full first-order power. Actually, we only need atomic feature Ξ_{mF}-expressions to state that a set is the subset of a unary, binary or tertiary product of other sets.*

Example 29 (CT: Expressions). *To support the shift of paradigm from string-based to diagrammatic logic was one of our main motivations to develop our framework. Therefore, we will spend a bit more space and put some more effort on this example.*

Representation and visualization of graph homomorphisms: For a finite graph A, we can represent and visualize a graph homomorphism $\varphi : A \to B$ by means of the corresponding graph of assignments $A^\varphi = (A_V^\varphi, A_E^\varphi, sc^{A^\varphi}, tg^{A^\varphi})$ with $A_V^\varphi := \{(v, \varphi_V(v)) \mid v \in A_V\}$, $A_E^\varphi := \{(e, \varphi_E(e)) \mid e \in A_E\}$ where sc^{A^φ} and tg^{A^φ} are defined for all $e \in A_E$ by $sc^{A^\varphi}(e, \varphi_E(e)) = (sc^A(e), \varphi_V(sc^A(e)))$ and $tg^{A^\varphi}(e, \varphi_E(e)) = (tg^A(e), \varphi_V(tg^A(e)))$, respectively. The graphs A and A^φ are isomorphic by construction. Note that we actually simply lift the idea of "tuples as associative arrays" to graphs instead of sets of indexes.

We consider the graph Y, visualized below on the left. For the graph morphism $\varphi : \alpha(\mathtt{cmp}) \to Y$, defined by the assignments $xv_1 \mapsto yv_3$, $xv_2 \mapsto yv_2$, $xv_3 \mapsto yv_4$, $xe_1 \mapsto ye_5$, $xe_2 \mapsto ye_4$, $xe_3 \mapsto ye_3$, the corresponding graph of assignments $\alpha(\mathtt{cmp})^\varphi$ is visualized below in the middle. In many cases, we can fortunately use for $\alpha(\mathtt{cmp})^\varphi$ the shorthand graph, on the right, without causing unambiguities.

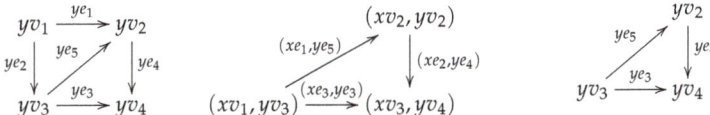

As proposed in [3], we can also work with a sequential representation of the shorthand graph (compare also Example 26): We can represent finite graphs by a list of edges plus a list of vertexes, respectively. Pursuing the idea of **tuples as associative arrays**, a graph homomorphism $\varphi : A \to B$ is then denoted by a list of image edges and a list of image vertexes in graph B.

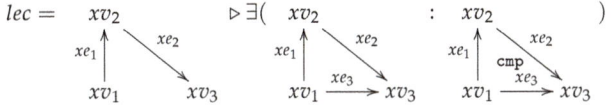

In such a way, we can visualize the atomic Ξ_{CT}-expression $\mathtt{cmp}(\varphi)$ by the graph above and represent it also by the string $\mathtt{cmp}(ye_5, ye_4, ye_3; yv_3, yv_2, yv_4)$. Since $\alpha(\mathtt{cmp})$ has no isolated vertexes, $\varphi : \alpha(\mathtt{cmp}) \to Y$ is uniquely determined by the edge-assignments; thus, we could even use the shorthand notation $\mathtt{cmp}(ye_5, ye_4, ye_3)$ instead.

Ξ_{CT}-*Expressions:* The *local property* composition is defined for a certain pair of edges can be formalized by the following feature Ξ_{CT}-expression:

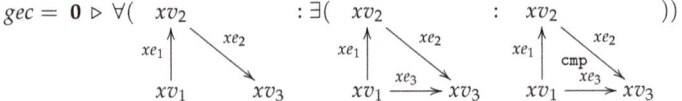

Universal quantification transforms this property into a general property composition is always defined *formalized by the following feature Ξ_{CT}-expression, where **0** is the empty graph:*

$gec = \mathbf{0} \triangleright \forall ($ <!-- diagram --> $: \exists ($ <!-- diagram --> $:$ <!-- diagram --> $))$

The general property composition is always unique *is given by the expression guc:*

$$guc = \mathbf{0} \triangleright \forall(xv_2 \xleftarrow{xe_1} xv_1 \xrightrightarrows[xe_4]{xe_3} xv_3 \xleftarrow{xe_2} : (\; xv_2 \xleftarrow{xe_1} xv_1 \xrightarrow{\mathtt{cmp}\; xe_3} xv_3 \xleftarrow{xe_2} \wedge \; xv_2 \xleftarrow{xe_1} xv_1 \xrightarrow{\mathtt{cmp}\; xe_4} xv_3 \xleftarrow{xe_2} \rightarrow \exists(\varphi, xv_2 \xleftarrow{xe_1} xv_1 \xrightarrow{xe} xv_3 \xleftarrow{xe_2} : \top)))$$

where φ simply maps xe_3 and xe_4 to xe. Analogously, we can also represent the other axioms of categories–existence and uniqueness of identity morphisms, both identity laws and the associativity law–by means of feature Ξ_{CT}-expressions. In addition, feature expressions are a handy tool to hide auxiliary items in diagrammatic specifications. The property **commutative square**, for example, is given by the feature Ξ_{CT}-expression csq, where we hide the diagonal:

$$csq = \; xv_2 \xrightarrow{xe_3} xv_4 \xleftarrow{xe_4} xv_1 \xrightarrow{xe_2} xv_3 \; \triangleright \; \exists(xv_2 \xrightarrow{xe_3} xv_4 \xleftarrow{xe_4} xv_1 \xrightarrow{xe_2} xv_3 \xleftarrow{xe_5} \; : \; xv_2 \xrightarrow{xe_3} xv_4 \xleftarrow{\mathtt{cmp}\, xe_5} xv_1 \; \wedge \; xv_4 \xleftarrow{xe_4} xv_1 \xrightarrow{\mathtt{cmp}\, xe_5} xv_2 \xrightarrow{xe_2} xv_3 \;)$$

That concepts and constructions are defined by **universal properties** is the crucial characteristic of Category Theory as a modeling technique. The concept **monomorphism**, for example, is defined by the feature Ξ_{CT}-expression mon:

$$mon = \; xv_1 \xleftarrow{xe} xv_2 \; \triangleright \; \forall(\; xv_1 \xleftarrow{xe_1} xv_3 \xrightarrow{xe_2/xe_3} xv_2 \; : \; xv_1 \xleftarrow{xe_1/\mathtt{cmp}\, xe} xv_3 \xrightarrow{xe_3} xv_2 \; \wedge \; xv_1 \xleftarrow{xe_2/\mathtt{cmp}\, xe} xv_3 \xrightarrow{xe_3} xv_2 \; \rightarrow \; \exists(\varphi, \; xv_1 \xleftarrow{xe_4/xe} xv_3 \xrightarrow{xe_3} xv_2 \; : \top))$$

where φ maps xe_1 and xe_2 to xe_4. In most cases, however, a universal property is the conjunction of a universally quantified existence assertion and a universally quantified uniqueness assertion (see Remark 10). The concept **final object**, for example, is defined by the feature Ξ_{CT}-expression fnl where φ maps xe_1 and xe_2 to xe:

$$fnl = xv \triangleright \forall(xv_1 \;\; xv : \exists(xv_1 \xrightarrow{xe} xv : \top)) \wedge \forall(\; xv_1 \xrightrightarrows[xe_2]{xe_1} xv \; : \; \exists(\varphi, xv_1 \xrightarrow{xe} xv : \top))$$

In case, we want to work with an explicit property **two parallel morphisms are equal**, we are free to utilize the Ξ_{CT}-expression $[=]$ where φ maps xe_1 and xe_2 to xe:

$$[=] = \; xv_1 \xrightrightarrows[xe_2]{xe_1} xv_2 \; \triangleright \; \exists(\varphi, xv_1 \xrightarrow{xe} xv_2 : \top)$$

Remark 10 (Limits and Colimits). *The fact that the universal properties in Category Theory do have a uniform and relatively simple logical structure shaped the theory of generalized sketches in [15]. The main ingredients of the definition of (co)limits are categorical diagrams, i.e., graph homomorphisms, thus we can beneficially use feature Ξ_{CT}-expressions to characterize the logical structure of the concept* (co)limit.

The universal property, defining a finite (co)limit, is a conjunction of two assertions–existence of mediators and uniqueness of mediators. We can express those assertions by feature Ξ_{CT}-expressions with the following structure (compare the definition of the concept **final object** in Example 29):

$$exist_I := C_I \triangleright \forall(C_I + C'_I : Ex_1 \longrightarrow \exists(C_I \overrightarrow{+} C'_I : Ex_2))$$
$$unique_I := C_I \triangleright \forall(C_I \overrightarrow{+} C'_I : Ex_3 \longrightarrow \exists(\varphi, C_I \overrightarrow{+} C'_I : \top))$$

I is the shape graph of the (co)limit, i.e., the empty graph in the case of final objects. C_I adds to I the shape of a (co)cone with base I while $C_I + C'_I$ extends C_I with the shape of a second (co)cone with base I. Ex_1 is the conjunction of all atomic $\mathtt{cmp}$-expressions on $C_I + C'_I$ turning both (co)cones into commutative ones. $C_I \overrightarrow{+} C'_I$ extends $C_I + C'_I$ by a single mediator while Ex_2 is the conjunction of all atomic $\mathtt{cmp}$-expressions on $C_I \overrightarrow{+} C'_I$ expressing the commutativity requirements for the mediator. $C_I \overrightrightarrows{+} C'_I$ extends $C_I + C'_I$ by two parallel mediators and Ex_3 is the conjunction of all atomic $\mathtt{cmp}$-expressions on $C_I \overrightrightarrows{+} C'_I$ expressing the commutativity requirements for both mediators. $\varphi : C_I \overrightrightarrows{+} C'_I \longrightarrow C_I \overrightarrow{+} C'_I$ simply identifies the two mediators in $C_I \overrightrightarrows{+} C'_I$.

Example 30 (RM: Expressions). *To formalize declarations of tables and data base schemes, respectively, we need only atomic feature Ξ_{RM}-expressions; thus, we consider in this example only atomic Ξ_{RM}-expressions. To deal also with so-called* business rules, *we would need, however, the full spectrum of first-order Ξ_{RM}-expressions.*

As seen in the examples, there are cases where we need only a restricted selection of first-order feature expressions. The freedom to select only the feature expressions we are interested in establishes a new parameter (see Figure 1).

Definition 9 (Sixth parameter: Choice of expressions). *As the sixth parameter of an Institution of Statements, we choose an Var_{Obj}-indexed family $\mathtt{XE}(\Xi)$ of subsets $\mathtt{XE}(\Xi, X) \subseteq \mathtt{FE}(\Xi, X)$ of first-order Ξ-expressions on $X \in \mathsf{Var}_{Obj}$.*

Despite the fact that the family $\mathtt{FE}(\Xi, X)$, $X \in \mathsf{Var}_{Obj}$ of sets of first-order feature expressions is defined by mutual induction, there is no explicit relationship between the different sets $\mathtt{FE}(\Xi, X)$ since we do not base the definition of our framework on translation maps induced by variables translations, i.e., morphisms in Var (see Definition A1 in Appendix A). Therefore, the choice of $\mathtt{XE}(\Xi, X)$ for a certain X can be made independently from all the other choices! However, if we also incorporate later translation maps, it will be reasonable to require that the choices of the different $\mathtt{XE}(\Xi, X)$ are compatible with translation maps!

What are natural choices? We could simply choose all first-order feature expressions, i.e., $\mathtt{XE}(\Xi, X) = \mathtt{FE}(\Xi, X)$ for all $X \in \mathsf{Var}_{Obj}$, as we will do it in the FOL-example as well as in the CT-example. The other extreme case is to forget about "first-order" and to restrict ourselves to atomic feature expressions. This we have done in [13] and in DPF [18,21] since first-order feature expressions have not been available. For the mFOL-example and the RM-example, it is sufficient to use atomic expressions only.

Besides these two extreme cases, we could, for example, exclude negation or we could choose a minimal set of logical connectives and so on. In the ALC-example, we choose only the first-order feature expressions necessary to encode ALC in first-order logic (compare Example 27).

If Base has an initial object, we could restrict ourselves to closed expressions only (see Remark 8). In this case, we are back to traditional institutions since we do not need contexts to utilize closed formulas for specification purposes. The definition of closed formulas and of the satisfaction relation for closed formulas goes, however, always via open formulas and therefore any deduction calculus for closed formulas is based on a manipulation of open formulas. In other words: We are convinced that the concept of a context, defined in Definition 11, is relevant and beneficial for any logic beyond propositional logic even for traditional first-order predicate logic!

3.4.2. Semantics of Feature Expressions

Due to Definition 5, a Ξ-structure $\mathcal{U} = (U, \Phi^{\mathcal{U}})$ fixes for each feature symbol $F \in \Phi$ its semantics in $\mathcal{U}$ as a set $[\![F]\!]^{\mathcal{U}} \subseteq \mathsf{Base}(\alpha F, U)$ of all valid interpretations of F in U.

Relying on the inductive definition of first-order feature expressions, we can extend the semantics of feature symbols and define the semantics of a feature expression $X \triangleright Ex$ in a Ξ-structure $\mathcal{U}$ as a set $[\![Ex]\!]^{\mathcal{U}}_X$ of all **valid interpretations (solutions)** of $X \triangleright Ex$ in $\mathcal{U}$. This semantics is a restriction of the semantics of X relative to the carrier U as defined by Equation (1), i.e., $[\![Ex]\!]^{\mathcal{U}}_X \subseteq [\![X]\!]^{U} = \mathsf{Base}(X, U)$. For **interpretations** $\iota : X \to U$, we will use, instead of $\iota \in [\![Ex]\!]^{\mathcal{U}}_X$, also the more traditional notation $\iota \models^{\mathcal{U}} X \triangleright Ex$.

Given a morphism $\varphi : X \to Y$ in Var, we say that an interpretation $\varrho : Y \to U$ is an **expansion** of an interpretation $\iota : X \to U$ **via** φ if, and only if, $\varphi; \varrho = \iota$.

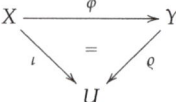

Definition 10 (Feature expressions: Semantics). *The semantics of feature Ξ-expressions in an arbitrary, but fixed, Ξ-structure $\mathcal{U} = (U, \Phi^{\mathcal{U}})$ is defined inductively:*

1. *Atomic expressions:* $\iota \in [\![F(\beta)]\!]_X^{\mathcal{U}}$ *iff* $\beta; \iota \in [\![F]\!]^{\mathcal{U}}$

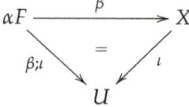

2. *Everything:* $[\![\top]\!]_X^{\mathcal{U}} := [\![X]\!]^{\mathcal{U}} = \mathsf{Base}(X, U)$
3. *Void:* $[\![\bot]\!]_X^{\mathcal{U}} := \emptyset$
4. *Conjunction:* $[\![(Ex_1 \wedge Ex_2)]\!]_X^{\mathcal{U}} := [\![Ex_1]\!]_X^{\mathcal{U}} \cap [\![Ex_2]\!]_X^{\mathcal{U}}$
5. *Disjunction:* $[\![(Ex_1 \vee Ex_2)]\!]_X^{\mathcal{U}} := [\![Ex_1]\!]_X^{\mathcal{U}} \cup [\![Ex_2]\!]_X^{\mathcal{U}}$
6. *Implication:* $\iota \in [\![Ex_1 \to Ex_2]\!]_X^{\mathcal{U}}$ *iff* $\iota \in [\![Ex_1]\!]_X^{\mathcal{U}}$ *implies* $\iota \in [\![Ex_2]\!]_X^{\mathcal{U}}$
7. *Negation:* $[\![\neg Ex]\!]_X^{\mathcal{U}} := \mathsf{Base}(X, U) \setminus [\![Ex]\!]_X^{\mathcal{U}}$
8. *Existential quantification:* $\iota \in [\![\exists(\varphi, Y : Ex)]\!]_X^{\mathcal{U}}$ *iff there exists an expansion ϱ of ι via φ such that* $\varrho \in [\![Ex]\!]_Y^{\mathcal{U}}$.

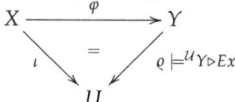

Universal quantification: $\iota \in [\![\forall(\varphi, Y : Ex)]\!]_X^{\mathcal{U}}$ *iff for all expansions ϱ of ι via φ we have* $\varrho \in [\![Ex]\!]_Y^{\mathcal{U}}$.

Remark 11 (Feature expressions: Semantics). *Every feature symbol F in Φ reappears as the Ξ-expression $\alpha F \triangleright F(id_{\alpha F})$ and Definition 10 ensures $[\![F(id_{\alpha F})]\!]_{\alpha F}^{\mathcal{U}} = [\![F]\!]^{\mathcal{U}}$.*

The universal quantification $X \triangleright \forall(\varphi, Y : Ex)$ is trivially valid if there is no expansion of ι via φ at all, while the existential quantification $X \triangleright \exists(\varphi, Y : Ex)$ is not valid, in this case.

*Two expressions $X \triangleright Ex_1$ and $X \triangleright Ex_2$ are **semantical equivalent**, $X \triangleright Ex_1 \equiv Ex_2$ in symbols, if, and only if, $[\![Ex_2]\!]_X^{\mathcal{U}} = [\![Ex_2]\!]_X^{\mathcal{U}}$ for all Ξ-structures $\mathcal{U}$ in $\mathsf{Sem}(\Xi)$. Definition 10 ensures that we do have the usual semantic equivalences available. In particular, conjunction and disjunction are associative; thus we can drop, for convenience, the corresponding parenthesis as we have done already at some places in the examples.*

Remark 12 (Closed expressions: Semantics). *For a closed expression $\mathbf{0} \triangleright Ex$ (see Remark 8), $[\![\mathbf{0}]\!]^{\mathcal{U}} = \mathsf{Base}(\mathbf{0}, U)$ is a singleton with the initial morphism $!_U : \mathbf{0} \to U$ as the only element. In such a way, we have either $[\![Ex]\!]_{\mathbf{0}}^{\mathcal{U}} = [\![\top]\!]_{\mathbf{0}}^{\mathcal{U}} = \{!_U\}$, i.e., $!_U \models^{\mathcal{U}} \mathbf{0} \triangleright Ex$, or $[\![Ex]\!]_{\mathbf{0}}^{\mathcal{U}} = [\![\bot]\!]_{\mathbf{0}}^{\mathcal{U}} = \emptyset$, i.e., $!_U \not\models^{\mathcal{U}} \mathbf{0} \triangleright Ex$.*

3.5. Institutions of Statements

Generalizing concepts like *set of generators* in Group Theory, *underlying graph of a sketch* in Category Theory, *set of individual names* in Description Logics and *underlying graph of a model* in Software Engineering, we introduce in this section the concept of a *context* as one of our main conceptual and methodological proposals. Furthermore, we introduce the concept *statement (in a context)* in generalizing the corresponding concepts defining relation in Group Theory, diagram in a sketch in Category Theory, concept/role assertion in Description Logic and constraint in Software Engineering. We use institutions [2,31] as a methodological guideline to define and present the formalisms build upon these new concepts.

3.5.1. Category of Contexts and Sentence Functor

As **abstract signatures** in an Institution of Statements, we introduce contexts.

Definition 11 (Seventh parameter: Contexts). *As the seventh parameter of an Institution of Statements, we choose another subcategory* Cxt *of* Base. *The objects in* Cxt *are called **contexts** while we refer to the morphisms in* Cxt *as **context morphisms**.*

If Base *has initial objects, we assume that* Cxt *contains, at least, one of them denoted by* **0**.

Even if Cxt is called the "seventh parameter", the choice of Cxt relies only on the chosen Base and does not depend on all the other parameters we introduced (see Figure 1)!

Remark 13 (Variables vs. context vs. carrier). *Introducing contexts, we establish a technological layer independent of "pure syntax" (variables) and "pure semantics" (carriers of structures) as we postulated it in Requirement 2 (p. 3). We prefer to consider variable declarations as something finite or enumerable while contexts can be arbitrary.*

In case Var *is a subcategory of* Cxt, *we perceive the inclusion* Var $\sqsubseteq$ Cxt *as a change of roles: Variables are essentially syntactic items but can also serve as generators of structures, like groups and (term) algebras, for example.*

If we are interested in completeness proofs and corresponding freely generated structures, we have to suppose Carr $\sqsubseteq$ Cxt. *Coming back to the discussion in Section 1.1.1, the introduction of contexts allows us to keep syntax and semantics separated and to avoid, in such a way, certain kinds of circularity in the definition of formalisms.*

Example 31 (FOL: Context). *PROLOG distinguishes between* atomic values (literals) *and* (logical) variables. *Literals can be either* number literals *or* symbolic literals.

Our choice of contexts reflects this line of tradition. We define Cxt_{FOL} *as the subcategory of* $\text{Carr}_{FOL} = \text{Base}_{FOL} = \text{Set}^S$ *given by all S-sets* $K = (K_s \mid s \in S)$ *with* K_s *a finite set of literals and logical variables for all* $s \in S$.

For the sample footprint $\Xi_{FOL} = (\Phi_{FOL}, \alpha_{FOL})$ *with* $S = \{prs, nat\}$ *(see Example 11), we consider a sample context* K *with* K_{nat} *the set of all natural numbers from 0 to 200 and* $K_{prs} = \{Anna, Michael, Dora, Heinz, Sorin, Gabi, Uwe\}$.

Example 32 (ALC: Context). *This example has been chosen since it works explicitly with contexts in our sense. ALC uses the term* individual name *instead of* symbolic literal *and contexts in ALC are sets* N_O *of individual names.*

Example 33 (mFOL: Context). *In this example, we describe the traditional formalism* many-sorted first-order logic without functions *as such; thus, a context should declare finite sets of sort and predicate symbols, respectively.*

Analogously to the definition of Var_{mF} *in Example 8, we assume an enumerable set PSym of admissible predicate symbols and an enumerable set SSym of admissible sort symbols.* Cxt_{mF} *is then the full subcategory of* Set/M_{mF} *given by all finite* M_{mF}-*typed sets* $(K, \tau_K : K \to M_{mF})$ *such that* $\tau_K^{-1}(S) \subseteq SSym$ *and* $\tau_K^{-1}(P) \subseteq PSym$.

To be able to reconstruct the sample FOL-footprint $\Xi_{FOL} = (\Phi_{FOL}, \alpha_{FOL})$ *(see Example 11), we choose for the sample mFOL-footprint* $\Xi_{mF} = (\Phi_{mF}, \alpha_{mF})$ *in Example 13 the sample context* $(K, \tau_K : K \to M_{mF})$ *with* $\tau_K^{-1}(S) := \{prs, nat\}$ *and* $\tau_K^{-1}(P) := \{\texttt{parent}, \texttt{male}, \texttt{age}, \texttt{less}\}$.

Example 34 (CT: Context). *We simply choose* $\text{Cxt}_{CT} := \text{Carr}_{CT} = \text{Base}_{CT} = \text{Graph}$. *As an example, we consider the following finite graph G.*

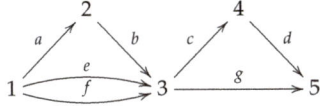

Example 35 (RM: Context). *A context in this example declares the items in a database schema, i.e., a finite graph with table identifiers, datatype identifiers, and column identifiers, respectively. Analogously to Example 33, we assume an enumerable sets TId of admissible table identifiers, DId of admissible datatype identifiers and CId of admissible column identifiers, respectively.*

As Cxt_{RM}, we choose the full subcategory of Graph/M_{RM} given by all finite M_{RM}-typed graphs $(K, \tau_K : K \to M_{RM})$ such that $\tau_K^{-1}(T) \subseteq TId$, $\tau_K^{-1}(D) \subseteq DId$ and $\tau_K^{-1}(c) \subseteq CId$. We intend to formalize the database schema, discussed in Section 3.1.5, and consider the sample RM-context (K, τ_K) as depicted in the following diagram.

$$\begin{array}{ccc}
Empl : T & & Addr : T \\
\text{\textit{name}:c} & A.\text{\textit{ssn}:c} & \\
eid:c \Big\downarrow \quad E.\text{\textit{ssn}:c} & \text{\textit{town}:c} & \Big\downarrow \text{\textit{street}:c} \\
Int : D & & String : D
\end{array}$$

Note that both tables do have a column with name ssn; thus, we distinguish between them by means of the table identifiers. □

Feature expressions can be utilized to make statements in a certain context. Those *statements in context* are the **sentences** in an Institution of Statements.

Definition 12 (Statement). *An $\text{XE}(\Xi)$-statement (X, Ex, γ) in context $K \in \text{Cxt}_{Obj}$ is given by a feature Ξ-expression $X \triangleright Ex$ in $\text{XE}(\Xi, X)$ and a binding morphism $\gamma : X \to K$ in Base.*

By $\text{Stm}(K)$, we denote the set of all $\text{XE}(\Xi)$-statements in K.

Statements are part of sketches and examples of sketches are presented in Section 5.

Remark 14 (Atomic statements). *For a feature symbol $F \in \Phi$ and a context K there can be different variable declarations X, X', morphisms $\beta : \alpha F \to X$, $\beta' : \alpha F \to X'$ and binding morphisms $\gamma : X \to K$, $\gamma' : X' \to K$ such that $\beta; \gamma = \beta'; \gamma'$. That is, the distinct statement expressions $(X, F(\beta), \gamma)$ and $(X', F(\beta'), \gamma')$ represent somehow the "same statement" in K.*

*We choose therefore a kind of **normal form** to define the concept atomic statement: **Atomic statements** in context K are statements of the form $(\alpha F, F(id_{\alpha F}), \gamma)$, $\gamma : \alpha F \to K$. For any context K we denote by $\text{At}(K)$ the set of all atomic statements in K.*

In abuse of notation, we will sometimes use for atomic statements the same notation $F(\gamma)$ as for atomic expressions. Thus, we can, in the examples, take advantage of our notational conventions based on the idea of "associative arrays".

Remark 15 (General statements and closed formulas). *If Base has an initial object $\mathbf{0}$, there is for any closed expression $\mathbf{0} \triangleright Ex$ (see Remarks 8 and 12) a unique initial morphism $\gamma =!_K : \mathbf{0} \to K$; thus, we have $(\mathbf{0}, Ex, !_K) \in \text{Stm}(K)$ for any context K and all the closed expressions $\mathbf{0} \triangleright Ex$ in $\text{XE}(\Xi, \mathbf{0})$. We call $(\mathbf{0}, Ex, !_K)$ a **general statement in** K.*

*The general statements in $\text{Stm}(\mathbf{0})$, i.e., statements of the form $(\mathbf{0}, Ex, id_\mathbf{0})$ are the precise formal counterpart of traditional **closed formulas** within our framework. Be aware that there may be statements $(X, Ex, \gamma : X \to \mathbf{0})$ in $\text{Stm}(\mathbf{0})$ with X non-initial.*

Remark 16 (Expression vs. statement). *The idea behind our definition of statements is to encapsulate the relatively intricate construction of first-order syntactic entities and do it once and for all. In such a way, we achieve the following objectives: (1) There is no need to lift arbitrary "semantic entities", like elements in the carrier of a structure, to the syntactic level. (2) We can define and work with first-order statements in arbitrary base categories. (3) We do not depend on translation maps (compare Definition A1 in Appendix A) to translate first-order statements. (4) The translation of first-order statements is simply performed by composition in the category Base!*

This encapsulation trick we have seen in [31] where it is used for "initial/free constraints".

Any morphism $\varphi\colon K \to G$ in Cxt induces a map $\mathtt{Stm}(\varphi)\colon \mathtt{Stm}(K) \to \mathtt{Stm}(G)$ defined by simple post-composition for all statements (X, Ex, γ) in K:

$$\mathtt{Stm}(\varphi)(X, Ex, \gamma) := (X, Ex, \gamma; \varphi) \qquad (2)$$

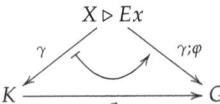

It is easy to show that the assignments $K \mapsto \mathtt{Stm}(K)$ and $\varphi \mapsto \mathtt{Stm}(\varphi)$ provide a functor $\mathtt{Stm}\colon \mathsf{Cxt} \to \mathsf{Set}$. This is the **sentence functor** of an Institution of Statements.

3.5.2. Model Functor

Interpretations of contexts are the **models** in an Institution of Statements.

Definition 13 (Context interpretations). *An **interpretation** $(\iota, \mathcal{U})$ of a context $K \in \mathsf{Cxt}_{Obj}$ is given by a Ξ-structure $\mathcal{U} = (U, \Phi^{\mathcal{U}})$ in $\mathsf{Sem}(\Xi)$ and a morphism $\iota\colon K \to U$ in Base.*

A morphism $\varsigma\colon (\iota, \mathcal{U}) \to (\varrho, \mathcal{V})$ between two interpretations of K is given by a morphism $\varsigma\colon \mathcal{U} \to \mathcal{V}$ in $\mathsf{Sem}(\Xi)$ such that $\iota; \varsigma = \varrho$ for the underlying morphism $\varsigma\colon U \to V$ in Carr.

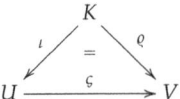

For any context K in Cxt we denote by $\mathtt{Int}(K)$ the category of all interpretations of K and all morphisms between them and by $\Pi_K\colon \mathtt{Int}(K) \to \mathsf{Sem}(\Xi)$ the obvious projection functor.

Note that, for an initial object $K = \mathbf{0}$, the projection functor $\Pi_0\colon \mathtt{Int}(\mathbf{0}) \to \mathsf{Sem}(\Xi)$ is an isomorphism.

For any Ξ-structure $\mathcal{U}$ in $\mathsf{Sem}(\Xi)$, the corresponding **fiber over** $\mathcal{U}$, i.e., the subcategory of $\mathtt{Int}(K)$ given by all interpretations of K in $\mathcal{U}$, is a discrete category representing the hom-set $\mathsf{Base}(K, U)$.

Remark 17 (Functorial semantics). *We present in this paper an abstract and general definition of Institutions of Statements covering a brought range of applications. Therefore, we are not assuming any structure on the hom-sets $\mathsf{Base}(K, U)$.*

In examples, following the path of Functorial Semantics, $\mathsf{Sem}(\Xi)$ will be constituted by Ξ-structures $\mathcal{U} = (U, \Phi^{\mathcal{U}})$ where U is provided by a category like Set or Par, for example. In those cases, $\mathsf{Base}(K, U)$ will be a category with morphisms reflecting the idea of natural transformations.

For those special cases, we can vary Definition 13 in such a way that a morphism between the two interpretations of K is given by a morphism $\varsigma\colon U \to V$ in Carr and a morphism in $\mathsf{Base}(K, V)$ from $\iota; \varsigma$ to ϱ. We are convinced that all the following constructions and results can be transferred, more or less straightforwardly, to this extended version of morphisms between interpretations. We let this as a topic of future research.

Any context morphism $\varphi\colon K \to G$ induces a functor $\mathtt{Int}(\varphi)\colon \mathtt{Int}(G) \to \mathtt{Int}(K)$ with:

$$\mathtt{Int}(\varphi); \Pi_K = \Pi_G : \mathtt{Int}(G) \to \mathsf{Sem}(\Xi) \qquad (3)$$

defined by simple pre-composition: $\mathtt{Int}(\varphi)(\varrho, \mathcal{V}) := (\varphi; \varrho, \mathcal{V})$ for all interpretations $(\varrho, \mathcal{V})$ of G, and for any morphism $\varsigma\colon (\iota, \mathcal{U}) \to (\varrho, \mathcal{V})$ between two interpretations of G the same underlying morphism $\varsigma\colon U \to V$ in Carr establishes a morphism $\mathtt{Int}(\varphi)(\varsigma) := \varsigma\colon (\varphi; \iota, \mathcal{U}) \to (\varphi; \varrho, \mathcal{V})$ between the corresponding two interpretations of K.

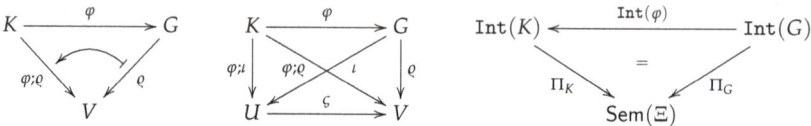

It is straightforward to validate that the assignments $K \mapsto \text{Int}(K)$ and $\varphi \mapsto \text{Int}(\varphi)$ define a functor $\text{Int}\colon \text{Cxt}^{op} \to \text{Cat}$. This is the **model functor** of an Institution of Statements.

3.5.3. Satisfaction Relation and Satisfaction Condition

The last two steps, in establishing an institution, are the definition of *satisfaction relations* and the proof of the so-called *satisfaction condition*. The satisfaction relations are simply given by the semantics of features expressions, as described in Definition 10.

Definition 14 (Satisfaction relation). *For any context $K \in \text{Cxt}$, any $\text{XE}(\Xi)$-statement (X, Ex, γ) in K and any interpretation $(\iota, \mathcal{U})$ of context K we define:*

$$(\iota, \mathcal{U}) \models_K (X, Ex, \gamma) \quad \textit{iff} \quad \gamma; \iota \models^{\mathcal{U}} X \triangleright Ex \quad (\textit{i.e.} \quad \gamma; \iota \in [\![Ex]\!]_X^{\mathcal{U}}) \tag{4}$$

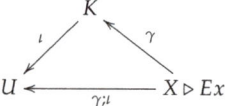

Remark 18 (Validity of Closed Formulas). *In case $X = K = \mathbf{0}$, we do have for any Ξ-structure $\mathcal{U} = (U, \Phi^{\mathcal{U}})$ in $\text{Sem}(\Xi)$ exactly one interpretation $(!_U, \mathcal{U})$ thus for any closed formula $(\mathbf{0}, Ex, id_{\mathbf{0}})$ (see Remark 15) $(!_U, \mathcal{U}) \models_{\mathbf{0}} (\mathbf{0}, Ex, id_{\mathbf{0}})$ means nothing but that the closed formula $(\mathbf{0}, Ex, id_{\mathbf{0}})$ is valid in $\mathcal{U}$ in the traditional sense. Therefore, we will also write $\mathcal{U} \models (\mathbf{0}, Ex, id_{\mathbf{0}})$ instead of $(!_U, \mathcal{U}) \models_{\mathbf{0}} (\mathbf{0}, Ex, id_{\mathbf{0}})$.*

Moreover, the validity of closed formulas is context independent *in the following sense: For any context K and any closed expressions $\mathbf{0} \triangleright Ex$, we have:*

$$(\iota, \mathcal{U}) \models_K (\mathbf{0}, Ex, !_K) \quad \textit{iff} \quad !_K; \iota =!_U \models^{\mathcal{U}} \mathbf{0} \triangleright Ex \quad \textit{iff} \quad [\![Ex]\!]_{\mathbf{0}}^{\mathcal{U}} = \{!_U\} \quad \textit{iff} \quad \mathcal{U} \models (\mathbf{0}, Ex, id_{\mathbf{0}})$$

After we developed everything in a systematic modular way, we obtain the satisfaction condition nearly "for free".

Corollary 1 (Satisfaction condition). *For any morphism $\varphi\colon K \to G$ in Cxt, any $\text{XE}(\Xi)$-statement (X, Ex, γ) in K and any interpretation $(\varrho, \mathcal{U})$ of context G we have:*

$$\text{Int}(\varphi)(\varrho, \mathcal{U}) \models_K (X, Ex, \gamma) \quad \textit{iff} \quad (\varrho, \mathcal{U}) \models_G \text{Stm}(\varphi)(X, Ex, \gamma). \tag{5}$$

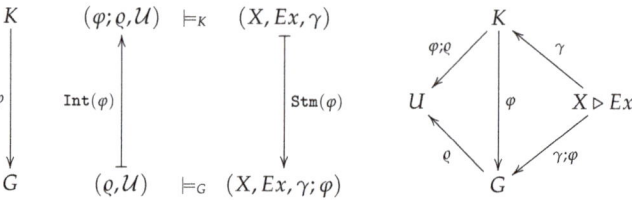

Proof. Due to the definition of the functors $\text{Int}\colon \text{Cxt}^{op} \to \text{Cat}$ and $\text{Stm}\colon \text{Cxt} \to \text{Set}$, we obtain the commutative diagram, above on the right, thus the satisfaction condition follows immediately from Definition 14. □

Remark 19 (Satisfaction Condition). *As mentioned in the introductory Section* 1.1.6, *the finding of corresponding assignments and corresponding evaluations enabled us to prove in [29] the satisfaction condition for four formalisms in a systematic, uniform and straightforward way. The proof of Corollary* 1 *mirrors the essence of this uniform and straightforward way at a very high abstraction level.*

Summarizing all definitions and results, we obtain the main result of this section:

Theorem 1 (Institution of Statements). *Any choice of a category* Base, *of subcategories* Var, Cxt, Carr *of* Base, *of a footprint* Ξ *over* Var, *of a category* Sem(Ξ) *of* Ξ-*structures and of an* Var$_{Obj}$-*indexed family* XE(Ξ) *of first-order* Ξ-*expressions establishes a corresponding* **Institution of Statements** $\mathcal{IS} = ($Cxt, Stm, Int, $\models)$.

Remark 20 (Indexed institutions). *We come back to the discussion in Remark* 5. *If we consider a category of footprints over* Var *we will obtain, due to Theorem* 1, *for each footprint a corresponding institution of statements. To lift morphisms between footprints to corresponding morphisms between institutions of statements, we have, however, to coordinate somehow the construction of the different institutions (consult Figure* 1).

All institutions should share, besides Base and Var also the same categories Carr and Cxt. We have to show that this assumption ensures that the assignments $\Xi \mapsto$ Str(Ξ) can be lifted to a functor Str. Analogously, the assignments $\Xi \mapsto$ FE(Ξ) should also provide a functor FE. Finally, the choices of Sem(Ξ) and XE(Ξ) have to be aligned in such a way that we obtain corresponding restrictions of the functors Str and FE, respectively.

Under these assumptions, we will hopefully be able to establish a category of institutions of statements indexed by the category of footprints; thus, we can benefit from all the nice results and constructions in [2]. In particular, the construction of the corresponding Grothendieck institution will surely become relevant.

4. Institutions of Equations

With this section about Institutions of Equational Statements, or short Institutions of Equations, we start to close the circle to the ideas and motivations discussed in the introductory Section 1.1.1 Universal Algebra and Algebraic Specifications. In these areas, substitutions play a central role and, analyzing the situation in these areas, we may obtain also some hints and guidelines for the future development of a more abstract and general account of substitutions in Logics of Statements.

Equations are the main conceptual tool in Universal Algebra. To define equational statements, we could again apply the encapsulation trick we have used in the last subsections to define statements for footprints with feature symbols only. That is, we could introduce atomic equations $X \triangleright t_1 = t_2$, define atomic equational statements $(X, t_1 = t_2, \gamma)$ in contexts K with $\gamma : X \to K$ and translate atomic equational statements along context morphisms by simple post-composition.

This idea works fine as long as we are only interested in formalisms to describe and specify algebraic structures. The encapsulation approach seems to be not appropriate, however, to describe and work with instances of equations w.r.t. substitutions of variables by terms. The construction of those instances is a crucial tool in any deduction calculus in Universal Algebra; thus, we decided to work instead of the encapsulation-based two-step approach with a one-step approach defining directly equations $K \triangleright t_1 = t_2$ in contexts K.

This means that we adapt for Institutions of Equations the construction scheme in Figure 1 in the following way: We have Str(Ξ) = Sem(Ξ). Step (6) is dropped and we construct directly Stm(K) as a set of equations in context K. Correspondingly, the satisfaction relations $\models_K$ are defined by means of the evaluation of terms in algebras.

As a complement to the FOL-example, we consider many-sorted total algebras and conditional equations. In this section, we define corresponding Institutions of Equations while conditional equations are formalized and discussed in Section 5.3.

In accordance with the FOL-example, we fix a finite set $S \in \mathsf{Set}_{Obj}$ of sort symbols and choose as Base_{EQ} the interpretation category $\mathsf{Set}^S = [S \to \mathsf{Set}]$. Var_{EQ} is the full subcategory of Base_{EQ} given by all finite and disjoint S-sets $X = (X_s \mid s \in S)$ with X_s a subset of the set $\{x, x_1, x_2, \ldots, y, y_1, y_2, \ldots\}$ for all $s \in S$.

4.1. Signatures, Algebras and Contexts

Signatures $\Sigma = (\Omega, in, out)$ correspond to traditional many-sorted algebraic signatures and are given by a set Ω of operation symbols, a map in assigning to each operation symbol $\omega \in \Omega$ an object $in(\omega)$ in Var_{EQ}, its **arity**, and a map $out : \Omega \to S$. For convenience, we assume that $\bigcup in(\omega) = \{x_1, x_2, \ldots, x_n\}$, $n \geq 0$; thus, we can represent $in(\omega)$ as a list $[x_1{:}s_1, x_2{:}s_2, \ldots, x_n{:}s_n]$ of variable declarations (compare Example 11).

We have $\mathsf{Carr}_{EQ} := \mathsf{Base}_{EQ}$. As structures, we consider Σ-**algebras** $\mathcal{A} = (A, \Omega^{\mathcal{A}})$ with an S-set $A = (A_s \mid s \in S)$ and a family $\Omega^{\mathcal{A}}$ of operations $\omega^{\mathcal{A}} : A^{in(\omega)} \to A_{out(\omega)}$, $\omega \in \Omega$, where $A^{in(\omega)}$ is a shorthand for the set $\mathsf{Set}^S(in(\omega), A)$ of all S-maps from $in(\omega)$ into A.

A **homomorphism** $\varsigma : \mathcal{A} \to \mathcal{B}$ between Σ-algebras $\mathcal{A}$ and $\mathcal{B}$ is given by an S-map $\varsigma = (\varsigma_s \mid s \in S) : A \to B$ such that $\omega^{\mathcal{A}}; \varsigma_s = \varsigma^{in(\omega)}; \omega^{\mathcal{B}}$ for all $\omega \in \Omega$ where the map $\varsigma^{in(\omega)} : A^{in(\omega)} \to B^{in(\omega)}$ is defined by $\varsigma^{in(\omega)}(\tau) := \tau; \varsigma$ for all S-maps $\tau \in A^{in(\omega)}$.

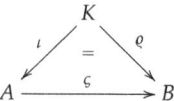

$\mathsf{Alg}(\Sigma)$ is the category of all Σ-algebras and all homomorphisms between them.

We choose $\mathsf{Cxt}_{EQ} := \mathsf{Carr}_{EQ} = \mathsf{Base}_{EQ} = \mathsf{Set}^S$. The model functor of an Institution of Equations is defined in full analogy to Institutions of Statements.

An interpretation $(\iota, \mathcal{A})$ of a context K in Cxt_{EQ}, i.e., of an S-set K, is given by a Σ-algebra $\mathcal{A} = (A, \Omega^{\mathcal{A}})$ and an S-map $\iota : K \to A$.

A morphism $\varsigma : (\iota, \mathcal{A}) \to (\varrho, \mathcal{B})$ between two interpretations of K is given by a homomorphism $\varsigma : \mathcal{A} \to \mathcal{B}$ such that $\iota; \varsigma = \varrho$ for the underlying S-map $\varsigma : A \to B$.

For any context K in Cxt_{EQ}, $\mathsf{Int}(K)$ denotes the category of all interpretations of K and all morphisms between them and $\Pi_K : \mathsf{Int}(K) \to \mathsf{Alg}(\Sigma)$ is the corresponding projection functor. The fiber over a Σ-algebra $\mathcal{A}$ represents the semantics of a context K in $\mathcal{A}$, i.e., the set $A^K := \mathsf{Set}^S(K, A)$ of all S-maps from K into the carrier of $\mathcal{A}$.

Note that, in the case of the empty S-set $K = \mathbf{0} = (\emptyset \mid s \in S)$ the projection functor $\Pi_0 : \mathsf{Int}(\mathbf{0}) \to \mathsf{Alg}(\Sigma)$ is an isomorphism.

Any S-map $\varphi : K \to G$ induces a functor $\mathsf{Int}(\varphi) : \mathsf{Int}(G) \to \mathsf{Int}(K)$ with:

$$\mathsf{Int}(\varphi); \Pi_K = \Pi_G : \mathsf{Int}(G) \to \mathsf{Alg}(\Sigma) \tag{6}$$

defined by simple pre-composition: $\mathsf{Int}(\varphi)(\varrho, \mathcal{B}) := (\varphi; \varrho, \mathcal{B})$ for all interpretations $(\varrho, \mathcal{B})$ of G, and for any morphism $\varsigma : (\iota, \mathcal{A}) \to (\varrho, \mathcal{B})$ between two interpretations of G the same underlying S-map $\varsigma : A \to B$ establishes a morphism $\mathsf{Int}(\varphi)(\varsigma) := \varsigma : (\varphi; \iota, \mathcal{A}) \to (\varphi; \varrho, \mathcal{B})$ between the corresponding two interpretations of K.

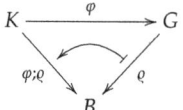 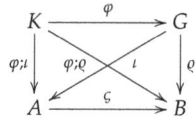 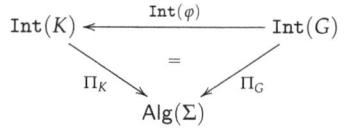

The assignments $K \mapsto \text{Int}(K)$ and $\varphi \mapsto \text{Int}(\varphi)$ define a functor $\text{Int}: \text{Cxt}_{EQ}^{op} \to \text{Cat}$. This is the **model functor** of an Institution of Equations.

4.2. Terms and Equations

To define equations, we need terms! For any S-set K the S-set $T_\Sigma(K)$ of all Σ-**terms on** K is defined inductively as the smallest S-set such that:

1. $K \subseteq T_\Sigma(K)$
2. $\omega\langle\rangle \in T_\Sigma(K)_{out(\omega)}$ for all $\omega \in \Omega$ with $in(\omega)$ the empty S-set $\mathbf{0} = (\emptyset \mid s \in S)$.
3. $\omega\langle\tau_{s_1}(x_1), \ldots, \tau_{s_n}(x_n)\rangle \in T_\Sigma(K)_{out(\omega)}$ for all $\omega \in \Omega$ with $in(\omega)$ non-empty and all S-maps $\tau: in(\omega) \to T_\Sigma(K)$ where $[x_1:s_1, x_2:s_2, \ldots, x_n:s_n]$ is the assumed representation of $in(\omega)$ as a list of variable declarations.

A Σ-**equation** $(K, t_1 = t_2)$ **in** K is given by two Σ-terms $t_1, t_2 \in T_\Sigma(K)_s$ for some $s \in S$ and $\text{Eq}(K)$ denotes the set of all Σ-equations $(K, t_1 = t_2)$ in K. In the usual way, the inductive definition of Σ-terms allows us to extend any S-map $\varphi: K \to G$ between S-sets to an S-map $\varphi^*: T_\Sigma(K) \to T_\Sigma(G)$ such that $\subseteq; \varphi^* = \varphi; \subseteq$ thus $\varphi: K \to G$ induces a map $\text{Eq}(\varphi) : \text{Eq}(K) \to \text{Eq}(G)$ with:

$$\text{Eq}(\varphi)(K, t_1 = t_2) := (G, \varphi^*(t_1) = \varphi^*(t_2)) \tag{7}$$

for all Σ-equations $(K, t_1 = t_2)$ in K.

Since $id_K^* = id_{T_\Sigma(K)}$ and $(\varphi; \psi)^* = \varphi^*; \psi^*$ for all $\varphi: K \to G$, $\psi: G \to H$, the assignments $K \mapsto \text{Eq}(K)$ and $\varphi \mapsto \text{Eq}(\varphi)$ define a functor $\text{Eq} : \text{Cxt}_{EQ} \to \text{Set}$. This is the **sentence functor** of an Institution of Equations.

The semantics of terms is based on the **evaluation of terms** in algebras: Due to the inductive definition of Σ-terms, we can extend any interpretation $\iota: K \to A$ of a context K in a Σ-algebra $\mathcal{A} = (A, \Omega^\mathcal{A})$ to an S-map $\iota^\circ : T_\Sigma(K) \to A$ such that:

$$\subseteq; \iota^\circ = \iota. \tag{8}$$

In such a way, we can define the semantics $t^\mathcal{A}$ of a Σ-term $t \in T_\Sigma(K)$, $s \in S$ in a Σ-algebra $\mathcal{A}$ as a map $t^\mathcal{A} : A^K \to A_s$ defined by $t^\mathcal{A}(\iota) := \iota^\circ(t)$ for all $\iota: K \to A$. Thus, feature expressions represent derived properties while terms represent *derived operations*!

4.3. Satisfaction Relation and Satisfaction Condition

Definition 15 (Satisfaction relation for equations). *For any context $K \in \text{Cxt}_{EQ}$, any Σ-equation $(K, t_1 = t_2)$ in K and any interpretation $(\iota, \mathcal{A})$ of context K in a Σ-algebra $\mathcal{A} = (A, \Omega^\mathcal{A})$, we define:*

$$(\iota, \mathcal{A}) \models_K (K, t_1 = t_2) \quad \textit{iff} \quad \iota^\circ(t_1) = \iota^\circ(t_2) \quad (i.e. \quad t_1^\mathcal{A}(\iota) = t_2^\mathcal{A}(\iota)) \tag{9}$$

The satisfaction condition is ensured by the well-behaved interplay of translations of terms along context morphisms and evaluations of terms.

Proposition 1 (Satisfaction condition for equations). *For any morphism $\varphi : K \to G$ in Cxt_{EQ}, any Σ-equation $(K, t_1 = t_2)$ in K and any interpretation $(\varrho, \mathcal{A})$ of context G in a Σ-algebra $\mathcal{A} = (A, \Omega^{\mathcal{A}})$, we have:*

$$\mathtt{Int}(\varphi)(\varrho, \mathcal{A}) \models_K (K, t_1 = t_2) \quad \textit{iff} \quad (\varrho, \mathcal{A}) \models_G \mathtt{Eq}(\varphi)(K, t_1 = t_2). \tag{10}$$

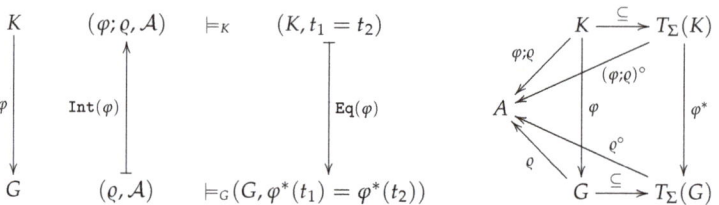

Proof. Due to the definition of the functors $\mathtt{Int} : \mathsf{Cxt}_{EQ}^{op} \to \mathsf{Cat}$, $\mathtt{Eq} : \mathsf{Cxt}_{EQ} \to \mathsf{Set}$ and the fact that $(\varphi; \varrho)^\circ = \varphi^*; \varrho^\circ$, we obtain the commutative diagram, above on the right, thus the satisfaction condition follows immediately from Definition 15. □

Summarizing all definitions and results, we obtain the main result in this section:

Proposition 2 (Institution of Equations). *Any choice of a finite set S and a signature $\Sigma = (\Omega, in, out)$ establishes a corresponding **Institution of Equations** $\mathcal{IE} = (\mathsf{Cxt}_{EQ}, \mathtt{Eq}, \mathtt{Int}, \models)$.*

5. Sketches

Any institution gives us a corresponding category of presentations and an extension of the model functor of the institution to the category of presentations at hand [2,31]. We outline this construction for Institutions of Statements and Institutions of Equations.

We would like to use a specific term to distinguish presentations for Institutions of Statements or Equations, resp., from presentations in general. Since many of our motivating examples are variants of sketches, we will simply use the term *sketch*. In Sections 5.1 and 5.2, we concentrate on sketches for Institutions of Statements while Section 5.3 outlines the corresponding variations for Institutions of Equations.

5.1. Sketches of Statements: Syntax and Semantics

To be prepared for the topics in Section 6, we introduce a very abstract and semantics-independent concept of *sketch*.

Definition 16 (Sketch). *Let us have a category Ct of contexts and a functor $\mathtt{St} : \mathsf{Ct} \to \mathsf{Set}$, assigning to each $K \in \mathsf{Ct}_{Obj}$ a set $\mathtt{St}(K)$ of all statements in context K.*

*An $\mathtt{St}$- **sketch** $\mathbb{K} = (K, St^{\mathbb{K}})$ is given by a context $K \in \mathsf{Ct}_{Obj}$ and a set $St^{\mathbb{K}} \subseteq \mathtt{St}(K)$ of statements in context K.*

In this subsection, we consider the case $\mathsf{Ct} = \mathsf{Cxt}$, $\mathtt{St} = \mathtt{Stm}$ with $\mathcal{IS} = (\mathsf{Cxt}, \mathtt{Stm}, \mathtt{Int}, \models)$ an arbitrary Institution of Statements according to Theorem 1.

All definitions and constructions are, however, institution-independent; thus, they apply analogously to the case $\mathsf{Ct} = \mathsf{Cxt}_{EQ}$, $\mathtt{St} = \mathtt{Eq}$ with $\mathcal{IE} = (\mathsf{Cxt}_{EQ}, \mathtt{Eq}, \mathtt{Int}, \models)$ an arbitrary Institution of Equations according to Proposition 2.

Example 36 (FOL: Sketches). *We extend the sample context K in Example 31 to an $\mathtt{Stm}_{FOL}$-sketch $\mathbb{K}$ with the atomic statements (facts) $\mathtt{parent}(Anna, Uwe, Gabi)$, $\mathtt{parent}(Uwe, Heinz, Dora)$, $\mathtt{male}(Michael)$ and the proper first-order statements $([y : prs], sbl, (y \mapsto Michael))$,*

$([y : prs], sbl, (y \mapsto Uwe))$, $([y : prs, x : nat], younger, (y \mapsto Michael, x \mapsto 12))$, $([y : prs], sbl, (y \mapsto Gabi))$. *The expression* $[y : prs] \triangleright sbl$, *representing the property* being sibling of someone, *and the expression* $[y : prs, x : nat] \triangleright younger$, *representing the property* younger than, *are defined in Example* 26.

Example 37 (ALC: Sketches). *Contexts in ALC are sets* N_O *of individual names as already mentioned in Example* 32. *A concept assertion in ALC, i.e., a statement of the form* $a : C$ *with* $a \in N_O$ *and* C *a (derived) concept, can be seen as a statement* $(\{x_1\}, C(x_1), (x_1 \mapsto a))$ *in* N_O *where the assignment* $(x_1 \mapsto a)$ *defines a binding* $\beta : \{x_1\} \to N_O$ *with* $\beta(x_1) = a$.

A role assertion, i.e., a statement of the form $(a, b) : R$ *where* $a, b \in N_O$ *and* R *is a role, can be seen as a statement* $(\{x_1, x_2\}, R(x_1, x_2), (x_1 \mapsto a, x_2 \mapsto b))$ *in* N_O. *An ABox in ALC is a finite set of* assertional axioms. *Thus, a pair* $(N_O, \mathcal{A})$ *of a set* N_O *of individual names and an ABox* $\mathcal{A}$ *of assertional axioms in* N_O *is just an* Stm_{ALC}*-sketch in our sense*.

Example 38 (mFOL: Sketches). *We extend the context* $(K, \tau_K : K \to M_{mF})$ *in Example* 33 *to an* Stm_{mF}*-sketch with the atomic statements* $\text{un}(male : P, prs : S)$, $\text{bin}(less : P, nat : S, nat : S)$, $\text{bin}(age : P, prs : S, nat : S)$ *and* $\text{trt}(parent : P, prs : S, prs : S, prs : S)$.

Obviously, this Stm_{mF}*-sketch describes exactly the sample footprint* Ξ_{FOL} *in Example* 11! *Actually, we can describe all FOL-footprints, declaring only unary, binary or tertiary predicate symbols, as* Stm_{mF}*-sketches. This fact confirms that the mFOL-example establishes indeed a metalevel for the FOL-example.*

We have to be aware, however, that not all Stm_{mF}*-sketches correspond to FOL-footprints. For each predicate symbol in a FOL-footprint, we have to declare an arity, and this arity should be unique! Therefore, only those* Stm_{mF}*-sketches, with exactly one atomic statement for each element in* $\tau_K^{-1}(P)$ *correspond to FOL-footprints. To describe those requirements concerning the structure of sketches, we can utilize* sketch implications, *introduced in the next subsection, and/or* sketch constraints *introduced in Section* 6.

Example 39 (CT: Sketches). *These are just the sketches, as we know them from Category Theory, with the essential difference that we are not restricting ourselves to commutative, limit and colimit statements only. We do not need to encode, for example, the concept* monomorphism *by means of pullbacks but can define it directly as a property of edges utilizing the* Ξ_{CT}*-expressions we discussed in Example* 29.

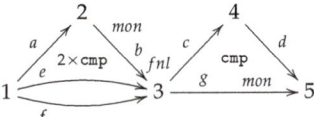

As an example, we consider the context G from Example 34 *and extend it to an* Stm_{CT}*-sketch* $\mathbb{G} = (G, St^{\mathbb{G}})$ *visualized above.* $St^{\mathbb{G}}$ *contains the atomic statements* $\text{cmp}(a, b, e)$, $\text{cmp}(a, b, f)$, $\text{cmp}(c, d, g)$ *and the proper first-order statements:*

$(xv, fnl, (xv \mapsto 3))$, $(xv_1 \xrightarrow{xe} xv_2, mon, (xe \mapsto b))$, $(xv_1 \xrightarrow{xe} xv_2, mon, (xe \mapsto g))$.

Example 40 (RM: Sketches). *We extend the sample context* (K, τ_K) *from Example* 35 *to an* Stm_{RM}*-sketch* $\mathbb{K} = (K, St^{\mathbb{K}})$. *First, we declare two tables, i.e.,* $St^{\mathbb{K}}$ *contains two atomic statements* $\text{tb}(3)(\gamma_1)$, $\text{tb}(3)(\gamma_2)$ *with bindings* γ_1 *and* γ_2 *visualized by the following typed graphs:*

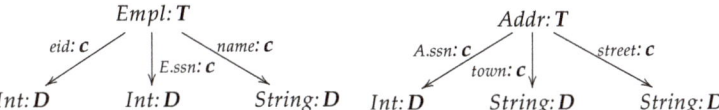

Then, we declare for each table a primary key, i.e., we add two atomic statements $\text{pk}(\gamma_3)$, $\text{pk}(\gamma_4)$ with bindings γ_3, γ_4 given by $\text{Empl}: T \xrightarrow{eid:c} \text{Int}: D$ and $\text{Addr}: T \xrightarrow{A.ssn:c} \text{Int}: D$. Moreover, we declare a foreign key $\text{fk}(\gamma_5)$ with γ_5 depicted by $\text{Empl}: T \xrightarrow{E.ssn:c} \text{Int}: D \xleftarrow{A.ssn:c} xt_2: T$.

We could also require that each employee has a name and add an atomic statement $\text{tot}(\gamma_6)$ with γ_6 given by $\text{Empl}: T \xrightarrow{name:c} \text{String}: D$.

Analogously to the requirements in Example 38, we do have the requirement that a table identifier can only appear once in a $\text{tb}(n)$-statement. There are, however, other database specific requirements: Any table should have exactly one primary key, a foreign key has to refer to a primary key, and others. As said before, to describe those kinds of structural requirements, we need **sketch implications** and/or **sketch constraints**. □

For any context K in Cxt, any set $S \subseteq \text{Stm}(K)$ of statements in K and any interpretation $(\iota, \mathcal{U})$ of context K in a Ξ-structure $\mathcal{U}$ we define, relying on Definition 14:

$$(\iota, \mathcal{U}) \models_K S \quad \text{iff} \quad (\iota, \mathcal{U}) \models_K (X, Ex, \gamma) \text{ for all } (X, Ex, \gamma) \in S. \tag{11}$$

Be aware that the statements in S may have different variable declarations X.

Definition 17 (Interpretation of sketch). *A **valid interpretation (model)** of an Stm-sketch $\mathbb{K} = (K, St^{\mathbb{K}})$ is an interpretation $(\iota, \mathcal{U})$ of context K such that $(\iota, \mathcal{U}) \models_K St^{\mathbb{K}}$.*

We denote by $\text{Int}(\mathbb{K})$ the full subcategory of $\text{Int}(K)$ determined by all valid interpretations of $\mathbb{K}$ and by $\Pi_{\mathbb{K}}: \text{Int}(\mathbb{K}) \to \text{Sem}(\Xi)$ we denote the corresponding restriction of the projection functor $\Pi_K: \text{Int}(K) \to \text{Sem}(\Xi)$.

Remark 21 (Traditional presentations). *If Base has an initial object $\mathbf{0}$, we can consider sketches $(\mathbf{0}, St)$ with St only containing **closed formulas**, i.e., statements of the form $(\mathbf{0}, Ex, id_\mathbf{0})$ (see Remark 15). As discussed before, the projection functor $\Pi_\mathbf{0}: \text{Int}(\mathbf{0}) \to \text{Sem}(\Xi)$, due to Definition 13, is an isomorphism. In such a way, $(\mathbf{0}, St)$ is not only determining the interpretation subcategory $\text{Int}(\mathbf{0}, St) \sqsubseteq \text{Int}(\mathbf{0})$ but can also be seen as a **presentation (specification)** of the corresponding full subcategory $\text{Sem}(\Xi, (\mathbf{0}, St)) := \Pi_\mathbf{0}(\text{Int}(\mathbf{0}, St))$ of $\text{Sem}(\Xi)$ isomorphic to $\text{Int}(\mathbf{0}, St)$.*

In other words: due to Remark 18, we can describe $\text{Sem}(\Xi, (\mathbf{0}, St))$ as the full subcategory of $\text{Sem}(\Xi)$ given by all Ξ-structures $\mathcal{U} = (U, \Phi^\mathcal{U})$ in $\text{Sem}(\Xi)$ such that $\mathcal{U} \models (\mathbf{0}, Ex, id_\mathbf{0})$ for all closed formulas $(\mathbf{0}, Ex, id_\mathbf{0})$ in St.

Example 41 (FOL: Interpretations). *If we interpret the symbolic literals in $K_{prs} = \{Anna, Michael, Dora, Heinz, Sorin, Gabi, Uwe\}$ by the real persons in our family in December 2021, we will not obtain a valid interpretation of the Stm_{FOL}-sketch $\mathbb{K}$ in Example 36 since the statement $([y: prs], sbl, (y \mapsto Gabi))$ is not satisfied by this interpretation. If we use, however, the statement $([y: prs], \neg sbl, (y \mapsto Gabi))$ instead, the interpretation becomes valid.*

Note that the statement $([y: prs], sbl, (y \mapsto Uwe))$ is satisfied by the interpretation even if there is no witness for this statement in the context. Uwe's only sister Brita is not present in the context K!

Example 42 (mFOL: Interpretations). *An interpretation of the sample context (K, τ_K) assigns to each element in $\tau_K^{-1}(S) := \{prs, nat\}$ and $\tau_K^{-1}(P) := \{\text{parent}, \text{male}, \text{age}, \text{less}\}$, respectively, a set. Since Base_{mF} is the slice category SET/M_{mF}, a certain set can either serve as a sort or as a predicate.*

Our choice of $\text{Sem}(\Xi_{mF})$ in Example 23 ensures, in addition, that the valid interpretations of the sample Stm_{mF}-sketch from Example 38 are in one-to-one correspondence to the Ξ_{FOL}-structures in $\text{Sem}(\Xi_{FOL}) = \text{Str}(\Xi_{FOL})$. We do have such a semantical one-to-one correspondence for any FOL-footprint, declaring only unary, binary or tertiary predicate symbols, and the corresponding

Stm_{mF}-sketch. This confirms that the mFOL-example establishes a meta-level for the FOL-example also w.r.t. semantics.

It is maybe worth mentioning that any Stm_{mF}-sketch with two different atomic statements for, at least, one element in $\tau_K^{-1}(P)$ has no valid interpretation at all in $\text{Sem}(\Xi_{mF})$.

Example 43 (Category Theory: Interpretations). *Since we defined in Example 24 a very liberal semantics, we do have interpretations* $(\iota, \mathcal{U})$, $\mathcal{U} = (U, \Phi_{CT}^{\mathcal{U}})$ *of the sample* Stm_{CT}-*sketch* $\mathbb{G} = (G, St^{\mathbb{G}})$ *in Example 39, where the graph homomorphism* $\iota : G \to U$ *maps the edges e and f to different edges in U even if both are declared as the composition of a and b.*

If we would have also included into the sketch $\mathbb{G}$ *the* **general statement** $(\mathbf{0}, guc, !_G)$ *with the closed expression* $\mathbf{0} \triangleright guc$ *expressing the property* compositiion is always unique *(see Example 29), $(\iota, \mathcal{U})$ could be only a valid interpretation of $\mathbb{G}$ if ι identifies e and f.*

Example 44 (RM: Interpretations). *Analogously to Example 42, our choice of $\text{Sem}(\Xi_{RM})$ in Example 25 ensures that the valid interpretations of "well-formed" Stm_{RM}-sketches, i.e., Stm_{RM}-sketches representing database schemata, formalize exactly the traditional semantics of database schemata as outlined in Subsection 3.1.5.*

Morphisms between sketches are defined by means of semantic entailment in a certain Institution of Statements $\mathcal{IS} = (\text{Cxt}, \text{Stm}, \text{Int}, \models)$.

Definition 18 (Statement entailment). *For any context K in Cxt and any sets $S, T \subseteq \text{Stm}(K)$ of statements in K, we say that S **entails** T **in a** Ξ- **structure** $\mathcal{U}$, $S \Vdash_K^{\mathcal{U}} T$ in symbols, if, and only if, for all interpretations $(\iota, \mathcal{U})$ of K in $\mathcal{U}$: $(\iota, \mathcal{U}) \models_K S$ implies $(\iota, \mathcal{U}) \models_K T$.*

*S **entails** T, $S \Vdash_K T$ in symbols, if, and only if, $S \Vdash_K^{\mathcal{U}} T$ for all Ξ-structures $\mathcal{U}$ in $\text{Sem}(\Xi)$.*

Definition 19 (Sketch morphism). *An $\mathcal{IS}$-morphism $\varphi : \mathbb{K} \dashrightarrow \mathbb{G}$ between two Stm-sketches $\mathbb{K} = (K, St^{\mathbb{K}})$, $\mathbb{G} = (G, St^{\mathbb{G}})$ is a morphism $\varphi : K \to G$ in Cxt such that $St^{\mathbb{G}} \Vdash_G \text{Stm}(\varphi)(St^{\mathbb{K}})$. An $\mathcal{IS}$-morphism $\varphi : \mathbb{K} \dashrightarrow \mathbb{G}$ is called **strict** if $St^{\mathbb{G}} \supseteq \text{Stm}(\varphi)(St^{\mathbb{K}})$.*

$\text{Sk}(\mathcal{IS})^m$ denotes the category of all Stm-sketches and all $\mathcal{IS}$-morphisms between them. Its subcategory of all Stm-sketches and all strict $\mathcal{IS}$-morphisms is denoted by $\text{Sk}(\mathcal{IS})_s^m$.

We will consider three different kinds of directed relationships between sketches distinguished by three different kinds of arrow-symbols. We choose the arrow-symbol "$\dashrightarrow$" for sketch morphisms since it is the kind of directed relationship we will mention the least.

If $\mathcal{IS}$ is clear from the context, we will also use the shorthand notations Sk^m and Sk_s^m instead of $\text{Sk}(\mathcal{IS})^m$ and $\text{Sk}(\mathcal{IS})_s^m$, respectively.

$\mathcal{IS}$-morphisms $\varphi : \mathbb{K} \dashrightarrow \mathbb{G}$ with $K = G$ and $\varphi = id_K$ simply reflect statement entailments. For any $\mathcal{IS}$-morphism $\varphi : \mathbb{K} \dashrightarrow \mathbb{G}$, the condition $St^{\mathbb{G}} \Vdash_G \text{Stm}(\varphi)(St^{\mathbb{K}})$ ensures, due to the satisfaction condition that the functor $\text{Int}(\varphi) : \text{Int}(G) \to \text{Int}(K)$ restricts to a functor from $\text{Int}(\mathbb{G})$ into $\text{Int}(\mathbb{K})$. In such a way, the assignments $\mathbb{K} \mapsto \text{Int}(\mathbb{K})$ extend to a functor $\text{Int}^{\text{Sk}} : (\text{Sk}^m)^{op} \to \text{Cat}$.

According to well-known general results (see Corollary 4.3 in [2]), we know that Sk^m has whatever limits or colimits the category Cxt has since limits and colimits in the category Sk^m of Stm-sketches and $\mathcal{IS}$-morphisms are constructed by means of limits and colimits in the category Cxt, respectively (compare Propositions 5 and 6). This ensures also that we do have *amalgamation* [1,2,38]: $\text{Int}^{\text{Sk}} : (\text{Sk}^m)^{op} \to \text{Cat}$ maps all colimits in Cxt that are preserved by the inclusion Cxt $\sqsubseteq$ Base, to limits in Cat.

The Theory of Institutions gives us "for free" Stm-sketches, $\mathcal{IS}$-morphisms, the category Sk^m as well as the *extended model functor* $\text{Int}^{\text{Sk}} : (\text{Sk}^m)^{op} \to \text{Cat}$.

However, to employ sketches as a specification formalism and to develop deduction calculi for sketches, we need a number of other concepts, constructions and results.

5.2. Sketches of Statements vs. Structures

In the Introduction, we discussed, among other things, two central motivations for the development of our framework: (1) We want to be able to give a general abstract account of the concept of free structures generalizing concepts like a group generated by a set of generators and a set of defining relations. (2) We want to provide an alternative general mechanism to encode structures "syntactically" that avoids the kind of circularity inherent to the technique of "signature extensions".

In the remaining part of this section, we outline proposals to meet these objectives.

5.2.1. Freely Generated Structures

To reconstruct the concept of a group generated by a set of generators and a set of defining relations, we need operations only. Those cases of free algebras are discussed in Section 5.3.1.

First, We Consider Structures Freely Generated in $\mathrm{Sem}(\Xi)$

A Ξ-structure $\mathcal{F} = (F, \Phi^{\mathcal{F}})$ is freely generated in $\mathrm{Sem}(\Xi)$ by an Stm-sketch $\mathbb{G} = (G, St^{\mathbb{G}})$ if, and only if, $\mathcal{F}$ is in $\mathrm{Sem}(\Xi)$ and there is a *valid interpretation* $(\eta_{\mathbb{G}}, \mathcal{F})$ of $\mathbb{G}$ in $\mathcal{F}$ that is *universal relative to* $\mathrm{Sem}(\Xi)$. That is, for all Ξ-structures $\mathcal{U} = (U, \Phi^{\mathcal{U}})$ in $\mathrm{Sem}(\Xi)$ and all valid interpretations $(\iota, \mathcal{U})$ of $\mathbb{G}$ in $\mathcal{U}$ there exists a unique morphism $\iota^* : \mathcal{F} \to \mathcal{U}$ in $\mathrm{Sem}(\Xi)$ such that $\eta_{\mathbb{G}}; \iota^* = \iota$ in Base, i.e., such that ι^* establishes an interpretation morphism $\iota^* : (\eta_{\mathbb{G}}, \mathcal{F}) \to (\iota, \mathcal{U})$ in $\mathrm{Int}(\mathbb{G}) \sqsubseteq \mathrm{Int}(G)$ according to Definition 13.

$$\mathrm{Int}(\mathbb{G}) \quad G \xrightarrow{(\eta_{\mathbb{G}}, \mathcal{F}) \models_{\mathbb{G}} St^{\mathbb{G}}} F \quad \mathcal{F} = (F, \Phi^{\mathcal{F}}) \quad \mathrm{Sem}(\Xi)$$

(with diagram showing $(\iota, \mathcal{U}) \models_{\mathbb{G}} St^{\mathbb{G}}$ going to U, and ι^* arrows)

A Ξ-structure, freely generated in $\mathrm{Sem}(\Xi)$ by an Stm-sketch $\mathbb{G} = (G, St^{\mathbb{G}})$, is obviously uniquely determined "up to isomorphism in $\mathrm{Sem}(\Xi)$" if it exists.

The universal property of $(\eta_{\mathbb{G}}, \mathcal{F})$ entails that $(\eta_{\mathbb{G}}, \mathcal{F})$ is initial in $\mathrm{Int}(\mathbb{G})$, thus the projection functor $\Pi_{\mathbb{G}} : \mathrm{Int}(\mathbb{G}) \to \mathrm{Sem}(\Xi)$ establishes a functor from $\mathrm{Int}(\mathbb{G})$ into the co-slice category $\mathcal{F}/\mathrm{Sem}(\Xi)$.

In the case that $St^{\mathbb{G}}$ contains only atomic statements, the definition of morphisms between Ξ-structures ensures $(\eta_{\mathbb{G}}; \varrho, \mathcal{U}) \models_G St^{\mathbb{G}}$ for any morphism $\varrho : \mathcal{F} \to \mathcal{U}$ in $\mathrm{Sem}(\Xi)$; thus, the assignments $(\varrho : \mathcal{F} \to \mathcal{U}) \mapsto (\eta_{\mathbb{G}}; \varrho, \mathcal{U})$ establish a functor from $\mathcal{F}/\mathrm{Sem}(\Xi)$ into $\mathrm{Int}(\mathbb{G})$. Due to the universal property of $(\eta_{\mathbb{G}}, \mathcal{F})$, we obtain $(\eta_{\mathbb{G}}; \varrho)^* = \varrho$. Together with the equation $\eta_{\mathbb{G}}; \iota^* = \iota$, this ensures that the two functors establish an isomorphism between $\mathrm{Int}(\mathbb{G})$ and $\mathcal{F}/\mathrm{Sem}(\Xi)$ (compare Proposition 4.10 in [2]). This justifies that we can call, in this *atomic case*, the pair $(\mathbb{G}, \eta_{\mathbb{G}})$ a **sketch representation** of $\mathcal{F}$.

Note that the Ξ-structure $(G, \Phi^{\varnothing})$ with $\Phi^{\varnothing}$ a Φ-indexed family of empty sets is trivially freely generated in $\mathrm{Sem}(\Xi)$ by $\mathbb{G} = (G, \varnothing)$.

Second, We Consider Structures Freely Generated Relative to a Subcategory D:

Let D be an arbitrary full subcategory of $\mathrm{Sem}(\Xi)$. A Ξ-structure $\mathcal{F} = (F, \Phi^{\mathcal{F}})$ is freely generated in D by an Stm-sketch $\mathbb{G} = (G, St^{\mathbb{G}})$ if, and only if, $\mathcal{F}$ is an object in D and there is a valid interpretation $(\eta_{\mathbb{G}}, \mathcal{F})$ of $\mathbb{G}$ in $\mathcal{F}$ that is universal relative to D. That is, for all Ξ-structures $\mathcal{U} = (U, \Phi^{\mathcal{U}})$ in D and all valid interpretations $(\iota, \mathcal{U})$ of $\mathbb{G}$ in $\mathcal{U}$ there exists a unique morphism $\iota^* : \mathcal{F} \to \mathcal{U}$ in D such that $\eta_{\mathbb{G}}; \iota^* = \iota$ in Base, i.e., such that ι^* establishes an interpretation morphism $\iota^* : (\eta_{\mathbb{G}}, \mathcal{F}) \to (\iota, \mathcal{U})$ in $\mathrm{Int}(\mathbb{G}) \sqsubseteq \mathrm{Int}(G)$.

$$\mathrm{Int}(\mathbb{G}) \downarrow D \quad G \xrightarrow{(\eta_{\mathbb{G}}, \mathcal{F}) \models_{\mathbb{G}} St^{\mathbb{G}}} F \quad \mathcal{F} = (F, \Phi^{\mathcal{F}}) \quad D$$

A Ξ-structure, freely generated in D by an Stm-sketch $\mathbb{G} = (G, St^G)$ is, obviously, uniquely determined "up to isomorphism in D" if it exists. In this case, the universal property of $(\eta_G, \mathcal{F})$ entails that $(\eta_G, \mathcal{F})$ is initial in the subcategory $\mathtt{Int}(\mathbb{G}) \downarrow D := \Pi_G^{-1}(D)$ of all valid interpretations of $\mathbb{G}$ in Ξ-structures in D. Analogous to the case $D = \mathtt{Sem}(\Xi)$, we obtain, moreover, an isomorphism between $\mathtt{Int}(\mathbb{G}) \downarrow D$ and the co-slice category $\mathcal{F}/D$ if St^G contains only atomic statements.

Third, We Consider Subcategories Described by Logical Means

One logical means to describe subcategories of $\mathtt{Sem}(\Xi)$ are Stm-sketches $(\mathbf{0}, St)$ with St only containing closed formulas, i.e., statements of the form $(\mathbf{0}, Ex, id_0)$. As discussed in Remark 21, those sketches can be seen as presentations in the traditional sense of the Theory of Institutions specifying subcategories $\mathtt{Sem}(\Xi, (\mathbf{0}, St))$ of $\mathtt{Sem}(\Xi)$.

As another logical means to describe subcategories of $\mathtt{Sem}(\Xi)$, we will introduce sketch implications in Section 5.2.3 (see Remark 27).

5.2.2. Elementary Diagrams

To establish sketch-based mechanisms to encode structures "syntactically", we have to assume an Institution of Statements $\mathcal{IS} = (\mathtt{Cxt}, \mathtt{Stm}, \mathtt{Int}, \models)$ with $\mathtt{Carr} \sqsubseteq \mathtt{Cxt}$ and $\mathtt{At}(K) \subseteq \mathtt{Stm}(K)$ for all contexts K in $\mathtt{Cxt}$, i.e., $\mathtt{Stm}(K)$ contains all atomic statements in K.

There are two canonical ways to transform a Ξ-structure $\mathcal{U} = (U, \Phi^{\mathcal{U}})$ into an Stm-sketch. The atomic variant $\mathbb{S}_\Phi^{\mathcal{U}} = (U, St_\Phi^{\mathcal{U}})$ encodes only the semantics of feature symbols and uses therefore only atomic statements:

$$St_\Phi^{\mathcal{U}} := \{(\alpha F, F(id_{\alpha F}), \gamma) \mid F \in \Phi, \gamma \in [\![F]\!]^{\mathcal{U}}\} \subseteq \mathtt{At}(U). \tag{12}$$

The full variant $\mathbb{S}^{\mathcal{U}} = (U, St^{\mathcal{U}})$ is available if $\mathtt{XE}(\Xi, X) = \mathtt{FE}(\Xi, X)$ for all $X \in \mathtt{Var}_{Obj}$ and encodes the semantics of all feature expressions:

$$St^{\mathcal{U}} := \{(X, Ex, \gamma) \mid X \in \mathtt{Var}_{Obj}, Ex \in \mathtt{FE}(\Xi, X), \gamma \in [\![Ex]\!]_X^{\mathcal{U}}\} \subseteq \mathtt{Stm}(U). \tag{13}$$

We obviously have $St_\Phi^{\mathcal{U}} \subset St^{\mathcal{U}}$. For any statement (X, Ex, γ) in U we obtain, according to (13) and the definition of satisfaction relations in Definition 14,

$$(X, Ex, \gamma) \in St^{\mathcal{U}} \quad \text{iff} \quad \gamma; id_U = \gamma \in [\![Ex]\!]_X^{\mathcal{U}} \quad \text{iff} \quad (id_U, \mathcal{U}) \models_U (X, Ex, \gamma). \tag{14}$$

thus $(id_U, \mathcal{U})$ is a valid interpretation of $\mathbb{S}_\Phi^{\mathcal{U}}$ as well as of $\mathbb{S}^{\mathcal{U}}$.

In traditional First-Order Logic, we meet the full variant in the form of elementary diagrams [39]. The difference to our encoding is that the carrier of a first-order structure is not considered as a context. Instead, each element of the carrier is added as a constant to the signature. The encoding of structures as sketches avoids this kind of circularity. The "signature extension trick" works only for first-order signatures with constants symbols and, more critically, it requires that the carriers of first-order structures are sets! It looks like the sketch encoding mechanism is much more flexible and general.

The elementary diagrams in [2] give an abstract account of the signature extension approach but are based on an atomic variant of encoding.

There are no structures at all in [15] only atomic sketches! In [13], we followed Makkai and have not considered structures either. Instead, we worked, directly, with the atomic sketch encodings $\mathbb{S}_\Phi^{\mathcal{U}}$ of structures.

To validate, in retrospective, the approaches in [13,15], a noticeable portion of the remaining part of the paper, will be spent to answer the following question:

> Question 4: Is there any justification to ignore completely the concept of semantic structure (model)?

By construction, any Ξ-structure $\mathcal{U} = (U, \Phi^{\mathcal{U}})$ in $\mathtt{Sem}(\Xi)$ is freely generated in $\mathtt{Sem}(\Xi)$ by the Stm-sketch $\mathbb{S}_\Phi^{\mathcal{U}} = (U, St_\Phi^{\mathcal{U}})$ with the universal interpretation $(id_U, \mathcal{U})$. $St_\Phi^{\mathcal{U}}$ contains only atomic statements thus $(\mathbb{S}^{\mathcal{U}}_{\Phi}, id_{\mathcal{U}})$ becomes a sketch representation of $\mathcal{U}$ in the sense of the last subsection. In particular, there is an isomorphism between $\text{Int}(\mathbb{S}^{\mathcal{U}}_{\Phi})$ and $\mathcal{U}/\text{Sem}(\Xi)$.

The crucial observation is, however, that the assignments $\mathcal{U} \mapsto \mathbb{S}^{\mathcal{U}}_{\Phi}$ define an embedding $\text{Enc}: \text{Str}(\Xi) \to \text{Sk}(\text{Stm})^a$ of $\text{Str}(\Xi)$ into the category $\text{Sk}(\text{Stm})^a$ of all Stm-sketches and all Stm-sketch arrows defined in the next subsection in Definition 20. This embedding establishes, moreover, an isomorphism between $\text{Str}(\Xi)$ and the subcategory $\text{atSk}(\text{Stm})^a_s$ of $\text{Sk}(\text{Stm})^a$ given by all atomic Stm-sketches and all strict Stm-sketch arrows between them. An Stm-sketch $\mathbb{K} = (K, St^{\mathbb{K}})$ is atomic if $St^{\mathbb{K}} \subseteq \text{At}(K)$ (see Remark 14).

The concepts (atomic) Stm-sketch and (strict) Stm-sketch arrow concern only the "structure" of sketches and are completely semantics-independent. That is, the transition along the encoding functor Enc from the category $\text{Str}(\Xi)$ to the isomorphic category $\text{atSk}(\text{Stm})^a_s$ implements an abstraction from the concept semantic structure (model) to the concept atomic sketch. In case $\text{Sem}(\Xi) = \text{Str}(\Xi)$, this abstraction is exhaustive. In case $\text{Sem}(\Xi)_{Obj} \subsetneq \text{Str}(\Xi)_{Obj}$, however, we need an additional semantics-independent, purely structural characterization identifying exactly all those atomic Stm-sketches $\mathbb{S}^{\mathcal{U}}_{\Phi}$ in $\text{atSk}(\text{Stm})^a_s$ with $\mathcal{U}$ in $\text{Sem}(\Xi)$, to make the abstraction complete (see Remark 29).

A sketch is constituted by a context and a set of statements. The informal term "structure of a sketch" takes into account the context; for each statement, the syntactic structure of the corresponding expression and its "location", i.e., its binding morphism, the set of statements as such and the "distribution" of the statements over the context.

5.2.3. Sketch Arrows and Sketch Implications

We can not only transform Ξ-structures $\mathcal{U}$ into the Stm-sketches $\mathbb{S}^{\mathcal{U}}_{\Phi}$ and $\mathbb{S}^{\mathcal{U}}$. We can even encode the validity of certain classes of "closed formulas" in $\mathcal{U}$ by means of semantics-independent, pure structural closedness properties of $\mathbb{S}^{\mathcal{U}}_{\Phi}$ or $\mathbb{S}^{\mathcal{U}}$, respectively. To see this, we need some preparations.

First, we have to take a step back and consider a very simple, semantics-independent relationship between sketches. To be prepared for Section 6, we define this relationship on the same level of abstraction as Definition 16 (Sketch).

Definition 20 (Sketch Arrow). *Let us be given a category Ct and a functor* $\text{St}: \text{Ct} \to \text{Set}$. *An arrow* $\varphi: \mathbb{K} \to \mathbb{G}$ *between two* St*-sketches* $\mathbb{K} = (K, St^{\mathbb{K}})$, $\mathbb{G} = (G, St^{\mathbb{G}})$ *is given by a context morphism* $\varphi: K \to G$. $\varphi: \mathbb{K} \to \mathbb{G}$ *is called* **strict** *if* $St^{\mathbb{G}} \supseteq \text{St}(\varphi)(St^{\mathbb{K}})$.

$\text{Sk}(\text{St})^a$ *denotes the category of all* St*-sketches and all* St*-sketch arrows between them. Its subcategory of all* St*-sketches and all strict* St*-sketch arrows is denoted by* $\text{Sk}(\text{St})^a_s$.

If St is clear from the context, we will also use the shorthand notations Sk^a and Sk^a_s instead of $\text{Sk}(\text{St})^a$ and $\text{Sk}(\text{St})^a_s$, respectively. If $K = G$ and $\varphi = id_K$, we will also just write $\mathbb{K} \to \mathbb{G}$ instead of $\varphi: \mathbb{K} \to \mathbb{G}$. We consider the case $\text{Ct} = \text{Cxt}$, $\text{St} = \text{Stm}$ with $\mathcal{IS} = (\text{Cxt}, \text{Stm}, \text{Int}, \models)$ an Institution of Statements.

Remark 22 (Sketch Morphisms vs. Sketch Arrows). *An $\mathcal{IS}$-morphism $\varphi: \mathbb{K} \dashrightarrow \mathbb{G}$ is a* Stm*-sketch arrow $\varphi: \mathbb{K} \to \mathbb{G}$ satisfying the semantical morphism condition $St^{\mathbb{G}} \Vdash_G \text{Stm}(\varphi)(St^{\mathbb{K}})$. Not every* Stm*-sketch arrow $\varphi: \mathbb{K} \to \mathbb{G}$ provides an $\mathcal{IS}$-morphism $\varphi: \mathbb{K} \dashrightarrow \mathbb{G}$, but each $\mathcal{IS}$-morphism $\varphi: \mathbb{K} \dashrightarrow \mathbb{G}$ has an underlying* Stm*-sketch arrow $\varphi: \mathbb{K} \to \mathbb{G}$.*

Any strict Stm*-sketch arrow $\varphi: \mathbb{K} \to \mathbb{G}$ satisfies, trivially, the morphism condition and provides, in such a way, a strict $\mathcal{IS}$-morphism $\varphi: \mathbb{K} \dashrightarrow \mathbb{G}$ due to Definition 19.*

There is, however, another semantical condition that is kind of dual to the morphism condition. We call this condition the implication condition and, as a "terminological sleight of hand", we introduce the concept of a "sketch implication", simply indicating that a sketch arrow is intended to be the subject of this dual semantical condition.

Definition 21 (Sketch implication). *An $\mathcal{IS}$- **implication** $\mathbb{P} \stackrel{\varphi}{\Rightarrow} \mathbb{C}$ is given by two Stm-sketches $\mathbb{P} = (P, St^P)$, $\mathbb{C} = (C, St^C)$ and a context morphism $\varphi : P \to C$.*

An $\mathcal{IS}$-implication $\mathbb{P} \stackrel{\varphi}{\Rightarrow} \mathbb{C}$ is called **strict** *if $St^C \supseteq \text{Stm}(\varphi)(St^P)$.*

$\text{Sk}(\mathcal{IS})^i$ *denotes the category of all Stm-sketches and all $\mathcal{IS}$-implications between them. Its subcategory of all Stm-sketches and all strict $\mathcal{IS}$-implications is denoted by $\text{Sk}(\mathcal{IS})^i_s$.*

If $\mathcal{IS}$ is clear from the context, we will also use the shorthand notations Sk^i and Sk^i_s instead of $\text{Sk}(\mathcal{IS})^i$ and $\text{Sk}(\mathcal{IS})^i_s$, respectively. If $P = C$ and $\varphi = id_P$, we will also simply write $\mathbb{P} \Rightarrow \mathbb{C}$ instead of $\mathbb{P} \stackrel{id_P}{\Rightarrow} \mathbb{C}$.

What we call the implication condition is nothing but the usual condition that an implication is valid if each "solution" of the premise gives rise to a "solution" of the conclusion.

Definition 22 (Validity of Sketch Implications). *Let us be given an $\mathcal{IS}$-implication $\mathbb{P} \stackrel{\varphi}{\Rightarrow} \mathbb{C}$ between two Stm-sketches $\mathbb{P} = (P, St^P)$ and $\mathbb{C} = (C, St^C)$.*

*An **interpretation** $(\iota, \mathcal{U})$ of context P in a Ξ-structure $\mathcal{U}$ **satisfies** $\mathbb{P} \stackrel{\varphi}{\Rightarrow} \mathbb{C}$, $(\iota, \mathcal{U}) \models \mathbb{P} \stackrel{\varphi}{\Rightarrow} \mathbb{C}$ in symbols, if, and only if, $(\iota, \mathcal{U}) \models_P St^P$ implies that there exists an interpretation $(\varrho, \mathcal{U})$ of context C in $\mathcal{U}$ with $\varphi; \varrho = \iota$ such that $(\varrho, \mathcal{U}) \models_C St^C$.*

*$\mathbb{P} \stackrel{\varphi}{\Rightarrow} \mathbb{C}$ is **valid in a** Ξ- **structure** $\mathcal{U}$, $\mathcal{U} \models \mathbb{P} \stackrel{\varphi}{\Rightarrow} \mathbb{C}$ in symbols, if, and only if, we have $(\iota, \mathcal{U}) \models \mathbb{P} \stackrel{\varphi}{\Rightarrow} \mathbb{C}$ for all interpretations $(\iota, \mathcal{U})$ of P in $\mathcal{U}$.*

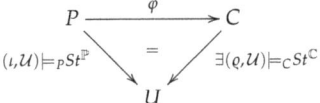

*$\mathbb{P} \stackrel{\varphi}{\Rightarrow} \mathbb{C}$ is **valid (in $\mathcal{IS}$)**, $\models \mathbb{P} \stackrel{\varphi}{\Rightarrow} \mathbb{C}$ in symbols, if, and only if, $\mathcal{U} \models \mathbb{P} \stackrel{\varphi}{\Rightarrow} \mathbb{C}$ for all Ξ-structures $\mathcal{U}$ in $\text{Sem}(\Xi)$.*

Remark 23 (Subcategories of valid Sketch Implications). *For any Ξ-structure $\mathcal{U}$ and any Stm-sketch $\mathbb{P}$ we have $\mathcal{U} \models \mathbb{P} \stackrel{id_P}{\Rightarrow} \mathbb{P}$. Moreover, $\mathcal{U} \models \mathbb{A} \stackrel{\varphi}{\Rightarrow} \mathbb{B}$ and $\mathcal{U} \models \mathbb{B} \stackrel{\psi}{\Rightarrow} \mathbb{C}$ implies $\mathcal{U} \models \mathbb{A} \stackrel{\varphi;\psi}{\Rightarrow} \mathbb{C}$. In such a way, the collection of all $\mathcal{IS}$-implications, valid in a Ξ-structure $\mathcal{U}$, defines a corresponding subcategory of Sk^i with the same objects as Sk^i.*

Intersecting all those subcategories for all Ξ-structures $\mathcal{U}$ in $\text{Sem}(\Xi)$, we obtain the subcategory $\text{Sk}^i(\text{Sem}(\Xi))$ of Sk^i given by all $\mathcal{IS}$-implications valid in $\mathcal{IS}$.

Remark 24 (Sketch Implications vs. Sketch Arrows). *An $\mathcal{IS}$-implication $\mathbb{P} \stackrel{\varphi}{\Rightarrow} \mathbb{C}$ is simply another notation for a Stm-sketch arrow $\varphi : \mathbb{P} \to \mathbb{C}$. The only difference is that we allow $\mathbb{P} \stackrel{\varphi}{\Rightarrow} \mathbb{C}$ to be the subject of semantical implication conditions, like $\mathcal{U} \models \mathbb{P} \stackrel{\varphi}{\Rightarrow} \mathbb{C}$, while the corresponding Stm-sketch arrow $\varphi : \mathbb{P} \to \mathbb{C}$ is considered as a pure structural entity without any semantical significance.*

In contrast to $\mathcal{IS}$-morphisms (compare Remark 22), a strict Stm-sketch arrow $\varphi : \mathbb{P} \to \mathbb{C}$ does not give, trivially, rise to an $\mathcal{IS}$-implication $\mathbb{P} \stackrel{\varphi}{\Rightarrow} \mathbb{C}$ satisfying semantical implication conditions.

For any Stm-sketch arrow $\varphi : \mathbb{P} \to \mathbb{C}$, we can construct a respective strict Stm-sketch arrow $\varphi : \mathbb{P} \to \mathbb{C}^\varphi$ with $\mathbb{C}^\varphi := (C, St^C \cup \text{Stm}(\varphi)(St^P))$. The satisfaction condition ensures that the corresponding $\mathcal{IS}$-implications $\mathbb{P} \stackrel{\varphi}{\Rightarrow} \mathbb{C}$ and $\mathbb{P} \stackrel{\varphi}{\Rightarrow} \mathbb{C}^\varphi$ are semantically equivalent: $\mathcal{U} \models \mathbb{P} \stackrel{\varphi}{\Rightarrow} \mathbb{C}$ if, and only if, $\mathcal{U} \models \mathbb{P} \stackrel{\varphi}{\Rightarrow} \mathbb{C}^\varphi$ for all Ξ-structures $\mathcal{U}$.

Remark 25 (Sketch Implications vs. Sketch Morphisms). *The concepts sketch morphism and sketch implication are skewed but kind of dual. Sketch morphisms talk about "reducts of models" while sketch implications state the existence of "model extensions".*

In case $P = \mathbb{C}$ and $\varphi = id_{\mathbb{P}}$, a Stm-sketch arrow $\varphi : \mathbb{P} \to \mathbb{C}$ provides an $\mathcal{IS}$-morphism $id_{\mathbb{P}} : \mathbb{P} \dashrightarrow \mathbb{C}$ if, and only if, $St^{\mathbb{C}} \Vdash_{\mathbb{P}} St^{\mathbb{P}}$ while the validity in $\mathcal{IS}$ of the corresponding $\mathcal{IS}$-implication $\mathbb{P} \Rightarrow \mathbb{C}$ means semantic entailment exactly in the opposite direction $St^{\mathbb{P}} \Vdash_{\mathbb{P}} St^{\mathbb{C}}$!

Remark 26 (Deduction Rules). *Attention, the exposition in the following remarks and examples, relies implicitly on the observation that sketch arrows can be utilized as* **deduction rules**. *A deduction rule, given by a* Stm*-sketch arrow* $\varphi : \mathbb{P} \to \mathbb{C}$, *is* **sound** *for a certain Institution of Statements* $\mathcal{IS} = (\mathsf{Cxt}, \mathsf{Stm}, \mathsf{Int}, \models)$ *if, and only if, the respective $\mathcal{IS}$-implication* $\mathbb{P} \stackrel{\varphi}{\Rightarrow} \mathbb{C}$ *is valid in $\mathcal{IS}$!*

The utilization of sketch arrows as deduction rules is triggered by Definition 23 as well as Proposition 3 and Corollary 2 at the end of this subsection and will be discussed shortly in Remark 32.

Remark 27 (Valid Sketch Implications and Axioms). *There are $\mathcal{IS}$-implications (or, more precisely, $\mathcal{IS}$-implication schemata) that are* **universal** *in the sense that they are valid in any Institution of Statements* $\mathcal{IS} = (\mathsf{Cxt}, \mathsf{Stm}, \mathsf{Int}, \models)$, *since they reflect the structure and semantics of feature expressions. In particular, the* **introduction** *and* **elimination** *rules for logical connectives can be described by those universal sketch implications. In case of* **conjunction** $\wedge$, *for example, we do have the two* Stm*-sketches* $\mathbb{L} = (X, \{(X, Ex_1 \wedge Ex_2, id_X)\})$ *and* $\mathbb{R} = (X, \{(X, Ex_1, id_X), (X, Ex_2, id_X)\})$. *In addition, the "elimination rule"* $\mathbb{L} \Rightarrow \mathbb{R}$ *as the "introduction rule"* $\mathbb{R} \Rightarrow \mathbb{L}$ *are universal sketch implications.*

For existential *quantification, we do also have a kind of* **modus ponens** *at hand described by the following universal sketch implication:*

$$(X, \{(X, Ex_1, id_X), (X, Ex_1 \to \exists(\varphi, Y : Ex), id_X)\}) \stackrel{\varphi}{\Longrightarrow} (Y, \{(Y, Ex_2, id_Y)\}). \quad (15)$$

The validity of other $\mathcal{IS}$-implications may only depend on the chosen base category Base *of an Institution of Statements. As long as* Base *is a presheaf topos, we do have, for example, $\mathcal{IS}$-implications at hand expressing reflexivity, symmetry and transitivity of* equality, *i.e., reflecting the properties of identifications of entities by means of maps (compare the definition of the Ξ_{CT}-expression $[=]$ in Example 29).*

Besides universal $\mathcal{IS}$-implications, we do also have $\mathcal{IS}$-implications that are valid in all Ξ-structures $\mathcal{U}$, and we have chosen to be in Sem(Ξ). *In case* Sem$(\Xi)_{Obj} \subsetneq$ Str$(\Xi)_{Obj}$, *we may be able to axiomatize* Sem(Ξ) *in the sense that there is a set SEM of $\mathcal{IS}$-implications such that* Sem$(\Xi) =$ Str(Ξ, SEM) *where* Str(Ξ, SEM) *is the full subcategory of* Str(Ξ) *given by all those Ξ-structures $\mathcal{U}$ such that $\mathcal{U} \models \mathbb{P} \stackrel{\varphi}{\Rightarrow} \mathbb{C}$ for all $\mathcal{IS}$-implications $\mathbb{P} \stackrel{\varphi}{\Rightarrow} \mathbb{C}$ in SEM.*

In the same way, we can utilize any set IMP of $\mathcal{IS}$-implications as a set of **axioms** *describing the full subcategory* Sem(Ξ, IMP) *of* Sem(Ξ) *given by all those Ξ-structures $\mathcal{U}$ in* Sem(Ξ) *such that $\mathcal{U} \models \mathbb{P} \stackrel{\varphi}{\Rightarrow} \mathbb{C}$ for all $\mathcal{IS}$-implications $\mathbb{P} \stackrel{\varphi}{\Rightarrow} \mathbb{C}$ in IMP.*

At the end of Section 5.2.1, we described a mechanism to define subcategories of Sem(Ξ) *by means of axioms in the traditional Hilbert-style, i.e., by* Stm*-sketches* $(\mathbf{0}, St)$ *with St only containing closed formulas, i.e., statements of the form* $(\mathbf{0}, Ex, id_\mathbf{0})$. *This mechanism can be integrated in the sketch implication based axiomatization mechanism, in a trivial way, by simply adding to IMP a corresponding* **introduction rule** $(\mathbf{0}, \varnothing) \Rightarrow (\mathbf{0}, St)$. *For certain classes of closed formulas, there exist more elaborated transformations of Hilbert-style axioms into sketch implication based axioms, as discussed in Section 5.2.4.*

Example 45 (FOL: Sketch implications). *Horn clauses are defined and utilized in PROLOG, in a way that it seems to be appropriate to consider them as sketch implications rather than universally quantified implications. That is, we consider a Horn clause not as a closed formula* $(\mathbf{0}, \forall (X : Ex \to Ex'), id_\mathbf{0})$ *with Ex a finite conjunction of atomic expressions* $X \triangleright F_i(\beta_i)$, $\beta_i : \alpha F_i \to X$ *with* $1 \leq i \leq n$ *and an atomic expression* $X \triangleright Ex' = F(\beta)$, $\beta : \alpha F \to X$, *but rather as the corresponding $\mathcal{IS}$-implication* $\mathbb{P} \Rightarrow \mathbb{C}$ *with* $\mathbb{P} = (X, St^{\mathbb{P}})$, $St^{\mathbb{P}} = \{(\alpha F_i, F_i(id_{\alpha F_i}), \beta_i) \mid 1 \leq i \leq n\}$ *and* $\mathbb{C} = (X, St^{\mathbb{C}})$, $St^{\mathbb{C}} = \{(\alpha F_i, F(id_{\alpha F}), \beta)\}$.

Example 46 (ALC: Sketch implications). *A so-called TBox in ALC is a finite set of terminological axioms, i.e., of* general concept inclusions $C \sqsubseteq D$. *For the way the semantics of general concept inclusions is defined in ALC, they correspond, analogous to Horn clauses, rather to sketch implications (than to closed formulas):*

$$(\{p_1\},\{(\{p_1\},C(p_1),id_{\{p_1\}})\}) \Longrightarrow (\{p_1\},\{(\{p_1\},D(p_1),id_{\{p_1\}})\})$$

Example 47 (Category Theory: Sketch implications). *There are, at least, three ways to axiomatize that all vertices do have an identity. First, we can require, due to Remark 18:*

$$\mathcal{U} \models (0, \forall(X : \exists(in, \alpha_{CT}(\text{id}) : \text{id}(id_{\alpha_{CT}(\text{id})}))), id_0)$$

where graph X consists only of a vertex xv and in : $X \to \alpha_{CT}(\text{id})$ is the inclusion of X into $\alpha_{CT}(\text{id})$ (see Examples 14 and 29). As proposed in Remark 27, we can equivalently add the introduction rule:

$$(0,\emptyset) \Longrightarrow (0, \{(0, \forall(X : \exists(in, \alpha_{CT}(\text{id}) : \text{id}(id_{\alpha_{CT}(\text{id})}))), id_0)\})$$

to our axioms. According to a general pattern, discussed in the next Section 5.2.4, we can use, instead, the equivalent rule:

$$(X,\emptyset) \Longrightarrow (X, \{(X, \exists(in, \alpha_{CT}(\text{id}) : \text{id}(id_{\alpha_{CT}(\text{id})})), id_X)\}).$$

In turn, this second rule can be composed with a simple variant of the modus ponens rule (15), and we obtain a third equivalent rule:

$$(X,\emptyset) \stackrel{in}{\Longrightarrow} (\alpha_{CT}(\text{id}), \{(\alpha_{CT}(\text{id}), \text{id}(id_{\alpha_{CT}(\text{id})})), id_{\alpha_{CT}(\text{id})})\})$$

Example 48 (RM: Sketch implication). *In DPF, we worked, until now, only with atomic statements and atomic sketch implications called* universal constraint. *In [18,21], the reader can find many examples of those sketch implications expressing properties like: any table should have exactly one primary key, a foreign key has to refer to a primary key, and many, many others. In Remark 28, we will relate the present DPF-terminology to the concepts introduced in this paper.* □

In the remaining part of the subsection, we demonstrate how to encode the validity of sketch implications by a semantics-independent, pure structural closedness property of the sketch encodings $\mathbb{S}^{\mathcal{U}} = (U, St^{\mathcal{U}})$ of Ξ-structures $\mathcal{U}$ as defined in (13).

For any context P any statement (X, Ex, β) in P and any interpretation $(\iota, \mathcal{U})$ of P in a Ξ-structure $\mathcal{U}$, we have $\text{Stm}(\iota)(X, Ex, \beta) = (X, Ex, \beta; \iota)$, due to (2), thus the satisfaction condition and the equivalences in (14) provide the following equivalence of statements:

$$(\iota,\mathcal{U}) \models_P (X, Ex, \beta) \quad \text{iff} \quad (id_U, \mathcal{U}) \models_U (X, Ex, \beta; \iota) \quad \text{iff} \quad \text{Stm}(\iota)(X, Ex, \beta) \in St^{\mathcal{U}} \quad (16)$$

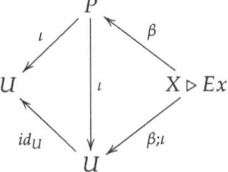

To be prepared for Section 6, we define the closedness property on the same level of abstraction as Definition 16 (Sketch) and Definition 20 (Sketch Arrow).

Definition 23 (Closedness). *Let us be given a category* Ct *and a functor* St : Ct → Set. *A* St-*sketch* $\mathbb{K} = (K, St^{\mathbb{K}})$ *is closed w.r.t. a* St- *sketch arrow* $\varphi : \mathbb{P} \to \mathbb{C}$ *relative to a strict*

St- *sketch arrow* $\iota : \mathbb{P} \to \mathbb{K}$ *if, and only if, there exists a strict* St*-sketch arrow* $\varrho : \mathbb{C} \to \mathbb{K}$ *such that* $\iota = \varphi ; \varrho$.

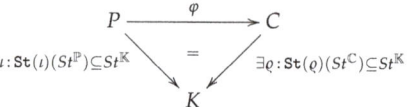

A St-*sketch* $\mathbb{K}$ *is* **closed w.r.t. a** St- ***sketch arrow*** $\varphi : \mathbb{P} \to \mathbb{C}$ *if, and only if, it is closed w.r.t.* $\varphi : \mathbb{P} \to \mathbb{C}$ *relative to each strict* St*-sketch arrow* $\iota : \mathbb{P} \to \mathbb{K}$.

We consider the case Ct = Cxt, St = Stm with $\mathcal{IS} = (\text{Cxt}, \text{Stm}, \text{Int}, \models)$ an Institution of Statements. From Definition 22, Definition 23 and Equation (16), we obtain immediately:

Proposition 3 (Validity $\cong$ Closedness). *For any* Stm*-sketch arrow* $\varphi : \mathbb{P} \to \mathbb{C}$, *the following two statements are equivalent for any* Ξ-*structure* $\mathcal{U}$:

1. *The corresponding* $\mathcal{IS}$-*implication* $\mathbb{P} \stackrel{\varphi}{\Rightarrow} \mathbb{C}$ *is valid in* $\mathcal{U}$, *i.e.*, $\mathcal{U} \models \mathbb{P} \stackrel{\varphi}{\Rightarrow} \mathbb{C}$.
2. *The* Stm-*sketch* $\mathbb{S}^{\mathcal{U}} = (U, St^{\mathcal{U}})$, *defined by* (13), *is closed w.r.t.* $\varphi : \mathbb{P} \to \mathbb{C}$.

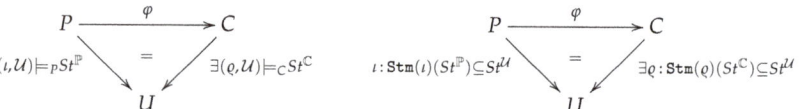

In case of arrows between atomic sketches, we can obviously replace $\mathbb{S}^{\mathcal{U}}$ by $\mathbb{S}^{\mathcal{U}}_{\Phi}$.

Corollary 2 (Validity $\cong$ Closedness). *For any* Stm*-sketch arrow* $\varphi : \mathbb{P} \to \mathbb{C}$ *with* $\mathbb{P}$ *and* $\mathbb{C}$ *atomic, the following two statements are equivalent for any* Ξ-*structure* $\mathcal{U}$:

1. *The corresponding* $\mathcal{IS}$-*implication* $\mathbb{P} \stackrel{\varphi}{\Rightarrow} \mathbb{C}$ *is valid in* $\mathcal{U}$, *i.e.*, $\mathcal{U} \models \mathbb{P} \stackrel{\varphi}{\Rightarrow} \mathbb{C}$.
2. *The atomic* Stm-*sketch* $\mathbb{S}^{\mathcal{U}}_{\Phi} = (U, St^{\mathcal{U}})$, *defined by Equation* (13), *is closed w.r.t.* $\varphi : \mathbb{P} \to \mathbb{C}$.

Remark 28 (DPF–Answer to Question 3). *In DPF, we worked, until now, only with atomic statements and we have not considered sketch arrows [18,21]. Having now the concept* sketch arrow *explicitly at hand, we can gain a better understanding of the present situation in DPF and are able to answer Question 3 (p. 7).*

The "specification morphisms" in DPF are strict sketch morphisms in the sense of Definition 19. "Specification entailments" in DPF are sketch implications in the sense of Definition 21 but only of the special kind $\mathbb{P} \stackrel{id_P}{\Rightarrow} \mathbb{C}$, i.e., we have, especially, $P = C$. The validity of specification entailments is defined analogously to the validity of sketch implications in Definition 22.

"Universal constraints" in DPF correspond to strict sketch arrows in the sense of Definition 20, and we defined the semantics of universal constraints in accordance with Definition 23. The crucial flaw is that we used, unfortunately and inadequately, the concept specification morphism *to define universal constraints and the closedness property. Effectively, we utilized only the pure structural "strict sketch arrow feature" of DPF specification morphisms for this purpose. However, because of the semantic denotation of the concept* specification morphism, *this was wrong and caused confusion.*

We touched upon the construction of strict sketch arrows $\varphi : \mathbb{P} \to \mathbb{C}^{\varphi}$, as discussed in Remark 24, but only in the skewed understanding that "each specification entailment gives rise to a universal constraint". Besides this, we have been aware and utilized the observation that "each universal constraint gives rise to a transformation rule" (compare Remarks 26 and 32).

5.2.4. Sketch Implications, Closed Formulas and Makkai's Generalized Sketches

A closer look at the definition of validity of sketch implications in Definition 22 and at the definition of the semantics of feature expressions in Definition 10 makes, straightforwardly, it apparent that the definition of the satisfaction relation in Definition 14 establishes an equivalence between finite sketch implications and universally quantified conditional existence statements (see also Remark 18).

Proposition 4 (Sketch Implications $\cong$ Closed Formulas). *For any Ξ-structure $\mathcal{U}$ and any closed expression $\mathbf{0} \triangleright \forall (X : Ex \to \exists(\varphi, Y : Ex'))$, the following two statements are equivalent:*

1. $\mathcal{U} \models (\mathbf{0}, \forall(X : Ex \to \exists(\varphi, Y : Ex')), id_0)$
2. $\mathcal{U} \models (X, \{(X, Ex, id_X)\}) \stackrel{\varphi}{\Longrightarrow} (Y, \{(Y, Ex', id_Y)\})$

In the case that Ex and Ex' are conjunctions, we can be even more specific.

Corollary 3 (Sketch Implications $\cong$ Closed Formulas). *For any Ξ-structure $\mathcal{U}$ and any closed expression $\mathbf{0} \triangleright \forall (X : Ex \to \exists(\varphi, Y : Ex'))$ with $Ex = Ex_1 \wedge \ldots \wedge Ex_n$ $1 \leq n$ and $Ex' = Ex'_1 \wedge \ldots \wedge Ex'_m$ $1 \leq m$, the following two statements are equivalent:*

1. $\mathcal{U} \models (\mathbf{0}, \forall(X : Ex \to \exists(\varphi, Y : Ex')), id_0)$
2. $\mathcal{U} \models (X, \{(X, Ex_1, id_X), \ldots, (X, Ex_n, id_X)\}) \stackrel{\varphi}{\Longrightarrow} (Y, \{(Y, Ex'_1, id_Y), \ldots, (X, Ex'_m, id_X)\})$

Finally, we can specialize the equivalence to conjunctions of atomic statements.

Corollary 4 (Sketch Implications $\cong$ Closed Formulas: Atomic-case). *For any Ξ-structure $\mathcal{U}$ and any closed expression $\mathbf{0} \triangleright \forall (X : Ex \to \exists(\varphi, Y : Ex'))$ with Ex a finite conjunction of atomic expressions $X \triangleright F_i(\beta_i), \beta_i : \alpha F_i \to X, 1 \leq i \leq n$ and Ex' a finite conjunction of atomic expressions $Y \triangleright F'_i(\beta'_i), \beta'_i : \alpha F'_i \to Y, 1 \leq i \leq m$, the following two statements are equivalent:*

1. $\mathcal{U} \models (\mathbf{0}, \forall(X : Ex \to \exists(\varphi, Y : Ex')), id_0)$
2. $\mathcal{U} \models (X, \{(\alpha F_i, F_i(id_{\alpha F_i}), \beta_i) \mid 1 \leq i \leq n\}) \stackrel{\varphi}{\Longrightarrow} (Y, \{(\alpha F'_i, F'_i(id_{\alpha F'_i}), \beta'_i) \mid 1 \leq i \leq m\})$

Now we are sufficiently prepared to give a reasonable answer to Question 4 (p. 39).

Remark 29 (Answer to Question 4). We discussed in Section 5.2.2 that the assignments $\mathcal{U} \mapsto \mathbb{S}^{\mathcal{U}}_{\Phi}$ establish an isomorphism between $\mathsf{Str}(\Xi)$ and the subcategory $\mathsf{atSk}(\mathsf{Stm})^a_s$ of $\mathsf{Sk}(\mathsf{Stm})^a$ given by all atomic Stm-sketches and all strict Stm-sketch arrows between them.

A sufficient condition to complete the abstraction from structures to atomic sketches is the existence of a set SEM of atomic (!) $\mathcal{IS}$-implications such that $\mathsf{Sem}(\Xi) = \mathsf{Str}(\Xi, SEM)$ (see Remark 27). The "purely structural characterization of exactly all those atomic Stm-sketches $\mathbb{S}^{\mathcal{U}}_{\Phi}$ in $\mathsf{atSk}(\mathsf{Stm})^a_s$ with $\mathcal{U}$ in $\mathsf{Sem}(\Xi)$", we have been asking for in Section 5.2.2, is then provided by Corollary 2 and is nothing but the closedness of an atomic Stm-sketch w.r.t. all the Stm-sketch arrows underlying the atomic $\mathcal{IS}$-implications in SEM.

If we are only interested in those subcategories $\mathsf{Sem}(\Xi, IMP) = \mathsf{Str}(\Xi, SEM \cup IMP)$ of $\mathsf{Sem}(\Xi)$ which can be axiomatized by a set IMP of atomic (!) $\mathcal{IS}$-implications, we can indeed completely forget about structures and can be content with the "universe of atomic sketches".

This is exactly Makkai's approach in [15]. He does not consider Ξ-structures at all. He relies, instead, on categories $\mathsf{atSk}(\mathsf{Stm})^a_s$ of atomic Stm-sketches and strict Stm-sketch arrows between them. He uses the term **sketch entailment** for those **strict sketch arrows** which are utilized for specification purposes. Note that the restriction to **strict sketch arrows** means that he works exclusively with sketch entailments of the form $\varphi : \mathbb{P} \to \mathbb{C}^{\varphi}$ (see Remark 24).

In the terminology of Institutions of Statements, Makkai's approach can be characterized by the choices $\mathsf{Base} = \mathsf{Var} = \mathsf{Cxt}$ and $\mathsf{Stm}(K) = \mathsf{At}(K)$ for all objects K in Cxt. In particular, he focuses on presheaf topoi, i.e., functor categories $\mathsf{Base} = [\mathsf{C} \to \mathsf{Set}]$, as base categories.

The structure of limit and colimit statements (see Remark 10) is strongly related to the structure of those closed formulas that can be equivalently described by atomic sketch implications (see Corollary 4). We guess that this is one of the underlying reasons that Makkai contents himself with atomic sketches and sketch arrows between them?

We should mention, however, that Makkai uses an additional mechanism to be able to reside in the "universe of atomic sketches". This mechanism (also known in Category Theory as the collage or the cograph of a distributor/profunctor) transforms atomic multi sketches for a presheaf topos Base $= [\mathbf{C} \to \mathsf{Set}]$ *and a certain footprint* $\Xi = (\Phi, \alpha)$ *on* Base *into plain contexts, i.e., into objects in another presheaf topos* Base'=Cxt'=$[\Phi\bar{\alpha}\mathbf{C} \to \mathsf{Set}]$ *with* $\Phi\bar{\alpha}\mathbf{C}$ *a category constructed out of* $\mathbf{C}$ *and* Ξ. *We explain and exemplify this construction in Remark* 41 *in Section* 6.

In cases where atomic sketch implications (and thus the corresponding universally quantified conditional existence statements *in Corollary* 3*) are not expressive enough to axiomatize the structures* $\mathcal{U}$*, we are interested in, and where we need more expressive first-order statements, to do the job, we can utilize the general first-order sketch constraints, introduced in Section* 6*, for a pure structural characterization of the respective atomic sketch encodings* $\mathbb{S}_\Phi^{\mathcal{U}}$ *(see Corollary* 7*).*

5.2.5. A Semantic Deduction Theorem

We consider semantic entailment between sketch implications.

Definition 24 (Entailment of Sketch Implications). *A set IMP of $\mathcal{IS}$-implications* **entails** *an $\mathcal{IS}$- implication* $\mathbb{P} \stackrel{\varphi}{\Rightarrow} \mathbb{C}$ **semantically**, $IMP \Vdash \mathbb{P} \stackrel{\varphi}{\Rightarrow} \mathbb{C}$ *in symbols, if, and only if, for all Ξ-structures $\mathcal{U}$ in* $\mathsf{Sem}(\Xi)$*, it holds that* $\mathcal{U} \models IMP$*, i.e.,* $\mathcal{U} \models \mathbb{K} \stackrel{\varphi}{\Rightarrow} \mathbb{G}$ *for all* $\mathbb{K} \stackrel{\varphi}{\Rightarrow} \mathbb{G}$ *in IMP, implies* $\mathcal{U} \models \mathbb{P} \stackrel{\varphi}{\Rightarrow} \mathbb{C}$.

Any Stm-sketch arrow $\varphi : \mathbb{P} \to \mathbb{C}$ can be factorized, i.e., can be obtained by composing the Stm-sketch arrows $\varphi : \mathbb{P} \to C^\varphi$ and $id_C : C^\varphi \to \mathbb{C}$, where $C^\varphi := (C, \mathtt{Stm}(\varphi)(St^\mathbb{P}))$.

Due to Definition 22, for any interpretation $(\iota, \mathcal{U})$ of context P in a Ξ-structure $\mathcal{U}$ the statement $(\iota, \mathcal{U}) \models \mathbb{P} \stackrel{\varphi}{\Rightarrow} C^\varphi$ means nothing but simply the existence of a morphism $\varrho : C \to U$ in Base such that $\varphi; \varrho = \iota$. That is, we have, especially, $IMP \Vdash \mathbb{P} \stackrel{\varphi}{\Rightarrow} C^\varphi$ if, and only if, $\varnothing \Vdash \mathbb{P} \stackrel{\varphi}{\Rightarrow} C^\varphi$ if, and only if, $\models \mathbb{P} \stackrel{\varphi}{\Rightarrow} C^\varphi$. Moreover, this allows for reformulating the validity of sketch implications.

Lemma 1 (Factorization of Sketch Implications). *For any set IMP of $\mathcal{IS}$-implications and any $\mathcal{IS}$-implication* $\mathbb{P} \stackrel{\varphi}{\Rightarrow} \mathbb{C}$, *the following two statements are equivalent:*

1. $IMP \Vdash \mathbb{P} \stackrel{\varphi}{\Rightarrow} \mathbb{C}$
2. $\varnothing \Vdash \mathbb{P} \stackrel{\varphi}{\Rightarrow} C^\varphi$ *and* $IMP \Vdash C^\varphi \Rightarrow \mathbb{C}$

Lemma 1 means, in practice, that we can restrict ourselves to $\mathcal{IS}$- implications of the form $\mathbb{K} \Rightarrow \mathbb{G}$ to specify (axiomatize) subcategories $\mathsf{Sem}(\Xi, IMP)$ of $\mathsf{Sem}(\Xi)$. By coincidence, we even have a semantic deduction theorem available for those special kinds of sketch implications.

Theorem 2 (Semantic Deduction Theorm). *For any set IMP of $\mathcal{IS}$-implications of the form $\mathbb{K} \Rightarrow \mathbb{G}$ and any $\mathcal{IS}$-implication* $\mathbb{P} \Rightarrow \mathbb{C}$*, the following two statements are equivalent:*

1. $IMP \Vdash \mathbb{P} \Rightarrow \mathbb{C}$
2. *For all Ξ-structures $\mathcal{U}$ in* $\mathsf{Sem}(\Xi)$ *and all interpretations $(\iota, \mathcal{U})$ of context $P = C$ in $\mathcal{U}$:* $\mathcal{U} \models IMP$ *and* $(\iota, \mathcal{U}) \models_P St^\mathbb{P}$ *implies* $(\iota, \mathcal{U}) \models_P St^\mathbb{C}$.

Theorem 2 guarantees that it is a reasonable idea to describe the deduction of sketch implications, which are semantically entailed by a given set IMP of sketch implications, by means of deduction calculi generating new sketches $(P, St^\mathbb{C})$ from a given sketch $(P, St^\mathbb{P})$ based on a utilization of the sketch implications in IMP as deduction rules. To deduce all (!) semantically entailed sketch implications, it may be necessary to also include deduction rules related to a set SEM of sketch implications representing the choice of Base, Ξ and $\mathsf{Sem}(\Xi)$, respectively (compare Remarks 27 and 29). This is exactly the approach in [6,7].

In [7], we also presented a deduction calculus which constructs directly sketch implications from a set of given sketch implications. Besides the composition of sketch implications, as mentioned in Remark 23, we could choose parallel composition and instantiation as the other basic constructions for such a deduction calculus:

- *Parallel composition:* $IMP \Vdash (P, St_1) \Rightarrow (P, St_1')$ and $IMP \Vdash (P, St_2) \Rightarrow (P, St_2')$ implies $IMP \Vdash (P, St_1 \cup St_2) \Rightarrow (P, St_1' \cup St_2')$
- *Instantiation:* For any context morphism $\mu : P \rightarrow R$: $IMP \Vdash (P, St) \Rightarrow (P, St')$ implies $IMP \Vdash (R, \mathtt{Stm}(\mu)(St)) \Rightarrow (R, \mathtt{Stm}(\mu)(St'))$.

Of course, we could also use, instead, more specialized and sophisticated constructions analogously to *resolution* in PROLOG or *parallel resolution* in [7], for example.

Remark 30 (Resolution in PROLOG). *In Example 45, we argued that Horn clauses in PROLOG should be rather considered as sketch implications than universally quantified implications.*

Concerning resolution, there is also a discrepancy between the theoretical justification and the actual effect of the resolution procedure in PROLOG. Resolution is explained as a special case of the general principle of "proof by refutation" [40]. Actually, PROLOG computes, however, (in a constructive way!) a Horn clause that is semantically entailed by the Horn clauses and the facts in the given PROLOG program (compare the Semantic Deduction Theorem 2).

5.3. Sketches of Equations

For an Institutions of Equations $\mathcal{IE} = (\mathsf{Cxt}_{EQ}, \mathsf{Eq}, \mathsf{Int}, \models)$ an Eq-sketch $\mathbb{E} = (X, E)$ is given by a context X in Cxt_{EQ}, i.e., an S-set X, and a set E of Σ-equations in X. A valid interpretation of $\mathbb{E} = (X, E)$ is an interpretation $(\iota, \mathcal{A})$ of context X in a Σ-algebra $\mathcal{A} = (A, \Omega^{\mathcal{A}})$ such that $(\iota, \mathcal{A}) \models_X E$, i.e., $(\iota, \mathcal{A}) \models_X (X, t_1 = t_2)$ for all Σ-equations $(X, t_1 = t_2)$ in E according to (9).

Based on these definitions, we can define $\mathcal{IE}$-morphisms, Eq-sketch arrows and $\mathcal{IE}$-implications, respectively, exactly in the same way as we have done it for Institutions of Statements $\mathcal{IS} = (\mathsf{Cxt}, \mathsf{Stm}, \mathsf{Int}, \models)$ in Sections 5.1 and 5.2. Moreover, we have, obviously, for Institutions of Equations also corresponding variants of Definition 22 (Validity of Sketch Implications), Definition 24 (Entailment of Sketch Implications), Lemma 1 (Factorization of Sketch Implications) and Theorem 2 (Semantic Deduction Theorem) available.

Abstract and Universal Algebra have been developed independent of First-Order Logic and conditional Σ-equations are usually not introduced as "universally quantified implications". They are rather described as $\mathcal{IE}$-implications $(Y, Prem) \Rightarrow (Y, Conc)$, in the sense of Definition 21 where $Prem$ represents the set of equations in the premise of a conditional Σ-equation and $Conc$ the single equation in the conclusion. In particular, the validity of conditional Σ-equations in Σ-algebras $\mathcal{A}$ is defined in perfect accordance with Definition 22 (Validity of Sketch Implications) (compare [6,7,41]). Therefore, we will also use the term **conditional Σ-equation** for $\mathcal{IE}$-implications $(Y, Prem) \Rightarrow (Y, Conc)$ with Y, $Prem$ finite and $Conc$ a singleton.

Finally, we reached the point where we can give an answer to Question 2 (p. 3): Yes, Theorem 2 is the general Semantic Deduction Theorem, we have been looking for and the equivalence, mentioned in the question, corresponds to the specialization of the general Semantic Deduction Theorem for conditional Σ-equations.

5.3.1. Freely Generated Algebras

The footprints in Institutions of Equations are algebraic signatures $\Sigma = (\Omega, in, out)$ and we have $\mathsf{Str}(\Sigma) = \mathsf{Sem}(\Sigma) := \mathsf{Alg}(\Sigma)$. Conditional Σ-equations are the traditional means to specify subcategories of $\mathsf{Alg}(\Sigma)$. Given a set CE of Conditional Σ-equations, we denote by $\mathsf{Alg}(\Sigma, CE)$ the subcategory of $\mathsf{Alg}(\Sigma)$ given by all those Σ-algebras $\mathcal{A}$ such that $\mathcal{A} \models CE$, i.e., $\mathcal{A} \models \mathbb{P} \Rightarrow \mathbb{C}$ (as defined in Definition 22) for all conditional Σ-equations $\mathbb{P} \Rightarrow \mathbb{C}$ in CE (compare Remark 27).

In case $\mathbb{P} = (Y, \emptyset)$, we may call $\mathbb{P} \Rightarrow \mathbb{C}$ a conditional Σ-equation with an empty premise. Note that there is a simply but crucial conceptual difference between a Σ-equation

$(Y, t_1 = t_2)$ and the corresponding conditional Σ-equation $(Y, \emptyset) \Rightarrow (Y, \{(Y, t_1 = t_2)\})$ with an empty premise. $(Y, t_1 = t_2)$ is just a simple *statement in context* Y while $(Y, \emptyset) \Rightarrow (Y, \{(Y, t_1 = t_2)\})$ is a tool to make statements about Σ-algebras. Being not aware of this difference is often a source of confusion!

First, We Consider Σ-Algebras Freely Generated in $\mathsf{Alg}(\Sigma)$

A Σ-algebra $\mathcal{F} = (F, \Omega^{\mathcal{F}})$ is freely generated by an Eq-sketch $\mathbb{G} = (X, R)$ if, and only if, there is a valid interpretation $(\eta_{\mathbb{G}}, \mathcal{F})$ of $\mathbb{G}$ in $\mathcal{F}$ that is universal relative to $\mathsf{Alg}(\Sigma)$. That is, for all Σ-algebras $\mathcal{A} = (A, \Omega^{\mathcal{A}})$ and all valid interpretations $(\iota, \mathcal{A})$ of $\mathbb{G}$ in $\mathcal{A}$ there exists a unique morphism $\iota^{\circ} : \mathcal{F} \to \mathcal{A}$ such that $\eta_{\mathbb{G}}; \iota^{\circ} = \iota$ in Base_{EQ}, i.e., such that ι° establishes an interpretation morphism $\iota^{\circ} : (\eta_{\mathbb{G}}, \mathcal{F}) \to (\iota, \mathcal{A})$ in $\mathsf{Int}(\mathbb{G}) \sqsubseteq \mathsf{Int}(X)$ (see Section 4.1).

$$\mathsf{Int}(\mathbb{G}) \quad X \xrightarrow{(\eta_{\mathbb{G}}, \mathcal{F}) \models_X R} F \qquad \mathcal{F} = (F, \Omega^{\mathcal{F}}) \qquad \mathsf{Alg}(\Sigma)$$

with morphisms $(\iota, \mathcal{A}) \models_X R$ down to A, ι°, and $\mathcal{A} = (A, \Omega^{\mathcal{A}})$.

The universal property of $(\eta_{\mathbb{G}}, \mathcal{F})$ entails that $(\eta_{\mathbb{G}}, \mathcal{F})$ is initial in $\mathsf{Int}(\mathbb{G})$, thus the projection functor $\Pi_{\mathbb{G}} : \mathsf{Int}(\mathbb{G}) \to \mathsf{Alg}(\Sigma)$ establishes a functor from $\mathsf{Int}(\mathbb{G})$ into the co-slice category $\mathcal{F}/\mathsf{Alg}(\Sigma)$.

In contrast to Institutions of Statements, we have for arbitrary (!) Eq-sketches $\mathbb{G} = (X, R)$ (and not only for atomic Eq-sketches) that the definition of homomorphisms between Σ-algebras ensures $(\eta_{\mathbb{G}}; \varrho, \mathcal{A}) \models_X R$ for any homomorphism $\varrho : \mathcal{F} \to \mathcal{A}$ in $\mathsf{Alg}(\Sigma)$ thus the assignments $(\varrho : \mathcal{F} \to \mathcal{A}) \mapsto (\eta_{\mathbb{G}}; \varrho, \mathcal{A})$ establish a functor from $\mathcal{F}/\mathsf{Alg}(\Sigma)$ into $\mathsf{Int}(\mathbb{G})$. Due to the universal property of $(\eta_{\mathbb{G}}, \mathcal{F})$, we obtain $(\eta_{\mathbb{G}}; \varrho)^{\circ} = \varrho$. Together with the equation $\eta_{\mathbb{G}}; \iota^{\circ} = \iota$, this ensures that the two functors establish an isomorphism between $\mathsf{Int}(\mathbb{G})$ and $\mathcal{F}/\mathsf{Alg}(\Sigma)$ (compare Proposition 4.10 in [2]). This justifies that we can call the pair $(\mathbb{G}, \eta_{\mathbb{G}}) = ((X, R), \eta_{\mathbb{G}})$ a sketch representation of $\mathcal{F}$.

For arbitrary Eq-sketches $\mathbb{G} = (X, R)$, a Σ-algebra $\mathcal{F}$, freely generated by $\mathbb{G}$, exists and is uniquely determined "up to isomorphism". In the introductory Subsection 1.1.1, we used the notation $\mathcal{F}(\Sigma, \emptyset, X, R)$ to denote those freely generated Σ-algebras.

The Σ-algebra, freely generated by $(X, \emptyset)$ is nothing but the Σ-term algebra $\mathcal{T}_{\Sigma}(X) = \mathcal{F}(\Sigma, \emptyset, X, \emptyset)$ on X and the unique morphism $\iota^{\circ} : \mathcal{T}_{\Sigma}(X) \to \mathcal{A}$ is simply the evaluation of terms (see Equation (8)). In general, $\mathcal{F}(\Sigma, \emptyset, X, R)$ can be constructed as a quotient of $\mathcal{T}_{\Sigma}(X)$.

Second, We Consider Σ-Algebras Freely Generated Relative to a Subcategory $\mathsf{Alg}(\Sigma, CE)$

Let CE be a set of conditional Σ-equations. A Σ-algebra $\mathcal{F} = (F, \Omega^{\mathcal{F}})$ is freely generated in $\mathsf{Alg}(\Sigma, CE)$ by an Eq-sketch $\mathbb{G} = (X, R)$ if, and only if, $\mathcal{F} \models CE$, and there is a valid interpretation $(\eta_{\mathbb{G}}, \mathcal{F})$ of $\mathbb{G}$ in $\mathcal{F}$ that is universal relative to $\mathsf{Alg}(\Sigma, CE)$. That is, for all Σ-algebras $\mathcal{A} = (A, \Omega^{\mathcal{A}})$ in $\mathsf{Alg}(\Sigma, CE)$ and all valid interpretations $(\iota, \mathcal{A})$ of $\mathbb{G}$ in $\mathcal{A}$ there exists a unique morphism $\iota^{\circ} : \mathcal{F} \to \mathcal{A}$ such that $\eta_{\mathbb{G}}; \iota^{\circ} = \iota$ in Base_{EQ}, i.e., such that ι° establishes an interpretation morphism $\iota^{\circ} : (\eta_{\mathbb{G}}, \mathcal{F}) \to (\iota, \mathcal{A})$ in $\mathsf{Int}(\mathbb{G}) \sqsubseteq \mathsf{Int}(X)$.

$$\mathsf{Int}(\mathbb{G}) \downarrow \mathsf{Alg}(\Sigma, CE) \quad X \xrightarrow{(\eta_{\mathbb{G}}, \mathcal{F}) \models_X R} F \qquad \mathcal{F} = (F, \Omega^{\mathcal{F}}) \qquad \mathsf{Alg}(\Sigma, CE)$$

with $(\iota, \mathcal{A}) \models_X R$ down to A, ι°, and $\mathcal{A} = (A, \Omega^{\mathcal{A}})$.

In this case, the universal property of $(\eta_{\mathbb{G}}, \mathcal{F})$ entails that $(\eta_{\mathbb{G}}, \mathcal{F})$ is initial in the subcategory $\mathsf{Int}(\mathbb{G}) \downarrow \mathsf{Alg}(\Sigma, CE) = \Pi_{\mathbb{G}}^{-1}(\mathsf{Alg}(\Sigma, CE))$ of $\mathsf{Int}(\mathbb{G})$ given by all valid interpretations of $\mathbb{G}$ in Σ-algebras in $\mathsf{Alg}(\Sigma, CE)$. Moreover, we obtain an isomorphism between $\mathsf{Int}(\mathbb{G}) \downarrow \mathsf{Alg}(\Sigma, CE)$ and the co-slice category $\mathcal{F}/\mathsf{Alg}(\Sigma, CE)$.

For arbitrary sets CE of conditional Σ-equations and arbitrary Eq-sketches $\mathbb{G} = (X, R)$, a Σ-algebra $\mathcal{F}$, freely generated by $\mathbb{G}$ in $\mathsf{Alg}(\Sigma, CE)$, exists and is uniquely determined "up to isomorphism". In the introductory Section 1.1.1, we used the notation $\mathcal{F}(\Sigma, CE, X, R)$ to denote those freely generated Σ-algebras. $\mathcal{F}(\Sigma, CE, X, R)$ can be constructed as a quotient of $\mathcal{T}_\Sigma(X)$.

In case of groups, CE is a set of conditional Σ-equations with an empty premise, representing the group axioms, and $\mathcal{F}(\Sigma, CE, X, R)$ is called the group freely generated by the set of generators X and the set R of defining relations.

5.3.2. Elementary Diagrams for Algebras

For Institutions of Equations, we have chosen $\mathsf{Cxt}_{EQ} = \mathsf{Carr}_{EQ} = \mathsf{Base}_{EQ} = \mathsf{Set}^S$. An atomic Σ-equation in a context K is a Σ-equation of the form:

$$(K, \omega\langle k_1, \ldots, k_n\rangle = k) \quad \text{with } \omega \in \Omega, \ k_i \in K_{s_i}, 1 \leq i \leq n \text{ and } k \in K_{out(\omega)} \tag{17}$$

where $[x_1\!:\!s_1, x_2\!:\!s_2, \ldots, x_n\!:\!s_n]$ is the assumed representation of $in(\omega)$ as a list of variable declarations (see Section 4.2). Note that the usual encoding of n-ary operations by (n + 1)-ary predicates establishes a one-to-one correlation between the corresponding atomic equations and atomic statements, respectively.

By $\mathtt{At}(K)$, we denote the subset of $\mathtt{Eq}(K)$ of all atomic Σ-equation in a context K. The assignments $K \mapsto \mathtt{At}(K)$ extend to a functor $\mathtt{At} : \mathsf{Cxt}_{EQ} \to \mathsf{Set}$.

In full analogy to Institutions of Statements, there are two canonical ways to transform a Σ-algebra $\mathcal{A} = (A, \Omega^\mathcal{A})$ into an Eq-sketch. The atomic variant $\mathbb{E}_\Omega^\mathcal{A} = (A, Eq_\Omega^\mathcal{A})$ encodes only the semantics of the operations in $\Omega^\mathcal{A}$:

$$Eq_\Omega^\mathcal{A} := \{(A, \omega\langle a_1, \ldots, a_n\rangle = \omega^\mathcal{A}(a_1, \ldots, a_n)) \mid \omega \in \Omega, a_i \in A_{s_i}, 1 \leq i \leq n\} \tag{18}$$

The full variant $\mathbb{E}^\mathcal{A} = (A, Eq^\mathcal{A})$ encodes the semantics of all terms (derived operations):

$$Eq^\mathcal{A} := \{(A, t_1 = t_2) \mid t_1, t_2 \in T_\Sigma(A)_s, s \in S, t_1^\mathcal{A}(id_A) = t_2^\mathcal{A}(id_A)\} \subseteq \mathtt{Eq}(A). \tag{19}$$

We have obviously $Eq_\Omega^\mathcal{A} \subset Eq^\mathcal{A}$ and $(id_A, \mathcal{A})$ is a valid interpretation of $\mathbb{E}_\Omega^\mathcal{A}$ as well as of $\mathbb{E}^\mathcal{A}$. Any Σ-algebra $\mathcal{A} = (A, \Omega^\mathcal{A})$ is freely generated by the Eq-sketch $\mathbb{E}_\Omega^\mathcal{A} = (A, Eq_\Omega^\mathcal{A})$ as well as by the Eq-sketch $\mathbb{E}^\mathcal{A} = (A, Eq^\mathcal{A})$ with the universal interpretation $(id_A, \mathcal{A})$. That is, $(\mathbb{E}_\Omega^\mathcal{A}, id_A)$ as $(\mathbb{E}^\mathcal{A}, id_A)$ are sketch representations of $\mathcal{A}$ in the sense of the last subsection.

Conditional Σ-equations are not atomic; thus, we have to rely on the full encodings of Σ-algebras to have a chance to express the validity of conditional Σ-equations by a closedness property analogously to Proposition 3.

Fortunately, the assignments $\mathcal{A} \mapsto \mathbb{E}^\mathcal{A}$ define an embedding of $\mathsf{Alg}(\Sigma)$ into the category $\mathsf{Sk}(\mathtt{Eq})^a$ of all Eq-sketches and all Eq-*sketch arrows* transforming each homomorphism between Σ-algebras into a strict Eq-sketch arrow.

5.3.3. Generalized Sketch Arrows and Sketch Implications

To be able to formulate a characterization of the validity of conditional Σ-equations by means of a closedness property, in the sense of Proposition 3, we have to consider more general sketch arrows based on the substitution of variables by terms. First, we extend the category Cxt_{EQ} by Kleisli morphisms.

Definition 25 (Generalized Context Morphisms). *We consider an Institution of Equations $\mathcal{IE} = (\mathsf{Cxt}_{EQ}, \mathtt{Eq}, \mathtt{Int}, \models)$ and a signature $\Sigma = (\Omega, in, out)$. A Σ-* **context morphism** *$\varphi : K \to G$ is given by an S-map $\varphi : K \to T_\Sigma(G)$. The composition $\varphi; \psi : K \to H$ of two Σ-context morphisms $\varphi : K \to G, \psi : G \to H$ is given by the S-map $\varphi; \psi^* : K \to T_\Sigma(H)$ where $\psi^* : T_\Sigma(G) \to T_\Sigma(H)$ is the usual translation of Σ-terms induced by the* **substitution** *$\psi : G \to T_\Sigma(H)$. Cxt_{EQ}^Σ denotes the category of all contexts and all Σ-context morphisms.*

By construction, Cxt_{EQ} is a subcategory of Cxt_{EQ}^{Σ} for any signature Σ. Second, the sentence functor $\text{Eq}: \text{Cxt}_{EQ} \to \text{Set}$ extends to a functor $\text{Eq}^{\Sigma}: \text{Cxt}_{EQ}^{\Sigma} \to \text{Set}$ with:

$$\text{Eq}^{\Sigma}(\varphi)(K, t_1 = t_2) := (G, \varphi^*(t_1) = \varphi^*(t_2)) \tag{20}$$

for all Σ-context morphisms $\varphi: K \to G$, i.e., for all S-maps $\varphi: K \to T_{\Sigma}(G)$, and all Σ-equations $(K, t_1 = t_2)$ in K. Since $id_K^* = id_{T_{\Sigma}(K)}$ and $(\varphi; \psi^*)^* = \varphi^*; \psi^*$ for all S-maps $\varphi: K \to T_{\Sigma}(G), \psi: G \to T_{\Sigma}(H)$, this defines indeed a functor.

Remark 31 (Generalized Sketch Implications). *We will use, implicitly, strict Eq^{Σ}-sketch arrows to formulate a characterization of the validity of conditional Σ-equations by means of a closedness property in the sense of Proposition 3.*

Besides this, it is very tempting to consider also "generalized sketch implications", defined by Eq^{Σ}-sketch arrows, and to study validity, entailment and factorization for those generalized sketch implications. In particular, it would be interesting to clarify the relation between those generalized sketch implications and the morphisms in the Lawvere theories for partial algebraic specifications we studied in [9].

For now, we overcome this temptation and postpone the study of generalized sketch implications to a following paper. We will concentrate on conditional Σ-equations and corresponding constructions and results.

*Before this, we would like to add a short side note: Σ-terms appear on an "internal level" as constituents of Σ-equations and on an "external level" as constituents of generalized context morphisms. Our ongoing studies around **graph algebras** indicate that we will probably need closely related, but different, concepts for these distinct levels if we want to generalize the idea of operations to graphs (and other kinds of presheaves).* □

To avoid headaches, we formulate explicitly the respective instance of Definition 23 for conditional Σ-equations (compare [7]).

Definition 26 (Closedness for Conditional Equations). *An Eq-sketch $\mathbb{E} = (X, E)$ is **closed** w.r.t. the underlying Eq-sketch arrow $(Y, \text{Prem}) \to (Y, \text{Conc})$ of a conditional Σ-equation $(Y, \text{Prem}) \Rightarrow (Y, \text{Conc})$ if, and only if, for all Σ-context morphisms $\iota: Y \to X$, i.e., all substitutions $\iota: Y \to T_{\Sigma}(X)$, it holds that $\iota^*(\text{Prem}) \subseteq E$ implies $\iota^*(\text{Conc}) \subseteq E$.*

In addition, here is the respective specialized instance of Proposition 3.

Corollary 5 (Validity $\cong$ Closedness for Conditional Equations). *For any Eq-sketch arrow $(Y, \text{Prem}) \to (Y, \text{Conc})$, the following two statements are equivalent for any Σ-algebra $\mathcal{A}$:*

1. *The corresponding conditional Σ-equation $(Y, \text{Prem}) \Rightarrow (Y, \text{Conc})$ is valid in $\mathcal{A}$, i.e., $\mathcal{A} \models (Y, \text{Prem}) \Rightarrow (Y, \text{Conc})$.*
2. *The Eq-sketch $\mathbb{E}^{\mathcal{A}} = (A, \text{Eq}^{\mathcal{A}})$, defined by Equation (19), is closed w.r.t. the Eq-sketch arrow $(Y, \text{Prem}) \to (Y, \text{Conc})$ according to Definition 26.*

Remark 32 (Sketch Arrows as Deduction Rules). *The most natural thing to do, if a structure is not closed w.r.t. a certain construction, is to repair this flaw by simply adding the missing parts. Applying this universal "repairing principle" to the closedness property in Definition 26, means nothing but to add new Σ-equations to a given set of Σ-equations by deploying Eq-sketch arrows as deduction rules.*

*To apply an Eq-sketch arrow $(Y, \text{Prem}) \to (Y, \text{Conc})$ as a deduction rule, we have, first, to find a **match** of the left-hand side (Y, Prem) of the rule in an Eq-sketch $\mathbb{E} = (X, E)$, i.e., a substitution $\iota: Y \to T_{\Sigma}(X)$ such that $\iota^*(\text{Prem}) \subseteq E$. Second, we apply the rule for this match and generate the Eq-sketch $(X, E \cup \iota^*(\text{Conc}))$. The resulting commutative square becomes a pushout in the category of all strict Eq^{Σ}-sketch arrows if $E \cap \iota^*(\text{Conc} \setminus \text{Prem}) = \emptyset$.*

$$\begin{array}{ccc} (Y, Prem) & \xrightarrow{id_Y} & (Y, Conc) \\ \iota \downarrow & = & \downarrow \tau^* \\ (X, E) & \xrightarrow{id_X} & (X, E \cup \iota^*(Conc)) \end{array}$$

Remark 33 (Answer to Question 1). *Based on the concepts* sketch, sketch implication, sketch arrow *and the related general definitions and results, we presented so far, we can give a kind of reasonable answer to Question 1 (p.3):*

Each sketch implication has an underlying sketch arrow and, the other way around, each sketch arrow gives rise to a sketch implication. Due to Proposition 3 (Validity ≅ Closedness), the validity of sketch implications in semantic structures can be, moreover, equivalently expressed by a closedness property of sketch encodings of semantic structures w.r.t. sketch arrows.

Each sketch arrow of the form $\mathbb{P} \to \mathbb{C}$ can be utilized as a rule allowing us to deduce new sketches from given sketches (as exemplified in Remark 32). Proposition 3 and Theorem 2 (Semantic Deduction Theorem) ensure that those deductions are sound and that they allow us, moreover, to deduce sketch implications semantically entailed by a given set of sketch implications.

6. Sketch Conditions and Constraints

In the preceding sections, we identified two main motivations to develop concepts and tools, deploying the expressiveness of first-order logic, to describe and reason about the structure of sketches. First, there is the need for those tools to specify the syntactic structure of software models. The second, more general, motivation concerns the structure of sketch encodings of semantic structures. If we use first-order tools to axiomatize the semantic structures we are interested in, it would be good to have corresponding first-order tools to axiomatize and reason about the sketch encodings of those semantic structures.

Software models are usually graph-based structures, thus we should not ignore the concepts and tools, developed in the area of Graph Transformations, to describe and axiomatize the structure of graphs. Therefore, we discuss in this section also four representative first-order based approaches to describe and axiomatize the structure of (different kinds of) graphs [22–25]. We will present a universal and fully first-order mechanism to describe the structure of sketches which unifies and generalizes all these approaches.

6.1. Abstract Sketches

In this section, we consider sketches independent of Institutions of Statements or Institutions of Equations, respectively. That is, we rely on Definition 16 (Sketch) and assume a category Ct of contexts and a functor $\mathrm{St} \colon \mathrm{Ct} \to \mathrm{Set}$ assigning to each $K \in \mathrm{Ct}_{Obj}$ a set $\mathrm{St}(K)$ of all statements in context K. An St-sketch $\mathbb{K} = (K, St^{\mathbb{K}})$ is given by a context K in Ct and a set $St^{\mathbb{K}} \subseteq \mathrm{St}(K)$ of statements in context K. For any statement $st \in \mathrm{St}(K)$, we will denote the image $\mathrm{St}(\varphi)(st) \in \mathrm{St}(G)$ also simply by $\varphi(st)$.

Guided by Definition 23 (Closedness) and Proposition 3 (Validity ≅ Closedness), we focus on the category Sk_s^a of all strict St-sketch arrows according to Definition 20 (Sketch Arrow). Generalizing the constructions and results in [19], one can prove that Sk_s^a has pushouts and pullbacks as long as Ct does.

Proposition 5 (Pushouts). *Let* $\mathbb{B} \xleftarrow{\mu} \mathbb{C} \xrightarrow{\varrho} \mathbb{A}$ *be a span of strict St-sketch morphisms. If there exists a pushout* $B \xrightarrow{\varrho^*} D \xleftarrow{\mu^*} A$ *of the span* $B \xleftarrow{\mu} C \xrightarrow{\varrho} A$ *of morphisms in* Ct, *then the diagram, below on the left, is a **pushout** in* Sk_s^a, *where:*

$$\mathbb{D} := (D, \mu^*(St^{\mathbb{A}}) \cup \varrho^*(St^{\mathbb{B}})) \tag{21}$$

$$\begin{array}{ccc} \mathbb{C} & \xrightarrow{\varrho} & \mathbb{A} \\ \mu \downarrow & PO & \downarrow \mu^* \\ \mathbb{B} & \xrightarrow{\varrho^*} & \mathbb{D} \end{array} \qquad \begin{array}{ccc} D & \xrightarrow{\mu^*} & A \\ \varrho^* \uparrow & PB & \uparrow \varrho \\ B & \xrightarrow{\mu} & C \end{array}$$

Proposition 6 (Pullbacks). *Let* $\mathbb{B} \xrightarrow{\mu} \mathbb{C} \xleftarrow{\varrho} \mathbb{A}$ *be a cospan of strict* St*-sketch morphisms. If there exists a pullback* $B \xleftarrow{\varrho^*} D \xrightarrow{\mu^*} A$ *of the cospan* $B \xrightarrow{\mu} C \xleftarrow{\varrho} A$ *of morphisms in* Ct, *then the diagram, above on the right, is a **pullback** in* Sk_s^a *where:*

$$\mathbb{D} := (D, \{st \in \mathsf{St}(D) \mid \mu^*(st) \in St^{\mathbb{A}}, \varrho^*(st) \in St^{\mathbb{B}}\}) \tag{22}$$

Remark 34 (Adhesiveness). *The concept of* **Adhesive Category** *has been introduced by Lack and Sobociński [42] and is based on the so-called Van-Kampen squares (see [14,20,43]). Adhesive categories are intensively used to present, systematize and generalize concepts, constructions and results in the area of Graph transformations [14]; thus, it seems to be worth including this remark.*

The category Sk_s^a *will be, in general, not adhesive, even if* Ct *is adhesive, since* $St^{\mathbb{D}}$ *in Proposition 5 is not constructed by a pushout in* Set *and in Proposition 6 not by a pullback in* Set *either.*

*To repair this deficiency, we can work with "multi sketches" where statements do have their own identity. A **multi** St-* ***sketch*** $\mathbb{K} = (K, I^{\mathbb{K}}, st^{\mathbb{K}})$ *is given by a context* K, *a set* $I^{\mathbb{K}}$ *of identifiers and a map* $st^{\mathbb{K}} : I^{\mathbb{K}} \to \mathsf{St}(K)$. *A **strict arrow*** $(\varphi, f) : \mathbb{K} \to \mathbb{G}$ *between two multi* St*-sketches* $\mathbb{K}$ *and* $\mathbb{G}$ *is given by a morphism* $\varphi : K \to G$ *in* Ct *and a map* $f : I^{\mathbb{K}} \to I^{\mathbb{G}}$ *such that* $\varphi(st^{\mathbb{K}}(i)) = st^{\mathbb{G}}(f(i))$ *for all* $i \in I^{\mathbb{K}}$. *Pushouts in the category* mSk_s^a *of multi* St*-sketches and strict arrows can always be constructed by componentwise pushouts of contexts in* Ct *and of sets of identifiers in* Set, *respectively. To ensure that componentwise pullbacks in* Ct *and* Set, *respectively, give us a pullback in* mSk_s^a, *we have to assume, however, that the functor* St: Ct $\to$ Set *preserves pullbacks.*

This is the case for the sentence functor Stm: $\mathsf{Cxt} \to$ Set *in any Institution of Statements as well as the sentence functor* Eq : $\mathsf{Cxt}_{EQ} \to$ Set *in any Institution of Equations.*

If St *preserves pullbacks, the monomorphisms in* mSk_s^a *are exactly the componentwise monomorphisms and* mSk_s^a *becomes adhesive if* Ct *is adhesive. Note that any topos is adhesive [44], thus especially the categories* $\mathsf{Cxt}_{EQ} = \mathsf{Set}^S$ *in Institutions of Equations are adhesive.*

Example 49 (Category Theory: Sketches (modified)). *For didactic reasons, we need for this section an example of an atomic sketch. We modify therefore the Category Theory example: We add to* Ξ_{CT} *in Example 14 the feature symbols* mon *with arity* $xv_1 \xrightarrow{xe} xv_2$ *and* fnl *with arity* xv. *Correspondingly, we vary the sample* Stm_{CT}*-sketch* $\mathbb{G} = (G, St^{\mathbb{G}})$ *in Example 39 by dropping the statement* $(xv, fnl, (xv \mapsto 3))$ *and replacing the statements* $(xv_1 \xrightarrow{xe} xv_2, mon, (xe \mapsto b))$, $(xv_1 \xrightarrow{xe} xv_2, mon, (xe \mapsto g))$ *by corresponding atomic statements* $\mathtt{mon}(b)$ *and* $\mathtt{mon}(g)$, *respectively.*

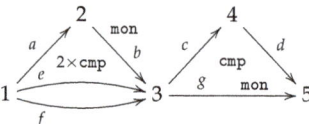

Example 50 (GraTra: Sketches). *Traditionally, there is no explicit use of "statements" in the area of Graph Transformations; thus sketches, in our sense, are just plain contexts where different kinds of graphs are chosen as contexts in the different approaches.*

In [23], Cxt *is a category of directed, labeled multi graphs and Ref. [24] restricts* Cxt *to a category of finite directed, labeled multi graphs. In contrast, Ref. [22] works with directed, labeled simple graphs in the sense that parallel edges with the same label are not allowed. Ref. [25] uses as* Cxt *a category* Graph_{TG} *of directed, labeled multi graphs typed over a graph TG.*

To a certain extent, we can, however, interpret the transition from graphs to labeled/typed graphs as the utilization of rudimentary forms of "statements", in our sense, where the choice of label alphabets or type graphs TG, respectively, corresponds to the choice of footprints. The encoding of binary relations by means of labeled edges in [22] makes this analogy apparent. In view of Institutions of Statements, we can reconstruct the concept of graph in [22] in the following way: Cxt *is the subcategory of* Set *given by all subsets of a "countable universe of nodes* Node*"* and Var $\sqsubset$ Cxt has a two-element set $\{x_1, x_2\} \subset$ Node as its only object. The footprint Ξ_R is given by a "countable universe Rel" of predicate symbols with $\alpha(P) = \{x_1, x_2\}$ for all $P \in$ Rel. An atomic Ξ_R-statement $P(\beta)$ in context $K \subseteq$ Node is, in such a way, given by a $P \in$ Rel and a binding $\beta : \{x_1, x_2\} \to K$ (see Remark 14 (Atomic Statements)). Relying on the isomorphism between the Cartesian product $K \times K$ and the set $K^{\{x_1,x_2\}}$ of maps, it is easy to check that the category Graph in [22] is isomorphic to the non-adhesive (!) category of all Ξ_R-sketches and all strict sketch arrows.

6.2. First-Order Sketch Conditions and Constraints

Generalizing different variants of graph conditions [14,22–25] as well as universal conditions and negative universal conditions in DPF [18,21], we define general first-order sketch conditions, which are redundant in the sense that we introduce, for example, as well existential as universal quantification and as well a symbol T for "true" as the the empty conjunction $\bigwedge \varnothing$. We define fully fledged first-order conditions and do not restrict ourselves to the traditional approach in Graph Transformations to define tree-like first-order conditions only (even if we see the practical relevance of those tree-like conditions). We define first-order sketch conditions in full analogy to the Definition 8 of first-order feature expressions. We underline, however, that feature expressions are "finitary syntactic entities" while sketch conditions have rather the flavor of sets of structural requirements!

Definition 27 (Sketch conditions: Syntax). *For a category* Ct *and a functor* St: Ct $\to$ Set, *we define inductively and in parallel a family* ST(K) *of sets of **first-order** St-* ***sketch conditions in context*** K, $c \in$ ST(K) *or* $K \blacktriangleright c$ *in symbols, where K varies over all objects in* Ct:

1. Statements: St(K) $\subset$ ST(K) for any context K.
2. True: $K \blacktriangleright T$ for any context K.
3. False: $K \blacktriangleright F$ for any context K.
4. Conjunction: $K \blacktriangleright \bigwedge C$ for any set $C \subset$ ST(K) of conditions in K.
5. Disjunction: $K \blacktriangleright \bigvee C$ for any set $C \subset$ ST(K) of conditions in K.
6. Implication: $K \blacktriangleright (c_1 \to c_2)$ for any conditions $K \blacktriangleright c_1$ and $K \blacktriangleright c_2$.
7. Negation: $K \blacktriangleright \neg c$ for any condition $K \blacktriangleright c$.
8. Quantification: $K \blacktriangleright \exists(\varphi, M : c)$ and $K \blacktriangleright \forall(\varphi, M : c)$ for any condition $M \blacktriangleright c$ and any morphism $\varphi : K \to M$ in Ct that is not an isomorphism.

Remark 35 (Sketch conditions: Syntax). *Non-monic morphisms* $\varphi : K \to M$ *are also used in [22–24] to express identifications.*

For sketch conditions, we apply the same notational conventions as described in Remark 6 for feature expressions.

If **0** *is an initial object in* Ct, *we call* **0** $\blacktriangleright c$ *a* ***closed*** St- ***sketch condition***.

Remark 36 (GraTra: Conditions). *If we drop in Definition 27 the "Implication" rule, we would obtain tree-like conditions analogously to the conditions in [23–25], where the tree structure is established by the context morphisms in the "Quantification" rule and the choice of the sets C in the "Conjunction" and/or "Disjunction" rule, respectively.*

To cover also the tree-like conditions in [22], we have, in addition, to replace the "Quantification" rule by a rule like:

Guarded quantification: $K \blacktriangleright (c_1 \to Q(\varphi, M : c_2))$ for $Q \in \{\exists, \forall\}$, any quantifier free condition $K \blacktriangleright c_1$, any condition $M \blacktriangleright c_2$ and any morphism $\varphi : K \to M$ in Ct.

Those tree-like conditions can be seen as a generalizing modification of the Q(*uantifier*)-*trees of the* language of diagrams *in [28].*

In [23,25], only existential quantification $\exists(\varphi, M : c)$ is used and $\forall(\varphi, M : c)$ is encoded by $\neg\exists(\varphi, M : \neg c)$. In [24], the symbols "$\exists$" and "$\forall$" are used in a bit unconventional, but consistent, way: In view of Definition 27, the symbol "$\exists$" in [24] combines "disjunction and existential quantification" while "$\forall$" combines conjunction and universal quantification. The conditions in [24] correspond to sketch conditions that can be generated by a single rule like:

$$\bigvee\{\exists(\varphi_i, M_i : c_i) \mid i \in I\}, \bigwedge\{\forall(\varphi_i, M_i : c_i) \mid i \in I\} \in \mathrm{ST}(K)$$

for any family $\{\varphi_i : K \to M_i \mid i \in I\}$ *of context morphisms and any conditions* $c_i \in \mathrm{ST}(M_i)$, $i \in I$. **T** *is encoded in [24] by the empty conjunction* $\bigwedge \emptyset$ *and* **F** *by the empty disjunction* $\bigvee \emptyset$, *respectively*.

Generalizing the traditional approaches [14,22–25] to define a satisfaction relation between graph morphisms and graph conditions, we can define a satisfaction relation between context morphisms and sketch conditions.

More precisely, we consider interpretations $(\tau : K \to G, \mathbb{G})$ of contexts K in St-sketches $\mathbb{G} = (G, St^\mathbb{G})$ and define valid interpretations of St-sketch conditions in K.

Definition 28 (Sketch conditions: Satisfaction). *We define inductively and in parallel a family* $\models_K$ *of satisfaction relations between interpretations* $(\tau, \mathbb{G})$ *of contexts* K *in* St-*sketches* $\mathbb{G} = (G, St^\mathbb{G})$ *and* St-*sketch conditions* $c \in \mathrm{ST}(K)$ *on* K:

1. *Statement:* For all $st \in \mathrm{St}(K) \subset \mathrm{ST}(K)$: $(\tau, \mathbb{G}) \models_K st$ iff $\mathrm{St}(\tau)(st) \in St^\mathbb{G}$.
2. *True:* $(\tau, \mathbb{G}) \models_K \mathbf{T}$
3. *False:* $(\tau, \mathbb{G}) \not\models_K \mathbf{F}$
4. *Conjunction:* $(\tau, \mathbb{G}) \models_K \bigwedge C$ iff $(\tau, \mathbb{G}) \models_K c$ *for every* $c \in C$.
5. *Disjunction:* $(\tau, \mathbb{G}) \models_K \bigvee C$ iff $(\tau, \mathbb{G}) \models_K c$ *for some* $c \in C$.
6. *Implication:* $(\tau, \mathbb{G}) \models_K (c_1 \to c_2)$ iff $(\tau, \mathbb{G}) \models_K c_1$ *implies* $(\tau, \mathbb{G}) \models_K c_2$
7. *Negation:* $(\tau, \mathbb{G}) \models_K \neg c$ iff $(\tau, \mathbb{G}) \not\models_K c$.
8. *Existential quantification:* $(\tau, \mathbb{G}) \models_K \exists(\varphi, M : c)$ iff *there exists a* $\varrho : Y \to G$ *with* $\varphi; \varrho = \tau$ *and* $(\varrho, \mathbb{G}) \models_M c$

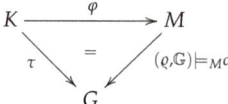

Universal quantification: $(\tau, \mathbb{G}) \models_K \forall(\varphi, M : c)$ iff *for all* $\varrho : Y \to G$ *with* $\varphi; \varrho = \tau$ *we have* $(\varrho, \mathbb{G}) \models_M c$

The satisfaction of graph/sketch conditions by a graph/context morphism is a powerful and practical useful tool to control the application of transformation rules. This is extensively demonstrated and validated in the Graph Transformation literature as in [14,22–25], for example. In DPF, we used until now only non-nested negative application conditions to control the application of non-deleting model transformation rules [18,21]. The paper paves the way for utilizing arbitrary first-order conditions to control model transformations in DPF. In this paper, we will, however, not explore this promising direction of applying first-order sketch conditions. We rather concentrate on two other aspects of diagrammatic modeling techniques–namely "syntactic structure" of models and "deducing information from and reason about models" in a diagrammatic manner.

Developing and applying DPF, we realized that typing mechanisms are not powerful enough to formalize all relevant restrictions concerning the syntactic structure of models. To overcome this deficiency, we introduced "universal constraints" and "negative universal constraints" [18,21] analogous to the non-nested graph constraints in [14].

Fortunately, sketch conditions and their satisfaction, as defined in Definition 28, now give us also more powerful general first-order sketch constraints at hand to describe the syntactic structure of models. The simple, but crucial, observation is that an assertion $(\tau, \mathbb{G}) \models_K c$ can be interpreted as well as an assertion concerning the structure of $\mathbb{G}$.

Definition 29 (Sketch constraints). *An* St- *sketch* K- *constraint* (c, τ) *on context* G *is given by a context* K, *a sketch condition* $K \blacktriangleright c$ *in context* K *and a context morphism* $\tau : K \to G$.

An St-sketch $\mathbb{G} = (G, St^\mathbb{G})$ **satisfies** the K-constraint (c, τ), $\mathbb{G} \models_K (c, \tau)$ in symbols, if, and only if, $(\tau, \mathbb{G}) \models_K c$.

Remark 37 (Attached Statements). *Only at this point and a few days before the paper deadline, we realized that it may be beneficial to apply the "reinterpretation principle" in Definition 29 also to structures. That is, for any Ξ-structure $\mathcal{U} = (U, \Phi^{\mathcal{U}})$, context K, morphism $\iota : K \to U$ and statement (X, Ex, γ) in K we can define:*

$$\mathcal{U} \models_K ((X, Ex, \gamma), \iota) \quad \text{iff} \quad (\iota, \mathcal{U}) \models_K (X, Ex, \gamma) \tag{23}$$

and may call the pair $((X, Ex, \gamma), \iota)$ a statement attached to $\mathcal{U}$ or a statement about $\mathcal{U}$.

To realize this idea, would, however, require a major revision of the paper.

If the sketch condition c does not contain any statements, as it usually the case in the area of Graph Transformations (compare Example 50), $\mathbb{G} \models_K (c, \tau)$ is just an assertion about the structure of the context G. In all other cases, $\mathbb{G} \models_K (c, \tau)$ tells us also something about the presence or non-presence of statements as well as the relations between the statements in $\mathbb{G}$.

Due to rule "Statement", all statements reappear as conditions. The following simple corollary illustrates that the requirement for strict sketch arrows to preserve statements "on the nose" encodes a structural constraint on the target.

Corollary 6 (Strict Sketch Arrow vs. Sketch Constraint). *A context morphism $\varphi : K \to G$ constitutes a strict St-sketch arrow $\varphi : \mathbb{K} \to \mathbb{G}$ between two St-sketches $\mathbb{K} = (K, St^\mathbb{K})$ and $\mathbb{G} = (G, St^\mathbb{G})$ if, and only if, $\mathbb{G} \models_K (\bigwedge St^\mathbb{K}, \varphi)$.*

Remark 38 (General constraints). *A K-constraint (c, τ) is, in general, only a **local constraint**, in the sense that it constrains the structure of $\mathbb{G}$ "around the image" of K w.r.t. τ. Thus, in case $K = G$ and $\tau = id_G$, (c, id_G) is an assertion about the structure of $\mathbb{G}$ as such.*

*If Ct has an initial object **0**, any closed condition $\mathbf{0} \blacktriangleright c$ gives rise to a sketch constraint $(c, !_G)$ with $!_G : \mathbf{0} \to G$ the initial morphism into G. $(c, !_G)$ is a **general constraint**, in the sense that the statement $\mathbb{G} \models_0 (c, !_G)$ can be seen as a characterization of the overall structure of $\mathbb{G}$. In the Graph Transformation literature, only general constraints have been considered [23,25].*

6.3. Statements and Sketch Constraints

In this subsection, we outline that first-order sketch constraints give us indeed the means at hand to express the validity of statements in semantic structures, in an equivalent way, by structural properties of sketch encodings of those semantic structures (see Remark 29). In particular, we are interested to extend Makkai's approach and to encode the validity of arbitrary first-order statements in semantic structures by structural properties of atomic sketch encodings.

Thus, we go back to the setting in Section 5.2.2 and assume an Institution of Statements $\mathcal{IS} = (\text{Cxt}, \text{Stm}, \text{Int}, \models)$ with Carr $\sqsubseteq$ Cxt, $\text{XE}(\Xi) = \text{FE}(\Xi)$ and thus $\text{At}(K) \subset \text{Stm}(K)$ for all contexts K in Cxt, i.e., $\text{Stm}(K)$ contains all *atomic statements* in K.

We consider the instances of Definition 27 and Definition 28, respectively, for the category Cxt of contexts and the functor At : Cxt $\to$ Set assigning to each context K the set $\text{At}(K)$ of all atomic statements in K as described in Remark 14.

Definition 27 of the syntax of sketch conditions follows exactly the same pattern as Definition 8 of the syntax of feature expression; thus, it should be possible to translate, for any context K, the statements in K into At-sketch conditions on K. This is indeed possible! However, to be able to translate *quantifications*, we have to assume that Cxt has pushouts (compare Appendix A).

Definition 30 (From Statements to Sketch conditions). *We assume that Cxt has pushouts. For an arbitrary but fixed choice of pushouts in Cxt we construct inductively and in parallel a* family of maps $tr_K : \text{Stm}(K) \to \text{AT}(K)$, where K varies over all objects in Ct: For arbitry variable declarations X and arbitrary binding morphism $\gamma: X \to K$, we define

1. Atomic expr.: $tr_K(X, F(\beta), \gamma) := F(\beta; \gamma) = (\alpha F, F(id_{\alpha F}), \beta; \gamma) \in \text{At}(K) \subset \text{AT}(K)$
2. Everything: $tr_K(X, \top, \gamma) := \mathbf{T} \in \text{AT}(K)$
3. Void: $tr_K(X, \bot, \gamma) := \mathbf{F} \in \text{AT}(K)$
4. Conjunction: $tr_K(X, (Ex_1 \wedge Ex_2), \gamma) := \bigwedge \{tr_K(X, Ex_1, \gamma), tr_K(X, Ex_2, \gamma)\} \in \text{AT}(K)$
5. Disjunction: $tr_K(X, (Ex_1 \vee Ex_2), \gamma) := \bigvee \{tr_K(X, Ex_1, \gamma), tr_K(X, Ex_2, \gamma)\} \in \text{AT}(K)$
6. Implication: $tr_K(X, (Ex_1 \to Ex_2), \gamma) := (tr_K(X, Ex_1, \gamma) \to tr_K(X, Ex_2, \gamma)) \in \text{AT}(K)$
7. Negation: $tr_K(X, \neg Ex, \gamma) := \neg\, tr_K(X, Ex, \gamma) \in \text{AT}(K)$
8. Quantification: $tr_K(X, Q(\varphi, Y : Ex), \gamma) := Q(\varphi^*, K_\gamma^\varphi : tr_{K_\gamma^\varphi}(Ex)) \in \text{AT}(K)$

for $Q \in \{\exists, \forall\}$ where $K \xrightarrow{\varphi^*} K_\gamma^\varphi \xleftarrow{\gamma^*} Y$ is the chosen pushout of $K \xleftarrow{\gamma} X \xrightarrow{\varphi} Y$.

Remark 39 (Translation of Feature Expressions). *Every feature expression $X \triangleright Ex$ reappears as the statement (X, Ex, id_X), thus we can consider $X \blacktriangleright tr_X(X, Ex, id_X)$ as the translation of the feature expression $X \triangleright Ex$ into a At-sketch condition.*

Besides syntax, also Definition 10 of the semantics of feature expressions (and thus Definition 14 of satisfaction of statements) and Definition 28 of satisfaction of sketch conditions (and thus Definition 29 of satisfaction of sketch constraints) follow exactly the same pattern. This enables us to prove straightforwardly that the family of translation maps $tr_K : \text{Stm}(K) \to \text{AT}(K)$ establishes an equivalence between first-order statements and first-order At-sketch conditions. Note that the proposal in Remark 37 would make the statement in the following proposition even more catchy.

Proposition 7 (Statements $\cong$ Sketch Constraints). *For any Ξ-structure $\mathcal{U} = (U, \Phi^\mathcal{U})$, context K, morphism $\iota: K \to U$ and statement (X, Ex, γ) in K we have:*

$$(\iota, \mathcal{U}) \models_K (X, Ex, \gamma) \quad \text{iff} \quad \mathbb{S}_\Phi^\mathcal{U} \models_K (tr_K(X, Ex, \gamma), \iota),$$

where $\mathbb{S}_\Phi^\mathcal{U} = (U, St_\Phi^\mathcal{U})$ is the atomic sketch encoding of structure $\mathcal{U}$ as defined by (12).

Instantiating this equivalence for the identity on U gives us exactly what we have been looking for, namely that the atomic sketch encoding of structures in an Institution of Statements encodes likewise all properties of structures that can be expressed by first-order statements and formulas.

Corollary 7 (Statements $\cong$ Sketch Constraints). *For any Ξ-structure $\mathcal{U} = (U, \Phi^\mathcal{U})$ and any statement (X, Ex, γ) in U we have:*

$$(id_U, \mathcal{U}) \models_U (X, Ex, \gamma) \quad \text{iff} \quad \mathbb{S}_\Phi^\mathcal{U} \models_K (tr_K(X, Ex, \gamma), id_U),$$

where $\mathbb{S}_\Phi^\mathcal{U} = (U, St_\Phi^\mathcal{U})$ is the atomic sketch encoding of structure $\mathcal{U}$ as defined by (12).

The case $X = 0$, and thus $\gamma =\, !_U$, corresponds to closed formulas and, due to Remark 18 (Validity of Closed Formulas), Corollary 7 ensures that we can detect all closed formulas that are valid in $\mathcal{U}$, by inspecting the atomic sketch encoding $\mathbb{S}_\Phi^\mathcal{U}$.

Proposition 7 and Corollary 7 are very good news for DPF and any other diagrammatic approach to Software Engineering. They ensure that we can describe both structure and constraints in the same diagrammatic, modelcentric format. There is, in principle, no need to combine diagrammatic models with dissimilar descriptions, like OCL code, for example, even if it comes to first-order properties. We can reason about and deal with a real system at a higher level of abstraction within one and the same diagrammatic paradigm!

Example 51 (CT: Sketch constraints). *Relying on Definition 30 and Remark 39, we can translate all the sample Ξ_{CT}-expressions in Example 29 into corresponding sketch conditions. Concerning the* visual representation, there is no essential difference between a Ξ_{CT}-expression and the corresponding sketch condition: We replace $\triangleright$ by $\blacktriangleright$ and $\top$ by $\mathbf{T}$. We rewrite $(\_\wedge\_)$ to $\bigwedge\{\_,\_\}$ and so on.

The Ξ_{CT}-expressions lec in Example 29 is transformed into the sketch condition

$$\overline{lec} = \begin{array}{c}xv_2\\ xe_1\uparrow \;\;\searrow xe_2\\ xv_1 \quad xv_3\end{array} \;\blacktriangleright\; \exists\left(\begin{array}{c}xv_2\\ xe_1\uparrow \;\;\searrow xe_2\\ xv_1 \xrightarrow{xe_3} xv_3\end{array} : \begin{array}{c}xv_2\\ xe_1\uparrow \;\underset{xe_3}{\overset{cmp}{\searrow}} xe_2\\ xv_1 \to xv_3\end{array}\right)$$

and the Ξ_{CT}-expressions gec, representing the property **composition is always defined**, is transformed into the sketch condition:

$$\overline{gec} = 0 \blacktriangleright \forall\left(\begin{array}{c}xv_2\\ xe_1\uparrow \searrow xe_2\\ xv_1 \quad xv_3\end{array} : \exists\left(\begin{array}{c}xv_2\\ xe_1\uparrow \searrow xe_2\\ xv_1 \xrightarrow{xe_3} xv_3\end{array} : \begin{array}{c}xv_2\\ xe_1\uparrow \underset{xe_3}{\overset{cmp}{\searrow}} xe_2\\ xv_1 \to xv_3\end{array}\right)\right)$$

For the sample sketch $\mathbb{G} = (G, St^{\mathbb{G}})$ in Example 49, we do have $\mathbb{G} \models (\overline{lec}, \tau_1)$, with τ_1 given by the assignments $xe_1 \mapsto a, xe_2 \mapsto b$, but $\mathbb{G} \not\models (\overline{lec}, \tau_2)$, with τ_2 given by $xe_1 \mapsto b, xe_2 \mapsto c$, thus $\mathbb{G} \not\models (\overline{gec}, !_{\mathbb{G}})$. General constraints imposing **uniqueness of composition**, independent of the existence of composition, can be formulated by the closed condition $\overline{guc}$:

$$0 \blacktriangleright \forall\left(\begin{array}{c}xv_2\\ xe_1\uparrow \searrow xe_2\\ xv_1 \underset{xe_4}{\overset{xe_3}{\rightrightarrows}} xv_3\end{array} : \left(\bigwedge\left\{\begin{array}{c}xv_2\\ xe_1\uparrow\underset{xe_3}{\overset{cmp}{\searrow}} xe_2\\ xv_1 \to xv_3\end{array}, \begin{array}{c}xv_2\\ xe_1\uparrow\underset{xe_4}{\overset{cmp}{\searrow}} xe_2\\ xv_1 \to xv_3\end{array}\right\} \to \exists\left(\varphi, \begin{array}{c}xv_2\\ xe_1\uparrow \searrow xe_2\\ xv_1 \xrightarrow{e} xv_3\end{array} : \mathbf{T}\right)\right)\right)$$

φ simply maps xe_3 and xe_4 to xe. $\mathbb{G}$ does not satisfy the constraint $(\overline{guc}, !_{\mathbb{G}})$ but would satisfy it if we delete the edge "f", for example. The remaining requirements–existence and uniqueness of identities, identity laws and associativity law–can be expressed analogously.

Besides formalizing the "laws of a category", we can also take advantage of our knowledge about the properties of the features in Ξ_{CT}–or to put it the other way around: We can formulate requirements that any intended semantics of the feature symbols in Ξ_{CT} has to comply with. For example, we can require that, for a final object, all outgoing morphisms are monic:

$$ct_1 := 0 \blacktriangleright \forall(xv : (xv^{\mathtt{fnl}} \longrightarrow \forall(xv \xrightarrow{xe} xv_1 : xv \xrightarrow[\mathtt{mon}]{e} xv_1)))$$

We can require that monomorphisms are closed under composition:

$$ct_2 := 0 \blacktriangleright \forall\left(\begin{array}{c}xv_2\\ xe_1\uparrow \searrow xe_2\\ xv_1 \quad xv_3\end{array} : \left(\bigwedge\left\{\begin{array}{c}xv_2\\ xe_1\uparrow\underset{\mathtt{mon}}{}\underset{xe_3}{\overset{cmp}{\searrow}}\underset{}{\mathtt{mon}}\, xe_2\\ xv_1 \to xv_3\end{array}\right\} \longrightarrow \begin{array}{c}xv_2\\ xe_1\uparrow \searrow xe_2\\ xv_1 \xrightarrow[\mathtt{mon}]{xe_3} xv_3\end{array}\right)\right)$$

Note that we use $\bigwedge\{\cdots\}$ because the single triangle between the curly brackets visualizes, actually, three atomic Ξ_{CT}-statements! We can also express our knowledge concerning the decomposition of monomorphisms:

$$ct_3 := 0 \blacktriangleright \forall\left(\begin{array}{c}xv_2\\ xe_1\uparrow \searrow xe_2\\ xv_1 \quad xv_3\end{array} : \left(\bigwedge\left\{\begin{array}{c}xv_2\\ xe_1\uparrow\underset{xe_3}{\overset{cmp}{\searrow}} xe_2\\ xv_1 \xrightarrow[\mathtt{mon}]{} xv_3\end{array}\right\} \longrightarrow \begin{array}{c}xv_2\\ xe_1\uparrow\underset{\mathtt{mon}}{} \searrow xe_2\\ xv_1 \xrightarrow{xe_3} xv_3\end{array}\right)\right)$$

$\mathbb{G} \models (ct_2, !_{\mathbb{G}})$ simply because there is no match in G of the triangular context in ct_2 satisfying the premise of the implication in ct_2. In contrast, $\mathbb{G} \not\models (ct_3, !_{\mathbb{G}})$ with the only counterexample given by the assignments $xe_1 \mapsto c, xe_2 \mapsto d, xe_3 \mapsto g$.

To be prepared for discussions, later in this section, we consider also the sketch condition $\overline{mon}$ defining the concept **monomorphism** and obtained by transforming the Ξ_{CT}-expressions mon in Example 29:

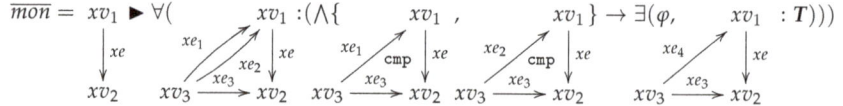

where φ maps xe_1 and xe_2 to xe_4.

6.4. Sketch Arrows, Constraints, Deduction, Meta-Modeling

In this subsection, we present vital observations, insights, concepts and ideas to establish a basis for the future further development of the "logic dimension" of Institutions of Statements and, especially of DPF, based on the new concepts and results presented in this paper.

Constraints in DPF at Present

Following [15] and analogous to [14], we use in DPF until now, instead of sketch constraints in the sense of Definition 29, only plain sketch arrows $\varphi : \mathbb{L} \to \mathbb{R}$ and call them (positive) universal constraints or negative universal constraints, respectively [18,21]. We define the satisfaction of universal constraints in DPF by means of the closedness property in Definition 23. That is, a sketch $\mathbb{G}$ satisfies the "universal constraint" $\varphi : \mathbb{L} \to \mathbb{R}$ if, and only if, for any strict sketch arrow $\tau : \mathbb{L} \to \mathbb{G}$ there is a strict sketch arrow $\varrho : \mathbb{R} \to \mathbb{G}$ such that $\varphi ; \varrho = \tau$.

By Proposition 7, we can transfer many findings in Sections 5.2.3 and 5.2.4 into the sketch constraints setting. Corollary 6 and Definition 28 ensure that the satisfaction of a universal constraint $\varphi : \mathbb{L} \to \mathbb{R}$ in a sketch $\mathbb{G}$ can be equivalently expressed by the assertion that $\mathbb{G}$ satisfies the general constraint $(uc, !_G)$ with (compare Corollary 3):

$$gc := \mathbf{0} \blacktriangleright \forall (L : (\bigwedge St^{\mathbb{L}} \to \exists (\varphi, R : \bigwedge St^{\mathbb{R}}))).$$

Be aware that the identifier φ in gc does not refer to the sketch arrow $\varphi : \mathbb{L} \to \mathbb{R}$ but to the underlying context morphism $\varphi : L \to R$. Note further that we can replace $St^{\mathbb{R}}$ by $(St^{\mathbb{R}} \setminus \varphi(St^{\mathbb{L}}))$ without losing the equivalence!

Furthermore, we say that a sketch $\mathbb{G}$ satisfies the "negative universal constraint" $\varphi : \mathbb{L} \to \mathbb{R}$ if, and only if, for any strict sketch arrow $\tau : \mathbb{L} \to \mathbb{G}$, there does not exist a strict sketch arrow $\varrho : \mathbb{R} \to \mathbb{G}$ such that $\varphi ; \varrho = \tau$. This requirement is equivalent to the statement that $\mathbb{G}$ satisfies the general constraint $(ngc, !_G)$ with:

$$ngc := \mathbf{0} \blacktriangleright \forall (L : (\bigwedge St^{\mathbb{L}} \to \neg \exists (\varphi, R : \bigwedge St^{\mathbb{R}})))$$

What can we do if a sketch $\mathbb{G}$ does not satisfy a general constraint $(c, !_G)$ for a simple condition of the form $c = \mathbf{0} \blacktriangleright \forall (L : (\bigwedge St^1 \to \exists (\varphi, R : \bigwedge St^2)))$ where St^1 is a set of statements in L and St^2 a set of statements in R, respectively?

We can repair this flaw by applying the sketch arrow $\varphi : (L, St^1) \to (R, St^2 \cup \varphi(St^1))$ as a transformation rule for all sketch morphisms $\tau : (L, St^1) \to \mathbb{G}$ not satisfying the conclusion in condition c. In other words, a match of the transformation rule is given by a context morphism $\tau : L \to G$ such that $\mathbb{G} \models (\bigwedge St^1, \tau)$ and $\mathbb{G} \models (\neg \exists (\varphi, R : \bigwedge St^2), \tau)$. Note that the negative application condition $\mathbb{G} \models (\neg \exists (\varphi, R : \bigwedge St^2), \tau)$ ensures that we do not apply the rule twice for the same match $\tau : (L, St^1) \to \mathbb{G}$. Applying the rule φ via the match τ means nothing but to construct a pushout in the category Sk_S^a of sketches and strict sketch arrows (compare Remark 32).

$$\begin{array}{ccc} (L, St^1) & \xrightarrow{\varphi} & (R, St^2 \cup \varphi(St^1)) \\ \tau \downarrow & \text{PO} & \downarrow \tau^* \\ \mathbb{G} & \xrightarrow{\varphi^*} & \mathbb{H} \end{array}$$

Depending on the properties of the context morphism $\varphi : L \to R$ the pushout construction may have different effects. The context G can be extended and/or factorized and, if $St^2 \neq \emptyset$, we will add new statements to the statements originating from $\mathbb{G}$.

In terms of sketch constraints, we can describe the crucial effect of the rule application as follows: $\mathbb{H}$ satisfies the constraint $(\bigwedge St^2, \tau^*)$ in addition to the constraint $(\bigwedge St^1, \tau; \varphi^*)$ inherited from $\mathbb{G}$.

Example 52 (Repairing Stm_{CT}-sketches). *As discussed in Example 51, there is one violation of the general constraints $(\overline{guc}, !_G)$ uniqueness of composition by the Stm_{CT}-sketch $\mathbb{G} = (G, St^{\mathbb{G}})$ in Example 49 and one violation of $(ct_3, !_G)$ decomposition of monomorphisms. Repairing these two violations by pushout constructions, as described above, will result in a Stm_{CT}-sketch $\mathbb{H}$ like the one visualized below.*

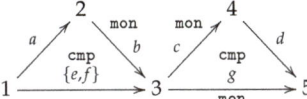

$\mathbb{G}$ *also does not satisfy the general constraint* $(\overline{gec}, !_G)$ *definedness of composition and the general constraint* existence of identities *that has not been formalized in Example 51. We do not want to require that any Stm_{CT}-sketch satisfies these two general constraints since we do not intend to use Stm_{CT}-sketches just as encodings of categories but rather as (hopefully finite) representations of (possibly infinite) categories. This is the original purpose of sketches in category theory. See also the later discussion in Remark 40.*

Deduction

Generating new statements from given statements by means of rules is the essence of deduction in logic. An interesting observation is that the "repairing procedure", discussed in the last paragraph, can be also described as a procedure deducing new sketch constraints from given sketch constraints.

We consider a sketch $\mathbb{G}$ together with a set $C^{\mathbb{G}}$ of sketch constraints on G. If $C^{\mathbb{G}}$ contains a general constraint $(c, !_G)$ with $c = \mathbf{0} \blacktriangleright \forall (L : (\bigwedge St^1 \to \exists (\varphi, R : \bigwedge St^2)))$, we can deduce a local sketch constraint $((\bigwedge St^1 \to \exists (\varphi, R : \bigwedge St^2)), \tau)$ on G for any context morphism $\tau : L \to G$. This step corresponds to the **universal elimination rule** in classical first-order logic.

We do have a sound "quasi-propositional" **modus ponens rule schemata** for sketch constraints at hand: For all contexts X, all sketch conditions $X \blacktriangleright c_1$, $X \blacktriangleright (c_1 \to c_2)$ and all context morphisms $\mu : X \to Y$, the sketch constraints (c_1, μ) and $((c_1 \to c_2), \mu)$ imply the sketch constraint (c_2, μ).

If there is a constraint $(\bigwedge St^1, \tau) \in C^{\mathbb{G}}$, we can apply this modus ponens rule and deduce the sketch constraint $(\exists (\varphi, R : \bigwedge St^2), \tau)$ on G. Keep in mind that $L \blacktriangleright \exists (\varphi, R : \bigwedge St^2)$! The pushout construction generates, finally, the constraint $(\bigwedge St^2, \tau^* : R \to H)$ on H. This looks very much like an analogon to **Skolemization** in classical first-order logic. More precisely, we can consider this pushout construction as a pendant to the introduction of Skolem constants. This is quite in accordance with the characterization of operations in graph term algebras by pushouts in [3].

As another example, motivating the use of sketch constraints as "first class citizens", we discuss atomic Ξ_{CT}-statements, as introduced and discussed in the Examples 39 and 49: We included now the feature symbols mon and fnl in our sample footprint Ξ_{CT} to exemplify, in a more appropriate way, the use of feature symbols in diagrammatic specifications in general. In Example 51, we discussed, first, that we can specify known or desired properties of features by means of sketch conditions. Later, we have shown that we can even express the universal properties, defining the concepts "monomorphism" and "final object", respectively, by means of sketch conditions.

Given a Stm_{CT}-sketch $\mathbb{G} = (G, St^{\mathbb{G}})$, the sketch condition $\overline{mon}$, defining the concept monomorphism, may help us to deduce from the cmp-statements, present in $St^{\mathbb{G}}$ that two parallel edges in G have to be identified. We need just a rule which generates for each atomic Ξ_{CT}-statement $(\alpha(\text{mon}), \text{mon}(id_{\alpha(\text{mon})}), \beta : \alpha(\text{mon}) \to G)$ in $St^{\mathbb{G}}$ a corresponding sketch constraint $(\overline{mon}, \beta)$ on $\mathbb{G}$. This works so easy, since we designed our examples in such a way that the context of $\overline{mon}$ is just $\alpha(\mathtt{mon})$. In general, any atomic Ξ-statement $(\alpha(\mathtt{mon}), \mathtt{mon}(id_{\alpha(\mathtt{mon})}), \beta)$ $(\alpha(P), P(id_{\alpha(P)}), \beta : \alpha(P) \to G)$ and any condition $K \blacktriangleright c$ may generate a sketch constraint $(c, \gamma; \beta)$ for any context morphism $\gamma : K \to \alpha(P)$. Since β binds all "free variables" in $\overline{mon}$, we just need to adapt the three steps (1) universal elimination, (2) modus ponens and (3) Skolemization, as discussed above for general constraints, to deduce identifications of parallel edges in G.

To keep Ξ_{CT} as small as possible, we have not included in Ξ_{CT} feature symbols for other limits and colimits like equ, pb, po, prod, for example. Employing sketch constraints we can even avoid to do this! As discussed in Remark 10, any (co)limit of shape I is axiomatized by the feature Ξ_{CT}-expressions $exists_I$ and $unique_I$.

Analogous to "anonymous functions" in programming, we can use the sketch condition $C_I \blacktriangleright \bigwedge \{tr_{C_I}(exists_I), tr_{C_I}(unique_I)\}$ as an **anonymous feature** representing the (co)limit concept that corresponds to the shape graph I. With anonymous features, we can not formulate statements, i.e., entities within a sketch $\mathbb{G}$, but constraints, like $(\bigwedge \{tr_{C_I}(exists_I), tr_{C_I}(unique_I)\}, \beta : C_I \to G)$ on the sketch $\mathbb{G}$.

There should be now sufficient evidence that it will be beneficial to work in future DPF with sketch constraints as first class citizens and our discussion suggests, especially, to employ pairs of a sketch $\mathbb{G} = (G, St^{\mathbb{G}})$ and a set $C^{\mathbb{G}}$ of sketch constraints on $\mathbb{G}$ as an appropriate formalization of software models. We call those pairs $((G, St^{\mathbb{G}}), C^{\mathbb{G}})$ **constrained sketches**.

Remark 40 (Constrained sketches in MDE). *Our approach to use and develop DPF as a theoretical foundation of MDE is based on the idea that any diagrammatic specification formalism/technique is characterized by a certain choice of a category* Cxt *and a footprint* Ξ *where the corresponding diagrams/models can be described as* Stm-*sketches. Sketch conditions and sketch constraints have been developed to provide the necessary additional means to describe/constrain the syntactic structure of diagrams/models. In such a way, we can characterize now a diagrammatic specification formalism not only by a certain category* Cxt *and a certain footprint* Ξ *but also by an additional set of* Stm-*sketch conditions.*

We should, however, distinguish between two kinds of Stm-*sketch conditions: The first kind of conditions is used to formulate those constraints on* Stm-*sketches* $\mathbb{G}$ *that can be legally used as elements in* $C^{\mathbb{G}}$. *For a constrained* Stm-*sketch* $(\mathbb{G}, C^{\mathbb{G}})$, *the occurrence of a constraint* (c, τ) *in* $C^{\mathbb{G}}$ *will certify that* $\mathbb{G} \models (c, \tau)$. *Requirements for the relational data model [18,21] like "every table must have a primary key" and "a foreign key should only refer to a primary key" will be formalized by conditions of this kind.*

Conditions formalizing requirements like "inheritance is transitive" or "a subclass inherits all attributes of all its superclasses", however, should not be included in any $C^{\mathbb{G}}$ *to avoid diagrams/models becoming too polluted with redundant information. Those additional conditions are part of the formalism as a whole and represent the background knowledge and rules that can be used to deduce for any constrained sketch information from the information given in* $St^{\mathbb{G}}$ *and* $C^{\mathbb{G}}$, *respectively, and to repair violations of the constraints in* $C^{\mathbb{G}}$.

Conceptual Hierarchy

Introducing constrained sketches teleports us "back to start" but on a higher conceptual level: We do have a category $\mathtt{Sk}_s^a$ of sketches. To any sketch $\mathbb{G} = (G, St^{\mathbb{G}})$, we can assign the set $\mathtt{Cstr}(\mathbb{G})$ of all sketch constraints $(c, \tau : K \to G)$ on context G with c a first-order sketch condition in $\mathtt{SC}(K)$ according to Definition 27. Analogously to the translation of statements in Institutions of Statements, we can define for any sketch morphism $\varphi : \mathbb{G} \to \mathbb{H}$ a map $\mathtt{Cstr}(\varphi) : \mathtt{Cstr}(\mathbb{G}) \to \mathtt{Cstr}(\mathbb{H})$ by simple post-composition with the underlying context morphism $\varphi : G \to H$: $\mathtt{Cstr}(\varphi)(c, \tau) := (c, \tau; \varphi)$ for all $(c, \tau) \in \mathtt{Cstr}(\mathbb{G})$. This gives us trivially a functor $\mathtt{Cstr} : \mathtt{Sk}_s^a \to \mathtt{Set}$ at hand.

This situation is, however, just an instance of the abstract pattern we started with in this section: The category $\mathtt{Sk}_s^a$ can be taken as an instance of Ct and the functor $\mathtt{Cstr} : \mathtt{Sk}_s^a \to \mathtt{Set}$ as an instance of St : Ct $\to$ Set, respectively. The constrained sketches are then nothing but the "abstract sketches" for this instance! We can now consider first-order sketch conditions and sketch constraints for this new instance and will finally obtain a further instance of the "abstract pattern". Potentially, we can even iterate this procedure ad infinitum.

Iterating this procedure is maybe not that relevant for DPF at the moment. We take it, however, as a good sign that our category independent approach allows us to move in and furnish the next higher level in the conceptual hierarchy whenever it is necessary and/or opportune.

Remark 41 (Makkai's Hierarchy of Sketches). *We continue the discussion in Remark 29 and rise the question: How is our conceptual hierarchy related to the "hierarchy of sketches" in [15]?*

Makkai considers only atomic statements and starts with a presheaf topos, i.e., a functor category Base = Var = Cxt = $[C \to Set]$. Note that topoi are adhesive [44]! As an example, we consider the presheaf topos:

$$\text{Graph} \cong [\; id_E \;\bigcirc\; E \xrightleftharpoons[t]{s} V \;\bigcirc\; id_V \;\longrightarrow\; \text{Set}].$$

Then, he describes an instance of a general construction in Category Theory: For any footprint $\Xi = (\Phi, \alpha)$, $\alpha \colon \Phi \to [C \to Set]_{Obj}$, there is a category $\Phi \vec{\alpha} C$ such that the category mSk_s^a of multi At-sketches (see Remark 34) is isomorphic to the presheaf topos $[\Phi \vec{\alpha} C \to Set]$.

$\Phi \vec{\alpha} C$ can be constructed as follows: We take the disjoint union of Φ (as a discrete category) and C. For any feature symbol $P \in \Phi$, any object C in C, and any $c \in \alpha(P)(C)$, we add an arrow $(P, c, C) \colon P \to C$. Finally, we define the composition for the new pairs of composable arrows: $(P, c, C); f := (P, \alpha(P)(f)(c), C')$ for all $f \colon C \to C'$ in C.

As an example, we take $\Phi = \{\text{mon}, \text{fnl}\}$ with arities as in Example 49. The category $\Phi \vec{\alpha} \text{Graph}$ is visualized below. Composition in $\Phi \vec{\alpha} \text{Graph}$ is defined by the equations $xe; s = xv_1$, $xe; t = xv_2$ and these equations encode the arity $xv_1 \xrightarrow{xe} xv_2$ of mon! The isomorphism transforms any multi At-sketch $\mathbb{K} = (K, I^{\mathbb{K}}, st^{\mathbb{K}})$ into a corresponding functor $\mathcal{K} \colon \Phi \vec{\alpha} \text{Graph} \to \text{Set}$.

$$\begin{array}{ccc}
\text{mon} & xv_1 & \text{fnl} \\
xe \downarrow \; xv_2 \searrow & & \downarrow xv \\
E & \xrightleftharpoons[t]{s} & V
\end{array}$$

$\mathcal{K}(\; E \xrightleftharpoons[t]{s} V \;)$ represents the graph K. The set $\mathcal{K}(\text{mon})$ holds all the identifiers $i \in I^{\mathbb{K}}$ with $st^{\mathbb{K}}(i) = (\alpha(\text{mon}), \text{mon}(id_{\alpha(\text{mon})}), \beta)$ while the maps $\mathcal{K}(xe), \mathcal{K}(xv_1), \mathcal{K}(xv_2)$ encode all the corresponding bindings $\beta \colon \alpha(\text{mon}) \to K$. Morphisms in $[\Phi \vec{\alpha} C \to \text{Set}]$, i.e., natural transformations, encode strict At-sketch arrows between multi At-sketches $\mathbb{K} = (K, I^{\mathbb{K}}, st^{\mathbb{K}})$.

After transforming mSk_s^a into $[\Phi \vec{\alpha} C \to \text{Set}]$, we can define another footprint $\Xi' = (\Phi', \alpha')$, $\alpha' \colon \Phi' \to [\Phi \vec{\alpha} C \to \text{Set}]_{Obj}$ on this next level of the hierarchy and start again but this time with atomic Ξ'-statements.

There are no sketch conditions in [15] but any multi At-sketch $\mathbb{K} = (K, I^{\mathbb{K}}, st^{\mathbb{K}})$ corresponds to the At-sketch condition $K \blacktriangleright \bigwedge \{st^{\mathbb{K}}(i) \mid i \in I^{\mathbb{K}}\}$ and any strict At-sketch arrow $\varphi \colon \mathbb{L} \to \mathbb{R}$ corresponds to a At-sketch condition of the form $\mathbf{0} \blacktriangleright \forall (L \colon (\bigwedge St^{\mathbb{L}} \to \exists (\varphi, R \colon \bigwedge St^{\mathbb{R}})))$. As we have seen, sketch conditions of this special form, and thus strict At-sketch arrows, allow us to axiomatize arbitrary limits or colimits, respectively.

In such a way, all the arities $\alpha'(P')$ in the footprint Ξ' correspond to very simple At-sketch conditions that are just conjunctions of At-statements and atomic At'-statements are simply conjunctions of those conjunctions of At-statements, which are introduced by the arities $\alpha'(P')$ and obtained the "label" P'.

As an example, we consider the footprint $\Xi = (\Phi, \alpha)$, $\alpha \colon \Phi \to \text{Graph}_{Obj}$ with $\Phi = \{\text{cmp}, \text{id}\}$ and arities as in Example 14. For the footprint $\Xi' = (\Phi', \alpha')$, $\alpha' \colon \Phi' \to [\Phi \vec{\alpha} \text{Graph} \to \text{Set}]_{Obj}$, we assume that, for any $P' \in \Phi'$, the arity $\alpha'(P')$ corresponds to an At-sketch that represents one of the commutative (co)cones described in Remark 10. In such a way, an atomic At'-sketch represents a graph with a set of commutative (co)cones labelled by feature symbols from Φ'. Strict atomic

At'-sketch arrows should allow us then to formulate propositions like: If we have binary products and equalizers, do we also have pullbacks!?

We close this remark with a revision of the concept of graph in [22]: For the footprint $\Xi_R = (\mathsf{Rel}, \alpha)$ in Example 50, we can consider α as a map $\alpha : \mathsf{Rel} \to [1 \to \mathsf{Set}]_{Obj}$ with V the only object in 1 and $\alpha(P)(V) = \{x_1, x_2\}$ for all $P \in \mathsf{Rel}$. $\Phi\vec{\alpha}1$ contains then for each $P \in \mathsf{Rel}$:

$$\cdots \quad P \xrightarrow[(P,x_2)]{(P,x_1)} V$$

an "edge sort" P and $[\Phi\vec{\alpha}1 \to \mathsf{Set}]$ is the category of graphs with an Rel-indexed family of edges. This category is adhesive in contrast to the category of Rel-labelled graphs in [22]! □

7. Conclusions

The paper presents an abstract framework allowing us to construct, in a uniform and universal way, specification formalisms in arbitrary categories enabling us to specify semantic structures while employing the full expressive power of first-order logic.

The framework is based upon a formalization of "open formulas" as statements in contexts and offers a freshly new and abstract view of logics and specification formalisms.

Relying on the new framework, we present a general and universal account of "syntactic" encodings and representations of semantic structures generalizing the idea of elementary diagrams in traditional first-order logic.

Guided by the top-down principle, we consider at this first stage of extension of our framework just simple categories. To extend a specification formalism to a proper logic, we also have to develop, however, appropriate deduction calculi. To establish those deduction calculi, we should have features, like the translation of statements along variable substitutions, for example, at hand. As exemplified in the paper, we have to assume at least the existence of pushouts to support those features. We are not logicians, but the extension of our framework by general deduction calculi will be one of the main topics in our future work.

Another main topic will be operations. At the present stage, our abstract framework does not comprise operations since it is not clear for us how to generalize the concept of operation from set-based structures to semantic structures defined in an arbitrary category. Already, the step from operations on sets to operations on graphs is not that trivial, and even the concepts, constructions and results we developed for graph operations in [3] are not fully satisfactory yet.

Funding: This research received no external funding.

Institutional Review Board Statement: Not applicable.

Data Availability Statement: Data sharing is not applicable.

Acknowledgments: I want to thank the guest editor of this special volume for encouraging me to write this paper.

Conflicts of Interest: The author declares no conflict of interest.

Appendix A. Translation of Feature Expressions

For a footprint Ξ and an object X in Var we denote by $\mathsf{FE}(\Xi, X)$ the set of all feature Ξ-expressions on X. In Example 26, we discussed the replacement of auxiliary feature symbols by feature expressions. To formalize those replacements, we consider footprint morphisms. A **morphism** $\eta : \Xi \to \Xi'$ between two footprints over the same category Var is given by a map η assigning to each feature symbol $F \in \Phi$ a feature Ξ'-expression $\eta(F) \in \mathsf{FE}(\Xi', \alpha(F))$. η is called **simple** if $\eta(F) = F'(id_{\alpha(F)})$, with $F' \in \Phi'$ and $\alpha'(F') = \alpha(F)$, for all $F \in \Phi$.

Any footprint morphism $\eta : \Xi \to \Xi'$ induces an Var_{Obj}-indexed family of maps $\eta_X : \mathsf{FE}(\Xi, X) \to \mathsf{FE}(\Xi', X)$. To define these maps for non-simple footprint morphisms, we have to rely, however, on a mechanism translating feature expressions along variable translations. Fortunately, we can establish such a mechanism, if Var has pushouts, and we fix a choice of pushouts in Var.

Definition A1 (Translation maps). *We define inductively and in parallel a family of* **translation maps** $\psi_\Xi : \mathrm{FE}(\Xi, X) \to \mathrm{FE}(\Xi, Z)$ *with ψ ranging over all variable translations $\psi : X \to Z$:*

1. *Atomic:* $\psi_\Xi(X \triangleright F(\beta)) := Z \triangleright F(\beta; \psi)$.
2. *Everything:* $\psi_\Xi(X \triangleright \top) := Z \triangleright \top$.
3. *Void:* $\psi_\Xi(X \triangleright \bot) := Z \triangleright \bot$.
4. *Conjunction:* $\psi_\Xi(X \triangleright (Ex_1 \wedge Ex_2)) := Z \triangleright (\psi_\Xi(Ex_1) \wedge \psi_\Xi(Ex_2))$.
5. *Disjunction:* $\psi_\Xi(X \triangleright (Ex_1 \vee Ex_2)) := Z \triangleright (\psi_\Xi(Ex_1) \vee \psi_\Xi(Ex_2))$.
6. *Implication:* $\psi_\Xi(X \triangleright (Ex_1 \to Ex_2)) := Z \triangleright (\psi_\Xi(Ex_1) \to \psi_\Xi(Ex_2))$
7. *Negation:* $\psi_\Xi(X \triangleright \neg Ex) := Z \triangleright \neg \psi_\Xi(Ex)$.
8. *Quantification:* $\psi_\Xi(X \triangleright Q(\varphi, Y : Ex)) := Z \triangleright Q(\varphi^*, Y_\psi^\varphi : \psi_\Xi^*(Ex))$

for $Q \in \{\exists, \forall\}$ where $Z \xrightarrow{\varphi^*} Y_\psi^\varphi \xleftarrow{\psi^*} Y$ is the chosen pushout of $Z \xleftarrow{\psi} X \xrightarrow{\varphi} Y$:

Note that the pushout construction formalizes and generalizes the "introduction of fresh variables" in traditional FOL! If we choose the cospan $Z \xrightarrow{\psi^{-1};\varphi} Y \xleftarrow{id_Y} Y$, whenever ψ is an isomorphism, we ensure, especially, that $(id_X)_\Xi$ becomes the identity map on $\mathrm{FE}(\Xi, X)$. Since the composition of chosen pushouts does not result, in general, in a chosen pushout, the assignments $\psi \mapsto \psi_\Xi$ constitute only a pseudo functor from Var into Set. This may be a hint to develop future deduction calculi for Institutions of Statements rather in a fibred setting (compare [45])?

The translation $\psi_{\Xi_{CT}}(mon)$ of the universal property *mon* of monomorphisms in Example 29 along the unique graph morphism $\psi : (xv_1 \xrightarrow{xe} xv_2) \to xv \circlearrowright xe$ gives us, for example, a definition of monic loops at hand.

For any footprint morphism $\eta : \Xi \to \Xi'$, we can define inductively and in parallel for all variable declarations X a **substitution map** $\eta_X : \mathrm{FE}(\Xi, X) \to \mathrm{FE}(\Xi', X)$ where the only non-trivial case is the base case :

1. *Atomic:* $\eta_X(F(\beta)) := \beta_{\Xi'}(\eta(F))$ for any $F \in \Phi$ and $\beta : \alpha F \to X$ in Var.

If η is simple, this base case degenerates, according to Definition A1, to a simple replacement of feature symbols:

1'. *Atomic':* $\eta_X(F(\beta)) := \beta_{\Xi'}(F'(id_{\alpha(F)})) = F'(id_{\alpha(F)}; \beta) = F'(\beta)$.

Thus, we do not need to employ translation maps to define substitution maps in case of simple footprint morphisms!

References

1. Ehrig, H.; Mahr, B. *Fundamentals of Algebraic Specification 1: Equations and Initial Semantics*; EATCS Monographs on Theoretical Computer Science; Springer: Berlin, Germany, 1985; Volume 6.
2. Diaconescu, R. *Institution-Independent Model Theory*; Studies in Universal Logic: Basel, Switzerland, 2008. [CrossRef]
3. Wolter, U.; Diskin, Z.; König, H. Graph Operations and Free Graph Algebras. In *Graph Transformation, Specifications, and Nets—In Memory of Hartmut Ehrig*; Springer: Cham, Switzerland, 2018; Volume 10800, pp. 313–331. [CrossRef]
4. Kaphengst, H.; Reichel, H. *Algebraische Algorithmentheorie*; WIB 1; VEB Robotron, Zentrum für Forschung und Technik: Dresden, Germany, 1971.
5. Reichel, H.; Hupbach, U.R.; Kaphengst, H. *Initial Algebraic Specification of Data Types, Parameterized Data Types, and Algorithms*; Technical Report 15; VEB Robotron, Zentrum für Forschung und Technik, Dresden: Dresden, Germany, 1980.
6. Reichel, H. *Initial Computability, Algebraic Specifications, and Partial Algebras*; Oxford University Press: Oxford, UK, 1987.
7. Wolter, U. An Algebraic Approach to Deduction in Equational Partial Horn Theories. *J. Inf. Process. Cybern.* **1990**, *27*, 85–128.
8. Lawvere, F.W. Functorial Semantics of Algebraic Theories. *Proc. Natl. Acad. Sci. USA* **1963**, *50*, 869–872. [CrossRef] [PubMed]
9. Claßen, I.; Große-Rhode, M.; Wolter, U. Categorical concepts for parameterized partial specifications. *Math. Struct. in Comp. Science* **1995**, *5*, 153–188. [CrossRef]
10. Barr, M.; Wells, C. *Category Theory for Computing Science*; Series in Computer Science; Prentice Hall International: London, UK, 1990.
11. Johnson, M.; Rosebrugh, R.; Wood, R. Entity-relationship-attribute designs and sketches. *Theory Appl. Categ.* **2002**, *10*, 94–112.

12. Wells, C. *Sketches: Outline with References*; Addendum 2009; Department of Mathematics, Case Western Reserve University: Cleveland, UH, USA, 1993.
13. Diskin, Z.; Wolter, U. A Diagrammatic Logic for Object-Oriented Visual Modeling. *Electron. Notes Theor. Comput. Sci.* **2008**, *203/6*, 19–41. [CrossRef]
14. Ehrig, H.; Ehrig, K.; Prange, U.; Taentzer, G. *Fundamentals of Algebraic Graph Transformations*; EATCS Monographs on Theoretical Computer Science; Springer: Berlin/Heidelberg, Germany, 2006. [CrossRef]
15. Makkai, M. Generalized Sketches as a Framework for Completeness Theorems. *J. Pure Appl. Algebra* **1997**, *115*, 49274. [CrossRef]
16. Cadish, B.; Diskin, Z. Heterogeneous view integration via sketches and equations. In Proceedigs of the 9th International Symposium on Methodologies for Intelligent Systems, Zakopane, Poland, 9–13 June 1996; Springer: Berlin/Heidelberg, Germany, 1996; pp. 603–612. [CrossRef]
17. Diskin, Z. Towards algebraic graph-based model theory for computer science. *Bull. Symb. Log.* **1997**, *3*, 144–145.
18. Rutle, A. Diagram Predicate Framework: A Formal Approach to MDE. Ph.D. Thesis, Department of Informatics, University of Bergen, Bergen, Norway, 2010.
19. Wolter, U.; Mantz, F. *The Diagram Predicate Framework in View of Adhesive Categories*; Technical Report 358; Department of Informatics, University of Bergen: Bergen, Norway, 2013.
20. König, H.; Wolter, U. Van Kampen Colimits and Path Uniqueness. *Log. Methods Comput. Sci.* **2018**, *14*, 1–27. [CrossRef]
21. Rutle, A.; Rossini, A.; Lamo, Y.; Wolter, U. A formal approach to the specification and transformation of constraints in MDE. *J. Log. Algebr. Program.* **2012**, *81/4*, 422–457. [CrossRef]
22. Rensink, A. Representing first-order logic using graphs. In Proceedings of the Graph Transformations, Second International Conference, ICGT 2004, Rome, Italy, 28 September–2 October 2004; Springer: Berlin/Heidelberg, Germany, 2004; Volume 3256, pp. 319–335. [CrossRef]
23. Habel, A.; Pennemann, K. Correctness of high-level transformation systems relative to nested conditions. *Math. Struct. Comput. Sci.* **2009**, *19*, 245–296. [CrossRef]
24. Bruggink, H.J.S.; Cauderlier, R.; Hülsbusch, M.; König, B. Conditional reactive systems. In Proceeding of the IARCS Annual Conference on Foundations of Software Technology and Theoretical Computer Science, FSTTCS 2011, Mumbai, India, 12–14 December 2011; Schloss Dagstuhl–Leibniz-Zentrum für Informatik: Wadern, Germany, 2011, Volume 13, pp. 191–203. [CrossRef]
25. Kosiol, J.; Strüber, D.; Taentzer, G.; Zschaler, S. Graph consistency as a graduated property–consistency-sustaining and -improving graph transformations. In Proceedings of the 13th International Conference, ICGT 2020, Bergen, Norway, 25–26 June 2020; Springer: Cham, Switzerland, 2020; Volume 12150, pp. 239–256. [CrossRef]
26. Makkai, M. First Order Logic with Dependent Sorts, with Applications to Category Theory. Available online: http://www.math.mcgill.ca/makkai/ (accessed on 31 January 2022).
27. Freyd, P.J. Properties invariant within equivalence types of categories. In *Algebra, Topology and Category Theory: A Collection of Papers in Honour of Samuel Eilenberg*; Heller, A., Tierney, M., Eds.; Academic Press: Cambridge, MA, USA, 1976; pp. 55–61.
28. Freyd, P.J.; Scedrov, A. *Categories, Allegories*; North-Holland Mathematical Library; North-Holland: Amsterdam, The Netherlands, 1990; Volume 39.
29. Wolter, U.; Klar, M.; Wessäly, R.; Cornelius, F. *Four Institutions—A Unified Presentation of Logical Systems for Specification*; Technical Report Bericht-Nr. 94-24; Fachbereich Informatik: Berlin, Germany, 1994.
30. Pawlowski, W. Context institutions. In Proceedings of the 11th COMPASS/ADT Workshop on Specification of Abstract Data Types Joint with the 8th COMPASS Workshop, Oslo, Norway, 19–23 September 1995; Springer: Cham, Switzerland, 1995; Volume 1130, pp. 436–457.
31. Goguen, J.A.; Burstall, R.M. Institutions: Abstract Model Theory for Specification and Programming. *J. ACM* **1992**, *39*, 95–146. [CrossRef]
32. Wolter, U. Institutional frames. In Proceedings of the 10th Workshop on Specification of Abstract Data Types Joint with the 5th COMPASS Workshop, Santa Margherita Ligure, Italy, 30 May–3 June1994; Springer: Cham, Switzerland, 1995; Volume 906, pp. 469–482. [CrossRef]
33. Martini, A.; Wolter, U.; Haeusler, E.H. Fibred and Indexed Categories for Abstract Model Theory. *Log. J. IGPL* **2007**, *15*, 707–739. [CrossRef]
34. Wolter, U.; Martini, A.; Haeusler, E.H. Towards a uniform presentation of logical systems by indexed categories and adjoint situations. *J. Log. Comput. Oxf. Univ. Press* **2015**, *25*, 57–93. [CrossRef]
35. McLarty, C. *Elementary Categories, Elementary Toposes*; Oxford Logic Guides (Book 21); Clarendon Press: Oxford, UK, 1991.
36. Baader, F.; Horrocks, I.; Sattler, U. Chapter 3. Description logics. In *Handbook of Knowledge Representation*; Elsevier: Amsterdam, The Netherland, 2007.
37. Goguen, J.A.; Meseguer, J. Order-sorted Algebra I: Equational Deduction for Multiple Inheritance, Overloading, Exceptions and Partial Operations. *Theor. Comput. Sci.* **1992**, *105*, 217–273. [CrossRef]
38. Ehrig, H.; Große-Rhode, M.; Wolter, U. Applications of Category Theory to the Area of Algebraic Specification in Computer Science. *Appl. Categ. Struct.* **1998**, *6*, 1–35. [CrossRef]
39. Chang, C.C.; Keisler, H.J. *Model Theory*; Studies in Logic and the Foundations of Mathematics; Elsevier: Amsterdam, The Netherland, 1990.
40. Lloyd, J.W. *Foundations of Logic Programming*, 2nd ed.; Springer: Cham, Switzerland, 1987.

41. Wechler, W. *Universal Algebra for Computer Scientists*; EATCS Monographs on Theoretical Computer Science; Springer: Berlin, Germany, 1992; Volume 25.
42. Lack, S.; Sobociński, P. Adhesive categories. In Proceedings of the FOSSACS 2004 International Conference on Foundations of Software Science and Computation Structures, Barcelona, Spain, 29 March–2 April 2004; Volume 2987, pp. 273–288.
43. Wolter, U. Indexed vs. fibred structures—A field report. *Rom. J. Pure Appl. Math.* **2020**, *66*, 813–830.
44. Lack, S.; Sobocinski, P. Toposes are adhesive. In Proceedings of the Third International Conference, ICGT 2006, Natal, Rio Grande do Norte, Brazil, 17–23 September 2006; Springer: Cham, Switzerland, 2006; Volume 4178, pp. 184–198. [CrossRef]
45. Wolter, U.; Martini, A.R.; Haeusler, E.H. Indexed and fibred structures for hoare logic. In *Electronic Notes in Theoretical Computer Science*; Elsevier: Amsterdam, The Netherland, 2020; pp. 125–145. [CrossRef]

Article
Representing 3/2-Institutions as Stratified Institutions

Răzvan Diaconescu

Simion Stoilow Institute of Mathematics of the Romanian Academy, 010702 Bucharest, Romania; razvansdiaconescu@gmail.com

Abstract: On the one hand, the extension of ordinary institution theory, known as the theory of stratified institutions, is a general axiomatic approach to model theories where the satisfaction is parameterized by states of the models. On the other hand, the theory of 3/2-institutions is an extension of ordinary institution theory that accommodates the partiality of the signature morphisms and its syntactic and semantic effects. The latter extension is motivated by applications to conceptual blending and software evolution. In this paper, we develop a general representation theorem of 3/2-institutions as stratified institutions. This enables a transfer of conceptual infrastructure from stratified to 3/2-institutions. We provide some examples in this direction.

Keywords: institution theory; category theory; stratified institutions; 3/2-institutions; categorical model theory

MSC: 18N10; 03C95; 68Q65; 68T27

1. Introduction
1.1. Stratified Institutions

Institution theory is a general axiomatic approach to model theory that was originally introduced in computing science by Goguen and Burstall [1]. In institution theory, all three components of logical systems—namely the syntax, the semantics, and the satisfaction relation between them—are treated fully abstractly by relying heavily on category theory. This approach has impacted significantly both theoretical computing science [2] and model theory as such [3] (Both mentioned monographs rather reflect the stage of development of institution theory and its applications at the moment they were published or even before that. In the meantime, a lot of additional important developments have already taken place. At this moment, the literature on institution theory and that around it has been developed over the course of four decades or so and is rather vast.) In computing science, the concept of institution has emerged as the most fundamental mathematical structure of logic-based formal specifications, a great deal of theory being developed at the general level of abstract institutions. In model theory, the institution theoretic approach meant an axiomatic-driven redesign of core parts of model theory at a new level of generality—namely that of abstract institutions—independent of any concrete logical system. institution theoretic approach Moreover, there is a strong interdependency between the two lines of developments.

The institution theoretic approach to model theory has also been refined in order to address directly some important nonclassical model theoretic aspects. One such direction is motivated by *models with states*, appear in myriad forms in computing science and logic. A typical important class of examples is given by the Kripke semantics (of modal logics), which itself comes in a wide variety of forms. Moreover, the concept of model with states goes beyond Kripke semantics, at least in its conventional acceptations. For instance, various automata theories provide another important class of examples. The institution theory answer to "models with states" is given by the theory of *stratified institutions* introduced in [4,5] and further developed or invoked in works such as [6–8], etc.

1.2. 3/2-Institutions

Although in mainstream institution theory signature morphisms are considered in their full generality, they are always implicitly assumed to be total. However, there are few contexts that on the one hand require partial translations between signatures, and on the other hand require an institution theoretic treatment. Two such contexts are conceptual blending [9–11] and software evolution [12]. In [13], we have developed an extension of the ordinary concept of institution [1,3] that accommodates implicitly partiality of the signature morphisms in order to constitute foundations for the above-mentioned application domains. This new structure is called *3/2-institution*, and mathematically, is significantly more complex than ordinary institutions. One way to develop the theory of 3/2-institutions is by representing them in another institution theory that enjoys a higher level of development, and through such a representation to import concepts and results from there. With this paper, we take a few steps in this direction.

The semantic effect of the (implicit) partiality of the signature morphisms in 3/2-institutions is that the reduct of a model with respect to a given signature morphism is a *set* of models rather than a single model. This goes at the heart of our representation of 3/2-institutions as stratified institutions: in the representation the states of a model consists of the set of its reducts (with respect to a given signature morphism).

1.3. Summary and Contributions

- In a preliminary section, we review (1) the category theory required by our work, (2) the concept of institution, (3) the concept of stratified institution, and (4) the concept of 3/2-institution. Examples are also discussed briefly.
- The main section of the paper defines a representation of 3/2-institutions as stratified institutions. We prove the correctness of this representation, i.e., that it satisfies the axioms of a stratified institution.
- One consequence is a further representation to ordinary institution theory via the adjunction from stratified institutions to ordinary institutions defined in [14] (formerly presented as a mere representation in [6]). Another consequence is the import of concepts of semantic connectives. The last consequence that we develop is about the relationship between model amalgamation properties in the representation and in the original 3/2-institution.

2. Preliminaries

2.1. Categories

In general, we stick to the established category theoretic terminology and notations, such as in [15]. However, unlike there, we prefer to use the diagrammatic notation for compositions of arrows in categories, i.e., if $f: A \to B$ and $g: B \to C$ are arrows, then $f;g$ denotes their composition. The domain of an arrow/morphism f is denoted by $\Box f$ while its codomain is denoted by $f\Box$. **Set** denotes the category of sets and functions and **CAT** the "quasi-category" of categories and functors (this means it is bigger than a category since the hom-sets are classes rather than sets). The class of objects of a category **C** is denoted by $|\mathbf{C}|$, and its class of arrows simply by **C** (so by $f \in \mathbf{C}$ we mean that f is an arrow in **C**).

The *dual* of a category **C** (obtained by formally reversing its arrows) is denoted by $\mathbf{C}^\ominus$.

The following functor from [13] extends the well-known power-set construction from sets to categories. Given a category **C**, the *power-set category* $\mathcal{P}\mathbf{C}$ is defined as follows:

- $|\mathcal{P}\mathbf{C}| = \{A \mid A \subseteq |\mathbf{C}|\}$ and $\mathcal{P}\mathbf{C}(A,B) = \{H \subseteq \mathbf{C} \mid \Box h \in A, h\Box \in B \text{ for each } h \in H\}$;
- Composition is defined by $H_1; H_2 = \{h_1; h_2 \mid h_1 \in H_1, h_2 \in H_2, h_1\Box = \Box h_2\}$; then $1_A = \{1_a \mid a \in A\}$ are the identities.

A *partial function* $f: A \nrightarrow B$ is a binary relation $f \subseteq A \times B$ such that $(a,b), (a,b') \in f$ implies $b = b'$. The *definition domain* of f, denoted $\mathrm{dom}(f)$ is the set $\{a \in A \mid \exists b\, (a,b) \in f\}$. A partial function $f: A \nrightarrow B$ is called *total* when $\mathrm{dom}(f) = A$. We denote by f^0 the restriction of f to $\mathrm{dom}(f) \times B$; this is a total function. Partial functions yield a subcategory of the category of binary relations, denoted **Pfn**. Note that $\mathrm{dom}(f;g) = \{a \in \mathrm{dom}(f) \mid$

$f^0(a) \in \text{dom}(g)$}. If $A' \subseteq A$ by $f(A')$, we denote the set $\{b \mid \exists a \in A', (a,b) \in f\}$. Then, $f(A)$ is denoted by $\text{Im}(f)$. It is easy to check the following (though not as immediate as in the case of the total functions): given partial functions $f : A \twoheadrightarrow B$ and $g : B \twoheadrightarrow C$ and $A' \subseteq A$, we have that $(f;g)(A') = g(f(A'))$.

A *3/2-category* is just a category such that its hom-sets are partial orders, and the composition preserves these partial orders. In the literature, 3/2-categories are also called *ordered categories* or *locally ordered categories*. In terms of enriched category theory [16], 3/2-category are just categories enriched by the monoidal category of partially ordered sets.

Given a 3/2-category **C** by $\mathbf{C}^{\ominus}$, we denote its "vertical" dual which reverses the partial orders, and by $\mathbf{C}^{\oplus}$ its double dual $\mathbf{C}^{\ominus\oplus}$. Given 3/2-categories **C** and **C**′, a *strict 3/2-functor* $F : \mathbf{C} \to \mathbf{C}'$ is a functor $\mathbf{C} \to \mathbf{C}'$ that preserves the partial orders on the hom-sets. *Lax functors* relax the functoriality conditions $F(h); F(h') = F(h;h')$ to $F(h); F(h') \leq F(h;h')$ (when $h\square = \square h'$) and $F(1_A) = 1_{F(A)}$ to $1_{F(A)} \leq F(1_A)$. If these inequalities are reversed, then F is an *oplax functor*. This terminology complies to [17] and to more recent literature, but in earlier literature [18,19] this is reversed. Note that oplax + lax = strict. In what follows, whenever we say "3/2-functor" without the qualification "lax" or "oplax" we mean a functor which is either lax or oplax.

Lax functors can be composed like ordinary functors; we denote by 3/2**CAT** the category of 3/2-categories and lax functors.

Most typical examples of a 3/2-category are **Pfn**—the category of partial functions in which the ordering between partial functions $A \twoheadrightarrow B$ is given by the inclusion relation on the binary relations $A \to B$ and **PoSET**—the category of partially ordered sets (with monotonic mappings as arrows) with orderings between monotonic functions being defined point-wise ($f \leq g$ if and only if $f(p) \leq g(p)$ for all p).

The following 3/2-category of [13] is instrumental for the concept of 3/2-institution. The category $\mathbf{CAT}_\mathcal{P}$ has categories as objects and has arrows/morphisms $\mathbf{C} \to \mathbf{C}'$ as mappings $\mathbf{C} \to \mathcal{P}\mathbf{C}'$. The composition in $\mathbf{CAT}_\mathcal{P}$ is defined as follows: given $F : \mathbf{C} \to \mathbf{C}'$ and $F' : \mathbf{C}' \to \mathbf{C}''$ in $\mathbf{CAT}_\mathcal{P}$, then their composition is the mapping $\mathbf{C} \to \mathcal{P}\mathbf{C}''$ that maps each arrow $f \in \mathbf{C}$ to the set $\bigcup_{f' \in Ff} F'f'$.

By considering the point-wise partial order on the class of the mappings $\mathbf{C} \to \mathcal{P}\mathbf{C}'$, we obtain a 3/2-category denoted $3/2(\mathbf{CAT}_\mathcal{P})$. Note that in the above definition, we do not require that the mappings $\mathbf{C} \to \mathcal{P}\mathbf{C}'$ are functors of any kind, not even morphisms of graphs, they are just mappings between classes of arrows. In fact, the above composition in general does not preserve functoriality properties.

2.2. Institutions

The original standard reference for institution theory is [1]. An *institution*

$$\mathcal{I} = (Sign^\mathcal{I}, Sen^\mathcal{I}, Mod^\mathcal{I}, \models^\mathcal{I})$$

consists of:

- A category $Sign^\mathcal{I}$ whose objects are called *signatures*.
- A sentence functor $Sen^\mathcal{I} : Sign^\mathcal{I} \to \mathbf{Set}$ defining for each signature a set whose elements are called *sentences* over that signature and defining for each signature morphism a *sentence translation* function.
- A model functor $Mod^\mathcal{I} : (Sign^\mathcal{I})^\ominus \to \mathbf{CAT}$ defining for each signature Σ the category $Mod^\mathcal{I}(\Sigma)$ of Σ-*models* and Σ-model homomorphisms, and for each signature morphism φ the *reduct* functor $Mod^\mathcal{I}(\varphi)$.
- For every signature Σ, a binary Σ-*satisfaction relation* $\models^\mathcal{I}_\Sigma \subseteq |Mod^\mathcal{I}(\Sigma)| \times Sen^\mathcal{I}(\Sigma)$.

Such that for each morphism φ, the *satisfaction condition*

$$M' \models^\mathcal{I}_{\Sigma'} Sen^\mathcal{I}(\varphi)\rho \text{ if and only if } Mod^\mathcal{I}(\varphi)M' \models^\mathcal{I}_\Sigma \rho \qquad (1)$$

holds for each $M' \in |Mod^{\mathcal{I}}(\varphi\square)|$ and $\rho \in Sen^{\mathcal{I}}(\square\varphi)$. This can be expressed as the satisfaction relation $\models$ being a natural transformation:

$$\begin{array}{ccc}
\square\varphi & Sen^{\mathcal{I}}(\square\varphi) \xrightarrow{\models^{\mathcal{I}}_{\square\varphi}} [|Mod^{\mathcal{I}}(\square\varphi)| \to 2] \\
\varphi \downarrow & Sen^{\mathcal{I}}(\varphi) \downarrow & \uparrow Mod^{\mathcal{I}}(\varphi) \\
\varphi\square & Sen^{\mathcal{I}}(\varphi\square) \xrightarrow[\models^{\mathcal{I}}_{\varphi\square}]{} [|Mod^{\mathcal{I}}(\varphi\square)| \to 2]
\end{array}$$

$([|Mod(\Sigma)| \to 2]$ represents the "set" of the "subsets" of $|Mod(\Sigma)|)$.

We may omit the superscripts or subscripts from the notations of the components of institutions when there is no risk of ambiguity. For example, if the considered institution and signature are clear, we may denote $\models^{\mathcal{I}}_{\Sigma}$ just by $\models$. For $M = Mod(\varphi)M'$, we say that M is the φ-reduct of M'. The institution is called *discrete* when the model categories $Mod(\Sigma)$ are discrete (i.e., do not posses nonidentity arrows).

The literature (e.g., [2,3]) shows myriads of logical systems from computing or from mathematical logic captured as institutions. In fact, an informal thesis underlying institution theory is that any "logic" may be captured by the above definition. While this should be taken with a grain of salt, it certainly applies to any logical system based on satisfaction between sentences and models of any kind.

2.3. Stratified Institutions

Informally, the main idea behind the concept of stratified institution, as introduced in [5], is to enhance the concept of institution with "states" for the models. Thus, each model M comes equipped with a *set* $[\![M]\!]$ that has to satisfy some structural axioms. The following definition has been given in [6] and represents an important upgrade of the original definition from [5], the main reason being to make the definition of stratified institutions really usable for doing in-depth model theory. The latter has suffered another different upgrade in [7], which is, however, strongly convergent to the upgrade proposed in [6].

A *stratified institution* $\mathcal{S}$ is a tuple

$$(Sign^{\mathcal{S}}, Sen^{\mathcal{S}}, Mod^{\mathcal{S}}, [\![\_]\!]^{\mathcal{S}}, \models^{\mathcal{S}})$$

consisting of:

- Category $Sign^{\mathcal{S}}$ of signatures;
- A sentence functor $Sen^{\mathcal{S}}: Sign^{\mathcal{S}} \to \mathbf{Set}$;
- A model functor $Mod^{\mathcal{S}}: (Sign^{\mathcal{S}})^{\ominus} \to \mathbf{CAT}$;
- A "stratification" lax natural transformation $[\![\_]\!]^{\mathcal{S}}: Mod^{\mathcal{S}} \Rightarrow SET$, where $SET: Sign^{\mathcal{S}} \to \mathbf{CAT}$ is a functor mapping each signature to $\mathbf{Set}$;
- A satisfaction relation between models and sentences which is parameterized by model states, $M \ (\models^{\mathcal{S}})^{w}_{\Sigma} \rho$, where $w \in [\![M]\!]^{\mathcal{S}}_{\Sigma}$ such that the following *satisfaction condition*

$$Mod^{\mathcal{S}}(\varphi)M' \ (\models^{\mathcal{S}})^{[\![M']\!]_{\varphi}w}_{\Sigma} \rho \text{ if and only if } M' \ (\models^{\mathcal{S}})^{w}_{\Sigma'} \ Sen^{\mathcal{S}}(\varphi)\rho \qquad (2)$$

holds for any signature morphism φ, $M' \in |Mod^{\mathcal{S}}(\varphi\square)|$, $w \in [\![M']\!]^{\mathcal{S}}_{\varphi\square}$, $\rho \in Sen^{\mathcal{S}}(\square\varphi)$. Like for ordinary institutions, when appropriate, we also use simplified notations without superscripts or subscripts that are clear from the context.

The lax natural transformation property of $[\![\_]\!]$ is depicted in the diagram below

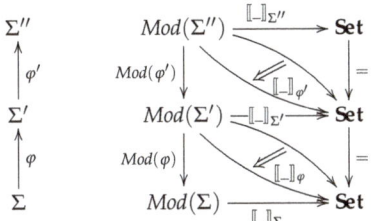

with the following compositionality property for each Σ''-model M'':

$$[\![M'']\!]_{(\varphi;\varphi')} = [\![M'']\!]_{\varphi'}; [\![Mod(\varphi')M'']\!]_{\varphi}. \tag{3}$$

Moreover, the natural transformation property of each $[\![\_]\!]_{\varphi}$ is given by the commutativity of the following diagram:

$$\begin{array}{ccc} M' & & [\![M']\!]_{\Sigma'} \xrightarrow{[\![M']\!]_{\varphi}} [\![Mod(\varphi)M']\!]_{\Sigma} \\ h' \downarrow & & [\![h']\!]_{\Sigma'} \downarrow \qquad\qquad\qquad \downarrow [\![Mod(\varphi)h']\!]_{\Sigma} \\ N' & & [\![N']\!]_{\Sigma'} \xrightarrow[{[\![N']\!]_{\varphi}}]{} [\![Mod(\varphi)N']\!]_{\Sigma} \end{array} \tag{4}$$

The satisfaction relation can be presented as a natural transformation $\models : Sen \Rightarrow [\![Mod(\_) \to \mathbf{Set}]\!]$, where the functor $[\![Mod(\_) \to \mathbf{Set}]\!] : Sign \to \mathbf{Set}$ is defined by

- For each signature $\Sigma \in |Sign|$, $[\![Mod(\Sigma) \to \mathbf{Set}]\!]$ denotes the set of all the mappings $f : |Mod(\Sigma)| \to \mathbf{Set}$ such that $f(M) \subseteq [\![M]\!]_{\Sigma}$;
- For each signature morphism $\varphi : \Sigma \to \Sigma'$

$$[\![Mod(\varphi) \to \mathbf{Set}]\!](f)(M') = [\![M']\!]_{\varphi}^{-1}(f(Mod(\varphi)(M'))).$$

A straightforward check reveals that the satisfaction condition (2) appears exactly as the naturality property of $\models$:

$$\begin{array}{ccc} \Sigma & Sen(\Sigma) \xrightarrow{\models_{\Sigma}} [\![Mod(\Sigma) \to \mathbf{Set}]\!] \\ \varphi \downarrow & Sen(\varphi) \downarrow \qquad\qquad\qquad \downarrow [\![Mod(\varphi) \to \mathbf{Set}]\!] \\ \Sigma' & Sen(\Sigma') \xrightarrow[\models_{\Sigma'}]{} [\![Mod(\Sigma') \to \mathbf{Set}]\!] \end{array}$$

Ordinary institutions are the stratified institutions for which $[\![M]\!]_{\Sigma}$ is always a singleton set. In the upgraded definition, we have removed the surjectivity condition on $[\![M']\!]_{\varphi}$ from the definition of the stratified institutions of [5] and rather make it explicit when necessary. This is motivated by the fact that most of the results developed do not depend upon this condition which, however, holds in all examples known by us. On the one hand, when modelling Kripke semantics abstractly, $[\![M']\!]_{\varphi}$ are even identities, which makes $[\![\_]\!]$ a strict rather than a lax natural transformation. However, on the other hand, there are interesting examples when the stratification is properly lax. One such example is provided by the representation result of this paper.

The following very expected property does not follow from the axioms of stratified institutions, hence we impose it explicitly.

Assumption 1. *In all considered stratified institutions, the satisfaction is preserved by model isomorphisms, i.e., for each Σ-model isomorphism $h: M \to N$, each $w \in [\![M]\!]_\Sigma$, and each Σ-sentence ρ,*

$$M \models^w \rho \text{ if and only if } N \models^{[\![h]\!]w} \rho.$$

The literature on stratified institutions shows many model theories that are captured as stratified institutions. Here, we recall some of them in a very succinct form; in a more detailed form, one may find them in [6,14].

1. In *modal propositional logic ($\mathcal{MPL}$)*, the category of the signatures is **Set**; $Sen(P)$ is the set of the usual modal sentences formed with the atomic propositions from P, and the P-models are the Kripke structures (W, M), where $W = (|W|, W_\lambda)$ consists of a set of "possible worlds" $|W|$ and an accessibility relation $W_\lambda \subseteq |W| \times |W|$, and $M : |W| \to 2^P$. The stratification is given by $[\![(W, M)]\!] = |W|$.

2. In *first-order modal logic ($\mathcal{MFOL}$)*, the signatures are first-order logic ($\mathcal{FOL}$) signatures consisting of sets of operation and relation symbols structured by their arities. The sentences extend the usual construction of $\mathcal{FOL}$ sentences with the modal connectives $\Box$ and $\Diamond$. The models for a signature Σ are Kripke structures (W, M), where W is like in $\mathcal{MPL}$ but $M : |W| \to |Mod^{\mathcal{FOL}}(\Sigma)|$ subject to the constraint that the carrier sets and the interpretations of the constants are shared across the possible worlds. The stratification is like in $\mathcal{MPL}$.

3. *Hybrid logics* refine modal logics by adding explicit syntax for the possible worlds such as *nominals* and @. Institutions of hybrid logics upgrade the syntactic and the semantic components of the institutions of modal logics accordingly.

4. *Multimodal logics* exhibit several modalities instead of only the traditional $\Diamond$ and $\Box$ and, moreover, these may have various arities. If one considers the sets of modalities to be variable, then they have to be considered as part of the signatures. Each of the stratified institutions discussed in the previous examples admit an upgrade to the multimodal case.

5. In a series of works on *modalization of institutions*, Refs. [20–22] modal logic and Kripke semantics are developed by abstracting away details that do not belong to modality, such as sorts, functions, predicates, etc. This is achieved by extensions of abstract institutions (in the standard situations meant in principle to encapsulate the atomic part of the logics) with the essential ingredients of modal logic and Kripke semantics. The result of this process, when instantiated to various concrete logics (or to their atomic parts only), generates uniformly a wide range of hierarchical combinations between various flavors of modal logic and various other logics. Concrete examples discussed in [20–22] include various modal logics over nonconventional structures of relevance in computing science, such as partial algebra, preordered algebra, etc. Various constraints on the respective Kripke models, many of them having to do with the underlying nonmodal structures, have also been considered. All these arise as examples of stratified institutions, such as the examples presented above in the paper. An interesting class of examples that has emerged quite smoothly out of the general works on *hybridization* (i.e., modalization including also hybrid logic features) of institutions is that of multilayered hybrid logics that provide a logical base for specifying hierarchical transition systems (see [23]).

6. *Open first order logic ($\mathcal{OFOL}$).* This is a $\mathcal{FOL}$ instance of $St(\mathcal{I})$, the "internal stratification" abstract example developed in [5]. An $\mathcal{OFOL}$ signature is a pair (Σ, X) consisting of $\mathcal{FOL}$ signature Σ and a finite block of variables. To any $\mathcal{OFOL}$ signature (Σ, X), there corresponds a $\mathcal{FOL}$ signature $\Sigma + X$ that adjoins X to Σ as new constants. Then, $Sen^{\mathcal{OFOL}}(\Sigma, X) = Sen^{\mathcal{FOL}}(\Sigma + X)$, $Mod^{\mathcal{OFOL}}(\Sigma, X) = Mod^{\mathcal{FOL}}(\Sigma)$, $[\![M]\!]_{\Sigma,X} = M^X$, i.e., the set of the "valuations" of X to M and for each (Σ, X)-model M, each $w \in M^X$, and each (Σ, X)-sentence ρ, we define $(M(\models^{\mathcal{OFOL}}_{\Sigma,X})^w \rho) = (M^w \models^{\mathcal{FOL}}_{\Sigma+X} \rho)$, where M^w is the expansion of M to $\Sigma + X$ such that $M^w_X = w$ (i.e., the new constants of X are interpreted in M^w according to the "valuation" w).

7. Various kinds of automata theories can be presented as stratified institutions. For instance, the deterministic automata (for regular languages) have the set of the input symbols as signatures, the automata A are the models and the words are the sentences. Then, $[\![A]\!]$ is the set of the states of A and $A \models^s \alpha$ if and only if α is recognized by A from the states s.

2.4. 3/2-Institutions

The concept of 3/2-institution has been introduced in [13]. Our presentation of 3/2-institutions follows that paper. A *3/2-institution* $\mathcal{I} = (Sign^{\mathcal{I}}, Sen^{\mathcal{I}}, Mod^{\mathcal{I}}, \models^{\mathcal{I}})$ consists of

- A 3/2-category $Sign^{\mathcal{I}}$—called the *category of the signatures*;
- A 3/2-functor $Sen^{\mathcal{I}} : Sign^{\mathcal{I}} \to \mathbf{Pfn}$—called the *sentence functor*;
- A lax 3/2-functor $Mod^{\mathcal{I}} : (Sign^{\mathcal{I}})^{\oplus} \to 3/2(\mathbf{CAT}_{\mathcal{P}})$ — called the *model functor*, such that $Mod(\varphi)$ is a lax functor for each signature morphism φ;
- For each signature $\Sigma \in |Sign^{\mathcal{I}}|$, a *satisfaction relation* $\models^{\mathcal{I}}_{\Sigma} \subseteq |Mod^{\mathcal{I}}(\Sigma)| \times Sen^{\mathcal{I}}(\Sigma)$.

Such that for each morphism $\varphi \in Sign^{\mathcal{I}}$, the *satisfaction condition*

$$M' \models^{\mathcal{I}}_{\varphi\square} Sen^{\mathcal{I}}(\varphi)\rho \quad \text{if and only if} \quad M \models^{\mathcal{I}}_{\square\varphi} \rho \tag{5}$$

holds for each $M' \in |Mod^{\mathcal{I}}(\varphi\square)|$, each $M \in |Mod^{\mathcal{I}}(\varphi)M'|$, and each $\rho \in \text{dom}(Sen^{\mathcal{I}}(\varphi))$.

The difference between 3/2-institutions and ordinary institutions, from now on called *1-institutions*, is determined by the 3/2-categorical structure of the signature morphisms which propagates to the sentence and to the model functors. Consequently, the satisfaction condition (5) takes an appropriate format. Thus, for each signature morphism φ, its corresponding sentence translation $Sen(\varphi)$ is a partial function $Sen(\square\varphi) \rightharpoonup Sen(\varphi\square)$ and, moreover, whenever $\varphi \leq \theta$, we have that $Sen(\varphi) \subseteq Sen(\theta)$. The sentence functor Sen can be either lax or oplax, and depending on how this is, we may call the respective 3/2-institution a *lax* or *oplax 3/2-institution*. In many concrete situations, it happens that Sen is strict, while some general results require it to be either lax, oplax or strict.

The model reduct $Mod(\varphi)$ is a lax functor $Mod(\varphi\square) \to \mathcal{P}Mod(\square\varphi)$, implying that for each Σ'-model M' we have a *class of reducts* M rather than a single reduct. In concrete examples, this is a direct consequence of the partiality of φ: in the reducts, the interpretation of the symbols on which φ is not defined is unconstrained, therefore there may be many possibilities for their interpretations. "Many" here includes also the case when there is no interpretation.

- The fact that Mod is a 3/2-functor implies also that whenever $\varphi \leq \theta$ we have $Mod(\theta) \leq Mod(\varphi)$, i.e., $Mod(\theta)M' \subseteq Mod(\varphi)M'$, etc.
- The lax aspect of Mod means that for signature morphisms φ and φ', such that $\varphi\square = \square\varphi'$, and for any $\varphi'\square$-model M'', we have that

$$Mod(\varphi)(Mod(\varphi')M'') \subseteq Mod(\varphi;\varphi')M''$$

and for each signature Σ and for each Σ-model M that

$$M \in Mod(1_{\Sigma})M.$$

- The lax aspect of the reduct functors $Mod(\varphi)$ means that for model homomorphisms h_1, h_2, such that $h_1\square = \square h_2$, we have that

$$Mod(\varphi)(h_1); Mod(\varphi)(h_2) \subseteq Mod(\varphi)(h_1; h_2)$$

and for each $M' \in Mod(\varphi\square)$ and each $M \in Mod(\varphi)M'$ that

$$1_M \in Mod(\varphi)1_{M'}.$$

The model homomorphisms do not yet play any role in conceptual blending or in other envisaged applications of 3/2-institutions. Hence, the lax aspect of model functors is for the moment a purely theoretical feature which is, however, supported naturally by all examples. Another technical note: according to the definition of 3/2-institutions. At the abstract level, there are several implicit ways to consider the "totality" of signature morphisms in terms of their syntactic and semantic effects. The following concepts have been introduced in [13]. A signature morphism φ in a 3/2-institution

- Is *Sen-maximal* when $Sen(\varphi)$ is total;
- Is *Mod-maximal* when for each $\varphi\square$-model M', $Mod(\varphi)M'$ is a singleton;
- Is *total* when it is both *Sen*-maximal and *Mod*-maximal;
- Is *Mod-strict* when for each signature morphism θ, such that $\theta\square = \square\varphi$, we have that

$$Mod(\varphi); Mod(\theta) = Mod(\theta; \varphi).$$

In general, in many concrete situations of interest, a signature morphism is *Mod*-strict whenever it is total. In [13], there is even a result of a general nature that supports this fact.

The seminal paper [13] presents in detail a series of examples of 3/2-institutions. Here, we recall from there three classes of examples in a very succinct form.

1. Common examples of institutions can be turned into 3/2-institutions by introducing explicit partiality at the level of the signature morphisms. This means that certain sort/operation/relation symbols are skipped by the respective (partial) signature morphism. This induces a further partiality on the sentence translations as only the sentences that does not contain "skipped" symbols can be translated. The model reducts may interpret freely the "skipped" symbols, hence in principle one model may have several reducts along the same signature morphisms. In [13], this procedure was illustrated on the institutions of propositional logic (hence 3/2$\mathcal{PL}$) and of many-sorted algebra (hence 3/2$\mathcal{MSA}$). In the latter case, several degrees of partiality can be introduced.
2. The *3/2-institutional seeds* of [13] provide a generic way to define 3/2-institutions. Some of the 3/2-institution that are based on some form of explicit partiality can also be presented in this way.
3. We may turn any abstract institution into a proper 3/2-institution by adding weights to the signature morphisms, which means that the signature morphisms come as pairs (φ, k) (in [13] denoted $\varphi \bullet k$), where φ is a signature morphism of the ordinary institution and $k \in \{0, 1\}$. The signatures stay the same. This construction is extended to sentences and models in a way that yields the sentence and the model functors proper lax functors. Although this is a mere technical construction without any known applications, it has an important theoretical significance because it provides a class of examples where the 3/2-categorical structures involved have nothing to do with any form of partiality.

3. The Canonical Stratified Institution Associated to a 3/2-Institution

The representation of 3/2-institutions as stratified institutions is in general partial in the sense that the signature morphisms that are subject to the representation have to satisfy certain technical conditions. Two of these are defined below. The second one appears as a 3/2-institution theoretic replica of a property from ordinary institution theory [3] with the same name but in a somewhat reverse form. While the former concept is a lifting concept, the 3/2-institution theoretic one may have an opposite appearance because it goes along the direction of the model reduct. However, this is misleading because in 3/2-institutions, due to the implicit partiality of the signature morphisms, reducts also have a nature of expansion. Towards the end of this section, we discuss what these two properties mean in concrete situations. The constructions and the results in this section are developed at the abstract level. It would be helpful if the reader would interpret them in the context of the examples of 3/2-institutions listed above. This should be a rather straightforward

Definition 1. *In any 3/2-institution, a signature morphism χ*

- *Is fiber-small when for each $\chi\square$-model M we have that $Mod(\chi)M$ is a set;*
- *Is quasi-representable when for each $\chi\square$-model homomorphism $h: M \to M_0$, and for each $N \in Mod(\chi)M$ there exists and unique model homomorphism $h^N \in Mod(\chi)h$, such that $\square h^N = N$.*

We now fix a 3/2-institution $\mathcal{I} = (Sign, Sen, Mod, \models)$ and gradually build the entities that define its associated stratified institution $\mathcal{I}^s = (Sign^s, Sen^s, Mod^s, [\![\_]\!], \models^s)$. The main idea of this representation is that the reducts of a model M are considered to be its states. In order to make precise sense of this idea, we have to change the concept of signature: in the stratified institution, a signature is a certain signature morphism χ in $\mathcal{I}$, such that M is a $\chi\square$-model. It is the abstract nature of the concept of institution that allows for such a conceptual twist.

Definition 2 (The category of the signatures). *The category $Sign^s$ has the objects the fiber-small quasi-representable signature morphisms χ of Sign. The arrows $\chi \to \chi'$ in $Sign^s$ are pairs of signature morphisms (φ, θ), such that*

- *Both φ and θ are total and Mod-strict;*
- *$\chi; \theta \leq \varphi; \chi'$.*

$$
\begin{array}{ccc}
\Sigma & \xrightarrow{\varphi} & \Sigma' \\
\chi \downarrow & \leq & \downarrow \chi' \\
\Omega & \xrightarrow{\theta} & \Omega'
\end{array}
\tag{6}
$$

The composition in $Sign^s$ is defined as pairwise composition in Sign, i.e., $(\varphi, \theta); (\varphi', \theta') = (\varphi; \varphi', \theta; \theta')$, as shown in the following diagram:

(7)

An arrow $(\varphi, \theta): \chi \to \chi'$ is strict when $\chi; \theta = \varphi; \chi'$.

We have the correctness of definition 1:

Proposition 1. *$Sign^s$ is a category.*

Proof. We have to prove that the composition preserves the preorder property. This follows from the monotonicity of the composition in *Sign* (we use the notations from (7)):

$$\chi; \theta; \theta' \leq \varphi; \chi'; \theta' \leq \varphi; \varphi'; \chi'.$$

It remains to note that totality and *Mod*-strictness when considered together are preserved by the composition of the signature morphisms. (*Mod*-strictness supports the preservation of *Mod*-maximality by the composition of signature morphisms.) □

Definition 3 (The sentence translation functor). *For any $Sign^s$ signature χ, we define $Sen^s(\chi) = Sen(\square\chi)$ and for any $Sign^s$-morphism (φ, θ), we define $Sen^s(\varphi, \theta) = Sen(\varphi)$.*

Proposition 2. Sen^s *is a functor* $Sign^s \to$ **Set**.

Proof. This is an immediate consequence of the functoriality of *Sen* and of the totality hypothesis, which guarantees that $Sen(\varphi)$ is indeed a total function. □

Definition 4 (The model reduct functor). *For any* $Sign^s$ *signature* χ, *we define* $Mod^s(\chi) = Mod(\chi\square)$ *and for any* $Sign^s$-*morphism* (φ, θ) *we define* $Mod^s(\varphi, \theta) = Mod(\theta)$.

Proposition 3. Mod^s *is a functor* $(Sign^s)^{\ominus} \to$ **CAT**.

Proof. This is an immediate consequence of the functoriality of *Mod* and of the *Mod*-maximality and *Mod*-strictness hypothesis (on θ). □

Definition 5 (The stratification). *For any* $Sign^s$ *signature* χ, *we define*
- $[\![M]\!]_\chi = Mod(\chi)M$ *for any* $M \in |Mod^s(\chi)| (= |Mod(\chi\square)|)$;
- $[\![h]\!]_\chi N = h^N \square$ *for any* $\chi\square$-*model homomorphism* $h \in Mod^s(\chi)(= |Mod(\chi\square)|)$ *and* $\square\chi$-*model* $N \in Mod(\chi)(\square h)$.

For each signature morphism $(\varphi, \theta) : \chi \to \chi'$ *in* $Sign^s$, *we define:*
- $[\![M']\!]_{(\varphi, \theta)} N' = Mod(\varphi) N'$ *for any* $M' \in |Mod^s(\chi')|$ *and any* $N' \in [\![M']\!]_{\chi'}$.

Proposition 4. $[\![\_]\!]$ *is a lax natural transformation* $Mod^s \Rightarrow SET$.

Proof. The correctness of definition 5 is justified as follows:
- $[\![M]\!]_\chi$ is a set by the fiber-small assumption on χ.
- The definition of $[\![h]\!]_\chi N$ relies on the quasi-representability assumption on χ.
- $[\![M']\!]_{(\varphi, \theta)} N'$ represents a single model because φ is Mod-maximal.
- That $[\![M']\!]_{(\varphi, \theta)}([\![M']\!]_{\chi'}) \subseteq [\![Mod^s(\varphi, \theta) M']\!]_\chi$ is shown as follows:

$$\begin{aligned}
[\![M']\!]_{(\varphi, \theta)}([\![M']\!]_{\chi'}) &= Mod(\varphi)(Mod(\chi')M') & \text{definition of } [\![\_]\!] \\
&\subseteq Mod(\varphi; \chi')M' & Mod \text{ lax} \\
&\subseteq Mod(\chi; \theta)M' & \chi; \theta \leq \varphi; \chi', Mod \text{ monotone} \\
&= Mod(\chi)(Mod(\theta)M') & \theta \; Mod\text{-strict} \\
&= [\![Mod(\theta)M']\!]_\chi & \text{definition of } [\![\_]\!]_\chi, \theta \; Mod\text{-maximal} \\
&= [\![Mod^s(\varphi, \theta)M']\!]_\chi & \text{definition of } Mod^s.
\end{aligned}$$

The *functoriality of* $[\![\_]\!]_\chi : Mod^s(\chi) \to$ **Set** means two things:
- That $[\![1_M]\!]_\chi N = N$ for each $\chi\square$-model M and each $N \in Mod(\chi)M$. This is shown by the following argument. Since $Mod(\chi)$ is lax, it follows that $1_N \in Mod(\chi) 1_M$, which by the uniqueness aspect of the quasi-representability property implies that $1_N = (1_M)^N$. Since $1_N \square = N$, the conclusion follows.
- That $[\![h; h_0]\!]_\chi = [\![h]\!]_\chi ; [\![h_0]\!]_\chi$ for any $\chi\square$-model homomorphisms $h : M \to M_0$ and $h_0 : M_0 \to M_1$. In order to show that, we consider any model $N \in Mod(\chi)M$ and denote by $N_0 = h^N \square$. We have that:

$$\begin{aligned}
h^N ; h_0^{N_0} &\in Mod(\chi) h \; ; \; Mod(\chi) h_0 & \text{definitions of } h_0^N, h_0^{N_0} \\
&\subseteq Mod(\chi)(h; h_0) & Mod(\chi) \text{ lax}.
\end{aligned}$$

From the uniqueness aspect of the quasi-representability property of χ, it follows that

$$h^N ; h_0^{N_0} = (h; h_0)^N. \tag{8}$$

Hence,

$$\begin{aligned}
[\![h;h_0]\!]_\chi N &= (h;h_0)^N \square & \text{definition of } [\![h;h_0]\!]_\chi N \\
&= (h^N; h_0^{N_0}) \square & (8) \\
&= h_0^{N_0} \square \\
&= [\![h_0]\!]_\chi ([\![h]\!]_\chi N) & \text{definitions of } N_0, [\![h_0]\!]_\chi N_0, [\![h]\!]_\chi N.
\end{aligned}$$

For proving the *lax natural transformation property of* $[\![\_]\!]$ (relation ((3))), we consider a composition of signature morphisms in $Sign^s$ such as in diagrams (7), an Ω''-model M'', and $N'' \in [\![M'']\!]_{\chi''} = Mod(\chi'')M''$. Note that since $N'' \in [\![M'']\!]_{\chi''}$, we have that

$$Mod(\varphi')N'' = [\![M'']\!]_{(\varphi',\theta')}N'' \in [\![Mod^s(\varphi',\theta')M'']\!]_{\chi'} = [\![Mod(\theta')M'']\!]_{\chi'} \quad (9)$$

Then, we have:
$[\![M'']\!]_{(\varphi,\theta);(\varphi',\theta')}N'' =$

$$\begin{aligned}
&= [\![M'']\!]_{(\varphi;\varphi',\theta;\theta')}N'' & \text{definition of } Sign^s \\
&= Mod(\varphi;\varphi')N'' & \text{definition of } [\![\_]\!] \\
&= Mod(\varphi)(Mod(\varphi')N'') & Mod \text{ functor, } \varphi \text{ Mod-strict} \\
&= [\![Mod(\theta')M'']\!]_{(\varphi,\theta)}(Mod(\varphi')N'') & (9), \text{definition of } [\![\_]\!] \\
&= [\![Mod^s(\varphi',\theta')M'']\!]_{(\varphi,\theta)}(Mod(\varphi')N'') & \text{definition of } Mod^s \\
&= [\![Mod^s(\varphi',\theta')M'']\!]_{(\varphi,\theta)}([\![M'']\!]_{(\varphi',\theta')}N'') & \text{definition of } [\![\_]\!].
\end{aligned}$$

For proving the *natural transformation property of* $[\![\_]\!]_{(\varphi,\theta)}$, under the notations from diagrams (7) by considering an Ω'-model homomorphism $h': M' \to M'_0$, we have to show that the diagram below commutes:

$$\begin{array}{ccccc}
M' & & Mod(\chi')M' & \xrightarrow{[\![M']\!]_{(\varphi,\theta)}} & Mod(\chi)(Mod(\theta)M') \\
{\scriptstyle h'}\downarrow & & {\scriptstyle [\![h']\!]_{\chi'}}\downarrow & & \downarrow{\scriptstyle [\![Mod(\theta)h']\!]_\chi} \quad (10)\\
M'_0 & & Mod(\chi')M'_0 & \xrightarrow[{[\![M'_0]\!]_{(\varphi,\theta)}}]{} & Mod(\chi)(Mod(\theta)M'_0)
\end{array}$$

Let $N' \in Mod(\chi')M'$, and let us denote $N = Mod(\varphi)N'$ and $h = Mod(\theta)h'$. Let us first prove that

$$Mod(\varphi)h'^{N'} = h^N. \quad (11)$$

On the one hand, we have:

$$\begin{aligned}
Mod(\varphi)h'^{N'} &\in Mod(\varphi)(Mod(\chi')h') & \text{definition of } h'^{N'} \\
&\subseteq Mod(\varphi;\chi')h' & Mod \text{ lax} \\
&\subseteq Mod(\chi;\theta)h' & Mod \text{ monotone, } \chi;\theta \leq \varphi;\chi' \\
&= Mod(\chi)(Mod(\theta)h') & \theta \text{ Mod-strict} \\
&= Mod(\chi)h.
\end{aligned}$$

On the other hand, we have:

$$\square Mod(\varphi)h'^{N'} = Mod(\varphi)(\square h'^{N'}) = Mod(\varphi)N' = N.$$

Then, (11) follows from $Mod(\varphi)h'^{N'} \in Mod(\chi)h$ and $\Box Mod(\varphi)h'^{N'} = N$ and from the uniqueness aspect of the quasi-representability property of χ. Now, the following argument completes the proof of the natural transformation property of $[\![\_]\!]_{(\varphi,\theta)}$:

$$\begin{aligned}
[\![Mod(\theta)h']\!]_\chi([\![M']\!]_{(\varphi,\theta)}N') &= [\![Mod(\theta)h']\!]_\chi(Mod(\varphi)N') & \text{definition of } [\![M']\!]_{(\varphi,\theta)} \\
&= h^N\Box & \text{definition of } [\![Mod(\theta)h']\!]_\chi = [\![h]\!]_\chi \\
&= (Mod(\varphi)h'^{N'})\Box & (11) \\
&= Mod(\varphi)(h'^{N'}\Box) & Mod(\varphi) \text{ functor} \\
&= [\![M'_0]\!]_{(\varphi,\theta)}(h'^{N'}\Box) & \text{definition of } [\![M'_0]\!]_{(\varphi,\theta)} \\
&= [\![M'_0]\!]_{(\varphi,\theta)}([\![h']\!]_{\chi'}N') & \text{definition of } [\![h']\!]_{\chi'}.
\end{aligned}$$

□

Definition 6 (The satisfaction relation). *For each signature χ in $Sign^s$, each $\chi\Box$-model M, each $\Box\chi$-model $N \in [\![M]\!]_\chi$, and each $\Box\chi$-sentence ρ,*

$$M(\models^s)_\chi^N \rho \text{ if and only if } N \models_{\Box\chi} \rho.$$

Proposition 5. *For any signature morphism $(\varphi,\theta) : \chi \to \chi'$ in $Sign^s$, any χ'-model M', any $N' \in [\![M']\!]_{\chi'}$, and any χ-sentence ρ:*

$$M' \models_{\chi'}^{N'} Sen^s(\varphi,\theta)\rho \text{ if and only if } Mod^s(\varphi,\theta)M' \models_\chi \rho.$$

Proof. By similarity to (9), we have that:

$$Mod(\varphi)N' \in [\![Mod(\theta)M']\!]_\chi \qquad (12)$$

Then, we have:

$$\begin{aligned}
M'(\models^s)_{\chi'}^{N'} Sen^s(\varphi,\theta)\rho &\Leftrightarrow N' \models_{\Box\chi'} Sen(\varphi)\rho & \text{definition of } \models^s \\
&\Leftrightarrow Mod(\varphi)N' \models_{\Box\chi} \rho & \text{Satisfaction Condition of } \mathcal{I} \\
&\Leftrightarrow Mod(\theta)M'(\models^s)_\chi^{Mod(\varphi)N'} \rho & (12), \text{definition of } \models^s \\
&\Leftrightarrow Mod(\theta)M'(\models^s)_\chi^{[\![M']\!]_{(\varphi,\theta)}N'} & \text{definition of } [\![\_]\!] \\
&\Leftrightarrow Mod^s(\varphi,\theta)M'(\models^s)_\chi^{[\![M']\!]_{(\varphi,\theta)}N'} & \text{definition of } Mod^s.
\end{aligned}$$

□

By putting together propositions 1–5, we obtain:

Corollary 1. $\mathcal{I}^s = (Sign^s, Sen^s, Mod^s, [\![\_]\!], \models^s)$ *is a stratified institution.*

The technical conditions underlying the construction of $\mathcal{I}^s$ imposes some restriction both on the $\mathcal{I}$ signature morphisms χ that play the role of $Sign^s$-signatures and on the $\mathcal{I}$ signature morphisms that make up the $Sign^s$ morphisms. Let us see their significance and what they might mean in concrete situations.

- The $\mathcal{I}$ signature morphisms that stand as $Sign^s$ signatures implicitly represent genuine partiality. By contrast, the $\mathcal{I}$ signature morphisms used for the $Sign^s$ morphisms implicitly represent genuine totality, the reason being that we want to achieve totality for the syntactic and of the semantic translations at the level of the resultant stratified institution.
- The $\mathcal{I}$ signature morphisms standing as $Sign^s$ signatures have to be fiber-small and quasi-representable. The former condition is necessary for the stratifications to be sets, and in the concrete situations is very mild. Only when we are in a many-sorted

context doe it amount to a certain restriction, namely that there is no partiality of the translation of the sorts.
- In the applications, the quasi-representability condition on a signature morphism χ is less stringent than how it appears in principle.
  - As it is about (proper) model homomorphisms, it holds trivially in their absence. This degenerated situation is in fact the norm in the applications of the 3/2-institutions, as until now there are not known applications that involve proper model homomorphisms.
  - When χ admits partiality only on the constants, then the quasi-representable holds.
  - When χ admits partiality only on the relation symbols and the model homomorphisms are "strong" (in the sense of [3]), then χ is quasi-representable, too.
- As an example that puts together some of the situations discussed above, if we consider the 3/2-institution of many sorted first-order logics with "strong" model homomorphisms, then any signature morphism that is total on the sorts and on nonconstant operation symbols qualifies as a $Sign^s$ signature.

4. Consequences of the Representation
4.1. Representing 3/2-Institutions as Ordinary Institutions

In [6], a general representation of stratified institutions as ordinary institutions was developed. In [14], it is shown that this constitutes a left adjoint functor from the category **SINS** of stratified institution morphisms to the category **INS** of ordinary institution morphisms. Let us recall this representation from either [6] or [14]. Given a stratified institution $\mathcal{S} = (Sign, Sen, Mod, [\![\_]\!], \models)$, the following institution $\mathcal{S}^\sharp = (Sign, Sen, Mod^\sharp, \models^\sharp)$ is defined by

- The objects of $Mod^\sharp(\Sigma)$ are the pairs (M, w), such that $M \in |Mod(\Sigma)|$ and $w \in [\![M]\!]_\Sigma$;
- The Σ-homomorphisms $(M, w) \to (N, v)$ are the pairs (h, w), such that $h: M \to N$ and $[\![h]\!]_\Sigma w = v$;
- For any signature morphism $\varphi: \Sigma \to \Sigma'$ and any Σ'-model (M', w')

$$Mod^\sharp(\varphi)(M', w') = (Mod(\varphi)M', [\![M']\!]_\varphi w');$$

- For each Σ-model M, each $w \in [\![M]\!]_\Sigma$, and each $\rho \in Sen(\Sigma)$

$$((M, w) \models_\Sigma^\sharp \rho) = (M \models_\Sigma^w \rho). \tag{13}$$

By "composing" the representation of 3/2-institutions as stratified institutions with the representation of stratified institutions as ordinary institutions, we obtain the following representation of 3/2-institutions as ordinary institutions.

Corollary 2. *Let* $\mathcal{I} = (Sign, Sen, Mod, \models)$ *be a 3/2-institution. Then,*

$$(\mathcal{I}^s)^\sharp = (Sign^s, Sen^s, (Mod^s)^\sharp, \models^\sharp)$$

defines an ordinary institution where
- $Sign^s$ *and* Sen^s *are given by definitions 2 and 3, respectively.*
- *For each* $\chi \in |Sign^s|$:
  - *A* $(Mod^s)^\sharp$ χ-*model is pair* (M, N) *such that* $M \in |Mod(\chi\square)|$, $N \in Mod(\chi)M$;
  - *A* χ-*model homomorphism* $(M, N) \to (M_0, N_0)$ *is a model homomorphism* $h: M \to M_0$, *such that* $N_0 = h^N\square$.
- *For each* $(\varphi, \theta): \chi \to \chi'$ *and any* $(Mod^s)^\sharp$ χ'-*model* (M', N')

$$(Mod^s)^\sharp(\varphi, \theta)(M', N') = (Mod(\theta)M', Mod(\varphi)N').$$

- For each $(Mod^s)^\sharp$ χ-model (M, N) and each Sen^s χ-sentence ρ

$$(M, N) \models^\sharp_\chi \rho \text{ if and only if } N \models^\mathcal{I}_{\Box\chi} \rho.$$

4.2. Semantic Connectives

Institution theory has developed its own general approach to logical connectives [3,24,25]. This was refined in [6] to stratified institution theory. With 3/2-institutions, there are two ways to approach this issue.

1. The straightforward way that mimics the semantic treatment of connectives from ordinary institution theory.
2. By using the stratified institution theoretic approach via the representation result given by corollary 1.

We argue that the straightforward approach does not work, which means that in order to have sound semantic connectives, we have to rely on the representation result. Our argument is based on an important property of the semantic connectives, namely that they should be preserved by the translations along signature morphisms. For instance, for a signature morphism φ, if ρ is a semantic disjunction of ρ_1 and ρ_2 in the signature $\Box\varphi$, then $Sen(\varphi)\rho$ should be a semantic disjunction of $Sen(\varphi)\rho_1$ and $Sen(\varphi)\rho_2$ in $\varphi\Box$. This holds naturally in ordinary institution theory as well as in stratified institution theory, the proof of this relying on the satisfaction condition. In fact, in the stratified institutions case, this property can be established from the corresponding ordinary institution theory property via the $\mathcal{S}^\sharp$ representation, since as noticed in [6], the common propositional connectives and the quantification connectives do coincide in $\mathcal{S}$ and in $\mathcal{S}^\sharp$.

In order to understand what is wrong with the straightforward approach to the semantic connectives in 3/2-institutions, let us attempt to establish the preservation property for the semantic disjunction. Let φ be a signature morphism and assume that ρ is a semantic disjunction of ρ_1 and ρ_2 in $\Box\varphi$, which means that for each $\Box\varphi$-model M, $M \models \rho$ if and only if $M \models \rho_k$ for some $k \in \{1, 2\}$. We have to establish the same property for $Sen(\varphi)\rho$, $Sen(\varphi)\rho_1$, and $Sen(\varphi)\rho_2$. A first issue with this is the existence of these translations. We can overcome this by requiring that $Sen(\varphi)\rho$ is a semantic disjunction of $Sen(\varphi)\rho_1$ and $Sen(\varphi)\rho_2$ when *all three translations do exist*. Let us attempt to prove the property under this new formulation. We have to prove that for any $\varphi\Box$-model M',

$$M \models Sen(\varphi)\rho \text{ if and only if } M' \models Sen(\varphi)\rho_k \text{ for some } k \in \{1, 2\}.$$

However, $M' \models Sen(\varphi)\rho$ means $M \models \rho$ for all $M \in Mod(\varphi)M'$. Since ρ is the semantic disjunction of ρ_1 and ρ_2, this further means that for each $M \in Mod(\varphi)M'$, there exists $k \in \{1, 2\}$, such that $M \models \rho_k$. At this point, we have to get back to $\varphi\Box$, i.e., to establish that there exists $k \in \{1, 2\}$ such that $M' \models Sen(\varphi)\rho_k$, which means that for all $M \in Mod(\varphi)M'$, $M \models \rho_k$ for the *same k*. This is a gap because for one M we may have $M \models \rho_1$ and for another M we may have $M \models \rho_2$. So, the property cannot be established.

This failure to prove the preservation of semantic disjunctions along signature morphisms also tells us about the crucial role played by the reducts; that in fact the satisfaction in 3/2-institutions has the reducts as an implicit parameter. This perspective provides a solution to our problem. Additionally, here we are; this situation calls for a stratified institution approach. In the particular case of the semantic disjunctions, this means that, under the representation given by corollary 1, we should define ρ as a semantic disjunction of ρ_1 and ρ_2, when for each χ-model M:

$$\{N \in [\![M]\!]_\chi \mid N \models \rho\} = \{N \in [\![M]\!]_\chi \mid N \models \rho_1\} \cup \{N \in [\![M]\!]_\chi \mid N \models \rho_2\}.$$

Similar definitions can be derived in the case of the other semantic connectives by following the stratified institutions approach [6].

4.3. Model Amalgamation

Model amalgamation is one of the most important concepts/properties in institution theory. The institution theory literature contains numerous works where model amalgamation is used decisively. Refs. [2,26], etc., are representative for computing science-oriented works, especially in the area of software modularisation, while in [3] and many other articles, one may find an abundance of uses of model amalgamation in institution-independent model theory. Regarding its role in 3/2-institution theory and applications, in [13], it is argued that model amalgamation squares in 3/2-institutions constitute a superior approach to the categorical modeling of conceptual blending than 3/2 or lax colimits.

The most notorious form of model amalgamation comes from ordinary institution theory. Given a diagram of signature morphisms, a model of that is a family $(M_i)_{i \in I}$ of models, indexed by the nodes of the diagram, such that M_i is a Σ_i-model, where Σ_i is the signature at node i, and such that for each signature morphism $\varphi : \Sigma_i \to \Sigma_j$ in the diagram, $M_i = Mod(\varphi) M_j$. A cocone μ of the diagram has the *model amalgamation* property when for each model $(M_i)_{i \in I}$ of the diagram there exists an unique model M of the vertex of the colimit, such that $Mod(\mu_i) M = M_i, i \in I$. Then M is called the *amalgamation* of $(M_i)_{i \in I}$.

The most frequent use of model amalgamation is for cocones of spans of signature morphisms (which are in fact commutative squares of signature morphisms). There are also variations of the concept of model amalgamation: when we do not require the uniqueness of the amalgamation M (called weak model amalgamation), or when we refer only to colimits (called exactness) or even to particular colimits such as pushout squares (called semiexactness).

In stratified institution theory, there is a specific concept of model amalgamation called *stratified model amalgamation*, which corresponds to model amalgamation in the flattening $S^\sharp$ of the respective stratified institution S. This has been introduced in [14]. When the stratified institution is strict, stratified model amalgamation collapses to ordinary model amalgamation. Though in our context, this does not happen because the stratifications of the representations of 3/2-institutions as stratified institutions are proper lax natural transformations.

The 3/2-institution theoretic concept of model amalgamation [13] represents another refinement of the ordinary concept of model amalgamation. Its definition just replaces the ordinary definition of model amalgamation equalities relations with membership relations (for instance $M_i = Mod(\varphi) M_j$ becomes $M_i \in Mod(\varphi) M_j$) and strict commutativity with lax commutativity. 3/2-institutional model amalgamation goes at the heart of the applications of 3/2-institutions because the 3/2-institution theoretic approach to conceptual blending comes with the proposal [13] to replace the original approach based on 3/2-categorical colimits [10,11] with model amalgamation cocones.

The following result establishes an equivalence relationship between stratified model amalgamation in $\mathcal{I}^s$ and 3/2-model amalgamation in $\mathcal{I}$.

Proposition 6. *Let* $\mathcal{I} = (Sign, Sen, Mod, \models)$ *be a stratified institution and let* $\mathcal{I}^s = (Sign^s, Sen^s, Mod^s, [\![\_]\!], \models^s)$ *be its representation as a stratified institution. Let the left hand square below represent a commutative diagram in* $Sign^s$, *such that its projection on the first component (the right hand side square below) is a model amalgamation square in* $\mathcal{I}$.

$$
\begin{array}{ccc}
\chi \xrightarrow{(\varphi,\theta)} \chi' & \quad & \Sigma \xrightarrow{\varphi} \Sigma' \\
{\scriptstyle (\zeta,\eta)} \downarrow \quad \downarrow {\scriptstyle (\zeta',\eta')} & & {\scriptstyle \zeta} \downarrow \quad \downarrow {\scriptstyle \zeta'} \\
\chi_1 \xrightarrow[(\varphi_1,\theta_1)]{} \chi'_1 & & \Sigma_1 \xrightarrow[\varphi_1]{} \Sigma'_1
\end{array}
\tag{14}
$$

Then, the square of $\mathcal{I}^s$-signature morphisms is a stratified model amalgamation square if and only if the following lax cocone of $\mathcal{I}$-signature morphisms has the model amalgamation property.

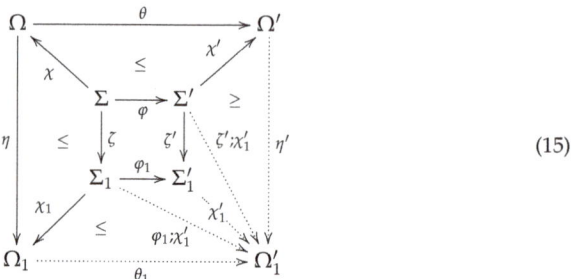

(15)

Proof. In this proof, we rely on the fact that stratified model amalgamation in $\mathcal{I}^s$ is the same as model amalgamation in $(\mathcal{I}^s)^\sharp$. First, we show that the model amalgamation in $\mathcal{I}$ implies that in $(\mathcal{I}^s)^\sharp$.

In $(\mathcal{I}^s)^\sharp$, we consider a χ'-model (M', N') and a χ_1-model (M_1, N_1), such that

$$(Mod^s)^\sharp(\zeta, \eta)(M_1, N_1) = (M, N) \text{ and } (Mod^s)^\sharp(\zeta', \eta')(M', N') = (M, N). \quad (16)$$

Let the Σ'_1-model N'_1 be the unique amalgamation of N' and N_1. Then, $(M_1, M, M', N_1, N, N', N'_1)$ is a model for the $Sign^s$ diagram with 7 vertices and 9 (full) arrows in (15). Let M'_1 be the Ω'_1-model that is the unique amalgamation of $(M_1, M, M', N_1, N, N', N'_1)$. We have that (M'_1, N'_1) is a χ'_1-model and that:

$$(Mod^s)^\sharp(\varphi_1, \theta_1)(M'_1, N'_1) = (M_1, N_1) \text{ and } (Mod^s)^\sharp(\zeta', \eta')(M'_1, N'_1) = (M', N').$$

The uniqueness of the amalgamation (M'_1, N'_1) follows from the uniquenesses of the amalgamations N'_1 and M'_1.

Conversely, we now assume the amalgamation property in $\mathcal{I}^s$ and prove it at the level of $\mathcal{I}$. Any model $(M_1, M, M', N_1, N, N', N'_1)$ for the $Sign^s$ diagram with 7 vertices and 9 arrows determines two $(\mathcal{I}^s)^\sharp$ models: an χ'-model (M', N') and an χ_1-model (M_1, N_1), such that (16) holds. By the stratified model amalgamation property in $\mathcal{I}^s$, interpreted in $(\mathcal{I}^s)^\sharp$, there exists an unique amalgamation (M'_1, N''_1) of (M', N') and of (M_1, N_1). Since $Mod(\eta)N_1 = Mod(\theta)N'$, $Mod(\theta_1)N''_1 = N_1$, $Mod(\eta')N''_1 = N'$, and because the same holds for N''_1 in the place of N'_1 by the uniqueness property of the $\mathcal{I}$-model amalgamation square (14), we have that $N''_1 = N'_1$.

Now, we show that M'_1 is the amalgamation of $(M_1, M, M', N_1, N, N', N'_1)$.

- $N'_1 \in Mod(\chi'_1)M'_1$ holds by the definition of $(Mod^s)^\sharp$ because (M'_1, N'_1) is an $(\mathcal{I}^s)^\sharp$ χ'_1-model.
- Since (M'_1, N'_1) is the amalgamation of (M_1, N_1) and (M', N'), it follows that $Mod(\theta_1)M'_1 = M_1$ and $Mod(\eta')M'_1 = M'$. It further follows that $Mod(\eta; \theta_1)M'_1 = Mod(\theta; \eta')M'_1 = M$.
- We also have that:

$$\begin{aligned} N' &= Mod(\zeta')N'_1 & \text{definition of } N'_1 \\ &\in Mod(\zeta')(Mod(\chi'_1)M'_1) & N'_1 \in Mod(\chi'_1)M'_1 \\ &\subseteq Mod(\zeta'; \chi'_1)M'_1 & Mod \text{ lax.} \end{aligned}$$

- By a similar argument to the above one, we establish that $N_1 \in Mod(\varphi_1; \chi'_1)M'_1$.

- Finally,

$$\begin{aligned} N &= Mod(\zeta;\varphi_1)N_1' & N &= Mod(\zeta)N_1,\ N_1 = Mod(\varphi_1)N_1' \\ &\in Mod(\zeta;\varphi_1)(Mod(\chi_1')M_1') & N_1' &\in Mod(\chi_1')M_1' \\ &\subseteq Mod(\zeta;\varphi_1;\chi_1')M_1' & & Mod\ \text{lax} \\ &\subseteq Mod(\zeta;\chi_1;\theta_1)M_1' & \chi_1;\theta_1 &\leq \varphi_1;\chi_1',\ Mod\ \text{3/2-functor} \\ &\subseteq Mod(\chi;\eta;\theta_1)M_1' & \chi;\eta &\leq \zeta;\chi_1,\ Mod\ \text{3/2-functor}. \end{aligned}$$

The uniqueness of M_1' follows from the uniqueness of the amalgamation (M_1', N_1') by relying on the first implication of the proposition. □

In the context of proposition 6, the following general result provides a sufficient condition for the lax cocone of $\mathcal{I}$-signature morphisms to have the model amalgamation property. Then, by the conclusion of proposition 6, this leads to the left-hand side square of diagrams (14) to be a stratified model amalgamation square. We need to recall from [13] two concepts as follows:

- In any 3/2-category, a strict commutative square

$$\begin{array}{ccc} \Sigma & \xrightarrow{\varphi_1} & A_1 \\ {\scriptstyle \varphi_2}\downarrow & & \downarrow{\scriptstyle \theta_1} \\ A_2 & \xrightarrow{\theta_2} & B \end{array}$$

    is a *3/2-pushout* when for any strict cocones (θ_1', θ_2') and (θ_1'', θ_2'') over the span (φ_1, φ_2), if $\theta_k' \leq \theta_k''$, $k = \overline{1,2}$, there exists unique mediating arrows $\mu' \leq \mu''$, such that $\theta_k;\mu' = \theta_k'$ and $\theta_k'';\mu'' = \theta_k''$, $k = \overline{1,2}$. Note that 3/2-pushouts are stronger than ordinary pushouts.
- *3/2-institutional seeds* were mentioned above when we discussed examples of 3/2-institutions. For the full definition, see [13]. For the purpose of proposition 7 below, we only need the property that there exists a signature Π, such that for each signature Σ

$$|Mod(\Sigma)| = \{M : \Sigma \to \Pi \mid Sen(M)\ \text{total}\}$$

and for each signature morphism φ and for each $\varphi\square$-model M',

$$Mod(\varphi)M' = \{M \in |Mod(\square\varphi)| \mid \varphi;M' \leq M\}.$$

Proposition 7. *Let us assume a 3/2-institution $\mathcal{I}$, such that when we remove its model homomorphisms it is generated by a 3/2-institutional seed. Let us consider a lax cocone of $\mathcal{I}$ signature morphisms such as in diagrams (15) with the following properties:*

- *The inner square (also known as the right-hand side square of diagram (14)) is a 3/2-pushout square;*
- *The outer square $(\eta, \theta, \eta', \theta_1)$ is a model amalgamation square;*
- *$(\varphi_1, \theta_1): \chi_1 \to \chi_1'$ and $(\zeta', \eta'): \chi' \to \chi_1'$ are strict.*

Then, the lax cocone of diagram (15) has the model amalgamation property.

Proof. Let us consider $(M_1, M, M', N_1, N, N', N_1')$, a model of the diagram of 7 vertices and 9 arrows of diagrams (14). Let M_1' be the amalgamation of M' and M_1 by using the model amalgamation property of the outer square $(\eta, \theta, \eta', \theta_1)$. We show that M_1' is also the amalgamation of $(M_1, M, M', N_1, N, N', N_1')$, and its uniqueness follows from the uniqueness as amalgamation of M' and M_1 only.

We first prove that $N'_1 \in Mod(\chi'_1)M'_1$. This goes as follows. Since $N' \in Mod(\chi')M'$, this means that $\chi'; M' \leq N'$. It follows that:

$$\zeta'; \chi'_1; M'_1 = \chi'; \eta'; M'_1 = \chi'; M' \leq N' = Mod(\zeta')N'_1 = \zeta'; N'_1. \tag{17}$$

Similarly,

$$\varphi_1; \chi'_1; M'_1 \leq \varphi_1; N'_1. \tag{18}$$

Because the inner square of diagram (15), i.e., the square $(\varphi, \zeta, \zeta', \varphi_1)$, is a 3/2-pushout square, from (17) and (18), we obtain that $\chi'_1; M'_1 \leq N'_1$, which means $N'_1 \in Mod(\chi'_1)M'_1$. From here, the proof that M'_1 is an amalgamation of $(M_1, M, M', N_1, N, N', N'_1)$ follows the same steps as in the second part of the proof of proposition 6. In particular, this means that the three specific conditions of the current proposition are not used anymore. □

In concrete situations, it is quite common that the 3/2-pushout condition on the inner square in proposition 7 implies the model amalgamation condition on the same square in proposition 6, a fact that enhances the applicability of proposition 7 within the context of the equivalence established by proposition 6.

Proposition 8. *In the context of a 3/2-institution generated by a 3/2-institutional seed, let us assume that Sen preserves and reflects maximality (i.e., φ is maximal if and only if $Sen(\varphi)$ is total). Then, any pushout cocone of signature morphisms determines a model amalgamation square.*

Proof. Let (φ_1, ζ') be a pushout cocone for a span (φ, ζ) of signature morphisms (such as in the diagram below).

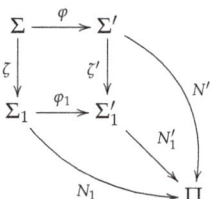

Given a Σ'-model N' and a Σ_1-model N_1, such that $Mod(\varphi)N' = Mod(\zeta)N_1$, we obtain a strict cocone (N', N_1) for the span (φ, ζ). By the pushout property of (φ_1, ζ'), there exists an unique $N'_1 : \Sigma'_1 \to \Pi$, such that $N' = \zeta'; N'_1$ and $N_1 = \varphi_1; N'_1$. It remains to prove that N'_1 qualifies as a Σ'_1-model, i.e., that $Sen(N'_1)$ is total.

By the hypothesis on Sen that it preserves maximality, it is enough to prove that N'_1 is maximal. Consider any $x : \Sigma'_1 \to \Pi$, such that $N'_1 \leq x$. It follows that $N' \leq \zeta'; x$ and $N_1 \leq \varphi_1; x$. By the hypothesis on Sen that it reflects maximality, we have that both N' and N_1 are maximal, hence $\zeta'; x = N'$ and $\varphi_1; x = N_1$. By the pushout hypothesis, it follows that $x = N'_1$. □

With respect to the conditions underlying proposition 8, note that:

- There are no restrictions on the signature morphisms that form the pushout square.
- Then, the condition of proposition 8 that Sen preserves and reflects maximality applies well in concrete situations. As an example, let us consider the case of 3/2$\mathcal{PL}$. There, $Sign = $ **Pfn**, and therefore it is evident that for any signature morphism φ $Sen(\varphi)$ is total if and only if φ is total.
- The 3/2-pushout condition of proposition 7 in general is stronger than the pushout condition of proposition 8.

Often, in concrete situations that are related to the basic context of proposition 6, the pushout squares of signature morphisms are already 3/2-pushout squares. The following result illustrates such a case that is emblematic for the concrete applications not only because it is sometimes involved as such (e.g., in 3/2$\mathcal{PL}$) but also because when it is not the case then the respective category of signature morphisms can be often treated in a similar way.

Proposition 9. *Any pushout square in* **Set** *is a 3/2-pushout square in* **Pfn**.

Proof. For this proof, it is convenient to use the representation of partial functions as homomorphisms between *pointed sets*. A pointed set A is a set with a universally designated element $\perp$. A homomorphism $f: A \to B$ of pointed sets is a function that preserves the designated element $\perp$, i.e., $f\perp = \perp$. This yields a category $\mathbf{Set}_\perp$ and a canonical isomorphism $\mathbf{Pfn} \cong \mathbf{Set}_\perp$ that:

- Maps any set A to the set $A_\perp = A \cup \{\perp\}$ (disjoint union);
- Maps any partial function $f: A \rightharpoonup B$ to the homomorphism $f_\perp: A_\perp \to B_\perp$ defined for each $x \in A$ by:

$$f_\perp x = \begin{cases} fx, & fx \text{ defined} \\ \perp, & fx \text{ undefined}. \end{cases}$$

Now, let us consider a pushout square in **Set** as follows.

$$\begin{array}{ccc} \Sigma & \xrightarrow{\varphi} & \Sigma' \\ \zeta \downarrow & & \downarrow \zeta' \\ \Sigma_1 & \xrightarrow{\varphi} & \Sigma'_1 \end{array} \qquad (19)$$

By mapping the pushout square (19) to $\mathbf{Set}_\perp$, we obtain the commutative square

$$\begin{array}{ccc} \Sigma_\perp & \xrightarrow{\varphi_\perp} & \Sigma'_\perp \\ \zeta_\perp \downarrow & & \downarrow \zeta'_\perp \\ (\Sigma_1)_\perp & \xrightarrow{(\varphi_1)_\perp} & (\Sigma'_1)_\perp \end{array}$$

This is a pushout square because $(\_)_\perp: \mathbf{Set} \to \mathbf{Set}_\perp$ is a left adjoint to the forgetful functor $\mathbf{Set}_\perp \to \mathbf{Set}$ and left adjoint functors preserve all colimits [15]. This left adjoint property can be either checked directly, or else it can be established by noticing that it is a special case of a free algebra construction corresponding to a reduct functor of categories of algebras for the signature inclusion of the signature consisting of one sort into the signature consisting of one sort and one constant.

This showed that (19) is a pushout square in **Pfn**. In order to prove that this is a 3/2-pushout square in **Pfn**, we let (a', a_1) and (b', b_1) be strict cocones for the span (φ, ζ), such that $a' \subseteq b'$ and $a_1 \subseteq b_1$. Let α and β be the unique mediating partial functions for (a', a_1) and (b', b_1), respectively. We have to show that $\alpha \subseteq \beta$. Note that $\alpha \subseteq \beta$ means that for each $x \in \Sigma'_1$, $\alpha_\perp x \neq \perp$ implies $\alpha_\perp x = \beta_\perp x$. However, $\alpha_\perp \neq \perp$ implies $x \neq \perp$. By the pushout property of (19), it follows that there exists y in Σ' or in Σ_1, such that $\zeta' y = x$ or $\varphi_1 x = y$. By symmetry, without any loss of generality, we may assume that $y \in \Sigma'$ and $\zeta' y = x$. We have that:

$$\alpha_\perp x = \alpha_\perp(\zeta' y) = ay = by \text{ (since } a \subseteq b) = \beta_\perp(\zeta' y) = \beta_\perp x.$$

□

5. Conclusions and Future Work

We have defined a representation of 3/2-institutions as stratified institutions in which the set of the reducts of a model with respect to a fixed signature morphism is assimilated to the set of its states. This representation is subject to some conditions on the signature morphisms. Then, we have explored three consequences of this general representation: a further representation to ordinary institutions, (stratified) semantic connectives in 3/2-institutions, and stratified model amalgamation in 3/2-institutions.

The results of our work also raise a series of issues to be addressed in the future. We mention a couple of them:

- The import of more model theory from stratified institution theory to 3/2-institutions.
- Find general ways, with good applicability in concrete situations, to generate model amalgamation cocones such as in diagrams (15).

As stratified institution theory continues to develop, our representation result may provide new enhancements of the theory of 3/2-institutions with concepts and results that come from stratified institutions.

Funding: This work was supported by a grant of the Romanian Ministry of Education and Research, CNCS—UEFISCDI, project number PN-III-P4-ID-PCE-2020-0446, within PNCDI III.

Acknowledgments: The comments of the reviewers helped improve the presentation of the results in the paper.

Conflicts of Interest: The author declares no conflict of interest.

References

1. Goguen, J.; Burstall, R. Institutions: Abstract Model Theory for Specification and Programming. *J. Assoc. Comput. Mach.* **1992**, *39*, 95–146. [CrossRef]
2. Sannella, D.; Tarlecki, A. *Foundations of Algebraic Specifications and Formal Software Development*; Springer: Berlin/Heidelberg, Germany, 2012.
3. Diaconescu, R. *Institution-Independent Model Theory*; Birkhäuser: Basel, Switzerland, 2008.
4. Diaconescu, R.; Stefaneas, P. Modality in Open Institutions with Concrete Syntax. *Bull. Greek Math. Soc.* **2004**, *49*, 91–101. Previously published as JAIST Tech Report IS-RR-97-0046, 1997.
5. Aiguier, M.; Diaconescu, R. Stratified institutions and elementary homomorphisms. *Inf. Process. Lett.* **2007**, *103*, 5–13. [CrossRef]
6. Diaconescu, R. Implicit Kripke Semantics and Ultraproducts in Stratified Institutions. *J. Log. Comput.* **2017**, *27*, 1577–1606. [CrossRef]
7. Aiguier, M.; Bloch, I. Logical dual concepts based on mathematical morphology in stratified institutions: Applications to spatial reasoning. *J. Appl. Non-Class. Log.* **2019**, *29*, 392–429. [CrossRef]
8. Găină, D. Forcing and Calculi for Hybrid Logics. *J. Assoc. Comput. Mach.* **2020**, *67*, 25:1–25:55. [CrossRef]
9. Fauconnier, G.; Turner, M. Conceptual integration networks. *Cogn. Sci.* **1998**, *28*, 133–187. [CrossRef]
10. Goguen, J. An Introduction to Algebraic Semiotics, with Application to User Interface Design. In *Computation for Metaphors, Analogy, and Agents*; Lecture Notes in Computer Science; Nehaniv, C.L., Ed.; Springer: Berlin/Heidelberg, Germany, 1999; Volume 1562, pp. 242–291.
11. Goguen, J.A. What Is a Concept? In *Conceptual Structures: Common Semantics for Sharing Knowledge. ICCS 2005*; Lecture Notes in Computer Science; Dau, F., Mugnier, M.L., Stumme, G., Eds.; Springe: Berlin/Heidelberg, Germany, 2005; Volume 3596, pp. 52–77.
12. Goguen, J. Categorical Approaches to Merging Software Changes. *Unpublished draft*.
13. Diaconescu, R. Implicit Partiality of Signature Morphisms in Institution Theory. In *Hajnal Andréka and István Németi on Unity of Science: From Computing to Relativity Theory Through Algebraic Logic*; Outstanding Contributions to Logic; Madarász, J., Székely, G., Eds.; Springer: Berlin/Heidelberg, Germany, 2021; Volume 19, pp. 81–123, ISBN 978-3-030-64186-3.
14. Diaconescu, R. Decompositions of Stratified Institutions. *arXiv* **2021**, arXiv:2112.12993.
15. Mac Lane, S. *Categories for the Working Mathematician*, 2nd ed.; Springer: Berlin/Heidelberg, Germany, 1998.
16. Kelly, M. *Basic Concepts of Enriched Category Theory*; Cambridge University Press: Cambridge, UK, 1982.
17. Borceux, F. *Handbook of Categorical Algebra*; Cambridge University Press: Cambridge, UK, 1994.
18. Kelly, M.; Street, R. Review of elements of 2-categories. In *Category Seminar Sydney 1972/1973*; Lecture Notes in Mathematics; Springer: Berlin/Heidelberg, Germany, 1974; pp. 75–103.
19. Jay, C.B. Partial Functions, Ordered Categories, Limits and Cartesian Closure. In *IV Higher Order Workshop, Banff 1990: Proceedings of the IV Higher Order Workshop, Banff, AB, Canada 10–14 September 1990*; Birtwistle, G., Ed.; Springer: London, UK, 1991; pp. 151–161.
20. Diaconescu, R.; Stefaneas, P. Ultraproducts and Possible Worlds Semantics in Institutions. *Theor. Comput. Sci.* **2007**, *379*, 210–230. [CrossRef]

21. Martins, M.A.; Madeira, A.; Diaconescu, R.; Barbosa, L. Hybridization of Institutions. In *Algebra and Coalgebra in Computer Science*; Lecture Notes in Computer Science; Corradini, A., Klin, B., Cîrstea, C., Eds.; Springer: Berlin/Heidelberg, Germany, 2011; Volume 6859, pp. 283–297.
22. Diaconescu, R. Quasi-varieties and initial semantics in hybridized institutions. *J. Log. Comput.* **2016**, *26*, 855–891. [CrossRef]
23. Madeira, A. Foundations and Techniques for Software Reconfigurability. Ph.D. Thesis, Universidades do Minho, Aveiro and Porto (Joint MAP-i Doctoral Programme), Aveiro, Portugal, 2014.
24. Tarlecki, A. On the Existence of Free Models in Abstract Algebraic Institutions. *Theor. Comput. Sci.* **1986**, *37*, 269–304. [CrossRef]
25. Diaconescu, R. Institution-independent Ultraproducts. *Fundam. Inform.* **2003**, *55*, 321–348.
26. Diaconescu, R.; Goguen, J.; Stefaneas, P. Logical Support for Modularisation. In *Logical Environments*; Huet, G., Plotkin, G., Eds.; Cambridge University Press: Cambridge, UK, 1993; pp. 83–130.

Review

The Axiomatic Approach to Non-Classical Model Theory

Răzvan Diaconescu

Simion Stoilow Institute of Mathematics of the Romanian Academy, 010702 Bucharest, Romania; razvan.diaconescu@imar.ro

Abstract: *Institution theory* represents the fully axiomatic approach to model theory in which all components of logical systems are treated fully abstractly by reliance on category theory. Here, we survey some developments over the last decade or so concerning the institution theoretic approach to non-classical aspects of model theory. Our focus will be on many-valued truth and on models with states, which are addressed by the two extensions of ordinary institution theory known as *L-institutions* and *stratified institutions*, respectively. The discussion will include relevant concepts, techniques, and results from these two areas.

Keywords: model theory; institution theory; category theory; stratified institutions; *categorical model theory*; many-valued truth institutions; *L*-institutions

MSC: 03C95; 03C40; 68Q65

1. From Classical Model Theory to Axiomatic Non-Classical Model Theory

In this introductory section, we will discuss briefly and informally the path leading from the most traditional form of model theory to the modern and non-classical one.

1.1. Model Theory

In a broader sense, model theory is the mathematical study of language interpretations, its main paradigm being Alfred Tarski's semantic definition of truth [1]. Thus, the occurrence of the symbol $\models$ always indicates that we are in the presence of some form of model–theoretical argument. In its most classical form, model theory deals with *first-order structures*. So, in first-order model theory, the relation $M \models \rho$ means that M is a first-order model and ρ is a first-order sentence. Tarski's approach was to determine the validity of this relation inductively on the structure of ρ. On the one hand, first-order model theory [2,3] is a vibrant and sophisticated area of mathematical research that brings logical methods to bear on deep problems of classical mathematics. Two early achievements of first-order model theory that brought it fame within the wider mathematical community were the modern and rigorous recovery of the approach to mathematical analysis of Newton, Leibniz and Euler—in the form of Robinson's non-standard analysis [4,5]—and the proof of the independence of the Continuum Hypothesis [6,7]. Moreover, first-order model theory has applications to other scientific areas, most notably to computing science. On the other hand, first-order model theory is the area in which many of the broader ideas of model theory were first worked out.

1.2. Axiomatic Model Theory

First-order model theory is also the most important example of the explicit and concrete approach to model theory. The axiomatic approach contrasts this as the concepts and defining properties are axiomatised rather than considered concretely. As with all other axiomatic approaches in mathematics, this achieves proper abstraction, relativisation, conceptual clarity, and structurally clean causality. In a sophisticated mathematical area such as model theory, these features are crucial. The very origins of the axiomatic approach to model theory may be traced back, although not in an explicit form, in Lindström's "external" characterisation of first-order logic [8]. Several explicit axiomatic developments followed, such as Barwise's *abstract model theory* [9,10] or the *categorical model theory* of the Budapest school [11–15], etc. In spite of their success in developing interesting results, all those approaches lacked full axiomatisability, as they would usually treat axiomatically some parts of the logical systems while considering concretely other parts. Consequently, they were not able to achieve the true power of the full axiomatic approach.

1.2.1. The Institution-Theoretic Trend

The definition in the late 1970s by Goguen and Burstall of the concept of *institution* as a formal definition of the intuitive notion of logic [16–18] achieved the *full axiomatic approach to model theory*. In institution theory, all three components of logical systems—namely, the syntax, the semantics, and the satisfaction relation between them—are treated fully abstractly by relying heavily on *category theory* [19]. Very briefly, the above-mentioned formalization is a category–theoretic structure $(Sign, Sen, Mod, \models)$, called *institution*, consisting of a category *Sign* (of so-called signatures), two functors (*Sen* for the syntax and *Mod* for the semantics), and a family $\models$ of binary relations, which are all bound to satisfy certain consistency axioms. We will clarify precisely this definition below in the paper. In our survey, we will follow this trend of axiomatic model theory known as *institution-independent model theory*, or *institutional model theory*, or *institution-theoretic model theory*. The first in this list of synonymous terminologies may be actually the most informative, as the word 'independent' suggests a model theory that is not confined to any particular logical system.

1.2.2. The Original Motivation

With institution theory, Goguen and Burstall addressed an important issue in computing science, and especially in formal–specification theory. There was an explosion of formal logical systems used, and there was a need for a uniform treatment of specification concepts and results across the increasing number of logic-based formal methods. There was also a strong feeling that much of the logic-based specification theory may actually be developed independently of an underlying concrete logical system. Over decades, this area undertook a massive development, and now, it is still vibrant and dynamic. It has fulfilled its original mission, even beyond expectations, as follows:

- The concept of institution has emerged as the *most fundamental mathematical structure of logic-based formal specifications* in the sense that virtually all modern specification languages/systems are rigorously based upon a logical system that is formally captured as an institution in such a way that each language construct corresponds exactly to a mathematical concept from that institution. In particular, this has been the principle underlying the design of specification languages and systems such as CASL [20], CafeOBJ [21,22], Hets [23], DOL [24], etc.
- A great deal of modern *formal specification theory has been developed at the general level of abstract institutions*, thus bringing an unprecedented high level of uniformity and clarity to an area that has witnessed a real explosion in the population of logical systems (cf. the monograph [25]).
- The institution–theoretic methods have been successfully *exported to other areas of computing science*, most notably to declarative programming [26–28] and ontologies [24,29]. In all these areas, in issues involving modularisation, stepwise refinement, or logical heterogeneity, the use of institution theory is practically without alternative.

1.2.3. Institutional Model Theory as Such

The abstract axiomatic development of institutional model theory goes back to [30–32]. Those early endeavours stemmed from computing science, addressing typical issues from formal specification (such as initial semantics), but they also led to strong model–theoretic results in themselves. Even so, a systematic programme for developing an in-depth institutional model theory beyond computing science motivations arose only after 2000.

- This meant an *axiomatic-driven redesign* of core parts of model theory at a new level of generality—namely, that of abstract institutions—independently of any concrete logical system. Those included institutional developments of some of the most important model–theoretic methods that were originally worked out in first-order model theory, such as diagrams [33], ultraproducts [34], elementary chains [35], saturated models [36], omitting types [37], forcing [38], etc.
- This institutional development has had at least three major consequences:
    1. A *new understanding* of model–theoretic phenomena that are uncontaminated by irrelevant concrete details; this led to revisions of well established concepts and facilitated access to difficult results;
    2. A consequence of (1) is a series of results about completeness [38,39], definability [40,41], interpolation [42–45], Löwenheim–Skolem [37,45], some instances of these representing *new important results* even in first-order model theory;
    3. A systematic and uniform development of *model theories for unconventional logics*, either new or older ones, which is a process of great difficulty within concrete frameworks.

    Moreover, in the case of (3), the institution–theoretic approach has also led to a better understanding of the respective logics sometimes accompanied by a conceptual resetting.

1.2.4. Logic by Translation

A specific general logical method that has gained prominence in the past few decades is that of logic by translation. By this method, one can overcome difficulties of developing results in a certain logical system by exporting the problem to another logical system where a solution is known or, for various reasons, is easier to obtain. This relies on translations/encodings between logical systems that have adequate properties both for the forward translation and for shifting the obtained result back to the source logic. Logic-by-translation has had many applications in logic and computer science, many of them through institution theory. That is mostly thanks to the fact that institution theory, with its category–theoretic build where logical systems arise as categorical objects, has come up with adequate mathematical concepts of structural mapping between institutions at an abstract level [18,46]. The value of the institution–theoretic proposal to logic-by-translation [47] has been awarded internationally by the scientific community at the *2nd World Congress of Universal Logic* (Xi'an, 2007).

1.3. Beyond Classical Institutional Model Theory

The concept of institution is abstract enough to accommodate any logical system based on satisfaction between sentences and models of any kind, including non-classical logics. However, the developments discussed above, albeit highly abstract and axiomatic, may be considered "classical" in the sense that they reflect concepts, methods and results that have been originally worked out at a concrete level in first-order model theory. Classical institutional model theory may be effective to some extent in non-classical contexts but not entirely satisfactory. For instance, non-classical logical situations that are beyond the usual binary satisfaction relation between models and sentences, such as local satisfaction in modal logics or many-valued satisfaction, admit classical institution–theoretic formalisations but at the cost of flattening the satisfaction relation to the binary case [44,48], which is a process that alters the nature of the respective logics. Consequently, there is a loss of information, and important non-classical logic developments cannot be completed naturally or not at all. For example, when considering institutions for modal logics, this is completed on the basis of global satisfaction, which is much less relevant than the local satisfaction relation. In addition, in the flattening of many-valued satisfaction, the possibility of grading the consequence relation [49] is lost. Moreover, logic encodings that are based on *theoroidal comorphisms* are difficult to define because of the multifaceted nature of the concept of theory in many-valued logics [49,50]. The answers to these challenges is given by the *stratified institutions* [51–53] and the *L-institutions* [49] that represent extensions of the ordinary concept of institution that accommodate properly models with states and local satisfaction, and many-valued semantic truth, respectively. Technically, these two new mathematical structures are generalisations of the ordinary concept of institution. This survey is about these two extensions of ordinary institution theory with emphasis on model theory-motivated developments rather than computing science. Regarding the technical level of this survey, while avoiding technical vagueness, we will also deliberately try to avoid intricate technicalities that pervade many institutional model theory works. In order to achieve such a balance in the presentation, we will employ more informal explanations while providing pointers to works where the respective technical details can be found.

Before surveying the theories of stratified and of *L*-institutions, respectively, we will review the ordinary concept of institution.

2. Institutions

In this section, we will first discuss the role played by category theory in institution theory, we will review some basic notational conventions, and finally, we will recall the concept of institution.

2.1. First, Some Category Theory

Category theory of Eilenberg and Mac Lane [19,54] constitutes the mathematical substance of institution theory. This situation is similar in other axiomatic approaches to model theory, such as in the above-mentioned Budapest school of abstract model theory. This means that the mathematical structures in institution theory are all categorical. On the other hand, the flow of ideas in institution theory is model theoretic. So, institution theory is a form of model theory that at the level of the mathematical structures is heavily based on categorical structures. This represents a sharp contrast to the widespread perception of category theory as a mere language that supports a clearer presentation and structuring of mathematical concepts that in fact do not have an inherent categorical nature. Institution theory without category theory is possible to the same extent as, for instance, group theory is possible without set theory!

Why such a reliance on category theory; is it indispensable for the axiomatic treatment of model theory? There are several reasons for this. One is that that set theoretical structures cannot support the required level of generality and abstraction. Another one is that category theory emphasises the relationships between objects rather than their internal structures. Moreover, category theory is conceptually a highly developed area of mathematics, so this brings in much conceptual and technical power.

However, the level of category theory involved in institution theory is rather elementary, as it hardly touches advanced concepts and techniques; the only slight exception being found in the area of stratified institutions. So, familiarity with concepts such as opposite (dual) of a category $\mathbf{C}$ (denoted $\mathbf{C}^\ominus$), comma category, functor, (lax) natural transformation, (co)limit, and adjunction may be enough to be able to engage with the study of institutional model theory. In this survey, with a few exceptions, in general, we follow the terminology and the notations of [19]. As regards the notational conventions,

- $|\mathbf{C}|$ denotes the class of objects of a category $\mathbf{C}$, $\mathbf{C}(A, B)$ and the set of arrows (morphisms) with domain A and codomain B;
- The domain of an arrow/morphism f is denoted by $\Box f$, while its codomain is denoted by $f\Box$;
- $f;g$ denotes the composition of arrows/morphisms in diagrammatic order, which in set theoretic orders reads as $g \circ f$;
- The category of sets (as objects) and functions (as arrows) is denoted by **Set**;
- The category of all categories (as objects) and functors (as arrows) is denoted by **CAT**. (Strictly speaking, **CAT** is only a 'quasi-category' living in a higher set-theoretic universe).

2.2. The Concept of Institution

The original standard reference for institution theory is [18]. An *institution*

$$\mathcal{I} = (Sign^{\mathcal{I}}, Sen^{\mathcal{I}}, Mod^{\mathcal{I}}, \models^{\mathcal{I}})$$

consists of

- A category $Sign^{\mathcal{I}}$ whose objects are called *signatures*;
- A sentence functor $Sen^{\mathcal{I}} : Sign^{\mathcal{I}} \to \mathbf{Set}$ defining for each signature a set whose elements are called *sentences* over that signature and defining for each signature morphism a *sentence translation* function;
- A model functor $Mod^{\mathcal{I}} : (Sign^{\mathcal{I}})^{\ominus} \to \mathbf{CAT}$ defining for each signature Σ the category $Mod^{\mathcal{I}}(\Sigma)$ of Σ-models and Σ-model homomorphisms, and for each signature morphism φ the *reduct* functor $Mod^{\mathcal{I}}(\varphi)$;
- For every signature Σ, a binary Σ-*satisfaction relation* $\models^{\mathcal{I}}_{\Sigma} \subseteq |Mod^{\mathcal{I}}(\Sigma)| \times Sen^{\mathcal{I}}(\Sigma)$;

such that for each morphism φ, the *Satisfaction Condition*

$$M' \models^{\mathcal{I}}_{\varphi\square} Sen^{\mathcal{I}}(\varphi)\rho \text{ if and only if } Mod^{\mathcal{I}}(\varphi) M' \models^{\mathcal{I}}_{\square\varphi} \rho \qquad (1)$$

holds for each $M' \in |Mod^{\mathcal{I}}(\varphi\square)|$ and $\rho \in Sen^{\mathcal{I}}(\square\varphi)$. This can be expressed as the satisfaction relation $\models$ being a natural transformation:

$$
\begin{array}{ccc}
\square\varphi & Sen^{\mathcal{I}}(\square\varphi) \xrightarrow{\models^{\mathcal{I}}_{\square\varphi}} [|Mod^{\mathcal{I}}(\square\varphi)| \to 2] \\
\varphi \downarrow & Sen^{\mathcal{I}}(\varphi) \downarrow & \uparrow Mod^{\mathcal{I}}(\varphi) \\
\varphi\square & Sen^{\mathcal{I}}(\varphi\square) \xrightarrow[\models^{\mathcal{I}}_{\varphi\square}]{} [|Mod^{\mathcal{I}}(\varphi\square)| \to 2]
\end{array}
$$

($[|Mod(\Sigma)| \to 2]$ represents the 'set' of the 'subsets' of $|Mod(\Sigma)|$).

We may omit the superscripts or subscripts from the notations of the components of institutions when there is no risk of ambiguity. For example, if the considered institution and signature are clear, we may denote $\models^{\mathcal{I}}_{\Sigma}$ just by $\models$. For $M = Mod(\varphi)M'$, we say that M is the φ-reduct of M'.

The literature shows myriads of logical systems from computing or from mathematical logic captured as institutions. Many of these are collected in [25,44]. In fact, an informal thesis underlying institution theory is that any 'logic' may be captured by the above definition. While this should be taken with a grain of salt, it certainly applies to any logical system based on satisfaction between sentences and models of any kind. In [44], one can read how propositional logic $\mathcal{PL}$, (many-sorted) first order logic $\mathcal{FOL}$ together with many of its fragments, partial algebra, various flavours of modal logic, intuitionistic logics, preordered algebra, multialgebras, membership algebra, higher-order logics with various semantics, many-valued logics, etc. can be captured as institutions. In all these cases, the effort to capture the (model theory of the) respective logical system as an institution implies a conceptual adjustment of some of its aspects in the direction of a higher mathematical rigour, an emblematic case being that of the variables (see for example the relevant discussion in [55]). In many cases, some important concepts have been extended, most notably concepts of signature morphisms. In order to fully understand these conceptual developments, it is worth looking in the literature at detailed examples of mainstream concrete institutions.

3. Stratified Institutions

Models with states appear in myriad forms in computing science and logic. Classes of examples include at least

- A wide variety of Kripke semantics as in [51,52,56,57];
- Various automata theories;
- Various model theories with partiality for signature morphisms [58], providing mathematical foundations to conceptual blending (see [59]).

The institution theory answer to this is given by the theory of *stratified institutions* introduced in [51,60] and further developed or invoked in works such as [52,53,56–58], etc. Informally, the main idea behind the concept of stratified institution as introduced in [51,60] is to enhance the concept of institution with 'states' for the models. Thus, each model M comes equipped with a *set* $[\![M]\!]$ that has to satisfy some structural axioms. The following definition has been given in [52] and represents an important upgrade of the original definition from [51], the main reason being to make the definition of stratified institutions really usable for conducting in-depth model theory. A slightly different upgrade has been proposed in [53], which is however strongly convergent to the upgrade proposed in [52].

A *stratified institution* $\mathcal{S}$ is a tuple $(Sign^{\mathcal{S}}, Sen^{\mathcal{S}}, Mod^{\mathcal{S}}, [\![\_]\!]^{\mathcal{S}}, \models^{\mathcal{S}})$ consisting of:

- A category $Sign^{\mathcal{S}}$ of signatures;
- A sentence functor $Sen^{\mathcal{S}} : Sign^{\mathcal{S}} \to \mathbf{Set}$;
- A model functor $Mod^{\mathcal{S}} : (Sign^{\mathcal{S}})^{\ominus} \to \mathbf{CAT}$.

Until this point, this definition is identical to that of an ordinary institution. However, now comes the additional structure that provides explicitly the states of the models.

- A "stratification" lax natural transformation $[\![\_]\!]^{\mathcal{S}} : Mod^{\mathcal{S}} \Rightarrow SET$, where $SET : Sign^{\mathcal{S}} \to \mathbf{CAT}$ is a functor mapping each signature to $\mathbf{Set}$; and
- A satisfaction relation between models and sentences which is parameterised by model states, $M \ (\models^{\mathcal{S}})_{\Sigma}^{w} \rho$ where $w \in [\![M]\!]_{\Sigma}^{\mathcal{S}}$ such that the following *Satisfaction Condition*

$$Mod^{\mathcal{S}}(\varphi)M' \ (\models^{\mathcal{S}})_{\Box\varphi}^{[\![M']\!]_{\varphi}w} \rho \text{ if and only if } M' \ (\models^{\mathcal{S}})_{\varphi\Box}^{w} Sen^{\mathcal{S}}(\varphi)\rho \tag{2}$$

holds for any signature morphism φ, $M' \in |Mod^{\mathcal{S}}(\varphi\Box)|$, $w \in [\![M']\!]_{\varphi\Box}^{\mathcal{S}}$, $\rho \in Sen^{\mathcal{S}}(\Box\varphi)$.

As for ordinary institutions, when appropriate, we shall also use simplified notations without superscripts or subscripts that are clear from the context.

The lax natural transformation property of $[\![\_]\!]$ is depicted in the diagram below

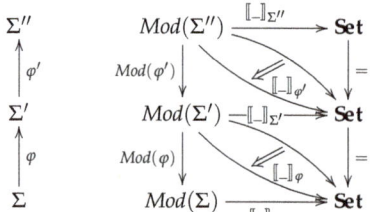

with the following compositionality property for each Σ''-model M'':

$$[\![M'']\!]_{(\varphi;\varphi')} = [\![M'']\!]_{\varphi'} ; [\![Mod(\varphi')M'']\!]_{\varphi}. \tag{3}$$

Moreover, the natural transformation property of each $[\![\_]\!]_{\varphi}$ is given by the commutativity of the following diagram:

$$\begin{array}{ccc} M' & [\![M']\!]_{\Sigma'} \xrightarrow{[\![M']\!]_{\varphi}} [\![Mod(\varphi)M']\!]_{\Sigma} \\ h' \downarrow & [\![h']\!]_{\Sigma'} \downarrow & \downarrow [\![Mod(\varphi)h']\!]_{\Sigma} \\ N' & [\![N']\!]_{\Sigma'} \xrightarrow[{[\![N']\!]_{\varphi}}]{} [\![Mod(\varphi)N']\!]_{\Sigma} \end{array} \tag{4}$$

The satisfaction relation can be presented as a natural transformation

$$\models : Sen \Rightarrow [\![Mod(\_) \to \mathbf{Set}]\!]$$

where the functor $[\![Mod(\_) \to \mathbf{Set}]\!] : Sign \to \mathbf{Set}$ is defined by

- For each signature $\Sigma \in |Sign|$, $[\![Mod(\Sigma) \to \mathbf{Set}]\!]$ denotes the set of all the mappings $f: |Mod(\Sigma)| \to \mathbf{Set}$ such that $f(M) \subseteq [\![M]\!]_\Sigma$; and
- For each signature morphism $\varphi: \Sigma \to \Sigma'$

$$[\![Mod(\varphi) \to \mathbf{Set}]\!](f)(M') = [\![M']\!]_\varphi^{-1}(f(Mod(\varphi)M')).$$

A straightforward check reveals that the Satisfaction Condition (2) appears exactly as the naturality property of $\models$:

$$\begin{array}{ccc} \Sigma & Sen(\Sigma) \xrightarrow{\models_\Sigma} [\![Mod(\Sigma) \to \mathbf{Set}]\!] \\ \varphi \downarrow & Sen(\varphi) \downarrow & \downarrow [\![Mod(\varphi) \to \mathbf{Set}]\!] \\ \Sigma' & Sen(\Sigma') \xrightarrow[\models_{\Sigma'}]{} [\![Mod(\Sigma') \to \mathbf{Set}]\!] \end{array}$$

Ordinary institutions are the stratified institutions for which $[\![M]\!]_\Sigma$ is always a singleton set. In the upgraded definition, the surjectivity condition on $[\![M']\!]_\varphi$ from [51] has been removed, as it can be made explicit when necessary. This is motivated by the fact that most of the results developed do not depend upon this condition which, however, holds in all examples known by us. On the one hand, in many important concrete situations (Kripke semantics, automata, etc.), $[\![M']\!]_\varphi$ are even identities, which makes $[\![\_]\!]$ a strict rather than a lax natural transformation. However, on the other hand, there are interesting examples when the stratification is properly lax, such as in the $\mathcal{OFOL}$ example below or the representation of 3/2 institutions as stratified institutions developed in [58].

The literature on stratified institutions shows many model theories that are captured as stratified institutions. Here, we recall some of them in a very succint form; for a more detailed form, one may find them in [52,57,58].

1. In *modal propositional logic* ($\mathcal{MPL}$), the category of the signatures is $\mathbf{Set}$, $Sen(P)$ is the set of the usual modal sentences formed with the atomic propositions from P, and the P models are the Kripke structures (W, M) where $W = (|W|, W_\lambda)$ consists of a set of 'possible worlds' $|W|$ and an accessibility relation $W_\lambda \subseteq |W| \times |W|$, and $M: |W| \to 2^P$. The stratification is given by $[\![(W, M)]\!] = |W|$.
2. In *first-order modal logic* ($\mathcal{MFOL}$), the signatures are first-order logic ($\mathcal{FOL}$) signatures consisting of sets of operation and relation symbols structured by their arities. The sentences extend the usual construction of $\mathcal{FOL}$ sentences with the modal connectives $\square$ and $\diamond$. The models for a signature Σ are Kripke structures (W, M) where W is like in $\mathcal{MPL}$ but $M: |W| \to |Mod^{\mathcal{FOL}}(\Sigma)|$ is subject to the constraint that the carrier sets, and the interpretations of the constants are shared across the possible worlds. The stratification is like in $\mathcal{MPL}$.
3. *Hybrid logics* ($\mathcal{HPL}$, $\mathcal{HFOL}$, etc.) refine modal logics by adding explicit syntax for the possible worlds such as *nominals* and @. Stratified institutions of hybrid logics upgrade the syntactic and the semantic components of the stratified institutions of modal logics accordingly. For instance, in the stratified institution of hybrid propositional logic ($\mathcal{HPL}$), the signatures are pairs of sets (Nom, P), the (Nom, P)-models are Kripke structures (W, M) like in $\mathcal{MPL}$, but where W adds interpretations of the nominals, i.e., $W = (|W|, (W_i)_{i \in Nom}, W_\lambda)$, and at the level of the syntax, for each $i \in Nom$, we have a new sentence i-sen, a new unary connective $@_i$, and existential quantifications over nominals variables. Then, $((W, M) \models^w i\text{-sen}) = (W_i = w)$, $((W, M) \models^w @_i \rho) = ((W, M) \models^{W_i} \rho)$, etc.
4. *Multi-modal logics* exhibit several modalities instead of only the traditional $\diamond$ and $\square$, and moreover, these may have various arities. If one considers the sets of modalities to be variable, then they have to be considered as part of the signatures. Each of the stratified institutions discussed in the previous examples admit an upgrade to the multi-modal case.

5. In a series of works on *modalization of institutions* [61–63], modal logic and Kripke semantics are developed by abstracting away details that do not belong to modality, such as sorts, functions, predicates, etc. This is achieved by extensions of abstract institutions (in the standard situations meant in principle to encapsulate the atomic part of the logics) with the essential ingredients of modal logic and Kripke semantics. The results of this process, when instantiated to various concrete logics (or to their atomic parts only) generate uniformly a wide range of hierarchical combinations between various flavours of modal logic and various other logics. Concrete examples discussed in [61–63] include various modal logics over non-conventional structures of relevance in computing science, such as partial algebra, preordered algebra, etc. Various constraints on the respective Kripke models, many of them having to do with the underlying non-modal structures, have also been considered. All these arise as examples of stratified institutions such as the examples presented above in the paper. An interesting class of examples that has emerged quite smoothly out of the general works on *hybridization* (i.e., modalization including also hybrid logic features) of institutions is that of multi-layered hybrid logics that provide a logical base for specifying hierarchical transition systems (see [64]). This construction will be discussed in more detail in a dedicated section below in the paper.

6. *Open first-order logic* ($\mathcal{OFOL}$). This is an $\mathcal{FOL}$ instance of $St(\mathcal{I})$, the 'internal stratification' abstract example developed in [51]. An $\mathcal{OFOL}$ signature is a pair (Σ, X) consisting of $\mathcal{FOL}$ signature Σ and a finite block of variables. To any $\mathcal{OFOL}$ signature (Σ, X) corresponds an $\mathcal{FOL}$ signature $\Sigma + X$ that adjoins X to Σ as new constants. Then, $Sen^{\mathcal{OFOL}}(\Sigma, X) = Sen^{\mathcal{FOL}}(\Sigma + X)$, $Mod^{\mathcal{OFOL}}(\Sigma, X) = Mod^{\mathcal{FOL}}(\Sigma)$, $[\![M]\!]_{\Sigma,X} = M^X$, i.e., the set of the "valuations" of X to M and for each (Σ, X)-model M, each $w \in M^X$, and each (Σ, X)-sentence ρ, we define $(M(\models^{\mathcal{OFOL}}_{\Sigma,X})^w \rho) = (M^w \models^{\mathcal{FOL}}_{\Sigma+X} \rho)$ where M^w is the expansion of M to $\Sigma + X$ such that $M^w_X = w$ (i.e., the new constants of X are interpreted in M^w according to the "valuation" w).

7. Various kinds of *automata theories* can be presented as stratified institutions. For instance, the stratified institution $\mathcal{SAUT}$ of deterministic automata (for regular languages) has sets of input symbols as signatures, the automata A are the models and the words are the sentences. Then, $[\![A]\!]$ is the set of the states of A and $A \models^s \alpha$ if and only if α is recognised by A from the state s.

8. In [51], the authors introduced an abstract approach to connectives that generalises the propositional and quantification connectives, modalities, nominals, and so on. A *connective signature* $\mathcal{C}$ is just a single sorted signature of operation symbols, which are called connectives. Let $T_\mathcal{C}$ denote the set of all $\mathcal{C}$-terms. A $\mathcal{C}$-algebra A consists of a set $[\![A]\!]$ and a mapping $A: T_\mathcal{C} \to \mathcal{P}[\![A]\!]$. A $\mathcal{C}$-homomorphism $h: A \to B$ is a function $h: [\![A]\!] \to [\![B]\!]$ such that $2^h \circ A = B$. If $\eta \in [\![A]\!]$ and $\rho \in T_\mathcal{C}$, then $A \models^\eta_\mathcal{C} \rho$ holds when $\eta \in A(\rho)$. All these define the stratified institution of abstract connectives $\mathcal{CON}$ that has the connectives signatures as its signatures, $\mathcal{C}$-algebras and $\mathcal{C}$-models, $T_\mathcal{C}$ as the set of $\mathcal{C}$-sentences, the stratification being given by $[\![A]\!]$ and the satisfaction relation defined as above.

9. In [58], there is a development of a general representation theorem of 3/2 institutions as stratified institutions. The theory of 3/2 institutions [59] is an extension of ordinary institution theory that accommodates the partiality of the signature morphisms and its syntactic and semantic effects, which is motivated by applications to conceptual blending and software evolution. The representation theorem is based, for each $\varphi\square$-model M, on setting $[\![M]\!]$ to the *set* its φ-reducts. This is possible because in 3/2 institutions, unlike in ordinary institution theory, a model may have more than one reduct with respect to a fixed signature morphism, this being the semantic effect of the (implicit) partiality of the signature morphisms.

That was the brief presentation of the concept of stratified institution together with a list of relevant concrete examples. In the remaining part of this section, we will present some of the most important model theoretic developments with stratified institutions as follows:

- A 'flattening' of stratified institutions to ordinary institutions as a universal construction, and on this basis, a general technique for establishing properties in some important class of stratified institution, which uses an axiomatic decomposition of the respective stratified institution.
- A general method to construct new stratified institutions out of existing stratified institutions by 'modalisation'.
- An axiomatic treatment of important model theoretic concepts such as propositional connectives, quantifiers, modalities, nominals, and interpolation.
- Some important model theoretic methods in the context of stratified institutions, including diagrams, ultraproducts, and Tarski's elementary chain theorem.
- Some more computing science-motivated uses of stratified institutions.

3.1. Flattening Stratified Institutions to Ordinary Institutions

Given any stratified institution $S = (Sign, Sen, Mod, [\![\_]\!], \models)$, in [52], we have built an ordinary institution $S^\sharp = (Sign, Sen, Mod^\sharp, \models^\sharp)$ as follows:

- The objects of $Mod^\sharp(\Sigma)$ are the pairs (M, w) such that $M \in |Mod(\Sigma)|$ and $w \in [\![M]\!]_\Sigma$;
- The Σ-homomorphisms $(M, w) \to (N, v)$ are the pairs (h, w) such that $h: M \to N$ and $[\![h]\!]_\Sigma w = v$;
- For any signature morphism $\varphi: \Sigma \to \Sigma'$ and any Σ'-model (M', w')

$$Mod^\sharp(\varphi)(M', w') = (Mod(\varphi)M', [\![M']\!]_\varphi w');$$

- For each Σ-model M, each $w \in [\![M]\!]_\Sigma$, and each $\rho \in Sen(\Sigma)$

$$((M, w) \models^\sharp_\Sigma \rho) = (M \models^w_\Sigma \rho). \tag{5}$$

In [57], the construction of $S^\sharp$ is explained as a categorical universal construction. That explanation involves the concept of *morphism of stratified institutions* which is an extension of the notorious concept of *morphism of institutions* (cf. [18,44,46], etc.). Both concepts represent mappings that preserve the mathematical structure of stratified institutions and of ordinary institutions, respectively, in the same way group homomorphisms preserve the group structure, or the continuous functions preserve the structure of topological spaces. Thus, $(\_)^\sharp$ arises as a left-adjoint functor from the category **SINS** of strict stratified institutions to the category **INS** of ordinary institutions. One way to present this is that for each institution $\mathcal{B}$, there exists a stratified institution $\widetilde{\mathcal{B}}$ and an institution morphism $\varepsilon_\mathcal{B}: \widetilde{\mathcal{B}}^\sharp \to \mathcal{B}$ such that for each morphism of institutions $(\Phi, \alpha, \beta): S^\sharp \to \mathcal{B}$, there exists a unique strict stratified institution morphism $(\Phi, \alpha, \widetilde{\beta}): S \to \widetilde{\mathcal{B}}$ such that the following diagram commutes:

(6)

The construction $S^\sharp$, called the *flattening of S*, on the one hand reduces stratified institutions to ordinary institutions without any loss of information. It is helpful for transferring concepts and results from the simpler world of ordinary institution theory to that of stratified institutions. One important example of that is given by the model amalgamation property, which is one of the most fundamental properties of institutions with vast consequences both in computing science and in institutional model theory (cf. [25,44,65], etc.). Model amalgamation in $S^\sharp$ defines the so-called *stratified model amalgamation* in S [57], which is more refined than plain model amalgamation in S and is a characteristic only to stratified institutions. On the other hand, it is important to avoid the trap of believing that in this way, the theory of stratified institutions can be dealt with entirely within the ordinary institution theoretic framework. The reason for this cannot be the case that the institutions $\mathcal{S}^\sharp$ are not any institutions, as they have a very specific structure given by the stratified structure of $\mathcal{S}$.

Another way to reduce a stratified institution to an ordinary institution is to flatten only the satisfaction relation, i.e.,

$$M \models^* \rho \text{ if and only if } M \models^w \rho \text{ for each } w \in \llbracket M \rrbracket.$$

This yields an institution when the stratification is surjective (i.e., for each signature morphism φ and each $\varphi\square$-model M', $\llbracket M' \rrbracket_\varphi$ is surjective). However, in this institution, denoted $\mathcal{S}^*$, the locality aspect of $\mathcal{S}$—which is very important—is lost. In the literature, $\mathcal{S}^*$ and $\mathcal{S}^\sharp$ are known as the *global* and the *local*, respectively, institutions associated to $\mathcal{S}$. They can be regarded as high abstractions of the global and of the local satisfaction in modal logic.

3.2. Decompositions of Stratified Institutions

In [57], we have introduced a technique for establishing properties of stratified institutions at the general level, which consists of projecting to simpler structures. This reflects a situation that occurs especially in the stratified institutions that are based on Kripke semantics, where the models are combined from two simpler components, of which one may think as a structure of the worlds on the one hand and a structure of primitive or base models placed in these worlds on the other hand. The actual definition of this is as follows.

Let $\mathcal{S}$ be any stratified institution and $(\Phi, \alpha, \beta) : \mathcal{S}^\sharp \to \mathcal{B}$ be a morphism of institutions (called a *base* for $\mathcal{S}$). By the natural isomorphism $\mathbf{INS}(\mathcal{S}^\sharp, \mathcal{B}) \cong \mathbf{SINS}(\mathcal{S}, \widetilde{\mathcal{B}})$ (given by the adjunction between **SINS** and **INS**), we obtain a morphism of stratified institutions $(\Phi, \alpha, \widetilde{\beta}) : \mathcal{S} \to \widetilde{\mathcal{B}}$ (cf. (6)). A *constraint model sub-functor* $Mod^C \subseteq Mod^{\widetilde{\mathcal{B}}}$ is a sub-functor such that for each signature Σ,

$$\widetilde{\beta}_\Sigma(Mod^\mathcal{S}(\Sigma)) \subseteq Mod^C(\Phi\Sigma).$$

Let $\widetilde{\mathcal{B}}^C$ denote the stratified sub-institution of $\widetilde{\mathcal{B}}$ induced by Mod^C. A *decomposition of* $\mathcal{S}$ consists of two strict stratified institution morphisms such as below

$$\mathcal{S}^0 \xleftarrow{(\Phi^0, \alpha^0, \beta^0)} \mathcal{S} \xrightarrow{(\Phi, \alpha, \widetilde{\beta})} \widetilde{\mathcal{B}}^C$$

such that for each $\mathcal{S}$-signature Σ

$$Mod^0(\Phi^0\Sigma) \xleftarrow{\beta^0_\Sigma} Mod^\mathcal{S}(\Sigma) \xrightarrow{\widetilde{\beta}_\Sigma} Mod^C(\Phi\Sigma)$$
$$\searrow_{\llbracket\_\rrbracket^0_{\Phi^0\Sigma}} \downarrow_{\llbracket\_\rrbracket^\mathcal{S}_\Sigma} \swarrow_{\llbracket\_\rrbracket^{\widetilde{\mathcal{B}}}_{\Phi\Sigma}}$$
$$\mathbf{Set}$$

is a pullback in **CAT**.

The following aspects emerge from the concept of decomposition.

- The models of $\mathcal{S}$ can be represented as pairs of $\mathcal{S}^0$ models and families of $\mathcal{B}$ models satisfying certain constraints (hence, $\widetilde{\mathcal{B}}^C$ models) such that the "worlds" of the corresponding $\widetilde{\mathcal{B}}^C$ model constitutes the stratification of the corresponding $\mathcal{S}^0$ model. This means that at the semantic level, $\mathcal{S}$ is completely determined by the two components of the decomposition.
- The situation at the syntactic level is different. The syntax (signatures and sentences) of each of the two components is represented in the syntax of $\mathcal{S}$, but the latter is not completely determined by the former syntaxes. In other words, $\mathcal{S}$ may have signatures and sentences that do not originate from either of the two components. This is what the definition gives us. However, while there are hardly any examples/applications where all sentences come from either of the two components, in many examples, the signatures of $\mathcal{S}$ are composed from the signatures of $\mathcal{S}^0$ and those from $\mathcal{B}$.

In the definition of decomposition, the role of the constraint model sub-functor Mod^C is strongly related to applications. For instance, in many concrete situations of interest, the Kripke models enjoy some form of sharing. Cases such as $\mathcal{MFOL}$ and $\mathcal{HFOL}$ are emblematic in this respect. If we consider the latter one, then:

- $\mathcal{S}^0 = \mathcal{RELC}^1$, which is the single-sorted sub-institution of $\mathcal{FOL}$ determined by the signatures without operation symbols other than constants. Consequently, $\Phi^0(\text{Nom}, P) = (\text{Nom}, \lambda : 2)$.
- α^0 is defined by

$$\alpha^0_{(\text{Nom},P)}\lambda(i,j) = @_i \diamond j (= @_i \neg \Box \neg j).$$

- $\mathcal{B} = \mathcal{AFOL}$, i.e., the sub-institution of $\mathcal{FOL}$ that admits only atoms as sentences.
- Mod^C restricts the $\widetilde{\mathcal{B}}$ models only to those for which the base $\mathcal{FOL}$ models share their underlying sets and the interpretations of the constants.
- α consists of canonical interpretations of the $\mathcal{FOL}$ atoms as $\mathcal{HFOL}$ sentences.

One of the consequences of decompositions is the possibility to obtain model amalgamation properties in $\mathcal{S}$ via model amalgamation properties in the components $\mathcal{S}^0$ and $\mathcal{B}$. This can be very useful in the applications as Kripke models are complex structures; therefore, their model amalgamation is a mathematically complicated matter, while model amalgamation in the components of a decomposition is much simpler. In [57], we have provided a general theorem that obtains model amalgamation through decompositions and which applies well in the examples. There have been also other applications of this decomposition technique which we will discuss later on in the paper.

Another important potential of the concept of decomposition is the possibility to apply it in a reverse way in the sense of constructing new stratified institutions starting from the components $\mathcal{S}^0$ and $\mathcal{B}$ (actually $\widetilde{\mathcal{B}}^C$). This can be a great source of new concrete stratified institutions serving various computing science purposes.

3.3. Modalised (Stratified) Institutions

The modalisation of institutions, already discussed as an item in the list of examples of stratified institutions, constitutes an example of reversing the decomposition concept in which $\mathcal{S}^0$ is rather concrete—its models being Kripke frames—while $\mathcal{B}$ is kept abstract, and it goes back essentially to [61].

In this context, the work [66] generalises the famous encoding of modal logic into first-order logic [67] in the sense that any abstract encoding $\mathcal{B} \to \mathcal{FOL}$ becomes lifted to an encoding $\mathcal{S}^* \to \mathcal{FOL}$ (the precise notion of encoding being what is known as *theoroidal comorphism*). This highly general encoding constitutes the foundations for the formal specification and verification language H [68], which is a language that is institution-independent in the sense that in principle, the base institution $\mathcal{B}$ can be any institution that can be plugged into the system.

Although the modalisation of institutions has been defined in the way presented above, in fact, it can be extended to a construction that takes an arbitrary stratified rather than an ordinary institution as input. So, it becomes a method for building new stratified institutions on top of proper stratified institutions. A brief description of this method is as follows:

- Let $\mathcal{S}$ be a stratified institution. The stratified institution to be constructed will be denoted $K(\mathcal{S})$.
- Then, we let $Sign^{K(\mathcal{S})} = Sign^{\mathcal{S}}$.
- For any signature Σ, $Sen^{K(\mathcal{S})}$ is the least set containing $Sen^{\mathcal{S}}(\Sigma)$ and which is closed under propositional connectives, quantifiers, and modalities ($\Box, \diamond$). We can chose what we need from those connectives, which means that they should be regarded as a parameter for $K(\mathcal{S})$. The quantifiers are treated abstractly in the typical institution theoretic manner (cf. [30,44] etc.) by using an abstract designated class of signature morphisms that obey some axioms known as *quantification space* [63,69].

- The models of $K(S)$ are the *Kripke models over* S, i.e., pairs (W, M) where W is a Kripke frame as in $\mathcal{MPL}$ or $\mathcal{MFOL}$, and $M = (M^w)_{w \in |W|}$ such that $[\![M^w]\!]_\Sigma^S = [\![M^v]\!]_\Sigma^S$ for all $w, v \in |W|$ (so the components of M share their 'internal states').
- The stratification is defined by $[\![(W, M)]\!]_\Sigma^{K(S)} = |W| \times [\![M]\!]_\Sigma^S$.
- The satisfaction relation of $K(S)$ is defined inductively on the structure of the respective sentences by following the common ideas of of Kripke semantics. For the base case, when the sentence is in S, we rely on the satisfaction relation of S.

In order to capture precisely various relevant examples, this construction can be refined in various ways by considering constrained models (axiomatically in the manner described in [63] or more concretely as in [61]), or by considering nominals structures or polyadic modalities. In the case of the latter two extensions, of course, the new category of signatures is a product between $Sign^S$ and some category of signatures for relations.

3.4. The Logic of Stratified Institutions

The development of an in-depth model theory in the axiomatic style relies also on the possibility to 'internalise' important logical concepts such as propositional connectives and quantifiers. In ordinary institution theory, this has been achieved very early in [30] (for a more comprehensive treatment, see also [44]). The axiomatic semantic definitions of the common propositional connectives and of quantifiers have been extended to stratified institutions in [52]. Although presented in a different form closer to [53], the definitions below are equivalent to those of [52]. The following notation is useful for what follows. For any Σ-model M and any Σ-sentence ρ, we let

$$[\![M, \rho]\!] = \{w \in [\![M]\!]_\Sigma \mid M \models^w \rho\}.$$

3.4.1. Propositional Connectives

Given a signature Σ in a stratified institution, a Σ-sentence ρ' is a *semantic*

- *Negation* of ρ when $[\![M, \rho']\!] = [\![M]\!] \setminus [\![M, \rho]\!]$;
- *Conjunction* of ρ_1 and ρ_2 when $[\![M, \rho']\!] = [\![M, \rho_1]\!] \cap [\![M, \rho_2]\!]$;
- *Disjunction* of ρ_1 and ρ_2 when $[\![M, \rho']\!] = [\![M, \rho_1]\!] \cup [\![M, \rho_2]\!]$;
- *Implication* of ρ_1 and ρ_2 when $[\![M, \rho']\!] = ([\![M]\!] \setminus [\![M, \rho_1]\!]) \cup [\![M, \rho_2]\!]$;
- etc.

for each Σ-model M. A stratified institution *has (semantic) negation* when each sentence of the institution has a negation. It has *(semantic) conjunctions* when each two sentences (of the same signature) have a conjunction. Similar definitions can be formulated for disjunctions, implications, and equivalences. As in ordinary institution theory, distinguished negations are usually denoted by $\neg\_$, distinguished conjunctions are usually denoted by $\_ \wedge \_$, distinguished disjunctions are usually denoted by $\_ \vee \_$ distinguished implications are usually denoted by $\_ \Rightarrow \_$ distinguished equivalences are usually denoted by $\_ \Leftrightarrow \_$, etc. Note that $\mathcal{MFOL}$, $\mathcal{MPL}$ together with their hybrid extensions $\mathcal{HFOL}$, $\mathcal{HPL}$, as well as $\mathcal{OFOL}$ have all these semantics propositional connectives. $\mathcal{SAUT}$ has conjunctions only.

When they exist, the semantic propositional connectives are inter-definable. Moroover, when they exist, the negations, conjunctions, disjunctions, implications, and negations coincide in S and $S^\sharp$.

3.4.2. Quantifiers

Given a morphism of signatures $\chi : \Sigma \to \Sigma'$, a Σ-sentence ρ is a *semantic*

- *Universal χ-quantification* of a Σ'-sentence ρ' when

$$[\![M, \rho]\!] = \bigcap_{Mod(\chi)M' = M} \{w \in [\![M]\!]_\Sigma \mid [\![M']\!]_\chi^{-1} w \subseteq [\![M', \rho']\!]\}, \text{ and}$$

- *Existential χ-quantification* of a Σ'-sentence ρ' when

$$[\![M, \rho]\!] = \bigcup_{Mod(\chi)M' = M} [\![M']\!]_\chi([\![M', \rho']\!]),$$

for any Σ-model M.

A stratified institution *has (semantic) universal $\mathcal{D}$-quantification* for a class $\mathcal{D}$ of signature morphisms when for each $(\chi: \Sigma \to \Sigma') \in \mathcal{D}$, each Σ'-sentence has a universal χ-quantification. A similar definition applies to existential quantification. Distinguished universal/existential quantifications are denoted by $(\forall \chi)\rho'/(\exists \chi)\rho'$.

When they exist, the universal and the existential χ-quantifications, respectively, coincide in $\mathcal{S}$ and $\mathcal{S}^\sharp$. So, on the one hand, the concepts of semantic propositional connectives and quantifications in ordinary institutions arise as an instance of those of stratified institutions when the underlying set of each $[\![M]\!]_\Sigma$ is a singleton set. On the other hand, we have seen that the stratified institution concepts of propositional connectives and quantifications are in substance no more general than their ordinary institution theoretic correspondents. Therefore, an alternative equivalent way to introduce the stratified institution semantics of propositional connectives is to define them on the basis of $\mathcal{S}^\sharp$ and then infer the above definitions as properties at the level of $\mathcal{S}$.

3.4.3. Modalities

While propositional and quantification connectives in stratified institutions can still be explained in terms of their ordinary institution theoretic counterparts, modalities and nominals can be defined only in the presence of stratifications because both of them rely semantically on models having internal states. Moreover, this is not enough; in both cases, some additional specific semantic infrastructure is also needed.

In order to define semantic possibility ($\Diamond$) and necessity ($\Box$) in a stratified institution, we have to be able to 'extract' Kripke frames from the stratification. Let $\mathcal{REL}$ denote the sub-institution of $\mathcal{FOL}$ determined by those signatures without function symbols. Let $\mathcal{REL}^1$ denote the single sorted version of $\mathcal{REL}$. Given a stratified institution $\mathcal{S}$, a *binary frame extraction* assumes that for each signature Σ, the stratification $[\![\_]\!]_\Sigma$ is a composition between a functor $Fr_\Sigma : Mod(\Sigma) \to Mod^{\mathcal{REL}^1}(\lambda : 2)$ and the forgetful functor $Mod^{\mathcal{REL}^1}(\lambda : 2) \to \mathbf{Set}$, where $Mod^{\mathcal{REL}^1}(\lambda : 2)$ is the category of the $\mathcal{FOL}$ models for a single sorted signature with one binary relation symbol λ.

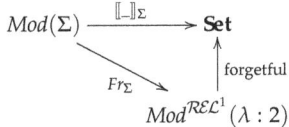

Note that the models of $Mod^{\mathcal{REL}^1}(\lambda : 2)$ are exactly the Kripke frames $W = (|W|, W_\lambda)$ of the modal logic examples $\mathcal{MPL}$, $\mathcal{MFOL}$, $\mathcal{HPL}$, and $\mathcal{HFOL}$. Since $|Fr_\Sigma(M)| = [\![M]\!]_\Sigma$, we can write $Fr_\Sigma(M) = ([\![M]\!]_\Sigma, (Fr_\Sigma(M))_\lambda)$. The Fr_Σ functors are also required to form a lax natural transformation from Mod to the constant functor mapping any signature to the category $Mod^{\mathcal{REL}^1}(\lambda : 2)$.

Concretely, in the stratified institutions $\mathcal{MFOL}$, $\mathcal{MPL}$, $\mathcal{HFOL}$, and $\mathcal{HPL}$, the Fr maps the Kripke models (W, M) to their underlying Kripke frames $W = (|W|, W_\lambda)$.

In the most general situation, when we allow *polyadic* modalities, i.e., modalities with more than one argument, first, we need a functor $L : Sign^\mathcal{S} \to Sign^{\mathcal{REL}^1}$ such that $L(\Sigma)$ represents the relation symbols corresponding to the modalities of Σ (we allow a flexible approach where the modalities may change with the signature). Then, we have a more general concept of frame extraction. In the binary case, $L(\Sigma)$ is always $\{\lambda : 2\}$ and hence, there is no reason to have λ as part of the signatures.

A *(general) frame extraction* (L, Fr) is a stratified institution morphism

$$(L, \varnothing, Fr) : \mathcal{S} \to \mathcal{REL}^1$$

where $\mathcal{REL}^1$ is considered as a stratified institution with no sentences, and for each $\mathcal{REL}^1$-model M, $[\![M]\!]$ is the underlying set of M and the satisfaction is invariant with respect to the states, i.e., $M \models^w \rho$ is $M \models \rho$. Commonly, in concrete examples, it happens that frame extractions are in fact strict institution morphisms.

In any stratified institution endowed with a binary frame extraction Fr, a Σ-sentence ρ' is a *semantic*

- *possibility* ($\Diamond$) of ρ when $[\![M, \rho']\!] = (Fr_\Sigma M)_\lambda^{-1} [\![M, \rho]\!]$;
- *necessity* ($\Box$) of ρ when $[\![M, \rho']\!] = \{i \mid (Fr_\Sigma M)_\lambda i \subseteq [\![M, \rho]\!]\}$,

for each Σ-model M.

Obviously, in $\mathcal{MPL}$, $\mathcal{MFOL}$, $\mathcal{HPL}$, and $\mathcal{HFOL}$, we have that each $\Diamond \rho / \Box \rho$ is a semantic possibility/necessity of ρ in the sense of our definitions above. The concept of semantic possibility/necessity admits an obvious extension to polyadic modalities by using general frame extractions.

3.4.4. Nominals

In order to define the semantics of hybrid features such as nominals and the satisfaction operator (@) in stratified institutions, we need to be able to extract nominals data from the corresponding stratification. Let $\mathcal{SETC}$ be the sub-institution of $\mathcal{FOL}$ that restricts the signatures to single-sorted ones and without relation symbols or function symbols of non-null arity, so only constants being admitted. Given a stratified institution $\mathcal{S}$, a *nominals extraction* assumes two additional data:

- A functor $N : \mathrm{Sign}^\mathcal{S} \to \mathrm{Sign}^{\mathcal{SETC}}$, i.e., each $N(\Sigma)$ is a single-sorted $\mathcal{FOL}$ signature having only constants; and
- That for each signature Σ, the stratification $[\![\_]\!]_\Sigma$ is a composition between a functor $Nm_\Sigma : \mathrm{Mod}^\mathcal{S}(\Sigma) \to \mathrm{Mod}^{\mathcal{SETC}}(N(\Sigma))$ and the forgetful functor $\mathrm{Mod}^{\mathcal{SETC}}(N(\Sigma)) \to \mathbf{Set}$,

$$\begin{array}{ccc} \mathrm{Mod}^\mathcal{S}(\Sigma) & \xrightarrow{[\![\_]\!]_\Sigma} & \mathbf{Set} \\ & \searrow_{Nm_\Sigma} & \uparrow \text{forgetful} \\ & & \mathrm{Mod}^{\mathcal{SETC}}(N(\Sigma)) \end{array}$$

such that the Nm_Σ functors are also required to form a lax natural transformation $\mathrm{Mod}^\mathcal{S} \Rightarrow N; \mathrm{Mod}^{\mathcal{SETC}}$.

Hence, a nominals extraction (N, Nm) is a stratified institution morphism

$$(N, \emptyset, Nm) : \mathcal{S} \to \mathcal{SETC}$$

where $\mathcal{SETC}$ is considered as a stratified institution in the same manner we considered $\mathcal{REL}^1$ as a stratified institution.

Concretely, in the stratified institutions of the hyrbid modal logics $\mathcal{HFOL}$, $\mathcal{HPL}$, we have that N maps each signature (Nom, Σ) to the single-sorted signature of constants Nom, and that $Nm_{(\mathrm{Nom},\Sigma)}$ maps each Kripke model (W, M) to the $\mathrm{Mod}^{\mathcal{SETC}}(\mathrm{Nom})$-model $(|W|, (W_i)_{i \in \mathrm{Nom}})$, so from the Kripke models, it forgets both the M part as well as the accessibility relation W_λ.

In any stratified institution endowed with a nominals extraction N, Nm, for each signature Σ and each $i \in N(\Sigma)$,

- A Σ-sentence ρ' is an *i-sentence* when $[\![M, \rho']\!] = \{(Nm_\Sigma M)_i\}$;
- A Σ-sentence ρ' is the *satisfaction of ρ at i* when

$$[\![M, \rho']\!] = \begin{cases} [\![M]\!], & (Nm_\Sigma M)_i \in [\![M, \rho]\!] \\ \emptyset, & (Nm_\Sigma M)_i \notin [\![M, \rho]\!] \end{cases}$$

for each Σ-model M.

In $\mathcal{HPL}$ and $\mathcal{HFOL}$, we have that each nominal i of the signature is an *i*-sentence and each sentence $@_i \rho$ is a satisfaction at i in the sense of the above definitions. In general, for the distinguished *i*-sentences and satisfaction at *i*, we may use the notations *i*-sen and $@_i\rho$, respectively.

3.5. Interpolation in Stratified Institutions

Interpolation is a notoriously important logical property which is easy to understand but difficult to establish. It also has a number of important applications in computing science, especially in formal specification theory [65,70–74] but also in databases (ontologies) [75], automated reasoning [76,77], type checking [78], model checking [79], structured theorem proving [80,81], etc. Computing science and model theoretic motivations have led to a very general approach to interpolation [30] within the theory of institutions that is completely independent of any concrete logical system. This direction of study and research has produced a substantial body of results reported in works such as [30,42,43,45,65,74,82–86]. In this context, the institution theoretic concept to interpolation had suffered a gradual evolution. At the level of ordinary institution theory, one way to express the end result of this evolution is that of 'interpolation square'. In its Craig interpolation version, this is as follows. In any given institution $\mathcal{I}$, a commutative square of signature morphisms as below

$$\begin{array}{ccc} \Sigma & \xrightarrow{\varphi_1} & \Sigma_1 \\ \varphi_2 \downarrow & & \downarrow \theta_1 \\ \Sigma_2 & \xrightarrow{\theta_2} & \Sigma' \end{array} \qquad (7)$$

is a *Craig interpolation square* when for each finite set E_k of Σ_k-sentences, $k = 1, 2$, such that when $\theta_1 E_1 \models \theta_2 E_2$, there exists a finite set E of Σ-sentences such that

$$E_1 \models \varphi_1 E \text{ and } \varphi_2 E \models E_2.$$

How can we lift this concept of interpolation square to stratified institutions? The obvious answer is to maintain the concept by apply it to a flattening of the respective stratified institution $\mathcal{S}$. However, here, we run into a problem: which of $\mathcal{S}^*$ and $\mathcal{S}^\sharp$ is the most appropriate for this? The answer is that this may be actually a wrong question, as both the local ($\models^\sharp$) and the global ($\models^*$) semantic consequences can be used legitimately to define interpolation concepts in stratified institutions. So, we naturally end up with two concepts of interpolation in stratified institutions.

Then, a natural question arises: what is the causal relationship between local and global interpolation? In [87], we have provided an answer to this question. Without some additional infrastructure, none of the two interpolation concepts causes the other one. However, the main result of [87] shows that local causes global interpolation when the respective stratified institution has some nominals infrastructure including universal quantification over the nominals. In [87], these properties are given precise mathematical sense through some rather intricate technicalities which we do not present here. This is only the first step toward a proper theory of interpolation specific to stratified institutions. More steps are needed in order to mature it at a level comparable to that of interpolation in ordinary institution model theory.

3.6. Diagrams in Stratified Institutions

In conventional model theory, the method of diagrams is one of the most important methods. The institution-independent method of diagrams plays a significant role in the development of a lot of model theoretic results at the level of abstract institutions, many of its applications being presented in [44]. These include the existence of co-limits of models, free models along theory morphisms, axiomatisability results, elementary homomorphisms results, filtered power embeddings results, saturated models results (including an abstract version of Keisler–Shelah isomorphism theorem), the equivalence between initial semantics and quasi-varieties, Robinson consistency results, interpolation theory, definability theory, proof systems, predefined types, etc.

In institution theory, diagrams had been introduced for the first time by Tarlecki in [31,32] in a form different from ours. In the form presented here, it has been introduced at the level of institution-independent model theory in [33] as a categorical property which formalises the idea that

> the class of model homomorphisms from a model M can be represented (by a natural isomorphism) as a class of models of a theory in a signature extending the original signature with syntactic entities determined by M.

Let us recall from [33,44] the main concept of the institution theoretic method of diagrams. An institution $\mathcal{I}$ has *diagrams* when for each signature Σ and each Σ model M, there exists a signature Σ_M and a signature morphism $\iota_\Sigma(M) : \Sigma \to \Sigma_M$, functorial in Σ and M, and a set E_M of Σ_M sentences such that $Mod(\Sigma_M, E_M)$ and the comma category $M/Mod(\Sigma)$ are naturally isomorphic, i.e., the following diagram commutes by the isomorphism $i_{\Sigma,M}$ that is natural in Σ and M

$$Mod(\Sigma_M, E_M) \xrightarrow{i_{\Sigma,M}} M/Mod(\Sigma) \qquad (8)$$
$$\searrow_{Mod(\iota_\Sigma(M))} \quad \downarrow \text{forgetful}$$
$$Mod(\Sigma)$$

The signature morphism $\iota_\Sigma(M) : \Sigma \to \Sigma_M$ is called the *elementary extension of Σ via M*, and the set E_M of Σ_M sentences is called the *diagram* of the model M.

This can be seen as a coherence property between the semantic and the syntactic structures of the institution. By following the basic principle that a structure is rather defined by its homomorphisms (arrows) than by its objects, the semantic structure of an institution is given by its model homomorphisms. On the other hand, the syntactic structure of an(y concrete) institution is based upon its corresponding concept of atomic sentence.

In [57], it has been proposed that the concept of a diagram in stratified institutions should be transferred to the flattenings:

the diagrams in a stratified institution $\mathcal{S}$ are the diagrams in $\mathcal{S}^\sharp$ (or in $\mathcal{S}^*$).

Based on this principle, in [57], we have developed a general result on the existence of diagrams at the level of abstract stratified institutions that is applicable to a wide class of concrete situations. Its underlying idea is to combine the diagrams in the two components of a decomposition. However, again, this requires some nominal infrastructure. Let us present briefly how we can obtain diagrams in $\mathcal{S}$ when this comes with a decomposition as in Section 3.2.

- For each Σ model of $\mathcal{S}$, let us define $\Sigma_0 = \Phi^0 \Sigma$, $\Sigma_1 = \Phi\Sigma$, $M_0 = \beta_\Sigma^0 M$, $M_1 = \widetilde{\beta}_\Sigma M$. We also let $\iota_{\Sigma_0} M_0 : \Sigma_0 \to (\Sigma_{0M_0}, E_{M_0})$ and (for each $i \in [\![M]\!]$) $\iota_{\Sigma_1} M_1^i : \Sigma_1 \to (\Sigma_{1M_1^i}, E_{M_1^i})$ be the diagrams of M_0 and M_1^i, respectively.
- We assume a coherence property that in the examples holds naturally in the case of models constrained by common forms of sharing (such as $\mathcal{MFOL}$, $\mathcal{HFOL}$, etc.): $\iota_{\Sigma_1} M_1^i = \iota_{\Sigma_1} M_1^j$ for all $i, j \in [\![M]\!]$.
- We further assume that

$$Sign^0 \xleftarrow{\Phi^0} Sign^\mathcal{S} \xrightarrow{\Phi} Sign^\mathcal{B}$$

is a product in **CAT**. This is a rather easy condition in concrete applications, typical examples being given by $\mathcal{HPL}$ and $\mathcal{HFOL}$.
- A final important assumption refers to each element $i \in [\![M]\!]$ of the underlying stratification having a syntactic designation $n_{\Sigma,M} i \in N(\Sigma_M)$. This is required to satisfy some natural conditions (details in [57]).
- Then, we define the $\mathcal{S}$ signature morphism $\iota_\Sigma M : \Sigma \to \Sigma_M$ by using the product property of (Φ^0, Φ):

$$\iota_\Sigma M = (\iota_{\Sigma_0} M_0, \iota_{\Sigma_1} M_1).$$

- Furthermore, we let

$$E_M = \alpha^0_{\Sigma_M} E_{M_0} \cup \bigcup_{i \in [\![M]\!]} @_i(\alpha_{\Sigma_M} E_{M_1^i})$$

where $@_i(\alpha_{\Sigma_M} E_{M_1^i})$ abbreviates $\{@_{n_{\Sigma,M}(i)} \alpha_{\Sigma_M} \rho \mid \rho \in E_{M_1^i}\}$. This gives the diagram M in $\mathcal{S}^*$.

- In order to obtain the diagram of a model (M, w) in $\mathcal{S}^\sharp$, it is enough to add the syntactic designation of w as a sentence to E_M.

Particular typical consequences of this general result are the existence of diagrams in hybrid logic institutions such as $\mathcal{HPL}, \mathcal{HFOL}$. The limitation of this result is represented by the general assumption on the availability of a nominals infrastructure. However, this seems to be an inherent limitation that has to do with the existence of diagrams; in other words, it is not a limitation of the way we have constructed the diagrams. This conclusion is supported toward the end of [57] by a proof showing that $\mathcal{MPL}$ and $\mathcal{MFOL}$ do not admit institution theoretic diagrams.

3.7. Ultraproducts in Stratified Institutions

The method of ultraproducts is renowned as extremely powerful and pervading a lot of deep results in model theory [2,88]. For instance, model ultraproducts are instrumental in the non-standard analysis [4,5] as the hyperreals are constructed by this technique. Chief among the ultraproduct method concepts and results that have been lifted to abstract institution theory is a very general version of Łoś theorem obtained as a puzzle of preservation results [34,44]. Then, general compactness results have been obtained as a consequence of this. Furthermore, in [61], all these have been extended to the framework of modalised institutions. In [52], we took another step by generalising the developments of [61] to arbitrary stratified institutions. In what follows, we present the milestones of this development:

- For any filter F over a set I and for any family $(M_i)_{i \in I}$ of Σ models, its F-product is defined categorically as the co-limit μ of a diagram of projections:

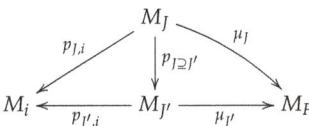

where for each $J \in F$, $(p_{J,j}: M_J \to M_j)_{j \in J}$ denotes a categorical product. This categorical approach on *filtered products* (called *ultraproducts* when F is an ultrafilter) has been used in various other categorical approaches to model theory such as [11,12,15,89], etc.

- The preservation of (the satisfaction of) a sentence ρ by F-filtered products is defined as follows. For any Σ sentence ρ, we introduce the following notation:

$$A_\mu(\rho) = \bigcup_{J \in F} [\![\mu_J]\!] \bigcap_{j \in J} [\![p_{J,j}]\!]^{-1} [\![M_j, \rho]\!].$$

Let $\mathcal{F}$ be a class of filters. Then, ρ is
- *Preserved by $\mathcal{F}$-products* when $A_\mu(\rho) \subseteq [\![M_F, \rho]\!]$, and it is
- *Preserved by $\mathcal{F}$-factors* when $[\![M_F, \rho]\!] \subseteq A_\mu(\rho)$,

for all filters $F \in \mathcal{F}$ and all families of models $(M_i)_{i \in I}$. When the F-products are *concrete*, which means that they are preserved by the stratification—a very common situation in the applications—the stratified concept of preservation in $\mathcal{S}$ reduces to the ordinary institution theoretic concept of preservation in $\mathcal{S}^\sharp$.

- Then, we have developed a series of results expressing the invariance of preservation, corresponding to various connectives. In the case of the propositional connectives, this invariance can be reduced to the corresponding invariance in ordinary institutions, which are already established in [34,44]. In the case of the quantifiers, this cannot be completed, but the proofs are similar to those from the ordinary institution theoretic framework. More interesting are the invariance results for modalities and nominals, as they do not have a counterpart in ordinary institutions, with the presence of stratification playing a key role. However, this is hardly unexpected, since the connectives are relevant only when models have internal states.

- In the applications, in order to obtain a preservation result for a certain sentence, we invoke corresponding invariance results through an inductive process on the structure of the respective sentence. For the base case, i.e., for the atomic sentences, we may use the ordinary institution theoretic preservation of the so-called *basic sentences* [34,44] via a decomposition of the stratified institution. Or else, we may establish their preservation directly.
- Each of the invariance results discussed above depends on some specific technical conditions involving model reducts, frame and nominals extractions, the class $\mathcal{F}$ of filters, etc. All of them are rather mild in the applications.

With respect to the compactness consequences of these invariances of preservation results, which together give a Łoś-style theorem for abstract stratified institutions, both in the local and global flattening (i.e., $\mathcal{S}^\sharp$ and $\mathcal{S}^*$, respectively), we usually obtain the model compactness property. However, the entailment–theoretic compactness of the semantic consequence may be obtained only for $\mathcal{S}^\sharp$, as in $\mathcal{S}^*$ negation, disjunction, existential quantifiers, etc., usually connectives that are related to negation in one form or another, pose some problems.

3.8. Abstract Connectives and Elementary Homomorphisms

In the list of examples of stratified institutions, we have presented the example $\mathcal{CON}$. We said that $\mathcal{CON}$ may provide foundations for an abstract theory of connectives. Let us see how this works by following some theory developed in [51]. The main idea is that we think of a stratified institution $\mathcal{S}$ as *having connectives* when we can 'extract' them from $\mathcal{S}$. Technically, this means that there exists a functor $C : \mathit{Sign}^\mathcal{S} \to \mathit{Sign}^{\mathcal{CON}}$ and for each $\Sigma \in |\mathit{Sign}^\mathcal{S}|$, a function $\beta_\Sigma : |\mathit{Mod}^\mathcal{S}(\Sigma)| \to |\mathit{Mod}^{\mathcal{CON}}(C\Sigma)|$ natural in Σ such that

$$Sen = T_- \circ C,\ [\![M]\!]^\mathcal{S}_\Sigma = [\![\beta_\Sigma M]\!]^{\mathcal{CON}}_{C\Sigma},\ M \models^\eta_\Sigma \rho \text{ if and only if } \beta_\Sigma M \models^\eta_{C\Sigma} \rho.$$

This means that any sentence of $\mathcal{S}$ is formed from connectives, each $\mathcal{S}$ model has an underlying connective algebra, and the satisfaction in $\mathcal{S}$ is given by evaluating the connective terms. In a more sophisticated terminology, $\mathcal{S}$ having connectives provides an example of morphism of stratified institutions.

$\mathcal{OFOL}$ provides a good example of this situation by letting the null-ary connectives consist of the atoms, the unary connectives consist of negation and quantifiers, the binary connectives being $\wedge, \vee, \ldots$, and that is all. Then, β maps to corresponding sets of valuations.

One of the consequences of these conceptual developments is the possibility of having a stratified institution theoretic alternative to the concepts of elementary homomorphism that is based on quasi-representability or on diagrams, such as in [35,44]. Thus, we say that a model homomorphism $h : M \to N$ in a stratified institution $\mathcal{S}$ is *elementary* when for each sentence ρ and each $\eta \in [\![M]\!]$, we have that

$$M \models^\eta_\Sigma \rho \text{ if and only if } N \models^{[\![h]\!]_\Sigma \eta}_\Sigma \rho.$$

The advantage of this concept of elementary homomorphism over the other ones from institution theory is that it does not depend on other properties that may be problematic in some cases. For instance, we have seen in Section 3.6 that diagrams are not always available especially in stratified contexts. So, in [51], there is a result that explains the common concept of elementary homomorphism in terms of stratified institution elementary homomorphism. Given a stratified institution with connectives, a Σ-homomorphism

$h: M \to N$ is elementary if and only if $[\![h]\!]$ is a connective algebra homomorphism $\beta_\Sigma M \to \beta_\Sigma N$.

In [51], this result had been used for providing a method for establishing Tarski's elementary chain/co-limit theorem for concrete model theories that can be captured as stratified institutions. This is one of the early model theoretic results in first-order logic [90] with manifold applications (these can be consulted in [2]), which has also received a proof in the abstract setting of arbitrary institutions in [35,44]. It says that the co-limit of a directed diagram of elementary homomorphisms consists of elementary homomorphisms, too. In the context of stratified institutions with connectives, this means that any co-limit of a directed diagram of elementary homomorphisms becomes mapped by the stratification to a co-limit in the category of connective algebra homomorphisms. Moreover, in [51], we can find examples on how this works in $\mathcal{MPL}$ and $\mathcal{OFOL}$.

3.9. Foundations for Formal Verification of Reconfigurable Systems

In [56], the author employs stratified institutions with frame and nominals extraction (presented above in Section 3.4) (rebranded as 'hybrid institutions') as a general foundational framework for a formal verification methodology for reconfigurable systems. The envisaged methodology would thus constitute an alternative to the methodology implemented by the language H [68] based on the generic translation concept of [66]. While in the latter case, the verification process is exported to first-order logic, and the result of that is imported back to the source logic, in the former case, the verification process happens right in the respective stratified institution. However, both approaches share the same verification goal: that of reconfigurable systems.

The substance of [56] consists of the definition of a generic proof calculi applicable to a relevant class of stratified institutions with frame and nominals extraction, which is proved complete (apparently) with respect to the local satisfaction relation $\models^\sharp$. The method to prove completeness is Cohen's forcing [6,7] adapted to abstract institutions [38].

3.10. Mathematical Morphology in Stratified Institutions

The mathematical morphology of [91,92] uses a pair of dual mappings between lattices called 'dilation' and 'erosion' in the context of some mathematical foundations for image analysis. In [53], the authors employ these concepts from mathematical morphology in order to derive pairs of dual connectives. This uses, for a given model M, the lattice on the quotient $Sen(\Sigma)/{\equiv_M}$, where $\rho \equiv_M \rho'$ when $[\![M,\rho]\!] = [\![M,\rho']\!]$ and the order on $Sen(\Sigma)/{\equiv_M}$ is given by $\rho/{\equiv_M} \leq \rho'/{\equiv_M}$ when $[\![M,\rho]\!] \subseteq [\![M,\rho']\!]$. When the respective stratified institution has conjunctions and disjunctions, $(Sen(\Sigma)/{\equiv_M}, \leq)$ is a lattice indeed. The authors provide a general abstract definition of 'dilation' and 'erosion' operators on sentences, $D_B\rho$ and $E_B\rho$, respectively, which are then extended as operations on $Sen(\Sigma)/{\equiv_M}$. Instances of D_B and E_B include the universal and existential quantifications in $\mathcal{OFOL}$ as well as the necessity and possibility in various modal logics. Moreover, the authors of [53] develop a general proof theory in stratified institutions based on abstract erosion and dilation operators, which is shown to be complete. Finally, ref. [53] offers some preliminary ideas regarding applications of this theory to qualitative spatial reasoning.

4. Many-Valued Truth Institution-Independent Model Theory

In standard institution theory, the satisfaction relation between models and sentences is considered to be binary, $M \models \rho$ either holds true or it does not. Many-valued institution theory considers a generalisation of ordinary institution theory where $M \models \rho$ is not necessarily binary. Such a generalisation can be achieved, and basic concepts such as semantic consequence, the Galois connection between syntax and semantics, internal logic, but also more advanced concepts such as filtered products, preservation, interpolation, definability, logic translation, etc. do "survive" it but in a subtler form. From a pure theoretical standpoint (there are also more practical motivations), this generalisation brings further clarifications to the complex network of causal relationships underlying model theory. This has to do with binary truth being a collapsed form of truth where many things happen somehow "by accident". Much institution-independent model theory may be developed in the many-valued truth fashion.

4.1. $\mathcal{L}$-Institutions

The extension of the concept of institution from binary to many-valued truth may be achieved at several structural levels. The most primitive level is to consider a plain set of truth values, either in general or in some particular form. At higher levels, we may consider various order theoretic structures. Traditionally, the binary situation is treated as a Boolean algebra in order to support the common logical connectives such as $\wedge, \vee, \neg$, etc. and their semantics. The many-valued approach treats the structure of truth values rather axiomatically, so we can consider order theoretic structures of various degrees of complexity. At the end, the most constrained such structure is in fact the binary Boolean algebra.

Given a set L, called the *space of the truth values*, an *L-institution*

$$\mathcal{I} = (Sign^{\mathcal{I}}, Sen^{\mathcal{I}}, Mod^{\mathcal{I}}, \models^{\mathcal{I}})$$

is like an ordinary institution with the only difference that the *Satisfaction Relation* is an indexed family of *L-fuzzy relation*, i.e., $\models^{\mathcal{I}}_{\Sigma} : |Mod^{\mathcal{I}}(\Sigma)| \times Sen^{\mathcal{I}}(\Sigma) \to L$ for each $\Sigma \in |Sign^{\mathcal{I}}|$. Then, the *Satisfaction Condition* obtains the following form: for each morphism $\varphi : \Sigma \to \Sigma' \in Sign^{\mathcal{I}}$,

$$(M' \models^{\mathcal{I}}_{\Sigma'} Sen^{\mathcal{I}}(\varphi)\rho) = (Mod^{\mathcal{I}}(\varphi)M' \models^{\mathcal{I}}_{\Sigma} \rho) \tag{9}$$

holds for each $M' \in |Mod^{\mathcal{I}}(\Sigma')|$ and $\rho \in Sen^{\mathcal{I}}(\Sigma)$. The Satisfaction Condition says that the *truth degree is an invariant with respect to change of notation*.

For $\mathcal{L} = (L, \leqslant)$ partial order, an $\mathcal{L}$-*institution* means just an L-institution. Evidently, the ordinary institutions are just $\mathcal{L}$-institutions for which $\mathcal{L}$ is the binary Boolean algebra. For this reason, in the context of the theory of $\mathcal{L}$-institutions, ordinary institutions may be refereed to as *binary institutions*. The step from classic binary institutions to many-valued institutions is hardly new; this idea had appeared already in the early age of institution theory in the form of the so-called 'galleries' of [93]. The 'generalised institutions' of [94] are very similar to $\mathcal{L}$-institutions; however, they introduce an additional monadic structure on the sentence functor meant to model substitution systems. A fully abstract treatment of many-valued semantics appears very early in [50]; however, it differs form the approach of $\mathcal{L}$-institutions in two quite important aspects. One is its single-signature feature. The other is the collapse of model theory modulo elementary equivalence, which makes it unusable for the development of a proper fully abstract many-valued model theory. In other words, Pavelka's approach in [50] would correspond to an $\mathcal{L}$-institution that has only one signature Σ and also such that $|Mod(\Sigma)| \subseteq L^{Sen(\Sigma)}$.

Now, we present the following examples from [48,49,95] very briefly; for more details, the reader should study them from these publications.

1. *Propositional many-valued logic* ($\mathcal{MVL}_0$) turns the institution of classical propositional logic (cf. [44]) into an $\mathcal{L}$-institution by adding $*$ as a new propositional connective and by letting models represent valuations of the propositional symbols of the signatures into L. $\mathcal{L}$ is required to be a residuated lattice.
2. *First-order many-valued logic* ($\mathcal{MVL}_1$) generalises the institution of classical first-order logic (cf. [18,25,44], etc.) in a way that resembles how $\mathcal{MVL}_0$ generalises the institution of classical propositional logic. For defining the satisfaction of quantified sentences, it is required that $\mathcal{L}$ is also complete.
3. *Temporal logic* ($\mathcal{TL}$). $\mathcal{L}$ is a fixed complete total order that models the 'time'. In the propositional version, the models interpret each propositional symbol as a subset of L. We have the usual temporal logic connectives, and the truth value of $M \models \rho$ is the supremum of all the time moments for which ρ holds in M at all moments of time before that.

4. *Fuzzy multi-algebras (𝓕𝓜𝓐)*. This 𝓛-institution generalises the institution of multi-algebras [96–98] (used for specifying non-determinism) to many-valued truth. Its main idea is that models M interpret an algebraic operation σ of arity n as an L-valued $(n+1)$-ary relation. Intuitively, $M_\sigma(x_1,\ldots,x_{n+1})$ is thought of as the truth degree of $\sigma(x_1,\ldots,x_n) = x_{n+1}$ in M.
5. *Abstract many-valued logic ($\mathcal{I}(\mathcal{L})$)*. This 𝓛-institution is more a model theoretic framework rather than a logical system as such. In [48], it is shown that $\mathcal{MVL}_0$, $\mathcal{MVL}_1$, and $\mathcal{FMA}$ can be conservatively embedded in $\mathcal{I}(\mathcal{L})$, which means that their semantics may be substituted by the generic categorical one provided by $\mathcal{I}(\mathcal{L})$.

In the rest of this section, we present the main developments that have happened in the area of 𝓛-institutions over the past decade or so. Our discussion includes the following aspects.

- A general 'flattening' of 𝓛-institutions to ordinary institution.
- A concept of semantic consequence that is genuinely many-valued and represents the most conceptually refined reflection of the binary semantic consequence of ordinary institution theory to many-valued truth.
- Unlike in binary institution theory, in 𝓛-institutions, the concept of theory is multifaceted. This is apparent especially when we consider closures of theories. This situation reflects also to concepts of consistency and compactness.
- We present the extension of the ordinary institution theoretic semantics of propositional and quantification connectives to 𝓛-institutions, both in their consequence and model theoretic forms.
- We present a series of preservation (by filtered products) results that have been recently developed for 𝓛-institutions. Consequences of these are general model compactness and initial semantics results.
- The graded concept of semantic consequence gives rise to a graded concept of interpolation specific to 𝓛-institutions. We discuss this new concept and its further impact to the whole conceptual environment of interpolation, including (Beth) definability and Robinson consistency. We re-establish the causality relationships between interpolation and these in the many-valued context.

4.2. Flattening 𝓛-Institutions to Binary Institutions

The general reduction of many-valued truth to binary truth advocated by the skeptics of many-valued truth can also be applied to 𝓛-institutions. It works as follows. Given any 𝓛-institution $\mathcal{I} = (Sign, Sen, Mod, \models)$, we define the binary institution $\mathcal{I}^\sharp = (Sign^\sharp, Sen^\sharp, Mod^\sharp, \models^\sharp)$:

- $Sign^\sharp = Sign$, $Mod^\sharp = Mod$;
- $Sen^\sharp(\Sigma) = Sen(\Sigma) \times L$;
- $M \models^\sharp_\Sigma (\rho, \kappa)$ if and only if $(M \models_\Sigma \rho) \geqslant \kappa$.

This flattening idea has been present in several places in the fuzzy logic literature. For instance, in [99], our pairs (ρ, κ) are called 'signed formulas' and given the same interpretation as here.

The flattening of 𝓛-institutions to binary institutions has the advantage of reducing things to a well-studied and matured framework and functions well in some aspects, but it falls short in several areas that involve some fine-grained aspects of multiple truth values. Thus, while the flattening $\mathcal{S}^\sharp$ of stratified institutions does not pose many limitations, the situation is different with the flattenings of 𝓛-institutions.

4.3. The Graded Semantic Consequence

Given an 𝓛 institution such that 𝓛 is a complete meet-semilattice, for each Σ-model M and each set E of Σ-sentences, we define

$$(M \models_\Sigma E) = \bigwedge \{M \models_\Sigma \rho \mid \rho \in E\}. \tag{10}$$

Given an $\mathcal{L}$-institution, there are two ways to extend the satisfaction relation to a semantic consequence relation between sets of sentences and single sentences, both of them generalising the semantic consequence relation of binary institution theory.

1. The *crisp semantic consequence*, defined by $E \models e$ if and only if for each model M, $(M \models E) = 1$ implies $(M \models e) = 1$ (where 1 denotes the top element of $\mathcal{L}$).
2. The *graded semantic consequence*, defined by

$$(E \models_\Sigma e) = \bigwedge \{(M \models_\Sigma E) \Rightarrow (M \models_\Sigma e) \mid M \in |Mod(\Sigma)|\}. \tag{11}$$

The graded semantic consequence is more subtle and more in the spirit of many-valued truth than the crisp one, although the definition of the latter requires more infrastructure on the space of the truth values, namely that $\mathcal{L}$ *is a residuated lattice* [100,101]. Hence, "$\Rightarrow$" of (11) represents the residuated implication operation. This difference in subtlety may be traced to the fact that while the crisp semantic consequence corresponds to the semantic consequence of the binary flattening $\mathcal{I}^\sharp$ of the $\mathcal{L}$-institution $\mathcal{I}$ (that $E \models e$ holds in $\mathcal{I}$ means $\{(\rho, 1) \mid \rho \in E\} \models (e, 1)$ in $\mathcal{I}^\sharp$), the graded semantic consequence is a concept beyond $\mathcal{I}^\sharp$. The graded semantic consequence appears in a disguised form in [50] within the context of Pavelka's theory of fuzzy consequence operators and in a form that is more explicitly similar to ours in [102] within the framework of 'graded consequence relations'. However, both these semantic frameworks are less general than ours, in both of them models being in fact fuzzy theories.

One of the important properties of the semantic consequence in binary institution theory is that it satisfies the axioms of entailment systems. The graded semantic consequence enjoys the same property but for the following refined many-valued concept of entailment. This has been proved in a full form in [49]. In a restricted single signature framework, this has also been proved in [102].

Graded Entailment

Let $\mathcal{L} = (L, \leq, *)$ such that $(L, \leq)$ is a complete meet-semilattice (with 1 denoting its upper bound) and $*$ is a binary operation on L. An $\mathcal{L}$-*entailment system* $(Sign, Sen, \vdash)$ consists of a functor $Sen : Sign \to \mathbf{Set}$ and a family $\vdash = (\vdash_\Sigma : \mathcal{P}Sen(\Sigma) \to Sen(\Sigma))_{\Sigma \in |Sign|}$ such that the following axioms hold:

$\{\gamma\} \vdash_\Sigma \gamma = 1$ reflexivity
$(E \vdash_\Sigma \gamma) \leq (E' \vdash_\Sigma \gamma)$ when $E \subseteq E'$ monotonicity
$(E \vdash_\Sigma \Gamma) * (\Gamma \vdash_\Sigma \rho) \leq (E \vdash_\Sigma \rho)$ (where $(E \vdash \Gamma) = \bigwedge_{\gamma \in \Gamma}(E \vdash \gamma)$.)   transitivity
$(E \vdash_\Sigma \gamma) \leq (Sen(\varphi)E \vdash_{\Sigma'} Sen(\varphi)\gamma)$ for any sign. morphism $\varphi : \Sigma \to \Sigma'$ translation.

When $\mathcal{L}$ is just the binary Boolean algebra (with $*$ being $\wedge$), $\mathcal{L}$-entailment systems are just ordinary entailment systems [44,103]/π-institutions [104]. In the graded context, the binary entailment systems will also be called *crisp entailment systems*. Previous to [49], the idea of graded entailment has appeared in various different forms in works such as [50,94,102,105]; in [49], there is a brief analysis on the differences between these several variants, which are in fact rather slight. Depending on actual applications, graded entailments may be interpreted in various ways: as provability degree, as degree of confidence in proofs, or even as a(n inverse) measure for the complexity of a proof. Moreover, in [49], there are also temporal interpretations of graded proofs. An important technical aspect worth mentioning is the use of $*$ rather than $\wedge$ in the *transitivity* axiom; in [49], it is shown that this choice is necessary for accommodating the semantic interpretations of graded entailment.

The result of [49] that the graded semantic consequence in an $\mathcal{L}$-institution $\mathcal{I}$ yields an $\mathcal{L}$-entailment system—called the *semantic entailment system of* $\mathcal{I}$—seems to suggest that $\mathcal{L}$-entailment systems are more abstract/general than $\mathcal{L}$-institutions. However, at least when $\mathcal{L}$ is a complete residuated lattice, this is a wrong impression, because a result from [49] shows that each $\mathcal{L}$-entailment system determines an $\mathcal{L}$-institution whose semantic entailment is precisely the respective $\mathcal{L}$-entailment system.

4.4. Many-Valued Theories, Consistency and Compactness

In binary institution theory, a Σ-theory is a set of Σ-sentences. (However, in many works, including [18,44], etc., this is called 'presentation', the word 'theory' being used for 'presentations' that are closed under semantic consequence. This owes to the algebraic specification tradition which considers theories that are 'presented' by (finite) sets of sentences, these being in fact specification modules.) Any theory may be represented by its characteristic function $Sen(\Sigma) \to 2$, which for each sentence gives a truth value for its membership to the respective theory. This new perspective on theories is the basis for the generalisation of the concept of theory to many-valued truth. For any fixed set L and for any functor $Sen : \mathbf{Sign} \to \mathbf{Set}$, a Σ-theory is just a function $X : Sen(\Sigma) \to L$. When $\mathcal{L} = (L, \leq, \wedge)$ is a complete meet-semilattice, for any Σ-theory $X : Sen(\Sigma) \to L$ and for any $E \subseteq Sen(\Sigma)$, we denote

$$X(E) = \bigwedge\{X(e) \mid e \in E\}. \tag{12}$$

Note that a theory in an $\mathcal{L}$-institution $\mathcal{I}$ corresponds exactly to a theory in its binary flattening $\mathcal{I}^\sharp$ by representing any function $X : Sen(\Sigma) \to L$ as the set $\{(\rho, X(\rho)) \mid \rho \in Sen(\Sigma), X(\rho) \neq 0\}$ (0 denotes the bottom element of $\mathcal{L}$).

The concept of Galois connection between syntax and semantics in binary institution theory admits a natural extension to many-valued truth. Let $\mathcal{L}$ be a complete meet-semilattice. In any $\mathcal{L}$-institution:

- For any Σ-model M, we let the theory $M^* : Sen(\Sigma) \to L$ such that $M^*(\rho) = (M \models \rho)$. For any class of models $\mathcal{M} \subseteq |Mod(\Sigma)|$, we let $\mathcal{M}^* = \bigwedge_{M \in \mathcal{M}} M^*$.
- For any Σ-theory $X : Sen(\Sigma) \to L$ we let $X^* = \{M \in |Mod(\Sigma)| \mid X \leq M^*\}$.

For each signature Σ, the mappings $(\_)^*$ defined above represent a Galois connection between $(\mathcal{P}|Mod(\Sigma)|, \supseteq)$ and $(L^{Sen(\Sigma)}, \leq)$.

4.4.1. Closure Systems

Concepts of closures of theories can be regarded as axiomatic treatments of consequence relations. This approach originates from Tarski's work [106] and later on was applied by Pavelka [50] to many-valued theories. The following definition from [49] extends the latter to the multi-signature framework. Given a partial order $\mathcal{L} = (L, \leq)$, an $\mathcal{L}$-closure system is a tuple $(\mathbf{Sign}, Sen, \mathcal{C})$ where

– $Sen : \mathbf{Sign} \to \mathbf{Set}$ is a functor, and
– $\mathcal{C}$ is a $\mathbf{Sign}$-indexed family of functions $\mathcal{C}_\Sigma : L^{Sen(\Sigma)} \to L^{Sen(\Sigma)}$ satisfying the following axioms (for $\varphi : \Sigma \to \Sigma'$ any signature morphism):

$X \leq \mathcal{C}_\Sigma X$ for each X	C-reflexivity
$\mathcal{C}_\Sigma X \leq \mathcal{C}_\Sigma Y$ when $X \leq Y$	C-monotonicity
$\mathcal{C}_\Sigma(\mathcal{C}_\Sigma X) = \mathcal{C}_\Sigma X$	C-transitivity
$\mathcal{C}_\Sigma(Sen(\varphi); X') \leq Sen(\varphi); \mathcal{C}_{\Sigma'}(X')$	C-translation.

In the binary framework, there is a straightforward equivalence between the concepts of entailment system and closure system: $E \vdash_\Sigma e$ if and only if $e \in \mathcal{C}_\Sigma E$. However, in the many-valued framework, the relationship between the two concepts is much more interesting. Let us present two of them from [49].

- Provided some conditions on $\mathcal{L}$ are fulfilled, the following closure applies to any graded entailment system. Let $\mathcal{L} = (L, \leq, *)$ be a complete meet-semilattice with a binary operation $*$ and let $(\mathbf{Sign}, Sen \vdash)$ be an $\mathcal{L}$-entailment system. The following definition draws inspiration from Goguen's many-valued interpretation of Modus Ponens [107]. A theory $X : Sen(\Sigma) \to L$ is *weakly closed* with respect to the entailment system when for each entailment $E \vdash_\Sigma \rho$,

$$X(E) * (E \vdash \rho) \leq X(\rho).$$

If $*$ is increasing monotone, then in [49], we have proved that the weakly closed theories are closed under arbitrary meets. This allows for the following definition: for any theory X, let $X°$, called the *weak closure* of X, denote the least weakly closed theory greater than X. In [49], we have also proved that the weak closure $(\_)°$ defines an $\mathcal{L}$-closure system.
- The second closure system on many-valued theories has a semantic nature, so its basic framework is now stronger than in the case of the previous closure system. Note that in any $\mathcal{L}$-institution, the Galois connection between $(\mathcal{P}|Mod(\Sigma)|, \supseteq)$ and $(L^{Sen(\Sigma)}, \leq)$ determines an $\mathcal{L}$-closure system $(Sign, Sen, (\_)^{**})$. This allows for the following definition. In any $\mathcal{L}$-institution, a Σ-theory is *strongly closed* when $X = X^{**}$. Moreover, X^{**} is called the *strong closure* of X. The relationship between the two closure systems has been established in [49] as follows. When $\mathcal{L}$ is a complete residuated lattice, in any $\mathcal{L}$-institution and for any Σ-theory X, if $X°$ denotes its weak closure with respect to the semantic $\mathcal{L}$-entailment system, then $X° \leq X^{**}$.

4.4.2. Consistency

The following is a generalisation of the concept of consistent theory from binary institution theory to $\mathcal{L}$-institutions. According to [49], in any $\mathcal{L}$-institution, a Σ-theory T is *consistent* when there exists a Σ-model M such that $T \leq M^*$. E is *consistent* when there exists $\kappa > 0$ such that E is κ-consistent; otherwise, it is *inconsistent*. Note that the concept of κ-consistency can be derived from the corresponding consistency concept from binary institution theory by considering the binary flattening of the respective $\mathcal{L}$-institution.

Now, we introduce another concept of consistency that is relative to a fixed truth value. First, we prepare some notations. For any truth value $\kappa \in L$, let T_κ denote the *constant theory* defined by $T_\kappa \rho = \kappa$ for each sentence ρ. For any Σ-theory T and $\Gamma \subseteq Sen(\Sigma)$, the theory $T|\Gamma$ is defined for each $\rho \in Sen(\Sigma)$ by

$$(T|\Gamma)\rho = \begin{cases} T\rho, & \rho \in \Gamma \\ 0, & \text{otherwise.} \end{cases}$$

In any $\mathcal{L}$-institution, for any truth value κ, a set E of Σ-sentences is κ-consistent when $T_\kappa | E$ is consistent. Note that this concept can also be reduced to binary consistency since E is κ-consistent if and only if $(E, \kappa) = \{(e, \kappa) \mid e \in E\}$ is consistent in the binary flattening of the respective $\mathcal{L}$-institution. Note also that in the binary case, both concepts of consistency defined above collapse to the same concept.

4.4.3. Compactness

Compactness can be thought both in semantic and consequence theoretic terms. This is what happens in every logic, and it extends also to many-valued truth.
- An $\mathcal{L}$-institution $\mathcal{I}$ is *m-compact* when its binary flattening $\mathcal{I}^\sharp$ is m-compact. This means that for each Σ-theory T, if $T|\Gamma$ is consistent for each finite $\Gamma \subseteq Sen(\Sigma)$, then T is consistent, too. This concept of compactness involves potentially all truth values. The following concept of compactness refers to an arbitrarily fixed truth value. In an $\mathcal{L}$-institution, let $\kappa \in L$ be any truth value. Then, the $\mathcal{L}$-institution is κ-*m-compact* when each set E of Σ-sentences is κ-consistent if E_0 is κ-consistent for each finite $E_0 \subseteq E$. Whilst in the binary case, the two concepts of compactness defined above collapse to the same concept, this is not the case in a proper many-valued context. However, in [49], we have established that the former is stronger than the latter: any m-compact $\mathcal{L}$-institution is κ-m-compact for each truth value κ.
- An $\mathcal{L}$-entailment system $(Sign, Sen, \vdash)$ is *compact* when for any entailment $E \vdash_\Sigma \gamma$, we have

$$E \vdash \gamma = \bigvee \{E_0 \vdash \gamma \mid E_0 \text{ finite} \subseteq E\}$$

The following characterisation from [49] brings closer to something that sounds more familiar. In any compact $\mathcal{L}$-entailment system $(Sign, Sen, \vdash)$ such that the meet operation $\wedge$ is join-continuous, for any finite $\kappa \in L$, if $\kappa \leq (E \vdash \gamma)$, then there exists finite $E_0 \subseteq E$ such that $\kappa \leq (E_0 \vdash \gamma)$.

4.5. The Logic of $\mathcal{L}$-Institutions

Many-valued logic in the institution theoretic framework can be approached at two different levels, namely that of consequence ($\mathcal{L}$-entailment systems) and that of semantics ($\mathcal{L}$-institutions). The former is of course more abstract than the latter, but the relationship between them is non-trivial. All these have been addressed in [49] as follows.

4.5.1. Entailment Theoretic Connectives

In an $\mathcal{L}$-entailment system $(Sign, Sen, \vdash)$, a Σ-sentence ρ is

- A *conjunction* of sentences ρ_1 and ρ_2 when for any set of sentences E,
$$E \vdash \rho = (E \vdash \rho_1) \wedge (E \vdash \rho_2);$$

- A *residual conjunction* of sentences ρ_1 and ρ_2 when for any set of sentences E,
$$E \vdash \rho = (E \vdash \rho_1) * (E \vdash \rho_2);$$

- An *implication* of sentences ρ_1 and ρ_2 when for any set of sentences E,
$$E \vdash \rho = E \cup \{\rho_1\} \vdash \rho_2;$$

- A *disjunction* of sentences ρ_1 and ρ_2 when $\mathcal{L}$ has joins and for any set of sentences E,
$$E \vdash \rho = (E \vdash \rho_1) \vee (E \vdash \rho_2);$$

- A *negation* of the sentence ρ' when for any sentence e,
$$\{\rho, \rho'\} \vdash e = 1;$$

- A *universal χ-quantification* of a Σ'-sentence ρ' for $\chi : \Sigma \to \Sigma'$ signature morphism when for any set of Σ-sentences E
$$E \vdash_\Sigma \rho = \chi(E) \vdash_{\Sigma'} \rho';$$

- An *existential χ-quantification* of a Σ'-sentence ρ' for $\chi : \Sigma \to \Sigma'$ signature morphism when for any Σ-sentence e
$$\rho \vdash_\Sigma e = \rho' \vdash_{\Sigma'} \chi(e).$$

These definitions can be extended at the level of the $\mathcal{L}$-entailment system. For instance, we say that the $\mathcal{L}$-entailment system *has conjunctions* when *any* two Σ-sentences have a conjunction and similarly for the other connectives.

When $\mathcal{L}$ is the binary Boolean algebra, the above definitions yield the usual entailment theoretic connectives from the institution theory literature (e.g., [108]). In binary logic, the inequalities that are implicit in the equation defining the entailment theoretic implication are known as *Modus Ponens* ($\leq$) and the *Deduction Theorem* ($\geq$). This terminology can be extended to $\mathcal{L}$-entailment systems.

As in the binary situation, we can consider the *least entailment system* that "contains" a given entailment system and that has some of the connectives defined above. This is supported by the following result from [49]: any intersection of entailment systems (that share the same sentence functor) is an entailment system. Moreover, the property of having a certain connective is invariant with respect to such intersections.

4.5.2. Model Theoretic Connectives

The many-valued semantic connectives mimic those defined for binary institutions [30,34,44,108], etc., but now, their interpretation is in a many-valued truth context. A Σ-sentence ρ is an $\mathcal{L}$-institution that is

- A *semantic conjunction* of sentences ρ_1 and ρ_2 when $\mathcal{L}$ has meets and for each Σ-model M,
$$(M \models \rho) = (M \models \rho_1) \wedge (M \models \rho_2);$$
- A *semantic residual conjunction* of sentences ρ_1 and ρ_2 when $\mathcal{L}$ is a residuated lattice and for each Σ-model M,
$$(M \models \rho) = (M \models \rho_1) * (M \models \rho_2);$$
- An *semantic implication* of sentences ρ_1 and ρ_2 when $\mathcal{L}$ is a residuated lattice and for each Σ-model M,
$$(M \models \rho) = (M \models \rho_1) \Rightarrow (M \models \rho_2);$$
- A *semantic disjunction* of sentences ρ_1 and ρ_2 when $\mathcal{L}$ has joins and for each Σ-model M,
$$(M \models \rho) = (M \models \rho_1) \vee (M \models \rho_2);$$
- A *semantic negation* of a sentence ρ' when $\mathcal{L}$ is a residuated lattice for each Σ-model M,
$$(M \models \rho') = (M \models \rho) \Rightarrow 0;$$
- A *semantic universal χ-quantification* of a Σ'-sentence ρ' for $\chi: \Sigma \to \Sigma'$ signature morphism when $\mathcal{L}$ is a complete meet-semilattice and for each Σ-model M
$$(M \models_\Sigma \rho) = \bigwedge \{M' \models_{\Sigma'} \rho' \mid Mod(\chi) M' = M\};$$
- An *semantic existential χ-quantification* of a Σ'-sentence ρ' for $\chi: \Sigma \to \Sigma'$ signature morphism when $\mathcal{L}$ is a complete join-semilattice and for each Σ-model M
$$(M \models_\Sigma \rho) = \bigvee \{M' \models_{\Sigma'} \rho' \mid Mod(\chi) M' = M\}.$$

These definitions can be extended at the level of the respective $\mathcal{L}$-institution. For instance, we say that the $\mathcal{L}$-institution *has conjunctions* when any two Σ-sentences have a conjunction, etc.

The semantic connectives represent yet another situation when the binary flattening diverges from the respective $\mathcal{L}$-institution. In general, it is not possible to establish a general causality relationship between the semantic connectives in the $\mathcal{L}$-institution and in its binary flattening.

4.5.3. Model Theoretic versus Entailment Theoretic Connectives

Given an $\mathcal{L}$-institution $\mathcal{I}$, when $\mathcal{L}$ is a complete residuated lattice, we thus have two different definitions for each connective: one in terms of satisfaction by models and another one in terms of the semantic $\mathcal{L}$-entailment system of $\mathcal{I}$. It is important to establish the relationship between these two in order to be able to have an entailment-based calculus for the semantic consequence.

Consider the semantic $\mathcal{L}$-entailment system of an $\mathcal{L}$-institution such that $\mathcal{L}$ is a complete residuated lattice. Let ρ be a Σ-sentence and $\varphi: \Sigma \to \Sigma'$ be a signature morphism. Then,

1. ρ is the entailment theoretic conjunction of ρ_1 and ρ_2 if it is the semantic conjunction of ρ_1 and ρ_2.
2. ρ is the entailment theoretic universal/existential χ-quantification of ρ' if it is its semantic universal/existential χ-quantification.

Let us further assume that $\mathcal{L}$ is a Heyting algebra. Then,

3. ρ is the entailment theoretic implication of ρ_1 and ρ_2 if it is the semantic implication of ρ_1 and ρ_2.
4. ρ is the entailment theoretic negation of ρ' if it is its semantic negation.

Let us further assume that $\mathcal{L}$ is a completely distributive Boolean algebra. Then

5. ρ is the entailment theoretic disjunction of ρ_1 and ρ_2 if it is the semantic disjunction of ρ_1 and ρ_2.

4.6. Preservation and Consequences

In [95], there is a development of a body of preservation results in the same style as had been conducted for ordinary institutions in [34] or for stratified institutions in [52]. The milestones of this development are as follows:

- The concept of a filtered product of models is the categorical one as discussed in Section 3.7 in the context of stratified institutions.
- The preservation of (the satisfaction of) a sentence ρ by filtered products/factors has been defined in [95] as follows. In any $\mathcal{L}$-institution, let Σ be any signature and let e be any Σ-sentence. In addition, let $\mathcal{F}$ be any class of filters and κ be any value in $\mathcal{L}$. Then,
    - e is κ-preserved by $\mathcal{F}$-products when for each F-product $(\mu_J : M_J \to M_F)_{J \in F}$ (where $F \in \mathcal{F}$ is a filter over I)
    $$\{i \in I \mid (M_i \models e) \geqslant \kappa\} \in F \text{ implies } (M_F \models e) \geqslant \kappa;$$
    - e is κ-preserved by $\mathcal{F}$-factors when for each F-product as above we have the reverse implication to the above.

    As a matter of terminology, when $\mathcal{F}$ is the class of all ultrafilters, we rather say directly "κ-preserved by ultraproducts/ultrafactors". When $\mathcal{F}$ is the class of all singleton filters, we rather say "κ-preserved by direct products/factors". In addition, when we do not specify the truth value κ and we just say "preserved by $\mathcal{F}$-products/factors", we mean that the sentence is κ-preserved for *all* truth values κ.

    Note that whilst κ-preservation represents just a rephrasing of the preservation concepts from binary institution theory because "ρ is κ-preserved by ..." is technically the same with "(ρ, κ) is preserved by ..." in the binary flattening, this is not the case for the preservation for *all* truth values. In other words "ρ is preserved by ..." in an $\mathcal{L}$-institution cannot be reduced to preservation in its binary flattening of a single sentence.

- The results in [95] that express the invariance of preservation with respect to connectives are restricted to
    - Invariance of preservation by $\mathcal{F}$-products under $\wedge$ and quantifications;
    - Invariance of preservation by $\mathcal{F}$-factors under $\wedge, \vee, *$ and quantifications; and
    - $\rho \Rightarrow \rho'$ is preserved by $\mathcal{F}$-products when ρ is preserved by $\mathcal{F}$-factors and ρ' is preserved by $\mathcal{F}$-products.

    Each of these results is subject to some specific conditions of various intensities of a general nature regarding $\mathcal{L}$, model reducts, $\mathcal{F}$, etc. All of them are manageable in concrete applications.

- As in the case of ordinary or stratified concrete institutions, when the sentences are constructed by iterative applications of connectives, in order to obtain their preservation, we invoke corresponding invariance results through an inductive process. However, in general, because the above-mentioned invariance results are less than in the binary truth case, it may happen that not all sentences of a respective $\mathcal{L}$-institution can be reached in this way. However, even under this less favourable situation, important classes of sentences are preserved by filtered products and factores. According to [95], these include an extended class of general Horn sentences.

- In this iterative process, the base cases are taken care of by corresponding preservation results for *basic sentences* in $\mathcal{L}$-institution theoretic sense as introduced in [95] as a generalisation of the ordinary concept of basic sentence from [34,44].

In [95], two main consequences of these preservation results have been derived.

- Initial semantics for a general class of Horn sentences.
- Model compactness for an extended general class of Horn sentences that do not necessarily admit initial semantics.

The former result involves also preservation by 'sub-models', which is a concept that is taken care of by the *inclusion systems* of [44,65], etc. (Such involvement of inclusion systems is common to all institution–theoretic approaches to quasi-varieties ([44]).)

For all this general theory, $\mathcal{FMA}$ presents itself as a special case when some general results cannot always be applied due to a lack of basic sentences. However, in [95], it is shown how an invariance of preservation results can still be used to obtain the preservation by filtered products for a relevant class of $\mathcal{FMA}$ sentences and consequently a model compactness result for those.

4.7. Around Graded Interpolation

In [109], the author developed a study of interpolation in the graded consequence framework. Envisaged applications include various forms of approximate reasoning. The starting point of this study is the extension of the classical concept of interpolation from the classical binary to the many-valued graded context. In any $\mathcal{L}$-entailment system, given a commutative square of signature morphisms

$$\begin{array}{ccc} \Sigma & \xrightarrow{\varphi_1} & \Sigma_1 \\ \varphi_2 \downarrow & & \downarrow \theta_1 \\ \Sigma_2 & \xrightarrow{\theta_2} & \Sigma' \end{array}$$

and finite sets $E_1 \subseteq Sen(\Sigma_1)$ and $E_2 \subseteq Sen(\Sigma_2)$, we say that a finite set $E \subseteq Sen(\Sigma)$ is a *Craig interpolant* of E_1 and E_2 when

$$\theta_1 E_1 \vdash \theta_2 E_2 \leq (E_1 \vdash \varphi_1 E) * (\varphi_2 E \vdash E_2). \tag{13}$$

When interpolants exist for all E_1, E_2, the respective commutative square of signature morphisms is called a *Craig interpolation square* (abbr. Ci square). When $\mathcal{L}$ is a residuated lattice, the concepts introduced in this definition extend also to $\mathcal{L}$-institutions by considering the graded semantic entailment system.

In [109], there are some proper examples of the graded interpolation concept, proof theoretic as well as model theoretic. Some of the examples suggest that graded interpolation is much more subtle than the crips (binary truth) interpolation, as there are natural situations when crisp interpolation non-problems may be good graded interpolation problems.

Craig–Robinson interpolation [110] is an extended version of common (Craig) interpolation, this extension being especially relevant in computing science applications [44,65,70,83] but not only. In the binary case, under the presence of implication, the two versions of interpolation can be established as equivalent (an institution-independent proof can be found in [44]). In [109], this has been extended to graded interpolation under the assumption that $\mathcal{L}$ is a Heyting algebra and only for the graded semantic consequence relation in $\mathcal{L}$-institutions.

Traditionally, model theoretic interpolation is causally related to Robinson consistency [2,111,112] and Beth definability [2,113]. These causalities have also been established in the abstract institution theoretic setting in [30,43,44]. Moreover, in [109], they have also been recovered at the many-valued truth level of $\mathcal{L}$-institutions. However, that enterprise required a significant conceptual and mathematical effort that we will briefly and rather informally review in what follows.

4.7.1. Graded Interpolation versus Many-Valued Robinson Consistency

Let us first have a look at the binary institution theoretic version of Robinson consistency (abbr. *Rc*). In an institution, a commutative square of signature morphisms such as below

$$\begin{array}{ccc} \Sigma & \xrightarrow{\varphi_1} & \Sigma_1 \\ \varphi_2 \downarrow & & \downarrow \theta_1 \\ \Sigma_2 & \xrightarrow{\theta_2} & \Sigma' \end{array}$$

is a *Robinson consistency (Rc) square* when any finite sets E_i of Σ_i-sentences, $i = 1, 2$, with 'inter-consistent reducts' (i.e., $\{\rho \in Sen(\Sigma) \mid E_1 \models \varphi_1\rho\} \cup \{\rho \in Sen(\Sigma) \mid E_2 \models \varphi_2\rho\}$ has a model) has 'inter-consistent Σ'-translations' (i.e., $\theta_1 E_1 \cup \theta_2 E_2$ has a model).

The many-valued version of this is based on a many-valued concept of 'inter-consistency' which is relative to arbitrary truth values and, very importantly, the two truth values of the inter-consistency of the reducts and of the translations, respectively, are in general not necessarily equal. Then, we obtain the expected bi-directional causality between Rc and a somehow stronger version of Ci. There are many aspects underlying this result that deserve mention.

- As expected, both directions rely on the respective $\mathcal{L}$-institution having conjunctions and negations.
- In the case of the implication of Ci from Rc, an additional compactness condition is required. This is different from the compactness concepts we discussed above, but a relationship with those is established at the general level, which also applies well in the concrete cases.
- Both directions require some relationships between the truth values of the two inter-consistencies, the two relationships being somehow dual. They also have an intersection such that one truth value determines uniquely the other one, which is relevant for the formulation of the causality relationship between Rc and Ci when formulated as an equivalence.

4.7.2. Graded Definability by Graded Interpolation

Both in the concrete classical case and in the institution theoretic context, interpolation constitutes a principal cause for the definability property, i.e., that implicitly implies explicit definability. In fact, in [44], it has been revealed that interpolation in the Craig–Robinson form is what is needed in order to establish definability. In this way, we can dispense with implications, and while implications plus Ci obtain Craig–Robinson interpolation, there are important situations when we have the latter in the absence of implications, such as in many-sorted Horn clause logics (cf. [44]).

In [109], we have extended both the implicit and the explicit definabilities from the their binary version of [40,44] to many-valued truth as follows.

- In any $\mathcal{L}$-entailment system, for any $\kappa \in L$, a signature morphism $\varphi : \Sigma \to \Sigma'$ is *defined κ-implicitly* by a set $E' \subseteq Sen(\Sigma')$ when for any diagram of pushout squares such as below

$$
\begin{array}{c}
\Sigma' \xrightarrow{\theta'} \Sigma'_1 \\
\varphi \nearrow \quad \nearrow \varphi_1 \quad \searrow u \\
\Sigma \xrightarrow{\theta} \Sigma_1 \quad \quad \Sigma'' \\
\varphi \searrow \quad \searrow \varphi_1 \quad \nearrow v \\
\Sigma' \xrightarrow{\theta'} \Sigma'_1
\end{array}
\tag{14}
$$

and for any Σ'_1-sentence ρ, we have that

$$u(\theta' E') \cup v(\theta' E') \cup u\rho \vdash v\rho \geq \kappa.$$

- In any $\mathcal{L}$-entailment system, for each $\kappa \in L$, a signature morphism $\varphi : \Sigma \to \Sigma'$ is *κ-explicitly defined* by a set of sentences $E' \subseteq Sen(\Sigma')$ when for each pushout square of signature morphisms such as

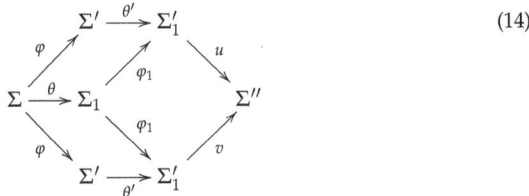

(15)

and each $\rho \in Sen(\Sigma_1')$, there exists a finite set of sentences $E_\rho \subseteq Sen(\Sigma_1)$ such that

$$(\theta'E' \cup \rho \vdash \varphi_1 E_\rho) * (\theta'E' \cup \varphi_1 E_\rho \vdash \rho) \geq \kappa.$$

The main result of this development is a theorem that generalises the binary truth result of [40]. It says that in any $\mathcal{L}$-institution with a form of model amalgamation and which enjoys Craig–Robinson interpolation (with respect to designated classes of signature morphisms), a signature morphism is defined κ-explicitly when it is defined ℓ-implicitly provided the truth values κ and ℓ are related by a condition similar to one of the conditions underlying the implication of Rc from Ci.

5. Conclusions

Standard institutional model theory has undergone a high level of development as partially shown in [44]. On the other hand, although non-classical institutional model theory, in its stratified and $\mathcal{L}$-institution forms, has advanced significantly over the past decade, it still lags behind the standard version. This is because of two main factors: time scale and mathematical difficulty. While standard institutional model theory has been developed over approximately four decades, the non-classical version is much younger. Then, of course, the latter is mathematically more difficult than the former; it is enough only to compare the basic definition in order to obtain an understanding of this. However, we have already seen that many non-classical developments may benefit from classical ones. At the same time, non-classical institution model theory has aspects that cannot be related to classical developments. All these mean that a lot of interesting theoretical problems await in non-classical institutional model theory, and we hope that in the next decade or so, many of them will be addressed.

In addition, there is something to be addressed that is at least as important as the theoretical problems: namely, to find new relevant applications. For instance, due to the highly abstract nature of this approach, which goes hand-in-hand with the axiomatic method, it has a strong potential to accomodate a wide class of old and new formalisms especially from computing science. However, all these require a thorough exploration.

Funding: This work was supported by a grant of the Romanian Ministry of Education and Research, CNCS–UEFISCDI, project number PN-III-P4-ID-PCE-2020-0446, within PNCDI III.

Conflicts of Interest: The author declares no conflict of interest.

References

1. Tarski, A. The Semantic Conception of Truth. *Philos. Phenomenol. Res.* **1944**, *4*, 13–47. [CrossRef]
2. Chang, C.C.; Keisler, H.J. *Model Theory*; North-Holland: Amsterdam, The Netherlands, 1990.
3. Hodges, W. *Model Theory*; Cambridge University Press: Cambridge, MA, USA, 1993.
4. Robinson, A. *Non-Standard Analysis*; North-Holland: Amsterdam, The Netherlands, 1966.
5. Goldblatt, R. *Lectures on Hyperreals*; Graduate Texts in Mathematics; Springer: New York, NY, USA; Berlin/Heidelberg, Germany, 1998; Volume 188.
6. Cohen, P.J. The independence of the Continuum Hypothesis. *Proc. Natl. Acad. Sci. USA* **1963**, *50*, 1143–1148. [CrossRef]
7. Cohen, P.J. The independence of the Continuum Hypothesis II. *Proc. Natl. Acad. Sci. USA* **1964**, *51*, 105–110. [CrossRef]
8. Lindström, P. On Extensions of Elementary Logic. *Theoria* **1969**, *35*, 1–11. [CrossRef]
9. Barwise, J. Axioms for Abstract Model Theory. *Ann. Math. Log.* **1974**, *7*, 221–265. [CrossRef]
10. Barwise, J.; Feferman, S. *Model-Theoretic Logics*; Springer: Berlin/Heidelberg, Germany, 1985.
11. Andréka, H.; Németi, I. Łoś Lemma Holds in Every Category. *Stud. Sci. Math. Hung.* **1978**, *13*, 361–376.
12. Andréka, H.; Németi, I. A General Axiomatizability Theorem Formulated in Terms of Cone-Injective Subcategories. In *Universal Algebra*; Csakany, B., Fried, E., Schmidt, E., Eds.; North-Holland: Amsterdam, The Netherlands, 1981; pp. 13–35.
13. Andréka, H.; Németi, I. *Generalization of the Concept of Variety and Quasivariety to Partial Algebras through Category Theory*; Dissertationes Mathematicae; Państwowe Wydawnictwo Naukowe: Warsaw, Poland, 1983; Volume 204.
14. Makkai, M.; Reyes, G. *First Order Categorical Logic: Model-Theoretical Methods in the Theory of Topoi and Related Categories*; Lecture Notes in Mathematics; Springer: Berlin/Heidelberg, Germany, 1977; Volume 611.
15. Makkai, M. Ultraproducts and Categorical Logic. In *Methods in Mathematical Logic*; Lecture Notes in Mathematics; DiPrisco, C., Ed.; Springer: Berlin/Heidelberg, Germany, 1985; Volume 1130, pp. 222–309.

16. Burstall, R.; Goguen, J. Semantics of Clear. In *Unpublished Notes Handed out at the 1978 Symposium on Algebra and Applications*; Stefan Banach Center: Warsaw, Poland, 1977.
17. Goguen, J.; Burstall, R. Introducing Institutions. In *Proceedings of the Logics of Programming Workshop*; Lecture Notes in Computer Science; Clarke, E., Kozen, D., Eds.; Springer: Berlin/Heidelberg, Germany, 1984; Volume 164, pp. 221–256.
18. Goguen, J.; Burstall, R. Institutions: Abstract Model Theory for Specification and Programming. *J. Assoc. Comput. Mach.* **1992**, *39*, 95–146. [CrossRef]
19. Mac Lane, S. *Categories for the Working Mathematician*, 2nd ed.; Springer: Berlin/Heidelberg, Germany, 1998.
20. Astesiano, E.; Bidoit, M.; Kirchner, H.; Krieg-Brückner, B.; Mosses, P.; Sannella, D.; Tarlecki, A. CASL: The Common Algebraic Specification Language. *Theor. Comput. Sci.* **2002**, *286*, 153–196. [CrossRef]
21. Diaconescu, R.; Futatsugi, K. *CafeOBJ Report: The Language, Proof Techniques, and Methodologies for Object-Oriented Algebraic Specification*; AMAST Series in Computing; World Scientific: Singapore, 1998; Volume 6.
22. Diaconescu, R.; Futatsugi, K. Logical Foundations of CafeOBJ. *Theor. Comput. Sci.* **2002**, *285*, 289–318. [CrossRef]
23. Mossakowski, T.; Maeder, C.; Lütich, K. The Heterogeneous Tool Set. In *Lecture Notes in Computer Science*; World Scientific Publishing: Singapore, 2007; Volume 4424, pp. 519–522.
24. Mossakowski, T.; Codescu, M.; Neuhaus, F.; Kutz, O. The Distributed Ontology, Modeling and Specification Language—DOL. In *The Road to Universal Logic*; Koslow, A., Buchsbaum, A., Eds.; Birkhauser: Cham, Switzerland, 2015.
25. Sannella, D.; Tarlecki, A. *Foundations of Algebraic Specifications and Formal Software Development*; Springer: Berlin/Heidelberg, Germany, 2012.
26. Diaconescu, R. Herbrand Theorems in arbitrary Institutions. *Inf. Process. Lett.* **2004**, *90*, 29–37. [CrossRef]
27. Țuțu, I.; Fiadeiro, J.L. From conventional to institution-independent logic programming. *J. Log. Comput.* **2017**, *27*, 1679–1716.
28. Țuțu, I.; Fiadeiro, J.L. Service-oriented Logic Programming. *Log. Methods Comput. Sci.* **2015**, *11*, lmcs:1579. [CrossRef]
29. Kutz, O.; Mossakowski, T.; Lücke, D. Carnap, Goguen, and the hyperontologies—Logical pluralism and heterogeneous structuring in ontology design. *Log. Universalis* **2010**, *4*, 255–333. [CrossRef]
30. Tarlecki, A. Bits and Pieces of the Theory of Institutions. In *Category Theory and Computer Programming, Proceedings of the Summer Workshop on Category Theory and Computer Programming, Guildford, UK, 16-20 September 1985*; Lecture Notes in Computer Science; Pitt, D., Abramsky, S., Poigné, A., Rydeheard, D., Eds.; Springer: Berlin/Heidelberg, Germany, 1986; Volume 240, pp. 334–360.
31. Tarlecki, A. On the Existence of Free Models in Abstract Algebraic Institutions. *Theor. Comput. Sci.* **1986**, *37*, 269–304. [CrossRef]
32. Tarlecki, A. Quasi-Varieties in Abstract Algebraic Institutions. *J. Comput. Syst. Sci.* **1986**, *33*, 333–360. [CrossRef]
33. Diaconescu, R. Elementary diagrams in institutions. *J. Log. Comput.* **2004**, *14*, 651–674. [CrossRef]
34. Diaconescu, R. Institution-independent Ultraproducts. *Fundam. Inform.* **2003**, *55*, 321–348.
35. Găină, D.; Popescu, A. An institution-independent generalization of Tarski's Elementary Chain Theorem. *J. Log. Comput.* **2006**, *16*, 713–735. [CrossRef]
36. Diaconescu, R.; Petria, M. Saturated models in institutions. *Arch. Math. Log.* **2010**, *49*, 693–723. [CrossRef]
37. Găină, D. Forcing, Downward Löwenheim-Skolem and Omitting Types Theorems, Institutionally. *Log. Universalis* **2014**, *8*, 469–498. [CrossRef]
38. Găină, D.; Petria, M. Completeness by Forcing. *J. Log. Comput.* **2010**, *20*, 1165–1186. [CrossRef]
39. Codescu, M.; Găină, D. Birkhoff completeness in institutions. *Log. Universalis* **2008**, *2*, 277–309. [CrossRef]
40. Petria, M.; Diaconescu, R. Abstract Beth definability in institutions. *J. Symb. Log.* **2006**, *71*, 1002–1028. [CrossRef]
41. Aiguier, M.; Barbier, F. An institution-independent proof of the Beth definability theorem. *Stud. Log.* **2007**, *85*, 333–359. [CrossRef]
42. Diaconescu, R. An institution-independent proof of Craig Interpolation Theorem. *Stud. Log.* **2004**, *77*, 59–79. [CrossRef]
43. Găină, D.; Popescu, A. An institution-independent proof of Robinson Consistency Theorem. *Stud. Log.* **2007**, *85*, 41–73. [CrossRef]
44. Diaconescu, R. *Institution-Independent Model Theory*; Birkhäuser: Basel, Switzerland, 2008.
45. Găină, D. Downward Löwenheim-Skolem theorem and interpolation in logics with constructors. *J. Log. Comput.* **2017**, *27*, 1717–1752. [CrossRef]
46. Goguen, J.; Roșu, G. Institution morphisms. *Form. Asp. Comput.* **2002**, *13*, 274–307. [CrossRef]
47. Mossakowski, T.; Diaconescu, R.; Tarlecki, A. What is a logic translation? *Log. Universalis* **2009**, *3*, 59–94. [CrossRef]
48. Diaconescu, R. Institutional semantics for many-valued logics. *Fuzzy Sets Syst.* **2013**, *218*, 32–52. [CrossRef]
49. Diaconescu, R. Graded consequence: An institution theoretic study. *Soft Comput.* **2014**, *18*, 1247–1267. [CrossRef]
50. Pavelka, J. On fuzzy logic I—Many-valued rules of inference. *Zeitscher Math. Log. Und Grund. Math.* **1979**, *25*, 45–52. [CrossRef]
51. Aiguier, M.; Diaconescu, R. Stratified institutions and elementary homomorphisms. *Inf. Process. Lett.* **2007**, *103*, 5–13. [CrossRef]
52. Diaconescu, R. Implicit Kripke Semantics and Ultraproducts in Stratified Institutions. *J. Log. Comput.* **2017**, *27*, 1577–1606. [CrossRef]
53. Aiguier, M.; Bloch, I. Logical dual concepts based on mathematical morphology in stratified institutions: Applications to spatial reasoning. *J. Appl.-Non-Class. Logics* **2019**, *29*, 392–429. [CrossRef]
54. Eilenberg, S.; Mac Lane, S. General Theory of Natural Equivalences. *Trans. Am. Math. Soc.* **1945**, *58*, 231–294. [CrossRef]
55. Diaconescu, R. From Universal Logic to Computer Science, and Back. In Proceedings of the Theoretical Aspects of Computing–ICTAC 2014, Bucharest, Romania, 17–19 September 2014; Lecture Notes in Computer Science; Ciobanu, G., Méry, D., Eds.; Springer: Berlin/Heidelberg, Germany, 2014; Volume 8687.
56. Găină, D. Forcing and Calculi for Hybrid Logics. *J. Assoc. Comput. Mach.* **2020**, *67*, 1–55. [CrossRef]

57. Diaconescu, R. Decompositions of Stratified Institutions. *arXiv* **2021**, arXiv:2112.12993.
58. Diaconescu, R. Representing 3/2-Institutions as Stratified Institutions. *Mathematics* **2022**, *10*, 1507. [CrossRef]
59. Diaconescu, R. Implicit Partiality of Signature Morphisms in Institution Theory. In *Hajnal Andréka and István Németi on Unity of Science: From Computing to Relativity Theory Through Algebraic Logic*; Outstanding Contributions to Logic; Madarász, J., Székely, G., Eds.; Springer: Berlin/Heidelberg, Germany, 2021; Volume 19, pp. 81–123. ISBN 978-3-030-64186-3.
60. Diaconescu, R.; Stefaneas, P. Modality in Open Institutions with Concrete Syntax. *Bull. Greek Math. Soc.* **2004**, *49*, 91–101.
61. Diaconescu, R.; Stefaneas, P. Ultraproducts and Possible Worlds Semantics in Institutions. *Theor. Comput. Sci.* **2007**, *379*, 210–230. [CrossRef]
62. Martins, M.A.; Madeira, A.; Diaconescu, R.; Barbosa, L. Hybridization of Institutions. In Proceedings of the Algebra and Coalgebra in Computer Science, Winchester, UK, 30 August–2 September 2011; Lecture Notes in Computer Science; Corradini, A., Klin, B., Cîrstea, C., Eds.; Springer: Berlin/Heidelberg, Germany, 2011; Volume 6859, pp. 283–297.
63. Diaconescu, R. Quasi-varieties and initial semantics in hybridized institutions. *J. Log. Comput.* **2016**, *26*, 855–891. [CrossRef]
64. Madeira, A. Foundations and Techniques for Software Reconfigurability. Ph.D. Thesis, Universidades do Minho, Aveiro and Porto (Joint MAP-i Doctoral Programme), Braga, Portugal, 2014.
65. Diaconescu, R.; Goguen, J.; Stefaneas, P. Logical Support for Modularisation. In *Logical Environments*; Huet, G., Plotkin, G., Eds.; Cambridge University Press: Cambridge, UK, 1993; pp. 83–130.
66. Diaconescu, R.; Madeira, A. Encoding Hybridized Institutions into First Order Logic. *Math. Struct. Comput. Sci.* **2016**, *26*, 745–788. [CrossRef]
67. Van Bentham, J. *Modal Logic and Classical Logic*; Humanities Press: London, UK, 1988.
68. Diaconescu, R. Introducing H, an institution-based formal specification and verification language. *Log. Universalis* **2020**, *14*, 259–277. [CrossRef]
69. Diaconescu, R. Quasi-Boolean encodings and conditionals in algebraic specification. *J. Log. Algebr. Program.* **2010**, *79*, 174–188. [CrossRef]
70. Bergstra, J.; Heering, J.; Klint, P. Module Algebra. *J. Assoc. Comput. Mach.* **1990**, *37*, 335–372. [CrossRef]
71. Dimitrakos, T. Formal Support for Specification Design and Implementation. Ph.D. Thesis, Imperial College, London, UK, 1998.
72. Bicarregui, J.; Dimitrakos, T.; Gabbay, D.; Maibaum, T. Interpolation in practical formal development. *Log. J. IGPL* **2001**, *9*, 231–243. [CrossRef]
73. Veloso, P. On pushout consistency, modularity and interpolation for logical specifications. *Inf. Process. Lett.* **1996**, *60*, 59–66. [CrossRef]
74. Borzyszkowski, T. Logical systems for structured specifications. *Theor. Comput. Sci.* **2002**, *286*, 197–245. [CrossRef]
75. Kutz, O.; Mossakowski, T. Modules in Transition. Conservativity, Composition, and Colimits. In Proceedings of the Second International Workshop on Modular Ontologies, Whistler, BC, Canada, 28 October 2007.
76. Nelson, G.; Oppen, D. Simplication by cooperating decision procedures. *ACM Trans. Program. Lang. Syst.* **1979**, *1*, 245–257. [CrossRef]
77. Oppen, D. Complexity, convexity and combinations of theories. *Theor. Comput. Sci.* **1980**, *12*, 291–302. [CrossRef]
78. Jhala, R.; Majumdar, R.; Xu, R.G. State of the Union: Type Inference Via Craig Interpolation. In Proceedings of the Tools and Algorithms for the Construction and Analysis of Systems, Braga, Portugal, 24 March–1 April 2007; Lecture Notes in Computer Science; Springer: Berlin/Heidelberg, Germany, 2007; Volume 4424, pp. 553–567.
79. McMillan, K. Applications of Craig interpolants in model checking. In Proceedings of the TACAS'2005, Edinburgh, UK, 4–8 April 2005; Lecture Notes in Computer Science; Springer: Berlin/Heidelberg, Germany, 2005; Volume 3440, pp. 1–12.
80. Amir, E.; McIlraith, S. Improving the Efficiency of Reasoning Through Structure-Based Reformulation. In Proceedings of the Symposium on Abstraction, Reformulation and Approximation (SARA'2000), Horseshoe Bay, TX, USA, 26–29 July 2000; Lecture Notes in Artificial Intelligence; Choueiry, B., Walsh, T., Eds.; Springer: Berlin/Heidelberg, Germany, 2000; Volume 1864, pp. 247–259.
81. McIlraith, S.; Amir, E. Theorem Proving with Structured Theories. In Proceedings of the 17th International Conference on Artificial Intelligence (IJCAI-01), Seattle, WA, USA, 4–10 August 2001; pp. 624–631.
82. Borzyszkowski, T. Generalized Interpolation in CASL. *Inf. Process. Lett.* **2001**, *76*, 19–24. [CrossRef]
83. Dimitrakos, T.; Maibaum, T. On a Generalized Modularization Theorem. *Inf. Process. Lett.* **2000**, *74*, 65–71. [CrossRef]
84. Diaconescu, R. Interpolation in Grothendieck Institutions. *Theor. Comput. Sci.* **2004**, *311*, 439–461. [CrossRef]
85. Diaconescu, R. Borrowing interpolation. *J. Log. Comput.* **2012**, *22*, 561–586. [CrossRef]
86. Diaconescu, R. Interpolation for predefined types. *Math. Struct. Comput. Sci.* **2012**, *22*, 1–24. [CrossRef]
87. Diaconescu, R. Concepts of Interpolation in Stratified Institutions. **2022**, submitted. [CrossRef]
88. Bell, J.L.; Slomson, A.B. *Models and Ultraproducts*; North-Holland: Amsterdam, The Netherlands, 1969.
89. Matthiessen, G. Regular and strongly finitary structures over strongly algebroidal categories. *Can. J. Math.* **1978**, *30*, 250–261. [CrossRef]
90. Tarski, A.; Vaught, R. Arithmetical extensions of relational systems. *Compos. Math.* **1957**, *13*, 81–102.
91. Serra, J. *Mathematical Morphology*; Academic Press: Cambridge, MA, USA, 1982.
92. Bloch, I.; Heijmans, H.; Ronse, C. *Handbook of Spatial Logics*; Chapter Mathematical Morphology; Springer: Berlin/Heidelberg, Germany, 2007; pp. 857–947.

93. Mayoh, B. *Galleries and Institutions*; Technical Report DAIMI PB-191; Aarhus University: Aarhus, Denmark, 1985.
94. Eklund, P.; Helgesson, R. Monadic extensions of institutions. *Fuzzy Sets Syst.* **2010**, *161*, 2354–2368. [CrossRef]
95. Diaconescu, R. Preservation in many-valued truth institutions. *Fuzzy Sets Syst.* **2021**, *submitted*. [CrossRef]
96. Walicki, M.; Meldal, S. Algebraic approaches to nondeterminism—An overview. *ACM Comput. Surv.* **1997**, *29*, 30–81. [CrossRef]
97. Lamo, Y.; Walicki, M. The general logic of Multialgebras. In Proceedings of the Workshop on Algebraic Development Techniques, Frauenchiemsee, Germany, 24–27 September 2002.
98. Lamo, Y. The Institution of Multialgebras—A General Framework for Algebraic Software Development. Ph.D. Thesis, University of Bergen, Bergen, Norway, 2003.
99. Gerla, G. *Fuzzy Logic: Mathematical Tools for Approximate Reasoning*; Kluwer: Alphen aan den Rijn, The Netherlands, 2001.
100. Ward, M.; Dilworth, R. Residuated lattices. *Trans. Am. Math. Soc.* **1939**, *45*, 335–354. [CrossRef]
101. Galatos, N.; Jipsen, P.; Kowalski, T.; Ono, H. *Residuated Lattices: An Algebraic Glimpse at Substructural Logics*; Elsevier: Amsterdam, The Netherlands, 2007.
102. Chakraborty, M.K. Graded Consequence: Further studies. *J. Appl.-Non-Class. Logics* **1995**, *5*, 127–137. [CrossRef]
103. Meseguer, J. General Logics. In *Logic Colloquium '87: Proceedings of the Colloquium (LOGIC COLLOQUIM// PROCEEDINGS), Granada, Spain, 20–25 July 1987*; Ebbinghaus, H.D., Fernandez-Prida, J., Garrido, M., Lascar, D., Eds.; North-Holland: Amsterdam, The Netherlands, 1989; pp. 275–329.
104. Fiadeiro, J.L.; Sernadas, A. Structuring Theories on Consequence. In *Recent Trends in Data Type Specification*; Lecture Notes in Computer Science; Sannella, D., Tarlecki, A., Eds.; Springer: Berlin/Heidelberg, Germany, 1988; Volume 332, pp. 44–72.
105. Chakraborty, M.K. Use of fuzzy set theory in introducing graded consequence in multiple valued logic. In *Fuzzy Logic in Knowledge-Based Systems, Decision and Control*; Gupta, M., Yamakawa, T., Eds.; Elsevier Science Publishers, B.V., North Holland: Amsterdam, The Netherlands, 1988; pp. 247–257.
106. Tarski, A. On some fundamental concepts of metamathematics. In *Logic, Semantics, Metamathematics*; Oxford University Press: Oxford, UK, 1956; pp. 30–37.
107. Goguen, J. The logic of inexact concepts. *Synthese* **1968**, *19*, 325–373. [CrossRef]
108. Mossakowski, T.; Goguen, J.; Diaconescu, R.; Tarlecki, A. What is a Logic? In *Logica Universalis*; Béziau, J.Y., Ed.; Birkhäuser: Basel, Switzerland, 2005; pp. 113–133.
109. Diaconescu, R. Generalized Graded Interpolation. **2022**, *submitted*.
110. Maehara, S. On the interpolation theorem of Craig. *Sugaku* **1962**, *12*, 235–237.
111. Robinson, A. A result on consistency and its applications to the theory of definition. *Indag. Math.* **1956**, *18*, 47–58. [CrossRef]
112. Mundici, D. Robinson's consistency theorem in soft model theory. *Trans. AMS* **1981**, *263*, 231–241.
113. Beth, E.W. On Padoa's method in the theory of definition. *Indag. Math.* **1953**, *15*, 330–339. [CrossRef]

MDPI
St. Alban-Anlage 66
4052 Basel
Switzerland
Tel. +41 61 683 77 34
Fax +41 61 302 89 18
www.mdpi.com

Mathematics Editorial Office
E-mail: mathematics@mdpi.com
www.mdpi.com/journal/mathematics

www.ingramcontent.com/pod-product-compliance
Lightning Source LLC
LaVergne TN
LVHW070154120526
838202LV00013BA/1094